Musical Notation in the West

Musical notation is a powerful system of communication between musicians, using sophisticated symbolic, primarily non-verbal means to express musical events in visual symbols. Many musicians take the system for granted, having internalized it and their strategies for reading it and translating it into sound over long years of study and practice. This book traces the development of that system by combining chronological and thematic approaches to show the historical and musical context in which these developments took place. Simultaneously, the book considers the way in which this symbolic language communicates to those literate in it, discussing how its features facilitate or hinder fluent comprehension in the real-time environment of performance. Moreover, the topic of musical as opposed to notational innovation forms another thread of the treatment, as the author investigates instances where musical developments stimulated notational attributes, or notational innovations made practicable advances in musical style.

JAMES GRIER is Professor of Music History at the University of Western Ontario and Fellow of the Royal Society of Canada. He has written The Critical Editing of Music (Cambridge University Press, 1996; Spanish translation 2008), and three books on the music of Adémar de Chabannes, eleventh-century Aquitanian monk.

A complete list of books in the series is featured at the back of this book.

Musical Notation in the West

JAMES GRIER
University of Western Ontario

CAMBRIDGE
UNIVERSITY PRESS

University Printing House, Cambridge CB2 8BS, United Kingdom

One Liberty Plaza, 20th Floor, New York, NY 10006, USA

477 Williamstown Road, Port Melbourne, VIC 3207, Australia

314–321, 3rd Floor, Plot 3, Splendor Forum, Jasola District Centre, New Delhi – 110025, India

79 Anson Road, #06–04/06, Singapore 079906

Cambridge University Press is part of the University of Cambridge.

It furthers the University's mission by disseminating knowledge in the pursuit of education, learning, and research at the highest international levels of excellence.

www.cambridge.org
Information on this title: www.cambridge.org/9780521898164
DOI: 10.1017/9781139034821

© Cambridge University Press 2021

This publication is in copyright. Subject to statutory exception and to the provisions of relevant collective licensing agreements, no reproduction of any part may take place without the written permission of Cambridge University Press.

First published 2021

A catalogue record for this publication is available from the British Library.

ISBN 978-0-521-89816-4 Hardback
ISBN 978-0-521–72642-9 Paperback

Cambridge University Press has no responsibility for the persistence or accuracy of URLs for external or third-party internet websites referred to in this publication and does not guarantee that any content on such websites is, or will remain, accurate or appropriate.

To Dr. Victoria L. Cooper

Contents

List of Figures [*page* ix]
List of Tables [xii]
List of Musical Examples [xiii]
Preface [xv]

1 Introduction: Musical Notation as a Symbolic Language [1]

2 Plainsong and the Origins of Musical Notation in the West [8]
  The Earliest Neumes [15]
  The Earliest Neumes: Directionality [17]
  The Earliest Neumes: Grouping and Ligation [22]
  The Earliest Neumes: Melodic Nuances [28]
  The Earliest Neumes: A Common Ancestor and Its Dissemination [35]
  Pitch [37]
  Later Chant Notation [40]

  Interlude 1: The Problem with Pitch [53]

3 Polyphony and Rhythmic Notation [61]
  The Rhythmic Modes [63]
  The Rhythmic Modes: *Proprietas et perfectio* [71]
  The Rhythmic Modes: Opposite Propriety and the Plica, *Fractio et collectio*, Individual Notes and Rests [78]
  Six Modes or Two? [81]
  Mensural Notation: Lambertus and Franco [85]
  The *ars noua* [96]
  Coloration and Proportion [111]
  Developments of the Fifteenth and Sixteenth Centuries [121]
  The Transition to Modern Rhythmic Notation in the Sixteenth and Seventeenth Centuries [128]
  Rests and Note Names [132]

  Interlude 2: Rhythm and Metre [135]

4 The Transition to the Modern Era: Instrumental Music and
  Performing Indications   [142]
  Keyboard Tablatures   [143]
  Lute Tablatures   [151]
  The Adoption of Vocal Notation by Instrumentalists   [160]
  Figured Bass Notation   [162]
  Idiosyncratic Notation for Instruments   [163]
  Bibliography of Notational Techniques   [164]
  Accidentals, Mode, Key and Signatures   [166]
  Dynamics, Tempo and Expression   [176]

  Interlude 3: The Score   [181]

5 Notational Nuance in the Twentieth Century
  and the Motives for Notational Innovation   [190]
  Performing Techniques   [193]
  Rhythm   [194]
  Pitch   [196]
  Aleatoric Notation   [197]
  The Tension between Composition and Performance,
     and Notational Innovation   [200]

  Coda: The Meaning of Musical Literacy   [206]

  Bibliography   [224]
  Index   [265]

Figures

2.1	Neumes in SG 359, Laon 239, Char 47 and Albi 44	
	Courtesy of Saint Gall, Stiftsbibliothek; Ville de Laon, Bibliothèque municipale; Albi, Bibliothèque municipale Rochegude; Médiathèque l'Apostrophe-Chartres. [*page* 18]	
2.2	Grouping and ligation in SG 359, Laon 239 and Char 47	[25]
2.3	The use of vertical space for melodic continuation in SG 359 and Char 47	[27]
2.4	Liquescents in SG 359, Laon 239, Char 47 and Albi 44	[28]
2.5	*Virga* and *cephalicus* in Char 47	[29]
2.6	*Oriscus* and *quilisma* in SG 359, Laon 239, Char 47 and Albi 44	[30]
2.7	*Oriscus* and *quilisma* in context	[30]
2.8	*Litterae significatiuae* in SG 359, Laon 239, Char 47 and Albi 44	[33]
2.9	Neumes in PaM 384, Pa 17296 and Pa 1107	
	Courtesy of Paris, Bibliothèque Mazarine, Photo by Bibliothèque Mazarine; Paris, Bibliothèque nationale de France. [42]	
2.10	*Alleluia* V *Video caelos* PaM 384 fol. 4v	[43]
2.11	Responsory *Missus est Gabriel* Pa 17296 fol. 2v	[45]
2.12	*Alleluia* V *Video caelos* Pa 1107 fol. XXIIra	[47]
3.1	F fol. 24r	
	Firenze, Biblioteca Medicea Laurenziana, Ms. Plut. 29.1, fol. 24r	
	Su concessione del MiBACT	
	E' vietata ogni ulteriore riproduzione con qualsiasi mezzo. [83]	
3.2	Mo H. 196 fols. 357v–358r	
	Bibliothèque interuniversitaire de Montpellier, BU historique de medicine	
	Copyright: BIU Montpellier / DIAMM, University of Oxford. [93]	
3.3	Pa 1584 fol. 455v, Pa 9221 fol. 152v	
	Courtesy of Paris, Bibliothèque nationale de France. [108]	
3.4	Chan 564 fol. 24v	
	Courtesy of Chantilly, Bibliothèque du château de Chantilly. [116]	
3.5	*Harmonice musices odhecaton* (1504 edition), fols. H 7v–8r	
	Courtesy of Paris, Bibliothèque nationale de France. [125]	

3.6 *Frottole intabulate* (1517)
Collection of the National Museum, National Museum Library, gg 19, fols. 2v, 3r, 6v, Prague, Czech Republic. [129]

3.7 Claudio Monteverdi, *Lamento della Ninfa*, bars 50–57, in *Madrigali guerrieri, et amorosi*, Basso continuo p. 57
Courtesy of Fondazione Claudio Monteverdi. [130]

3.8 Francesco Cavalli, *Il novello Giasone*, Sinfonia Avanti il Prologo, Si L.V.33 fol. 3v
Courtesy of Siena, Biblioteca Communale degli Intronati di Siena. [131]

3.9 Francesco Cavalli, *Scipione Africano*, act 1, scene 7, Ven 371 fol. 21r
Courtesy of Venice, Biblioteca nazionale Marciana. [131]

4.1 Buxheimer Orgelbuch, Mü 3725 fol. 87r
Bayerische Staatsbibliothek München, Mus.ms. 3725. [144]

4.2 Elias Nikolaus Ammerbach, *Orgel oder Instrument Tabulaturbuch*, p. 33
Bayerische Staatsbibliothek München, 4 Mus.pr. 130. [146]

4.3 Antonio Valente, *Intavolatura de cimbalo*, p. xxxiiii
Courtesy of Naples, Biblioteca nazionale. [147]

4.4 Antonio de Cabezón, *Obras de música*, fol. 39r
Courtesy of Madrid, Biblioteca Nacional de España. [148]

4.5 *Intabulatura de lauto libro primo*, fol. 9r
Courtesy of Paris, Bibliothèque nationale de France. [152]

4.6 Pierre Attaingnant, *Tres breue et familiere introduction*, fol. v v
Courtesy of Berlin, Staatsbibliothek Preußischer Kulturbesitz. [155]

4.7 Hans Newsidler, *Ein newgeordent küntslich Lautenbuch*, fol. l iii r
Bayerische Staatsbibliothek München, 4 Mus.pr. 439. [157]

Coda.1 Francis Poulenc, Sonata for Flute and Piano, third movement, p. 6
Sonata For Flute and Piano
Composed by Francis Poulenc
© Copyright 1958, 1992 Chester Music Limited.
All Rights Reserved. International Copyright Secured.
Used by Permission of Hal Leonard Europe Limited. [212]

Coda.2 Arnold Schoenberg, *Five Pieces for Orchestra*, Opus 16, no. 2, p. 26
Five Pieces for Orchestra, Opus 16 by Arnold Schoenberg
© Copyright 1952 by Henmar Press Inc. Used by permission C.F. Peters Corporation. All Rights Reserved. [216]

Coda.3   Igor Stravinsky, *Variations, Aldous Huxley in Memoriam*, p. 16
         "Variations: Aldous Huxley in Memoriam" by Igor Stravinsky
         ©1965 by Boosey & Hawkes Music Publishers Limited.
         All Rights Reserved. Used With Permission.   [218]
Coda.4   SG 359, p. 26
         Courtesy of Saint Gall, Stiftsbibliothek.   [219]

I am very grateful to the libraries and publishers listed above who kindly granted me permission to reproduce materials in their holdings.

Tables

3.1 Rhythmic modes [*page* 66]
3.2 Substitution in trochaic and iambic metres [70]
3.3 Propriety and perfection in binary and ternary ligatures [75]
3.4 Propriety and perfection according to Franco [78]
3.5 Morphology of ligatures to show propriety and perfection according to Franco [90]
3.6 Table of values in perfect and imperfect mensurations [101]
3.7 The commonly used mensuration signs, according to Prosdocimus de Beldemandis [110]
3.8 Note names [134]
Interlude 3.1 Placement of solo piano in scores for concerti [188]

Musical Examples

3.1 *Alleluia* V *Pascha nostrum*, portion of verse, F fol. 24r   [*page* 83]
3.2 *Se ie chante / Bien doi amer / Et sperabit*, Mo H. 196 fols. 357v–359v   [92]
3.3 Guillaume de Machaut, *Biaute qui toutes autres pere*, Pa 1584 fol. 455v   [107]
3.4 *Medee fu*, Chan 564 fol. 24v   [113]
3.5 Loyset Compere, *Garisses moy, Harmonice musices odhecaton*, fols. H 7v–8r   [123]
4.1 Pitch values in the tablatures of Valente and Cabezón   [150]

Preface

I write this volume on musical notation at the invitation of Dr. Victoria L. Cooper, then music editor at Cambridge University Press. It grows out of my book on editing where I explored in a limited way the idea that musical notation in the West constituted a semiotic system, an idea introduced to me by the ever creative, imaginative and innovative scholarship of Leo Treitler. At an early stage in this project, I decided that the core of the investigation would revolve around the semiotic properties of musical notation and how they communicate to the musically literate. As I considered each phase in the development of Western notation, I wondered how a musically literate user could have benefited from it and how it contributed to the efficient and effective communication of the sounds it was intended to encode. How, in effect, it contributed to the functioning of musical notation as a symbolic language, as a semiotic system transparent to musicians both contemporary and at present. I have attempted to emphasize consistently the historical and musical environment in which these developments took place so that performers who would wish to recreate pieces written in period notations or scholars executing critical acts on them would bring a heightened awareness of these considerations to their endeavours.

I am very grateful to several institutions for generous support while I pursued this project. First and foremost, the combination of a Killam Research Fellowship and Fellowships from the National Endowment of the Humanities and the American Council of Learned Societies permitted me a three-year research leave 2009–12. I also received Standard Research Grants from the Social Sciences and Humanities Research Council of Canada in 2006 and 2010, and an Insight Grant in 2014. This ongoing support has enabled me to enjoy much freedom and underwritten many research trips to distant libraries that greatly facilitated and expedited the progress of the project.

The librarians and collections of many libraries materially aided this study, most of all the Bibliothèque nationale de France, where I conducted a great deal of the research for this book. I have benefited from many kindnesses on the part of the librarians there at the Salle des manuscrits, Département de la musique and the très grande bibliothèque at Tolbiac.

I am and continue to be very grateful. Many other libraries have generously shared their resources with me, including those geographically closest to me, the University of Western Ontario, the University of Windsor and the University of Michigan. Librarians at the Pontifical Institute of Mediaeval Studies in Toronto, the Library of Congress, the New York Public Library and Columbia University have also extended to me many courtesies, and I thank them.

Many colleagues have generously shared their expertise and opinions along the way and offered support in countless other ways, including Charles M. Atkinson, Gunilla Björkvall, Daniel F. Callahan, John Check, the late John A. Emerson, Bryan Gillingham, the late Michel Huglo, Gunilla Iversen, Ritva Jacobsson, Thomas Forrest Kelly, the late Kenneth Levy, Judith Peraino, the late Alejandro Enrique Planchart, Susan Rankin, Anne Walters Robertson, Leo Treitler and Craig Wright. At the Press, Kate Brett and her staff have proved themselves to be extremely patient and supportive throughout this long process. I remain grateful.

When Vicki Cooper invited me to undertake this volume, she saw it as a complement to my volume on editing music, a sentiment I shared with her, as I explain above. I was eager, although very slow, to comply, but I am very anxious to acknowledge my debt to Vicki for the original inspiration and, since our first introduction, decades of support for several projects including the current one. In my experience, she is a singular individual in the publishing world, combining scholarly erudition with a creative imagination and much sympathy, at least for this author. Any credit for the success of my book on editing, my study of the musical career of my eleventh-century alter ego, Adémar de Chabannes, and this volume must be shared with her. I am very pleased to dedicate this book to her in small repayment for all the support and encouragement she has afforded me over these many years.

To my dear friends Claire Harrison and Peter Jarrett, I extend a warm thanks for their wonderful hospitality in Paris, where their home served as a base for many research trips to the BnF and a refuge for writing. And finally, I acknowledge the support of my wife and daughter, who have continuously offered extraordinary support for the time and attention I have lavished on these projects. They have attended every step of the journey with good humour, boundless affection and love.

1 | Introduction: Musical Notation as a Symbolic Language

By the early twenty-first century, Western musical notation has developed into an extraordinarily rich and complex piece of visual communication. Modern musicians expend considerable time and energy to create strategies for its more efficient comprehension. Simultaneously, musicians are continuously inventing new symbols and systems of symbols for two very different reasons. Some wish to communicate with ever greater precision the instructions necessary for the reproduction of a musical work. Others are seeking ways of recording in writing musics whose origins are not necessarily rooted in notation. Charles Seeger identified these two streams as, respectively, "prescriptive" and "descriptive" forms of notation.[1]

Like many useful binary oppositions, these two categories function better as the two endpoints of a continuum instead of mutually exclusive classifications. As helpful as they are in understanding many of the applications of musical notation in the West, they have not rested in static relation throughout the history of Western music. Scribes, typesetters, engravers and now computer-literate users of musicprocessors have striven to clarify, render more precise and otherwise improve the efficiency and the manner in which musical notation communicates to its audiences, functioning as intermediaries between the sounds themselves and their representation in writing. In some cases, they have started with a composer's prescriptive notation and finished by issuing an interpretative version that more closely recalls Seeger's descriptive notation.

Another factor that prevents Seeger's classifications from being hermetically sealed is the fluidity of musical practice itself. Composers, despite Wagner's and Stravinsky's protests to the contrary, inevitably leave some aspects of the performance to the discretion of the performer.[2] Stravinsky explicitly and implicitly denies these concessions in his *Poetics*, consciously avoiding, in the French text, the conventional word for "performer," namely "interprète," and substituting for it "exécutant."[3] Nevertheless, even the most detailed score leaves aspects of articulation, tempo and

---

[1]. Seeger, "Prescriptive and Descriptive Music-Writing."
[2]. Grier, "Authority of the Composer."   [3]. Strawinsky, *Poétique musicale*, pp. 82–92.

dynamics to be determined by the realities of performance in response to such factors as ambient room acoustics and the taste, sensitivity and education of the performer. To achieve an indicated *forte* might require two very different efforts on the part of the same musician performing in two acoustically different environments. Similarly, the transcription of orally conceived musics into notation, Seeger's "descriptive" notation, potentially involves significant compromises, as Philip Bohlman eloquently argues.[4] In fact, as Leo Treitler remarked, the transcription of such music by practitioners (as opposed to scholars from a foreign culture) often blurs the distinction between composing, performing and writing.[5]

Here I shall investigate some aspects of the tension between musical sounds, the musical practices that generate them and the role of notation in mediating between the two. In particular, I would like to address the way in which the marks or signs that make up musical notation function within conventional and arbitrarily determined systems to communicate to their users. Semiotics, taken literally from the Greek το σημεῖον, refers to the theory and history of signs per se, and the systems operating in musical notation closely accord with two of the principal concepts that Ferdinand de Saussure proposed in his seminal work on the discipline: notational symbols derive their meaning equally from convention and from their relative position within a system of symbols.[6] Both concepts are arbitrary. For example, it is conventional and arbitrarily determined that the position of a note on the vertical axis indicates its pitch while its position on the horizontal axis shows its relative position in the rhythmic framework of the music (respectively, action in space and action in time, to use Paul Hindemith's pithy formulation).[7]

Naturally, the convention of reading from left to right derives from the customary inscription of language in the West. The earliest notations in the medieval West record the melodies of vocal music and usually accompany the sung literary text. Scribes write the literary text, of course, from left to right, and so the melody written above the text proceeds in the same manner. Likewise, the placing of pitch on the vertical axis accords simultaneously with our subjective conception of high and low, already present in medieval music theory, and with the quantitative measurement of pitch in Hertz, or cycles per second of the vibrating body: subjectively higher pitches vibrate at quantitatively higher frequencies. Despite these

---

[4.] Bohlman, "Musicology as a Political Act."
[5.] Treitler, "Oral, Written, and Literate Process" and "Observations on the Transmission."
[6.] Saussure, *Cours de linguistique générale*, ed. Bally and Sechehaye, esp. pp. 23–35, 100–2, 180–84.
[7.] Hindemith, *Elementary Training for Musicians*.

circumstantial reasons for inscribing music in this way along the vertical and horizontal axes, the arrangement, nevertheless, is entirely arbitrary and finds meaning only through convention.

Similarly, the symbols for relative duration also derive meaning from convention. Their morphology permits us to recognize their relative values. In the first instance, however, those relative values are determined arbitrarily and entirely by convention. In the second instance, the relativity of the values operates within the system of symbols. There is no intrinsic value in the graphic shape of the half note, for example, that makes it longer than the quarter note, but convention dictates it. That convention then extends across the entire system of durational symbols to govern the relationships among the members that constitute the whole.

The symbols that make up musical notation form a number of interacting systems. Leo Treitler usefully adopts Charles Sanders Peirce's theoretical framework for classifying signs.[8] Peirce identifies three categories of signs, iconic, indexical and symbolic, of which he offers concise definitions. "An *Icon* is a sign which refers to the Object that it denotes merely by virtue of characters of its own, and which it possesses, just the same, whether any such Object actually exists or not." "An *Index* is a sign which refers to the Object that it denotes by virtue of being really affected by that Object." "A *Symbol* is a sign which refers to the Object that it denotes by virtue of a law, usually an association of general ideas, which operates to cause the Symbol to be interpreted as referring to that Object."[9]

So, iconic signs resemble in some way the object they are respresenting. The marks conventionally used for articulation (slurs, dots, tenuto marks, wedges, etc.) offer visual cues to the way in which the notes are to be executed, and so may be considered iconic; iconic also is the conventional notation for the use of the damper pedal on the piano, whose shape graphically resembles the motions made by the player's foot as it depresses, holds and releases the pedal. Indexical symbols represent some aspect of action between the object and its referent. Some systems of notation use indexical signs, which dictate a specific physical action: instrumental tablatures, for example, that indicate which finger to use or at which fret to stop the string, or fingering instructions for keyboard and string

---

[8.] Treitler, "The Early History of Music Writing." Treitler, focusing on chant notation, applies two of Peirce's three categories, iconic and symbolic.

[9.] Quotation: Peirce, "A Second Trichotomy of Signs," in *Collected Papers of Charles Sanders Peirce*, 2: *Elements of Logic*, ed. Hartshorne and Weiss, Book 2 "Speculative Grammar," Chapter 2 "Divisions of Signs," §5, paragraphs 247–49, pp. 143–44; see also Book 2 "Speculative Grammar," Chapter 3 "The Icon, Index, and Symbol," paragraphs 274–308, pp. 156–73.

instruments. Symbolic marks derive their meaning from pure convention, for example, the modern signs for duration I discuss above.

In complex notation, several systems operate simultaneously, offering guidance over several independent aspects of the execution of a given note or pattern of notes. Moreover, these systems and their interrelations have changed over time, and so a third element enters the equation, alongside the concepts of convention and system, and that is context. The meaning of the individual symbol can change from one context to another, one era to the next. But even more important, entire systems can change or be replaced by new ones. Experienced musicians learn to apprehend these interacting systems at a glance and incorporate the suggestions each presents into their playing. Simultaneously, musicians cultivate a historical awareness of notational systems, how they change over time and in different contexts, and how their meaning affects the sounds generated. By analyzing the semiotic components of the systems that constitute musical notation, we can achieve a fuller understanding of how and what it communicates.

Musical notation, therefore, constitutes a language of signs, a symbolic language that must, therefore, in order to communicate efficiently and effectively, accord with various principles that determine whether symbols and signs function appropriately.[10] Four basic principles emerge from the study of signs and their effectiveness. First and determinant for the other principles, users must be able to read the symbols efficiently in real time. Users do not have time to consult a table or legend and should not have to reflect on the meaning of the symbol. To achieve this goal, two strategies present themselves. Either the meaning of the symbol must be so entirely self-evident that no doubt may arise regarding its meaning (Peirce's category of iconic symbols), or the users must have internalized the system and the meanings of the symbols so completely that no delay arises in their comprehension and application. Commonly used signs, like those governing traffic or the symbols for toilets, fall into the first category while musical notation belongs squarely in the second. As I said at the outset, musicians spend significant quantities of time internalizing the meanings of notational symbols so that they can read efficiently during performance.

The three remaining principles all descend from this first one. The design of individual symbols must enable immediate identification on the part of users and so distinguish them from all other symbols in the system.

[10.] On symbols and their language, see Frutiger, *Der Mensch und seine Zeichen*; Jean, *Langage de signes*; and Pierce, *The International Pictograms Standard*.

The durational signs of modern notation achieve that goal through a complex system of void and filled-in noteheads, stems and flags or beams. More complicated relationships find expression through numerals, such as the numeral 3 imposed above notes to indicate a relationship of three of one durational level in the time of two of the same level. As I discuss in Chapter 3, fourteenth-century notation of the *ars noua* period did not normally distinguish between durations divisible in three or two equal parts; the same grapheme served for both, and so theorists devised complex rules so that musicians could recognize which notes of the same physical appearance were triple and which ones duple in nature. Modern notation simply uses the dot to achieve the same goal: a dotted note at one level equals three equal notes of the next lower level; one without a dot, two.

Next, classes of symbols within the same system must exhibit clear interrelations between one another in order to facilitate their comprehension and efficient apprehension. Again, the durational signs of modern notation provide a good example. I mentioned above that the morphology of these symbols contains no intrinsic, or iconic, meaning regarding their durational value. Convention and convention alone, reinforced by centuries of usage, dictates the relative meaning of the symbols. Here, then, is another instance of how musicians must work within the historical conventions of the notation to internalize the arbitrary relationships between the various durational values. The interrelations between the symbols only become clear through pedagogy and long exposure, but clear they do become to musically literate musicians.

Finally, when the prevailing system combines classes of symbols, the interrelations among the classes must remain clear. Such combinations in musical notation usually signify modifications to the meaning of the notes that form the central core of the system. Time and key signatures indicate the way performers should group the durational values and what chromatic adjustments to apply. Again, nothing intrinsic in either type of symbol conveys those meanings, although a logic does inform the arrangement of numerals in the time signature that resemble an equation. And so, the relationships between the classes of symbols, as Saussure would say, are arbitrary and governed by convention. Musicians must learn and practise them in order to internalize their meanings and apply them as needed in real time during performance.

The system of musical notation we know and that I am critiquing evolved over centuries; no musician set out to design the system from a blank sheet of paper, with the result that many of its attributes do not evince absolute transparency. They developed over time through a certain amount of trial and error, and so they do not uniformly embrace the principles that an efficient system would require. Instead, as I note several times above, musicians must devote significant time and effort to the internalization of these symbols and their meaning to use them effectively. This circumstance generates two results that impose limitations on musical practice. First, because of the great investment of time and effort musicians must make to master notation and musical literacy, they are reluctant to invent or adopt new symbols or systems, as I show in Chapter 5, where I discuss developments in the twentieth and early twenty-first centuries. From this situation emerges the second limiting circumstance, and that is that traditional musical notation imposes a relatively rigid grid of pitch and temporal relationships. Modern attempts to decrease the rigidity of the system have generally failed.

These limitations have caused musicians to question the purpose and function of notation. In articles originally published side by side in the journal *Critique*, Pierre Boulez and Hugues Dufourt, both musically literate and highly proficient musicians and composers, suggest that musical notation imposes significant restraints on musical practice.[11] Boulez points out that the writing of music transforms the art from a dynamic to a static form. Similarly, Dufourt avers that the transformation renders music an art for the eye instead of one for the ear. "L'oeil admet l'oreille aux disponibilités relationnelles enclose dans la sphere des sons. L'oeil introduit l'oreille dans l'espace des opérations et des fonctions."[12] ("The eye admits the ear to the relational possibilities that are enclosed in the sphere of sounds. The eye introduces the ear into the space of these operations and functions.") He observes that neumes, in their original invention, attempt to convey melodic movement, with all its subtleties and nuances. As notation came to represent more aspects of music (pitch, rhythm, metre, dynamics and so on), however, the intimacy of that relationship with melodic motion and the spontaneity of the interaction between sound and the symbols used to represent it became more remote.[13]

If Boulez and Dufourt are correct, then, why write a book like this one about a technology that impedes instead of enabling musical practice? As the careers of these two distinguished musicians unequivocally

---

[11] Boulez, "L'écriture du musician"; and Dufourt, "L'artifice de l'écriture."

[12] Dufourt, "L'artifice de l'écriture," p. 465; compare Karlheinz Stockhausen's conception of "read" music ("*gelesene Musik*"), "Musik und Graphik," p. 13 (Stockhausen's italics); I discuss this article further in Chapter 5 and the Coda below.

[13] Dufourt, "L'artifice de l'écriture," pp. 468–69.

demonstrate, musical notation, with all its imperfections, still remains a relatively efficient means of communicating musical events between musically literate individuals. Those efficiencies depend, as I argue above, on the devotion of musicians to obtain and cultivate musical literacy, but many musicians, Boulez and Dufourt among them, are willing to expend that devotion. And so scholars are obliged to continue to investigate and critique the nature of musical notation as a system of signs and as a reality both historical and actual for practising musicians.

By studying the semiotic import of musical notations, I hope that practitioners of music will gain an increased critical awareness of how musical notation relates to the musical events it attempts to represent, how it communicates those events to musically literate practitioners and how practitioners have shaped notation to serve their needs. The critical investigation of the interaction between musical events, the practitioners who create them and the notational symbols that represent them will assist musically literate musicians at all levels to gain an increased sensitivity to the way in which they use musical notation in their professional activities. Musical notation is not a passive conduit through which a musically literate individual apprehends the musical events the notation attempts to represent. Notation actively shapes that apprehension by engaging in dialogue with musical style, genre and the actions required to animate it in performance. It is this critical engagement with the manner in which notation communicates to practitioners that I hope to encourage and even facilitate.

2 | Plainsong and the Origins of Musical Notation in the West

The continuous history of musical notation in the West begins in the ninth century. Two groups of competing theories prevent more definitive statements about those origins, and their critical treatment serves as a starting point for the narrative. One group of theories concerns the origin of the neumes themselves, of which the most recent scholarship recognizes three possible sources: punctuation signs in Latin, Latin accentual signs and a form of graphic notation that was eventually replaced by one that represented the melodic contours of the chant.[1] The other concerns the date at which notation originated in the Latin West, and the two competing theories present the opposite ends of the ninth century for its beginning.[2] One theory, supported only by narrative and circumstantial evidence, situates the beginning of notation in the educational and cultural reforms of Charlemagne's court around the turn of the ninth century. The other begins with the oldest surviving practical sources with musical notation from the medieval West, all of which date from the last quarter or so of the ninth century, and interprets them as products of the first medieval attempts to record music in writing.

On one matter, all recent scholarship agrees, namely that, no matter what the ultimate origins of notation may be or at what date musicians devised it, the invention of notation took place amid the rich intellectual and cultural environment of the Carolingian Empire.[3] To meet the administrative needs of a growing empire with increasing centralization of power, first under Pippin the Short and then his son Charlemagne during the second half of the eighth century, the Carolingian rulers required a bureaucracy that depended on literacy for its efficient operation. Accordingly, Charlemagne launched a broad

---

[1] The chief proponent of the derivation of neumes from punctuation signs is Leo Treitler; see "The Early History of Music Writing," esp. pp. 269–72, and "Reading and Singing," esp. pp. 186–206. On accentual signs, Atkinson, "*De Accentibus Toni*," "Glosses on Music and Grammar," and "The Anonymous Vaticanus *in speculo*," pp. 36–45; and Rankin, *Writing Sounds*, pp. 303–17. On a graphic system that was supplanted by a gestural system, Levy, "On the Origins of Neumes."

[2] Kenneth Levy prefers a date around A.D. 800, "Charlemagne's Archetype." The principal advocate for a date at the end of the century is Helmut Hucke, "Toward a New Historical View."

[3] Rankin, *Writing Sounds*, pp. 337–61.

educational programme that placed at its centre the study of Latin.[4] Simultaneously, Charlemagne, or possibly Pippin before him, initiated liturgical reforms that some scholars attribute to a desire to Romanize the Frankish liturgy for political or religious reasons.[5] All, however, agree that both Pippin and Charlemagne, as part of this reform, required the Frankish clergy to adopt the chant sung at the papal curia in Rome.

Scholars differ as to the role notation played in the adoption of the Roman chant by the Franks, largely on the basis of the date they believe notation came into widespread use, either around A.D. 800 or the end of the ninth century. For example, Leo Treitler deduces from the complex verbal descriptions of melodic motion provided by Aurelian of Réôme (writing around the middle of the ninth century) several propositions regarding their significance for the history of notation.[6] He first notes that the descriptions pertain to the quality of the melodic gesture as singers would realize it in performance rather than pitch content; second, that had Aurelian and his readers known a musical notation that could represent these melodic nuances, "such elaborate verbal descriptions would have been the more inefficient medium";[7] and third, that his treatise may mark the date after which such a musical notation developed. Treitler concludes, "Aurelian certainly knew the chant tradition as an oral tradition."[8] So, he would push the origins of this nuanced notation to the second half of the ninth century, in agreement with Helmut Hucke, to a second phase of dissemination of chant throughout the Frankish Empire.[9]

(Not all scholars understand Aurelian in this way. Kenneth Levy sees, in Aurelian's references to visual representations of music, sophisticated

---

[4.] For an overview of Charlemagne's educational programme, see Riché, *Écoles et l'enseignement*, pp. 47–118. On the importance of literacy, see Martin, *Histoire et pouvoirs*, pp. 128–33; McKitterick, *The Carolingians and the Written Word*; and Nelson, "Literacy in Carolingian Government." On the study of Latin, see Law, "The Study of Grammar." Roger Wright, *Late Latin and Early Romance*, shows that, beginning around A.D. 800 as a result of the educational innovations of Alcuin, the Carolingians adopted a standardized orthography, pronunciation and Latin usage for texts that formed part of the liturgy; see esp. pp. 45–144.

[5.] Klauser, "Die liturgischen Austauschbeziehungen"; Vogel, *La reforme cultuelle* and "Les motifs"; P. Bernard, *Du chant romain*, pp. 639–709; and Hen, *The Royal Patronage of Liturgy*, pp. 42–95.

[6.] Treitler, "Reading and Singing," pp. 156–61. He cites, *ibid.*, pp. 156–57, the following passages from Aurelian: *Musica disciplina* 19, 13 and 19 (a second time), ed. Gushee, pp. 122–23, 97–98 and 120–21, respectively; trans. Ponte, pp. 49, 33–34 and 48, respectively.

[7.] Treitler, "Reading and Singing," p. 160.   [8.] Treitler, "Reading and Singing," p. 161.

[9.] Hucke, "Toward a New Historical View," pp. 446–47, 466.

knowledge of musical notation.[10] And Charles M. Atkinson shows that his explanation of terms borrowed from the vocabulary of prosodic accents accords very closely with the graphic attributes of palaeofrankish notation.)[11]

Kenneth Levy, on the other hand, would link the origins and rapid dissemination of musical notation throughout the Frankish Empire with the adoption of Roman chant there during the second half of the eighth century.[12] Levy maintains that the Frankish cantors needed a firm written record of an unfamiliar repertory of chant that royal command obliged them to learn. Accordingly, his reconstruction involves, in the first instance, a form of notation that accurately represents the constituent pitches and intervals of the melodies, which he calls a graphic form of notation and identifies with the palaeofrankish script. Eventually, a second type of notation that attempted to capture the nuances and gestures of the chant replaced this graphic form. All this happened around the turn of the ninth century, and certainly no later than A.D. 822, the latest possible date of the letter from Abbot Helisachar to Archbishop Nibridius of Narbonne in which Helisachar makes what I consider to be an unequivocal statement about the compilation of a noted antiphoner for the Divine Office.[13]

My own reconstruction, which accords largely with Levy's interpretation of the literary evidence, especially his understanding of Helisachar's letter, places the invention of notation squarely in the Frankish Empire around the turn of the ninth century.[14] I differ from Levy's view, however, in seeing as the impetus for the development of notation not the necessity to master the pitch sequences of the melodies, but rather the difficulties the Frankish singers experienced in executing the melodic nuances of the chant repertory imported from Rome. The literary sources suggest a very narrow range of dates between which Frankish musicians began their experiments with musical notation. Helisachar's letter provides, in my opinion, a firm *terminus post quem non* of A.D. 822. The antiphoner he was preparing must have included musical notation, as I mention above.

The literary sources give strong indications as to when it may have become necessary for Frankish musicians to adopt musical notation,

---

[10.] Levy, "Charlemagne's Archetype," pp. 9–10, and *Gregorian Chant*, pp. 187–94.
[11.] Atkinson, "De Accentibus Toni," pp. 40–42; also Rankin, *Writing Sounds*, pp. 303–17.
[12.] Levy, "Charlemagne's Archetype," and "On the Origins of Neumes."
[13.] Levy, "Abbot Helisachar's Antiphoner"; P. Bernard, *Du chant romain*, 739–45; and Grier, "Adémar de Chabannes, Carolingian Musical Practices, and *Nota Romana*," pp. 71–74.
[14.] Grier, "Adémar de Chabannes, Carolingian Musical Practices, and *Nota Romana*."

without mentioning the technology specifically. Pippin the Short, Charlemagne's father, received a gift of chant books from Pope Paul I, who also sent Simeon, prior of the Roman schola cantorum, to teach singing in the Frankish kingdom, unsuccessfully, as it turns out, and as I discuss below.[15] Chant received legislative attention in the following reign, that of Charlemagne himself, who mandated, in the *Admonitio generalis* of 23 March 789, that every monastery and cathedral possess a corrected book or books of chants, and that every cleric fully learn Roman chant.[16] He returned to the matter in a capitulary issued to the *missi* (his regional delegates) at Thionville in A.D. 805, in which he instructed them to oversee the churches on various concerns, including chant.[17] I would therefore date the origins of a notation for plainsong between the promulgation of the *Admonitio generalis* in 789 and Helisachar's letter to Nibridius, 822 at the latest, perhaps in the last decade of the eighth century or the first of the ninth.

I diverge from Levy's narrative, however, in the motivations I assign for the development of notation and therefore its character. Literary evidence, scant though it may be, indicates that the Franks experienced difficulties in mastering the nuances of singing the chant that their monarchs, beginning with Pippin, required them to sing. Pope Paul I, writing to Pippin, noted that monks under the instruction of Simeon in the Frankish kingdom had not been able to learn the "singing of psalmody" ("psalmodii modulationem").[18] The late ninth-century commentators John the Deacon and the monk of Saint Gall (often identified as the composer Notker Balbulus), writing, respectively, in their biographies of Pope Gregory the Great and Charlemagne, both remark on the challenges faced by the Frankish singers in learning Roman chant.[19] John blames the Franks for their technical inability, while the monk of Saint Gall

---

[15] Grier, "Adémar de Chabannes, Carolingian Musical Practices, and *Nota Romana*," pp. 61–62; and Page, *The Christian West and Its Singers*, pp. 301–2, 313, 327–28.

[16] *Admonitio generalis* 72 and 80; text, translation and discussion, together with other bibliography, in Grier, "Adémar de Chabannes, Carolingian Musical Practices, and *Nota Romana*," pp. 63–69.

[17] Grier, "Adémar de Chabannes, Carolingian Musical Practices, and *Nota Romana*," p. 70.

[18] Grier, "Adémar de Chabannes, Carolingian Musical Practices, and *Nota Romana*," pp. 61–62. On the technical meaning of the nouns *modulatio* and *modulamen*, and verb *modulo*, both here and in other Carolingian documents, see *ibid.*, pp. 66–67.

[19] For translations of the texts and commentary, see Treitler, "Homer and Gregory," pp. 338–40; see also the translations and commentary by James McKinnon in *Source Readings in Music History*, ed. Strunk and Treitler, nos. 21–22, pp. 178–83; further, van Dijk, "Papal Schola *versus* Charlemagne," pp. 23–30, and McKitterick, "Royal Patronage," pp. 121–23.

suggests that their Roman mentors deliberately misled them. All agree that the Franks could not sing the Roman chant.

The eleventh-century historian and musician Adémar de Chabannes offers a narrative based on that of John the Deacon, which he elaborates with considerable historical and musical precision.[20] He expands on John's comments about the singing of the Franks by remarking that "[they] could not perfectly express the tremulous or the sinuous notes, or the notes that are to be elided or separated, breaking the notes in the throat, with a natural barbaric voice, rather than expressing them."[21] For the first of these, the "tremulous notes," Adémar uses the technical term *tremulus*, by which several music theorists describe the effect required by the *quilisma*, a symbol found in most early notational dialects. Adémar, therefore, seems to be referring to specific vocal techniques that the Franks found difficult to execute. From his statement, therefore, in combination with the similar remarks of John the Deacon and the evidence for Simeon's failed pedagogical expedition to the Frankish kingdom in the eighth century, I deduce that the inability of the Franks to perform these nuances compelled musicians at Charlemagne's court to develop a form of musical notation that indicated where and how to introduce those nuances into their renditions of the Roman chant.[22]

This deduction, if valid, may illuminate Aurelian of Réôme's purpose in offering the detailed verbal descriptions that Treitler suggested he could have more efficiently achieved with noted musical examples, had a nuanced notation been available to him. Two of the passages Treitler cites refer to vocal effects Adémar specified as difficult for the Franks to execute: the tristrophe, which I believe corresponds to Adémar's "notes that are to be separated," and the *quilisma*, the tremulous notes mentioned above.[23] Aurelian, aware that his Frankish colleagues found these awkward to produce, felt it useful to explicate them, their meaning and manner of execution first through verbal descriptions and then by invoking passages that both exemplified them and were well known to his audience. The less efficient verbal description outweighs the more efficient musical symbol, in

---

[20] For text, translation and commentary, see Grier, "Adémar de Chabannes, Carolingian Musical Practices, and *Nota Romana*," esp. pp. 46–61.

[21] Grier, "Adémar de Chabannes, Carolingian Musical Practices, and *Nota Romana*," p. 48 for text and translation, and pp. 54–56 for commentary.

[22] This is also the conclusion of Timothy J. McGee; see "'Ornamental' Neumes and Early Notation," pp. 61–64, and *The Sound of Medieval Song*, pp. 121–25.

[23] Tristrophe: Aurelian, *Musica disciplina* 19, ed. Gushee, pp. 122–23; trans. Ponte, p. 49 (see Treitler, "Reading and Singing," pp. 156–57). Quilisma: Aurelian, *Musica disciplina* 13, ed. Gushee, pp. 97–98; trans. Ponte, pp. 33–34 (see Treitler, "Reading and Singing," pp. 157–58).

Aurelian's calculation, because his audience needed help in understanding how to execute these difficult vocal effects.

This interpretation finds support in the statement of the music theorist Hucbald of Saint Amand (†930) regarding the relative purposes of the musical notations known to him. He notes that the signs Boethius attached to the Greek names of the musical notes indicate with precision what pitches to sing, such that "every melody that is noted through them, even without anyone teaching, after once they have been learned, may be sung" ("sic per has omne melos adnotatum, etiam sine docente, postquam semel cognitae fuerint, ualeat decantari").[24] Hucbald contrasts the utility of this system with that which "usage has transmitted" ("usus tradidit"). They appear in various forms in different geographical areas and, although they serve as a memory aid, they do not permit the accurate reconstruction of the pitches of a melody.[25]

Nevertheless, they do offer important information about the execution of the chant: where to slow down, where to speed up, where to use the "tremulous" note ("tremulam ... notam"), sounds that are joined or separated, and where to cadence.[26] Hucbald's list includes both nuances discussed by Aurelian, the *quilisma* and the tristrophe, and three of the four Adémar would mention in the eleventh century, excluding only the turning or sinuous note, characterized by Adémar with the adjective *uinnolus*. Whether those who designed the system intended it principally to communicate this information does not interest Hucbald, who focuses more attention on the problem of accurately conveying pitch relations. Still, he acknowledges the importance of such performing indications, even if he expresses it somewhat obliquely: "These customary notes, nevertheless, are held to be not entirely unnecessary" ("Hae tamen consuetudinariae notae non omnino habentur non necessariae").[27] Hucbald's comments indicate that musicians of his generation had fully integrated into their musical consciousness the key purpose of neumatic notation, namely to indicate

---

[24] Hucbald, *Musica* 44, ed. Chartier, p. 194; trans. Babb, p. 36. Hucbald names Boethius as his source and gives the full table of signs at *Musica* 47, ed. Chartier, p. 198; trans. Babb, pp. 37–38. See Boethius, *De institutione musica* 4.3, ed. Friedlein, pp. 309–14; trans. Bower, pp. 123–26. On Hucbald's treatment of notation, see Chartier, "Hucbald de Saint-Amand"; Sullivan, "Alphabetic Notation"; and Rankin, *Writing Sounds*, pp. 359–60.

[25] Hucbald, *Musica* 44, ed. Chartier, p. 194; trans. Babb, p. 36. Rankin, "Identity and Diversity," pp. 375–77, shows that manuscripts containing several regional dialects of notation were present at Saint Amand during Hucbald's lifetime, and that therefore he may well have known some or all of them firsthand.

[26] Hucbald, *Musica* 46, ed. Chartier, p. 196; trans. Babb, p. 37.

[27] Hucbald, *Musica* 46, ed. Chartier, p. 196; trans. Babb, p. 37.

where and how to supply the problematic vocal nuances in performance, something Aurelian could not take for granted a half century earlier.

Finally, strong circumstantial evidence suggests that the invention of musical notation may have occurred in Metz.[28] Already during the reign of Pippin the Short, Bishop Chrodegang had introduced Roman chant to his diocese and implemented a stational liturgy in close imitation of that practised in Rome.[29] Charlemagne's Thionville capitulary of A.D. 805 received a gloss in the late ninth century that strongly associated singers from Metz with the imperial dissemination of Roman chant. Late in Charlemagne's reign, in 813 or 814, Archbishop Leidrad of Lyon wrote to the emperor requesting that he send a cleric from Metz who might reform singing in his province.[30] Moreover, three of our narrative sources, John the Deacon, the monk of Saint Gall and Adémar de Chabannes, all name Metz as an important centre for the practice of singing in the Roman style. None of these sources mentions notation, but it seems logical that if the empire's most authoritative practitioners of singing resided in Metz, they would be the ones most likely to undertake, or be asked to undertake, the invention of musical notation.

And so, I deduce that musicians in the Latin West began using musical notation around the turn of the ninth century, and that the singers at Metz, who had been practising Roman chant for half a century by then, invented it either on their own initiative or, as I believe, at the request or command of their monarch.[31] That notation focused on specifying the vocal nuances the Franks found so difficult to negotiate, a circumstance that would explain the postures of Aurelian and Hucbald toward notation and the manner in which it depicted musical information. Likewise a notation that did not specify the pitch content of the chants would help to explain the ongoing interaction

---

[28] The derivation of the surviving regional notational dialects from a centrally mandated notation forms a central facet of Levy's theory of the origins of chant notation; see n. 12 above. More recently, Ferretti ("Molti dialetti") and Rankin ("Typologies," pp. 42–48, "Identity and Diversity," especially pp. 382–93, and *Writing Sounds*, pp. 170–73, 269–76, 328–30) delineate the similarities of the chant dialects in morphology.

[29] Our source for Chrodegang's adoption of Roman chant is the near-contemporary historian Paul the Deacon, writing in the late eighth century; for references and bibliography, see Grier, "Adémar de Chabannes, Carolingian Musical Practices, and *Nota Romana*," p. 62. See also P. Bernard, *Du chant romain*, pp. 725–29; P.-E. Wagner, "Chant romain et chant messin"; Claussen, *The Reform of the Frankish Church*, pp. 271–76; and Page, *The Christian West and Its Singers*, pp. 339–53. On the stational liturgy, see Claussen, *The Reform of the Frankish Church*, pp. 276–89.

[30] For references and bibliography regarding the glosses to the Thionville capitulary and Leidrad's letter, see Grier, "Adémar de Chabannes, Carolingian Musical Practices, and *Nota Romana*," pp. 70–71.

[31] See also McKitterick, "Royal Patronage," pp. 120–26.

between oral and written processes that Leo Treitler sees in the transmission of chant well after the introduction of musical notation. Musicians depended on other means, principally memory, but also other resources, such as their general knowledge of the musical idioms of chant, its genres and the modal system, to retain and reconstruct that information.[32]

The largest problem with this reconstruction is the absence of any surviving evidence for the kind of complete noted books that I suggest Abbot Helisachar possessed in the first quarter of the ninth century. The earliest full books with musical notation date from the last decades of the century, and so my hypothesis about the origins of notation would therefore require that all the manuscripts in use throughout the Carolingian Empire for as much as three-quarters of a century have perished, a deafening silence, as I put it elsewhere.[33] It is true, as Kenneth Levy points out in answer to this objection, that music books suffered a high rate of destruction in the Middle Ages as they became obsolete.[34] And an equally distressing silence hangs over chant books from the eighth century, noted or otherwise. We know that Pope Paul I sent two such volumes to Pippin the Short around A.D. 760, an antiphonale and a responsale, and the *Admonitio generalis* stipulates that books of chants be corrected, but no physical remains of these eighth-century manuscripts survive.[35] In this context, it seems less remarkable that the following century should have witnessed similar losses of music books.

The Earliest Neumes

The surviving witnesses of chant indicate that, by the earliest years of the tenth century, at least four regional notational dialects had come into use: in the eastern region of the Frankish Empire, exemplified by SG 359; the central area, Laon 239; the northwest, Char 47; and the southwest region, Albi 44.[36] Of these earliest witnesses, only Albi 44 does not include music for all or most

---

[32.] Treitler's most important contribution on this subject is "Homer and Gregory."
[33.] Grier, "Adémar de Chabannes, Carolingian Musical Practices, and *Nota Romana*," p. 81. Rankin, *Writing Sounds*, pp. 93–123, identifies a number of ninth-century neumed manuscripts, some of which may represent fragments of fully neumed books, although the notation is not always coeval with the literary texts they contain.
[34.] Levy, "Charlemagne's Archetype," pp. 5–7, and *Gregorian Chant*, p. 242.
[35.] Grier, "Adémar de Chabannes, Carolingian Musical Practices, and *Nota Romana*," p. 81.
[36.] Rankin, *Writing Sounds*, pp. 99–102, citing a number of ninth-century fragments (see esp. Table 3, pp. 101–2), shows that Breton notation, exemplified by Char 47, was practised over a relatively large area.

of its chants, and its layout, with relatively little vertical space between the lines of text, inhibits the accurate inscription of the music. For some of the chant texts, however, the scribe left horizontal space between syllables or words that permits the entry of melismata, and so we can deduce that he anticipated including some music.[37] Fortunately, the notation it does contain exhibits the principal features of the Aquitanian dialect, and so we can make meaningful comparisons with the other three, more fully represented styles of notation.

These four dialects share three important characteristics that might reveal attributes of the notation I believe originated in Metz around A.D. 800: directionality, grouping or ligation, and the depiction of vocal nuances such as liquescence and the *quilisma*. I deal with each of these in turn, but first, I address the absence of any precision in the indication of pitch. By the time these manuscripts were produced, at least two notational systems had originated that are able to show pitch with some precision: palaeofrankish notation and the dasian system. The former indicates relative pitch by the placement of the note on the vertical axis of writing, precisely the system that came into use during the eleventh century and led directly to the modern convention of pitch notation.[38] The dasian system also uses the vertical dimension to show pitch relations, regulated with horizontal lines to each of which is attached a form of the dasian symbol that indicates a particular note.[39] The syllable of text to be sung on a note is written on the corresponding line.

In fact, the capacity of palaeofrankish notation to indicate pitch persuaded Kenneth Levy that the initial codification of chant carried out under Charlemagne must have employed this type of notation in order to convey the intervallic content of the melodies accurately.[40] Treitler points out, however, that most of the sources that use palaeofrankish notation fall into two categories: either liturgical books intended for use by the celebrant or performers other than the singers of the choir, or pedagogical or theoretical texts illustrated by examples that use the notation to indicate pitch relations.[41] It shares this last attribute, of course, with dasian notation, which seems to have been created

---

[37] Emerson, *Albi, Bibliothèque Municipale Rochegude, Manuscript 44*, pp. lviii–lxv.
[38] See Handschin, "Eine alte Neumenschrift"; Jammers, "Die palaeofraenkische Neumenschrift"; Atkinson, "*De Accentibus Toni*," pp. 30–42; Ferretti, *Una notazione neumatica*; Arlt, "A propos de la notation «paléofranque»"; and Rankin, *Writing Sounds*, pp. 94–98, 255–71, 303–17.
[39] See Unverricht, "Die Dasia-Notation"; Phillips, "The Dasia Notation," and "Notationen und Notationslehren," pp. 305–25; Hebborn, *Die Dasia-Notation*; and Ostheimer, "Die Niederschrift von Musik."
[40] Levy, "On the Origin of Neumes," esp. pp. 65–78; and *Gregorian Chant*, pp. 218–41, 249–52.
[41] Treitler, "Reading and Singing," pp. 142–78.

specifically for this purpose. Finally, Atkinson provides examples where palaeo-frankish notation does not always convey accurate pitch information.[42]

The Earliest Neumes: Directionality

To return to the three shared characteristics, I begin with directionality, the capacity of the notation to indicate the contours of the melody.[43] All four notational dialects employ two features to represent melodic direction, the morphology of the graphemes and their relative vertical position on the page, or heighting. The latter, of course, is self-explanatory: notes placed higher on the page are higher in pitch than those below them, a semiotic attribute Treitler would analyze as iconic in nature.[44] In the first instance, these relationships operate within neumes that represent more than a single note, compound neumes as they are usually termed. When a syllable of text carries more than one note, all notations used in plainsong group the notes to convey this relationship, a trait I discuss in more detail below when I consider grouping and ligation. Within these compound neumes, the signs that represent individual notes, or the portions of conjunct signs that do the same, occupy positions on the vertical axis of writing that correspond to their relative pitch.

The notational dialects differ, however, as to how they use heighting to indicate the relationships between neumes, either those that represent single notes or compound neumes.[45] At opposite ends of the scale stand Aquitanian notation and that used at Saint Gall. The former, already in Albi 44, attempts to relate individual neumes consistently by their relative position in the melodic contour, whereas the latter, represented by SG 359, tends to place all neumes on more or less the same horizontal plane irrespective of their relative pitch.[46] Somewhere between these two

---

[42.] Atkinson, "*De Accentibus Toni*," pp. 35–40.
[43.] The term directionality is Treitler's; see "The Early History of Music Writing," pp. 250–54. See also Duchez, "La representation spatio-verticale."
[44.] Treitler, "The Early History of Music Writing," pp. 239–40, observes that the notion of placing higher pitches at a higher position on the vertical axis of writing (and for that matter, notes that occur later in the temporal structure of the piece farther to the right on the horizontal axis) is a conventional, arbitrary and therefore symbolic means of representation. But once that notion becomes conventional, the relative position of those notes to indicate pitch (and temporal succession) becomes an iconic mode.
[45.] Rankin, "On the Treatment of Pitch."
[46.] On Albi 44, see Grier, *The Musical World*, p. 42. On SG 359, Rankin, "On the Treatment of Pitch," pp. 139–64, esp. 150–64, where she develops the "x-height syllable rule" to describe the

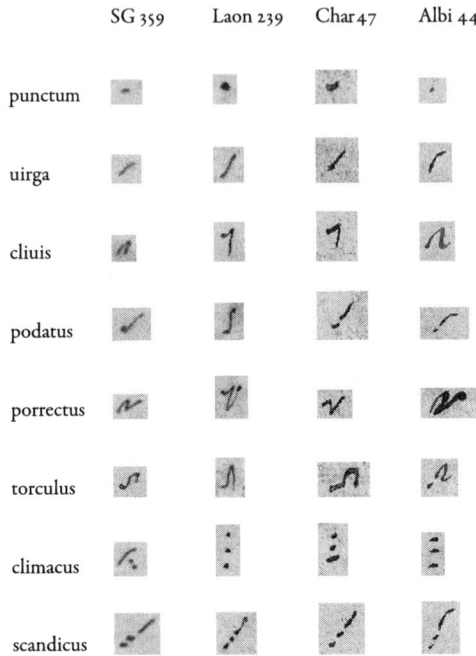

Figure 2.1 Neumes in SG 359, Laon 239, Char 47 and Albi 44
Courtesy of Saint Gall, Stiftsbibliothek; Ville de Laon, Bibliothèque municipale; Albi, Bibliothèque municipale Rochegude; Médiathèque l'Apostrophe-Chartres.

extremes lie the notations used in Char 47 and Laon 239, both of which attempt to show directionality between discrete neumes to some degree by relative heighting.[47]

The four dialects all share the second feature that represents melodic direction, namely morphology, by using the *punctum*, either round or a horizontal stroke, and *uirga*, an oblique line rising from left to right, to denote falling and rising motion respectively.[48] Figure 2.1 presents the principal morphological forms of the four notational dialects. Not only

---

orientation of the neumes along the horizontal axis; also R. Fischer, "Einführung in Handschriften."

[47] On Laon 239, see Rankin, "On the Treatment of Pitch," pp. 128–39; also R. Fischer, "Laon, Bibl. de la ville, 239"; and Rumphorst, "Verhältnis von St. Galler und Metzer Notation." On Char 47, R. Fischer, "Chartres, Bibliothèque Municipale, cod. 47."

[48] *PalMus* 11:55–58 (repeated at Sunyol, *Introducció a la paleografia*, pp. 91–96), conveniently provides a chart with the notational symbols in SG 359, Laon 239 and Char 47 laid out in parallel columns. See also the tables at Stäblein, *Schriftbild der einstimmigen Musik*, between pp. 32 and 33; Corbin, *Die Neumen*, p. 233; and Hiley and Szendrei, "Notation, §III, 1: History of Western Notation: Plainchant," Table 1.

does this practice accord with Treitler's concept of symbolic representation, but it also fulfills the two conditions Saussure identified as characterizing semiotic systems: the meaning of the signs is arbitrary, fixed by convention, and they operate within a system. Although, the form of the *uirga* does depict rising melodic motion, that of the *punctum* does not indicate descending motion; on the basis of its graphic form, it could represent, if anything, the lack of motion, or standing on the unison. And so the meaning, at least of the *punctum*, is arbitrary. Moreover, each sign derives its meaning from the immediately surrounding signs in the context: the *uirga* rises in relation to the note that precedes; the *punctum* falls on the same criterion.

These observations, incidentally, make it difficult to sustain the theory of the origin of the earliest neumes from the prosodic accents used in grammar. While the *uirga* resembles to some degree the acute accent, the *punctum* bears no similarity to the grave, which ought to descend from left to right. Moreover, as Atkinson perceptively observes, the palaeofrankish neumes that do look like the prosodic accents (the *pes* or *podatus* resembles the acute,[49] the *cliuis* the grave, and the *torculus* the circumflex) represent not single notes (as would be the case if the *uirga* and *punctum* were taken as cognates of the acute and grave, respectively) but two, in the case of the *podatus* and the *cliuis*, or three notes, in the case of the *torculus*.[50] Therefore, although prosodic accents might have influenced the graphemes used in this idiosyncratic dialect, they cannot lie at the basis of the other, more widely used notations in the ninth and tenth centuries.

Although the four early dialects agree in the morphology they use for a higher or lower note, they apply it differently in compound neumes that begin with descending motion: the *cliuis* and *climacus*, which represent, respectively, two and three descending notes, and the *porrectus*, the ternary

---

[49.] Medieval sources use both terms for the ascending binary neume, but *podatus* has earlier attestation, and so I use it alone for this neume. See Bernhard, "Die Überlieferung der Neumennamen," pp. 42, 44–48, 52–56, 67–68, 70–79, the tables at pp. 49, 56, 79 and especially 87–88, although the last (p. 88) reverses the terms used for this neume in "Tabula brevis" (which should read *podatus*) and "Tabula Vindobonensis" (which should read *pes*).

[50.] Atkinson, "De Accentibus Toni," pp. 30–42. Without making the connection with the prosodic accents, Levy, "On the Origins of Neumes," Figure 8, p. 75, makes the graphic relationships clear. Rankin, *Writing Sounds*, pp. 317–19, building on Atkinson's observations regarding the binary ascending neume that resembles the acute accent, avers that the palaeofrankish notation denotes motion (in this case from low to high) as opposed to discrete notes. To me, the distinction seems more semantic than substantive because the grapheme could equally represent the two discrete notes that constitute the ascent as opposed to the motion between them.

neume in which the middle note is lower than the first and last notes and so opens with descending motion. The Saint Gall notation places as the first note in each of these neumes the *uirga*, whereas the other three dialects begin them with a *punctum*. Treitler felt the difference to be so great that he placed the Saint Gall notation in a different classification from the other three, class A for the former and B for the other three, in his terms.[51]

He further differentiates these dialects by characterizing class A notations as symbolic and class B as iconic, principally on the basis of their treatment of the *uirga*. "The A scripts are based on a convention that a Virga, alone or in compounds, represents a high note and the Punctum a low one. . . . The B scripts are based on the principle of directionality: the vertical position of the note-signs vis-à-vis one another and the use of the Virga-like stroke to represent the motion to a high note."[52] But the class A dialects also use the "position of the note-signs vis-à-vis one another" to indicate relative pitch and not just morphology, because in each instance cited above, the Saint Gall notation places the *uirga* that begins each compound neume, *cliuis*, *climacus* and *porrectus*, above the next note in the neume. Thus, in the context of the neume, all four early dialects, including that used at Saint Gall, represent relative pitch by iconic means. It is only at the level of the individual sign, *punctum* and *uirga*, that they invoke a symbolic means of representation, and then in the strictest sense only for the *punctum*.

Furthermore, to differentiate the two classes of dialects as symbolic or iconic according to whether the *uirga* means "motion to a high note" (class B) or the note itself (class A) seems to confuse the two semiotic classifications, unless Treitler is implying a distinction he does not explicitly state. Atkinson observes that the palaeofrankish *podatus* resembles the acute accent and represents two notes, the second higher than the first. The more common *uirga* looks very much like the palaeofrankish *podatus* but represents only one note. Thus, the former, the binary palaeofrankish neume, iconically represents rising motion, from the first note to the second, while the latter, the *uirga* of the four early dialects, represents "motion to a high note," also iconic but because it signifies a single note, with a different iconic meaning. Therefore, I reject Treitler's two classes, A and B, at least with regard to the distinction, among these four early dialects, between the Saint Gall notation on the one hand and the other three.

---

[51] Treitler, "The Early History of Music Writing," pp. 245–54, esp. 251–54 and Table I, pp. 246–47, based, as Treitler notes, p. 245 n. 20 (the note extends to p. 248), on that in Corbin, *Die Neumen*, p. 233.

[52] Treitler, "The Early History of Music Writing," p. 253.

Finally, I address the matter of the independent *uirga*. Codices SG 359 and Char 47 often use the *uirga* as an isolated note, representing either a single note set to a single syllable of text or individual notes within a melisma. In contrast, Laon 239 rarely uses it in either fashion, for which reason, Susan Rankin resists applying the term *uirga* to it, noting the similarity between its use in Laon and the Aquitanian dialect.[53] In Aquitaine, however, the independent *uirga* appears frequently in disjunct compound neumes and occasionally as an isolated note, but only in syllabic textures such as those found commonly in the texted sequence, a genre that remains unrepresented in Laon 239.[54] In fact, the only sequence Jacques Hourlier identifies in Messine notation before the eleventh century is *Summa pia gratia*, added on a page that had been left blank in the Compiègne manuscript.[55]

And this neumation does use an isolated note that bears identification as the *uirga*. In appearance, it does not resemble the corresponding neume in Laon 239, but it is precisely the same as the note used elsewhere in this neumation as the second note of the *podatus*.[56] While I recognize the dangers of basing an interpretation of notational practice on two instances in a single neumation, which could be idiosyncratic, it is clear that, in all other respects, the scribe of Laon 239 uses this note just like the scribes of SG 359 and Char 47, only less often and without incorporating any examples of the genre where it finds most frequent application as an isolated note, namely the texted sequence. Further, at least one Messine scribe, in Pa 17436, the Compiègne manuscript, felt that it could be used alone when the circumstances permit.

In all early dialects, therefore, the *uirga* stands for a note higher than those immediately adjacent to it. In practice, this distinction most often applies to the note that directly precedes the *uirga*, *ex parte ante*, to use Eugène Cardine's phrase, but it can also affect the note that follows, *ex parte post*.[57] In the Messine and Aquitanian dialects, of course, the heighting of the adjacent notes

---

[53] Rankin, "On the Treatment of Pitch," pp. 132–34, and *Writing Sounds*, pp. 247–48; cf. R. Fischer, "Laon, Bibl. de la ville, 239," p. 78, and Rumphorst, "Verhältnis von St. Galler und Metzer Notation," p. 69, who apply the term in disjunct compound neumes. Treitler, "The Early History of Music Writing," p. 251, also notes the rarity of the *uirga* as an isolated note in these two dialects.

[54] On the use of the isolated *uirga* in Aquitanian notation, see Grier, *The Musical World*, pp. 43–44, 68, and *Ademarus Cabanennsis monachus et musicus*, p. 102.

[55] Pa 17436 fol. 24r; see Hourlier, "Le domaine," pp. 110–11; also Huglo, "Observations codicologiques sur l'antiphonaire de Compiègne," p. 121.

[56] Isolated *uirga*: line 1 above "nos," line 2 above the first syllable of "nostra." As second note of *podatus*: line 1 above third syllable of "conseruando," first syllable of "corpora" and elsewhere.

[57] Cardine, *Semiologia gregoriana*, pp. 10–12; see also Rankin, "On the Treatment of Pitch," pp. 132–33.

helps to indicate when the *uirga* stands above the note that precedes, that follows or both. All four dialects, then, preserve a relationship between the *punctum* and *uirga* as notes that indicate relative melodic direction.

The Earliest Neumes: Grouping and Ligation

The second shared characteristic, grouping and ligation of neumes, functions principally to show the relationship between text and music. That is, by grouping notes together or literally binding them by connecting them with lines, the scribes delimited the length of the setting of a single syllable of text. The theorists offer scant evidence for this idea, and Guido d'Arezzo, in particular, bluntly contradicts it: "Likewise, sometimes one syllable would have one or more neumes, sometimes one neume would be divided in several syllables."[58] Hucbald, however, writing a century earlier, provides a more conventional approach: "These artificial notes are able to show ... either how the sounds themselves are joined in one or separated from one another."[59] Nevertheless, all four early dialects use a range of similar strategies to depict graphically the relation between text and music, to show which notes are to be sung with which syllables.

Again, just as the various dialects use heighting to a greater or lesser extent to indicate directionality, so do they use ligation, the physical binding of the neumes with penstrokes, to show text–music relations. And again, the Aquitanian and Saint Gall notations occupy opposite ends of the continuum, with the Breton and Messine dialects falling in between. Aquitanian notation represents most notes with individual signs, most often with the *punctum* or *uirga*, using only two ligatures with any regularity, the *cliuis*, indicating two notes in a descending pattern, and the *porrectus*, a ternary neume in which the middle note is lower than the first and last. Neither neume, however, customarily stands alone, but instead forms part of a larger group that normally begins with one or more *puncta*.[60]

[58.] "Item aliquando una syllaba unam vel plures habeat neumas, aliquando una neuma plures dividatur in syllabas." Guido, *Micrologus* 15.30, ed. Smits van Waesberghe, p. 169; trans. Babb, p. 71.

[59.] "Vel qualiter ipsi soni iungantur in unum uel distinguantur ab inuicem ... hae artificiales notae ualent ostendere." Hucbald, *Musica* 46, ed. Chartier, p. 196; trans. Babb, p. 37.

[60.] Grier, *The Musical World*, pp. 69–70, and *Ademarus Cabanennsis monachus et musicus*, pp. 107–9.

Moreover, Aquitanian scribes often replace these ligatures with disjunct forms, so that the *torculus*, in which the middle note is higher than the first and last, is sometimes written *punctum-cliuis*, sometimes *punctum-uirga-punctum* and sometimes with three *puncta*. I consider these options to be semiotic equivalents; that is, the graphic form of the neume does not alter its semiotic meaning.[61] The Aquitanian scribes, of course, use the vertical placement of the notes to indicate the melodic direction irrespective of the morphology of the neumes. Scribes at Saint Gall, however, normally ligated both binary neumes, *cliuis* and *podatus* (showing rising motion), and the ternary neumes that involve a change of melodic direction, *porrectus* and *torculus*. More important, though, these four neumes can all stand alone, unlike the custom in Aquitaine, as well as forming part of a longer melisma.

The Messine and Breton dialects mediate these extremes by employing alternative forms of the four neumes: all occur as ligatures that, as at Saint Gall, appear independently or within a melisma. All four also have disjunct forms in Laon 239, as do the *cliuis*, *podatus* and *porrectus* in Char 47; this scribe breaks the *torculus* into a *punctum* followed by a *cliuis*.[62] Although it is not clear whether the alternatives in Char 47 are semiotic equivalents, Heinrich Rumphorst avers that the *uncinus*, the note used in Laon 239 for the disjunct binary and ternary neumes, carries the same meaning as the *tractulus* in SG 359.[63] If the *tractulus* indicates a note of longer rhythmic duration, as some believe, then so would the *uncinus* of Laon 239 and, by extension, its disjunct forms of the binary and ternary neumes.[64] As in Aquitanian notation, the scribes of Char 47 and Laon 239 use heighting to indicate melodic direction in the disjunct forms.

The question remains as to why some dialects use more ligatures with greater frequency than others. The choice lies between greater precision in the alignment of text and music, which ligation affords, and the greater clarity with which disjunct neumes show melodic direction, as Michel Huglo pointed out in regard to Aquitanian notation.[65] It is true that

---

[61] In general, see Grier, *The Critical Editing of Music*, pp. 42–43.

[62] On Laon 239, see R. Fischer, "Laon, Bibl. de la ville, 239," pp. 77–80; and Rumphorst, "Verhältnis von St. Galler und Metzer Notation," pp. 68–75. On Char 47, see R. Fischer, "Chartres, Bibliothèque Municipale, cod. 47," pp. 77–79.

[63] On the equivalence of the *tractulus* and *uncinus*, see Rumphorst, "Verhältnis von St. Galler und Metzer Notation," pp. 62–64; on the durations suggested by the disjunct forms in Laon 239, ibid., pp. 68–75; also Rankin, *Writing Sounds*, pp. 241–45.

[64] On the *tractulus* and its potential rhythmic significance, see P. Wagner, *Neumenkunde*, pp. 115–17, 381–408 (who calls it *uirga iacens*); Sunyol, *Introducció a la paleografia*, pp. 78–79, 85, 88, 289–91; Vollaerts, *Rhythmic Proportions*, pp. 28–57; Jammers, *Tafeln*, pp. 33–35; and Cardine, *Semiologia gregoriana*, pp. 9–16.

[65] Huglo, "La tradition musicale aquitaine," pp. 261–62 and 265.

ligatures also indicate direction through the relative height of the constituent strokes that comprise the neume, but the resolution of the gesture into discrete notes makes visual comprehension of the melodic shape more immediate. Therefore, the choice to use ligation or disjunct neumes must reflect local preferences, conventions and above all needs. Some scriptoria observed that members of their musical community felt more comfortable reading notation that prescribed text–music relations with greater precision, while others preferred to show melodic contour with more clarity.

All four dialects use similar strategies to define groups of neumes. Ligation, of course, requires the scribes to join the individual notes with penstrokes. The disjunct forms, however, employ other procedures, which the *scandicus* and *climacus*, ternary neumes that ascend and descend, respectively, exemplify. The former takes the same shape in each of the four dialects: two *puncta* precede a final *uirga*, which designates the highest note of the group, all ascending obliquely to the right so that morphology and heighting reinforce each other. The *climacus* in Aquitaine, Char 47 and Laon 239 consists of three *puncta* in vertical alignment that the singer reads downwards. At Saint Gall, it begins with a *uirga*, again designating the highest note, and then continues with two *puncta* descending obliquely to the right.

The Saint Gall *climacus*, therefore, provides a good example of iconic representation in comparison with the other three dialects, in contradiction to Treitler's characterization of his class A notations as symbolic, because no singer could read the Saint Gall *climacus* as an ascending figure: it clearly begins with a higher note, represented by the *uirga*, followed by two notes that can only descend because they are written successively lower and farther to the right. Convention alone, however, dictates that the *climacus* in the other dialects be read downwards instead of upwards. Their use of heighting identifies them as iconic (higher notes occur higher in the vertically aligned stack), but the convention to read them downwards is entirely symbolic, and only emerges from a comparison with the arrangement of notes in ascending motion, which always, in all four dialects, rise obliquely to the right, as mentioned above.

Each of the four early dialects, therefore, shares the principles of ligation and, for ascending gestures, disjunct neumes rising obliquely from left to right ending in a *uirga* to indicate groups. Descending gestures show little more variation: the Aquitanian, Breton and Messine dialects all use vertically stacked neumes, read top to bottom, while notation at Saint Gall uses

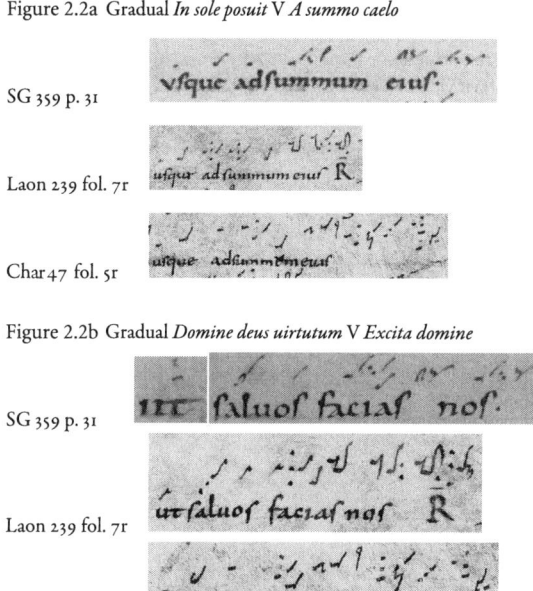

Figure 2.2a Gradual *In sole posuit* V *A summo caelo*

SG 359 p. 31

Laon 239 fol. 7r

Char 47 fol. 5r

Figure 2.2b Gradual *Domine deus uirtutum* V *Excita domine*

SG 359 p. 31

Laon 239 fol. 7r

Char 47 fol. 5r

Figure 2.2 Grouping and ligation in SG 359, Laon 239 and Char 47

disjunct neumes beginning with a *uirga* and descending obliquely from left to right, precisely the opposite of the convention for ascending figures. By these simple procedures for forming groups, all four dialects could create melismata of varying lengths to show precisely which notes were to be sung with which syllables of text. Figure 2.2 illustrates how three of the dialects, the Breton, Messine and Saint Gall, achieve these results.

In Figure 2.2a for the phrase "usque ad," all three witnesses use a ligated *podatus* to indicate that the second syllable of "usque" carries two notes.[66] The more elaborate setting for the first syllable of "summum" exhibits the usual conventions for grouping descending notes: the scribes of Char 47 and Laon 239 stack them vertically (two in the former, three in the latter), while the scribe of SG 359 begins the descent with a *uirga* and follows with two further *puncta* descending obliquely to the right. All three scribes commence the melisma with a *punctum* and end it with a *uirga*, the scribe of SG 359 adding a liquescent. All three also agree in the setting of the next two syllables, with a ligated *podatus* on the second syllable of "summum" and two ligated binary neumes (a *cliuis* and

66. For "ad," Laon 239 gives the same music as that for the first syllable of "summum," an error of assimilation through anticipation.

a *podatus*) on the first syllable of "eius," before evincing some variation on its second syllable.

The longer melisma on the second syllable of "eius" shows how scribes could join these various techniques for grouping into longer gestures. Some of the smaller units within the longer melismata might, as Cardine points out, indicate places where the singer could consider making an articulation, that is, dividing the melisma into shorter phrases.[67] For example, the scribe of Char 47 ends two consecutive ascents with a *uirga*, choosing not to link the end of the first ascent to the beginning of the second by using a *cliuis*. He may thereby be indicating to the singer a brief articulation, possibly a pause on the *uirga* followed by a short silence and a new glottal attack on the following *punctum*, although I acknowledge that this interpretation may not correspond to a medieval sense of how phrasing might work.

The phrase "ut saluos facias nos," in Figure 2.2b, exhibits the same strategies, but also an idiosyncrasy of scribal practices in SG 359. The text scribes of all three witnesses write "facias" without any separation between the syllables to accommodate the musical setting. In Char 47 and Laon 239, separation is unnecessary because their scribes write the three descending notes that constitute the bulk of the setting of the first syllable in vertical alignment, as is customary. Equally customary is the behaviour of the musical scribe of SG 359, who inscribes these three notes in an oblique descent. The extra horizontal space this configuration occupies requires the setting to continue above the last two syllables of the word, however, and the scribe compensates by writing the setting of the middle syllable below that of the first syllable.

Two conclusions follow from this circumstance. First, the text scribe was aware of the space requirements for the music, but often left insufficient room for it. If he was copying from a written exemplar, it might not have contained music. Second, the music scribe uses the vertical space above the text in an imaginative way, as Susan Rankin points out, to extend the horizontal space required for melismatic settings in response to the fact that the vertical space is not needed to indicate pitch.[68] Figure 2.3a shows this scribe continuing a single melisma, that for the middle syllable of "intende," on two horizontal planes due to the lack of space left by the text scribe.

[67.] Cardine, *Semiologia gregoriana*, pp. 56–65.
[68.] Rankin, "On the Treatment of Pitch," pp. 148–49, and *Writing Sounds*, p. 326. See also Rankin, "Calligraphy and the Study," pp. 55–57, where she shows that the music scribe of Cdg 473 also writes the neumes on a slant rising from left to right.

Figure 2.3a Gradual *Excita domine* V *Qui regis israhel*,
SG 359 p. 31

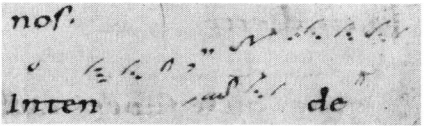

Figure 2.3b Gradual *Viderunt omnes* V *Notum fecit*,
Char 47 fol. 6v

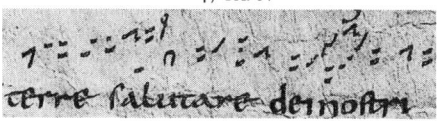

Figure 2.3 The use of vertical space for melodic continuation in SG 359 and Char 47

The scribe of Char 47 similarly tucks the setting for a subsequent syllable under the continuing melismatic setting of a previous syllable, as Figure 2.3b shows in two places. The melisma on the second syllable of "terre" rises above the first syllable of the following word, "salutare," the setting of whose first syllable then lies below the end of the melisma. The scribe secures the pitch relationship with the end of the preceding melisma by placing the *littera significatiua q* (meaning "equaliter" or unison) at the end of the melisma. He uses the vertical space above the literary text in the same way immediately after, on the phrase "dei nostri." The melisma on the second syllable of "dei" continues above the first syllable of "nostri," the setting of whose first syllable he places below the rising neumes of the melisma.

With these strategies of ligation and grouping, therefore, these early scribes provided information of great importance to the singers who used these manuscripts, namely the alignment between text and the melody to which they were to sing it. That these scribes rendered this relationship with a good deal more precision than they did the intervallic content of the melodies indicates how they conceived the music they were recording and how best to transmit it to those who would use these books: they could trust the memories of the singers to preserve the melodies, but those same singers depended much more on the written record to assure a correct correspondence between literary text and melody.

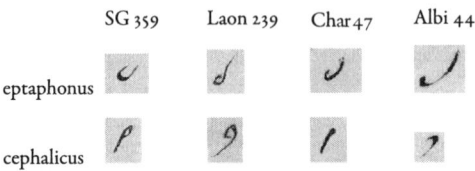

Figure 2.4 Liquescents in SG 359, Laon 239, Char 47 and Albi 44

The Earliest Neumes: Melodic Nuances

Finally, all four early dialects provide supplementary information about performing nuances in three principal forms: liquescents, special neumes such as the *quilisma*, and *litterae significatiuae*. Liquescents facilitate the delivery of diphthongs and certain combinations of consonants in the text.[69] Figure 2.2a shows that the scribe of SG 359 ends the setting of the first syllable of "summum" with a liquescent to aid the singer in enunciating the double consonant *mm* between the syllables, whereas the scribes of Char 47 and Laon 239 do not. Similarly, the scribe of Char 47 alone among these three witnesses indicates a liquescent, in Figure 2.2b, on the first syllable of "saluos," again to aid in the declamation of a difficult pair of consonants, *l* and consonantal *u* in this case. These variations indicate to what degree the use of liquescents in specific cases was subject to the tastes and needs of the individual musician, singer or scribe.[70]

Nevertheless, the appearance of liquescents in all four early dialects and their application to similar combinations of letters in the literary text show that their adoption was widespread in the late ninth and early tenth centuries.[71] Figure 2.4 shows the various forms of the liquescent neumes used in Char 47, Laon 239, SG 359 and Albi 44.[72] While the *eptaphonus*

---

[69] On liquescence in general, see R. Fischer, "Epiphonus oder Cephalicus?"; Haug, "Zur Interpretation der Liqueszenzneumen"; Bielitz, *Zum Bezeichneten der Neumen*; Phillips, "Notationen und Notationslehren," pp. 385–403; Betteray, *Quomodo cantabimus*; Białkowski, "Alcune osservazioni"; and Debrock and Mannaerts, "Liquescence et force articulatoire."

[70] On the idiosyncratic treatment of liquescence by Adémar de Chabannes, see Grier, *The Musical World*, pp. 74–77, 162–74, 282–83, and *Ademarus Cabanennsis monachus et musicus*, pp. 113–18.

[71] In Figure 2.4 and elsewhere, I use the term *eptaphonus* for the upwards liquescent. The term used by most scholars, *epiphonus*, appears to be a modern invention of Louis Lambillotte; see Floros, *Universale Neumenkunde*, 2:124–27. Odenkirchen, "13 Neumentafeln," p. 261 n. 11 and Abb. 2 facing p. 263, and Bernhard, "Die Überlieferung der Neumennamen," pp. 42–43, both document the medieval attestation of *eptaphonus*.

[72] For specifics on these forms, see, on SG 359, R. Fischer, "Einführung in Handschriften," pp. 64–65; on Laon 239, R. Fischer, "Laon, Bibl. de la ville, 239," pp. 78–82; on Char 47, R. Fischer, "Chartres, Bibliothèque Municipale, cod. 47," pp. 75–79; on Albi 44, Emerson, *Albi*,

Introit *Etenim sederunt*, Char 47 fol. 6v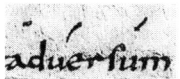

Figure 2.5 *Virga* and *cephalicus* in Char 47

takes a similar shape in all four dialects, the *cephalicus* falls into two forms that are differentiated on the grounds of whether the first, principal note is a *punctum*, as in Laon 239 and Albi 44, or a *uirga*, as in SG 359. In these three dialects, scribes add a downward curving stroke to indicate the second, liquescent note. The *cephalicus* in Char 47 presents another problem because of its marked resemblance to the *uirga* (see Figure 2.5).

The second and third syllables of "aduersum" use the *cephalicus* and *uirga*, respectively. Both ascend obliquely from left to right, but the latter curves upwards as it ascends, while the former curves downwards, a distinction Rupert Fischer makes implicitly.[73] The similarity of the two neumes and the fact that the form of the *cephalicus* does not make it clear, unlike that of the other three dialects, that it consists of two notes, creates a certain amount of ambiguity between *uirga* and *cephalicus* for the modern scholar and, I would submit, the tenth-century musician reading from this manuscript. The modern scholar can always compare the neumations in Char 47 with those in other early manuscripts, such as SG 359 and Laon 239, to determine which neume is a *uirga*, which a *cephalicus*, a luxury the tenth-century musician did not enjoy.

A similar ambiguity afflicts the *quilisma* in this manuscript, whose form is identical with that of the *oriscus*, to which I return below.[74] Both neumes indicate nuances of vocal delivery, the *quilisma* some kind of tremulous note, the *oriscus* a repeated note on the same pitch without changing syllable of text.[75] All four dialects use completely different forms of the two neumes from one another, as Figure 2.6 shows, even though they all

---

Bibliothèque Municipale Rochegude, Manuscript 44, pp. lxiv–lxv; further on SG 359 and Laon 239, Rumphorst, "Verhältnis von St. Galler und Metzer Notation," p. 78.

[73.] R. Fischer, "Chartres, Bibliothèque Municipale, cod. 47," pp. 75 and 78.

[74.] Rankin, *Writing Sounds*, pp. 252–54.

[75.] Medieval writers name the *oriscus* without defining its meaning; see Bernhard, "Die Überlieferung der Neumennamen," especially pp. 42–43, 46–47, 52, 54. Several authors including Guido d'Arezzo speak of a "tremulous" note; see Grier, "Adémar de Chabannes, Carolingian Musical Practices, and *Nota Romana*," p. 54. The passage in Guido, *Micrologus* 15.10, ed. Smits van Waesberghe, p. 164 (trans. Babb, p. 70), received two glosses in the late eleventh century in which the "tremulous" note is identified as the *quilisma*: Aribo, *De musica*, ed. Smits van Waesberghe, p. 66; repeated at *Commentarius anonymus in Micrologum Guidonis Aretini*, ed. Smits van Waesberghe, p. 153.

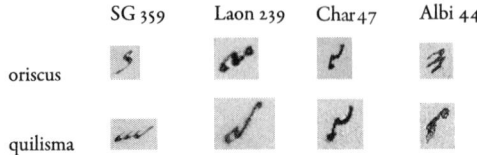

oriscus

quilisma

Figure 2.6 *Oriscus* and *quilisma* in SG 359, Laon 239, Char 47 and Albi 44

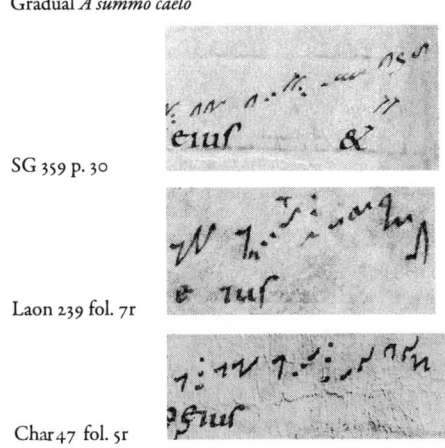

Gradual *A summo caelo*

SG 359 p. 30

Laon 239 fol. 7r

Char 47 fol. 5r

Figure 2.7 *Oriscus* and *quilisma* in context

carry the same meaning. While *oriscus* and *quilisma* differ from each other at Saint Gall and in Aquitaine, the Breton and Messine dialects use almost exactly the same form for each. The context in which these neumes occur may have helped the tenth-century singer distinguish them, as a higher note normally follows the *quilisma,* and the *oriscus* is usually preceded by a note at the same pitch. Still, I would suggest that the similarity of the morphology would pose problems for contemporary users of these manuscripts.

Figure 2.7 shows the same passage from the Gradual *A summo caelo* in SG 359, Laon 239 and Char 47. We see from the first named that, toward the end of the melisma on the second syllable of "eius," a *quilisma* occurs followed by an *oriscus* after the intervening *cliuis*. The singer reading from either Laon 239 or Char 47 would find it difficult, I would suggest, to see at a glance the difference between the two neumes.[76] Again, the modern

---

[76] R. Fischer, "Laon, Bibl. de la ville, 239," pp. 82–83, recognizes both *quilisma* and *oriscus* in Laon 239, but does not acknowledge the presence of the *quilisma* in Char 47; see R. Fischer,

scholar can identify them by consulting SG 359 or another source written in a dialect that distinguishes the two neumes, but I hardly suggest that as a practicable solution in the tenth century. To a degree, the context illuminates the identity of the neumes in Laon 239, as the *quilisma* definitely precedes a higher note, while the *oriscus* follows one of the same pitch, but I am hard pressed to apply the same criteria to the configuration of the neumes in Char 47.

In all four dialects, then, the *quilisma* and *oriscus* are symbolic in semiotic nature as no graphic feature of the neume suggests the nature of the musical gesture it represents, with one possible exception, the *quilisma* in SG 359, whose swirls might hint at the tremulous nature of its execution and so qualify as an iconic representation. Conversely, the liquescent neumes all seem to fall into the iconic category as their morphology suggests the direction of melodic motion, and the curving extension of the line that represents the liquescent note might hint at its mode of delivery. Again, there is an exception, the *cephalicus* in Char 47, which so closely resembles the *uirga* in that manuscript as possibly to cause confusion in the manuscript's users.

One issue remains with the *quilisma*, and that is its purported resemblance to the question mark in certain notational dialects and regions, an idea that seems to stem from an observation of Bernhard Bischoff's.[77] Leo Treitler amplifies Bischoff's remark to make the identity between either the *porrectus* or the *quilisma* and the question mark the central piece of evidence for his theory of the derivation of neumes from punctuation marks.[78] Treitler notes that the morphology of the question mark varies from region to region and that scribes use the question mark specific to their region as either *porrectus* or *quilisma* in their musical notation. From this agreement, Treitler extrapolates the derivation of the entire system of neumes from the corresponding system of punctuation marks.

A problem of logic vexes this theory. By what mechanism or motivation did scribes in different regions of the Carolingian Empire more or less simultaneously arrive at the idea of using the question mark, and by extension the rest of their conventional punctuation marks, as musical symbols? Only that coincidence would explain the regional differentiation in the two

---

"Chartres, Bibliothèque Municipale, cod. 47"; on the *oriscus*, ibid., pp. 82–83. Further on these two neumes in Laon 239, Rumphorst, "Verhältnis von St. Galler und Metzer Notation," pp. 76–78.

[77] Bischoff, *Paläographie des römischen Altertums*, p. 215; see also Treitler, "The Early History of Music Writing," p. 271.

[78] Treitler, "Reading and Singing," pp. 198–203.

types of signs because if the adaptation of punctuation marks as neumes occurred in a single place, say Metz, as I suggest above regarding the origin of neumes, then the regional variation in the symbols would have been minimal or nil altogether. Moreover, the palaeographic evidence does not seem to support Treitler's view. He does not print a table of neumes to show the parallels between them and the various regional question marks he does present.[79] The table of neumes he does print elsewhere does not include the *quilisma*, and the only neume in it that does resemble any of the question marks is the Saint Gall *porrectus*.[80] Other tables that do include the *quilisma* show that its Saint Gall iteration also resembles the question mark.[81]

Finally, what is clear from nearly every survey of medieval neumes is that many regional instances of the *quilisma* and *porrectus* bear not the slightest resemblance to any form of the question mark, whether from the same region or not. Another tantalizing piece of evidence might, however, shed some light on another observation of Treitler's. Lisa Fagin Davis shows that Gottschalk, music scribe at Lambach in the eleventh century, used neumes as omission marks in purely textual manuscripts.[82] Treitler states, "many of the signs were used in other connections beside punctuation in the eighth century and neumes in the ninth."[83] Scribes clearly exercised a certain commerce in signs, borrowing and adapting according to their needs and local practices. Morphological similarities alone do not prove historical connections.

The last of the three shared features that indicate vocal nuances is the use of *litterae significatiuae*. These letters, typically written above the neumes they affect, stand for words and expressions whose meanings, sometimes obscure, offer guidance on virtually every aspect of performance, including pitch, speed, duration and the character of the vocal sound.[84] All four early

---

[79.] Table of question marks, Treitler, "Reading and Singing," p. 198.

[80.] Treitler, "The Early History of Music Writing," pp. 246–47, derived from Corbin's table, as noted above, n. 51. The Saint Gall *porrectus* given there resembles question mark (a) at Treitler, "Reading and Singing," p. 198, which, according to the table of manuscripts, *ibid.*, p. 200, is used at Corbie.

[81.] See n. 48 above. The Saint Gall *quilisma* resembles question mark (f) at Treitler, "Reading and Singing," p. 198, also found at Corbie, *ibid.*, p. 200.

[82.] Davis, *The Gottschalk Antiphonary*, p. 51 and Figure 16, p. 53.

[83.] Treitler, "Reading and Singing," p. 198.

[84.] The bibliography on *litterae significatiuae* is extensive. Notker Balbulus offers a catalogue with definitions that apply to the signs as they were used at Saint Gall; see Froger, "L'épitre de Notker" (Rosenfeld's English translation in McGee, *The Sound of Medieval Song*, pp. 32–33). See also Mocquereau, *Le nombre musical grégorien*, 1:163–69, 171–74; P. Wagner, *Neumenkunde*, pp. 233–51; Sunyol, *Introducció a la paleografia*, pp. 79–90; Van Doren, *Étude sur l'influence*, pp. 94–118; Smits van Waesberghe, *Muziekgeschiedenis*, 2: *Verklaring der Letterteekens (litterae significatiuae)*; Rankin, "The Song School of St Gall," pp. 173–77, 181–84;

SG 359 p. 25, Gradual *Vniuersi qui*

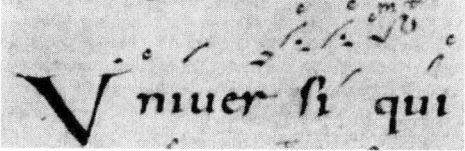

Laon 239 fol. 9v, Offertory *Deus enim firmauit* V *Dominus regnauit*

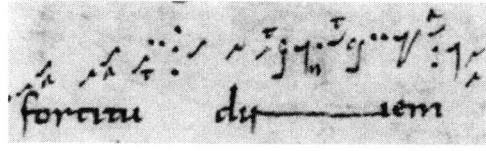

Char 47 fol. 6r, Offertory *Deus enim firmauit* V *Mirabilis in excelsis*

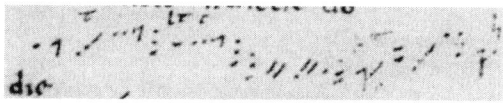

Albi 44 fol. 93v, Responsory *Ego sicut uitis*

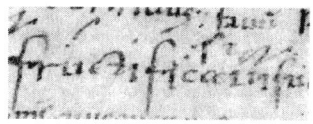

Figure 2.8 *Litterae significatiuae* in SG 359, Laon 239, Char 47 and Albi 44

dialects use at least some of these signs, perhaps the East Frankish more than the others and exploiting a wider range of them (see Figure 2.8). Although the four witnesses display many of the same signs, notably *t*, meaning "trahere" or "tenere" ("hold") in all four witnesses, and *c*, "cito" or "celeriter" ("quickly") in SG 359 (which also uses *m*, "mediocriter" ["with moderation"] meaning neither long not short, but in between), Laon 239 and Char 47, the signs do not invariably share meanings.[85]

For example, *a* according to Notker's epistle means "altius" ("higher") in pitch, but it seems unlikely that it retains that meaning in Laon 239. I note above that the scribe of Laon 239 uses heighting to indicate melodic direction and the first two instances of the letter *a* in Figure 2.8 appear under notes placed higher than those that immediately precede them; the

Phillips, "Notationen und Notationslehren," pp. 408–22; Huglo and Haggh-Huglo, "Des lettres de la passion"; and Llewellyn, "Grammar, Writing and Chant."

[85] On *litterae significatiuae* in Laon 239, see Billecocq, "Lettres ajoutées."

sign would therefore appear to be redundant. The third one, however, stands above a note that lies at the same height as the preceding one, and the sign seems to contradict the scribe's heighting. André Mocquereau provides a solution: by comparing its appearances with parallel passages in SG 359, he suggested that it must mean "auge" ("increase"), acting as a synonym for *t*.[86] Similarly, *n*, which according to Notker means "notare" ("note"), Mocquereau takes to mean "naturaliter" ("naturally") here in Laon 239, again affecting duration, equivalent to the *m* in SG 359.[87] So, the passage in Figure 2.8 shows a series of signs that indicate the relative durations of several notes, longer ones by *t* and *a*, shorter ones by *c*, and normal duration by *n*.

The passage in Figure 2.8 from Char 47 shows a slightly more varied approach to the use of the signs. In addition to *t* and *c* for longer and shorter notes, respectively, the scribe also combines two letters, *lt*, apparently with the same meaning as these individual signs have in Notker's epistle, "leuare" and "tenere" ("raise" and "hold"), affecting both the pitch and duration.[88] He also uses *h*, which Notker defines as indicating an aspirant sound for the note.[89] The editors of Paléographie Musicale 11 aver that in Char 47, it stands for "humiliter" ("low") in pitch, the meaning Mocquereau assigns it in Laon 239.[90] I stress that these alternative definitions for *a*, *n* and *h* in Laon 239 and Char 47 are hypotheses based on the melodic contexts in which they occur, as well as comparisons with parallel passages in SG 359.

The varied manifestations and applications of the system of *litterae significatiuae* in these three early chant witnesses suggest that even though the system and the principles of its use may have originated centrally, the specifics of their implementation varied across the regions in which these witnesses were produced, according to local needs and conventions. I would make much the same argument regarding the extremely varied morphology of the neumes, as well as the manner in which directionality,

---

[86]. Mocquereau, *Le nombre musical grégorien*, 1:172; see also R. Fischer, "Laon, Bibl. de la ville, 239," p. 86.

[87]. Mocquereau, *Le nombre musical grégorien*, 1:173; see also R. Fischer, "Laon, Bibl. de la ville, 239," p. 87. Billecocq, "Lettres ajoutées," pp. 20–28, esp. p. 21, is equivocal about the meaning of *n*.

[88]. *PalMus* 11:46–47. R. Fischer, "Chartres, Bibliothèque Municipale, cod. 47," pp. 83–84, does not include this combination among the *litterae significatiuae* he lists in this manuscript. On the *litterae significatiuae* in Char 47 in general, see *PalMus* 11:45–55.

[89]. See Llewellyn, "Grammar, Writing and Chant," pp. 228–31.

[90]. *PalMus* 11:46–47. On *h* in Laon 239, see Mocquereau, *Le nombre musical grégorien*, 1:171. See also R. Fischer, "Laon, Bibl. de la ville, 239," p. 87; and R. Fischer, "Chartres, Bibliothèque Municipale, cod. 47," p. 84.

grouping and ligation, and liquescence find application in the early, regional notational dialects. The dialects share clear principles, but the details of their use and functionality vary considerably across the regions.

The Earliest Neumes: A Common Ancestor and Its Dissemination

From these observations, we can make some deductions about the notation I posit as originating at Metz around A.D. 800, from which descended, I suggest, the early notational dialects attested by SG 359, Laon 239, Char 47 and Albi 44.[91] The four dialects derived from that notation the shared characteristics discussed above: directionality to show melodic motion; grouping and ligation to indicate the distribution of music above the sung literary text; and a preoccupation with melodic nuance through the specification of liquescence, special neumes such as the *quilisma*, and the *litterae significatiuae*. As I note above, the variety of ways in which the early dialects applied these characteristics demonstrates their adaptation to local circumstances, but it may equally indicate a degree of resistance to the centrally imposed practice of liturgical chant, particularly as the central authority of the Carolingian Empire progressively unravelled during the ninth century and individual centres could assert their independence.

It remains an open question as to whether that centrally mandated notation employed iconic or symbolic modes of representation because its surviving descendants freely mix these semiotic characteristics. The notation of SG 359, for example, uses symbolic gestures for the most part to represent pitch relations, but its form of the *climacus*, which shows three descending notes, is more clearly iconic than the cognate forms in the other three dialects, as I discuss above. So, although the semiotic analysis of the neume forms remains a powerful tool for understanding how they communicate to their users, one cannot be dogmatic about its application to an

---

[91.] Rankin, *Writing Sounds*, pp. 170–73 and 328–30, also posits, on the basis of similarities in the morphology of the graphemes used by the different dialects, a common ancestor for the various regional dialects, but proposes palaeofrankish script for the role. She then suggests that two distinct groups descended from this common ancestor, a dialect she calls Frankish that includes notations used widely in both the eastern and western regions of the Carolingian Empire and its successor states, on the one hand, and the Breton and Messine scripts on the other, *ibid.*, pp. 269–76, 330–36.

entire notational dialect or expect perfect consistency on the part of our tenth-century scribes.

The shared characteristics of these four early notational dialects indicate one central concern that they adopted from the notation devised at Metz, and that is the relationship between the sung text and its music. Several scholars observe that the principal purpose of chant and its notation is to facilitate the successful delivery of the text.[92] In particular, I would point to the use of grouping and ligation to indicate which notes set which syllables of text, and liquescence to aid the clear declamation of difficult combinations of letters. These features address specific problems in text–music relations and offer guidance to the singer who would negotiate them in the accurate presentation of the text within the larger sonic context of the sung chant. The common occurrence of these features in all four early dialects suggests that they derived these attributes from their shared ancestor.

Simultaneously, these shared traits indicate the importance of memory and the orally transmitted melodic tradition in the communication of melodies among musicians. Without specific pitch information, which all the early dialects lack, notation offers only mnemonic support and then in the three areas mentioned above, where ninth-century musicians, therefore, felt their memory needed the greatest written support. So, with the help of a notation that indicates melodic direction accurately, musicians were able to reconstruct the melodies with precision from their memory. Treitler would characterize the type of notation found in these early dialects as representative of a written, as opposed to a literate, tradition because musicians could not read it without prior knowledge of the melody.[93]

Outside or at the edge of the Carolingian Empire, similar dialects of chant notation appeared contemporaneously with the four just discussed or soon after. Visigothic notation occurs in manuscripts from northern Spain beginning in the late ninth or early tenth century.[94] Italian sources with notation and the earliest music sources from Anglo-Saxon England date from the late tenth or early eleventh century.[95] All these dialects,

---

[92.] This is the central concern of Jammers, "Studien zu Neumenschrift"; see also Treitler, "The Early History of Music Writing," pp. 243–45; and Rankin, "On the Treatment of Pitch," pp. 109–12, 166–68.

[93.] Treitler, "Oral, Written, and Literate Process."

[94.] Zapke, "Notation Systems in the Iberian Peninsula," pp. 208b–215a.

[95.] On notation in Anglo-Saxon England, see Planchart, *The Repertory of Tropes*, 1:61–66; Rankin, "Neumatic Notations"; and Rankin, ed., *The Winchester Troper*, pp. 22a–35b. No comprehensive treatment of early Italian notation exists; for overviews, see Sunyol, *Introducció*

including the various ones that came into use in the regions of Italy, differ in morphology, as do the four dialects described above, and they all share the three critical characteristics that mark those Carolingian notations: directionality, grouping and ligation, and signs for melodic nuance. I would aver that these traits indicate that these dialects, too, descend from the notation I believe originated at Metz around 800 at the request or command of Charlemagne.

Although the political power of the Frankish Empire had waned significantly by the time the earliest surviving examples of these notations appeared, the cultural capital that the empire had created and accumulated still held powerful sway over ecclesiastical institutions, such that churches neighbouring on it would aspire to imitate and acquire the cultural manifestations that still flourished in the aftermath of the empire, much like the Germanic tribes on the margins of the Roman Empire who emulated Latin culture even as the political and military power of Rome ebbed away at the conclusion of the antique period. The power of notation to preserve chant made it attractive to institutions whose welfare depended on the successful celebration of the liturgy. Thus, by the early years of the eleventh century, musicians throughout the territory that had formerly comprised the Carolingian Empire, and many not far from its borders, used musical notation principally to indicate the successful delivery of the sacred literary text.

Pitch

The development of a technology for the accurate inscription of pitch, first relative and then fixed pitch, holds a central position in the history of Western music. In comparison with musics of many other cultures, Western art music places higher importance on the role of pitch in its artistic formulations, as opposed to other elements such as timbre or rhythm. Therefore, musicians in Western culture devoted a great deal of thought to the creation of mechanisms for controlling pitch, in sound through tuning systems, or in writing through notation. As a result, I reserve a detailed consideration of the origins of notation with accurate pitch indications to Interlude 1. Here, I shall treat two preliminary issues,

a la paleografia, pp. 101–38; Stäblein, *Schriftbild der einstimmigen Musik*, pp. 34–38, 122–45; Corbin, *Die Neumen*, pp. 141–71; and Phillips, "Notationen und Notationslehren," pp. 477–94; see also Baroffio, "Music Writing Styles in Medieval Italy," for an introductory treatment of some dialects. On Beneventan notation, see Kelly and Peattie, eds., *The Music of the Beneventan Rite*, pp. 49–84.

first that of the motivation for these notational developments, and second, the steps that constituted them.

I begin with a consideration of precedence. Did the aesthetic concern for controlling pitch lead to developments in notation (or tuning systems), or did the notation enable musicians to introduce the control of pitch into their practices, in both performance and composition? My observations in Aquitanian notation suggest that preservation precedes creative initiatives.[96] Adémar de Chabannes wrote the earliest surviving manuscripts in Aquitanian notation that record accurate relative pitch information, beginning with Pa 1121, written between the summer of 1027 and late winter 1028.[97] In that manuscript, he uses notation to preserve the melodic contours of several liturgical repertories then practised at the abbey of Saint Martial in Limoges, including Proper and Common tropes of the Mass, Alleuias, Tracts and Offertories. The codex does include a handful of chants I identify as original compositions of Adémar's, but these hold a secondary position to the older items that occupy the majority of the manuscript.[98]

The next manuscript Adémar undertook, Pa 909, contains more original compositions where he exploits the technology of musical notation and its accurate representation of relative pitch to assist in a material way with his compositional process. First, in a couple of instances, he sketches and revises the melody, even as he is creating a fair copy. The most extensive examples occur in the newly composed Gradual and Alleluia for the Feast of Saint Martial, *Principes populorum* and *Alleluia V Beati oculi*, respectively.[99] Second, he exploits accurate pitch representation to explore relatively remote tonalities, by chant standards, most notably in the verse *Designatus a domino* of the Offertory *Diligo uirginitatem*, also for the Feast of Saint Martial.[100] These techniques would have been impossible to apply without the accurate representation of relative pitch, and so the technology here enabled the creative innovation.

The steps to the creation of accurate pitch representation involved one significant conceptual shift in the way the two-dimensional plane of the page represented musical action and then several incremental refinements.

---

[96] Grier, "Adémar de Chabannes (989–1034) and Musical Literacy," pp. 623–30.

[97] Grier, "The Musical Autographs," pp. 130–56; and *Ademarus Cabanennsis monachus et musicus*, pp. 22–25, 33–42.

[98] On these original compositions, see Grier, "The Musical Autographs," pp. 151–52; and *Ademarus Cabanennsis monachus et musicus*, pp. 40–41.

[99] Grier, *The Musical World*, pp. 264–69; and Adémar, *Opera liturgica et poetica*, ed. Grier, 1: II.9. B–C, pp. 196–200 (music) and 2:241–42 (commentary), and 1: App. B, pp. 642–44 (music) and 2:348–49.

[100] Grier, "Adémar de Chabannes (989–1034) and Musical Literacy," pp. 626–30.

That conceptual shift is the use of the vertical dimension to represent not just the direction of melodic motion (already present in the ninth- and tenth-century notations) but the musical distance between notes, the interval that separates them. Scribes early in the eleventh century, Adémar among them, began regulating the vertical position at which they wrote the neumes to indicate their relative pitch level, always within a diatonic framework. That is, a major or minor second required the same vertical distance, a major or minor third, and so on. This concept of space accurately reflected the medieval understanding of musical space on the gamut. Notes were adjacent regardless of whether they were separated by a major or minor second both in musical conceptualization and on the page.[101]

Once scribes grasped this conceptual shift, and it took a single generation at Saint Martial where the scribes were working with Aquitanian notation, they rapidly imposed a horizontal guideline to regulate the heighting of the neumes, a single line at first, but eventually a multi-line staff with notes placed on the lines or between them, just as in the modern system.[102] At first, they did not identify the value of the line, but by the middle of the twelfth century, Aquitanian scribes had put in place a multi-line staff with clefs fixing the pitch value of the lines. The first stages of these developments took place at precisely the same time as Guido d'Arezzo was formulating his notational system in the Prologue to his antiphoner, which we date to around 1030.[103]

Guido proposes a grid of horizontal lines within which scribes could affix notes either on the lines or between them, and they establish the pitch value by adding a clef or providing colour for one or more of the lines. Thus, the notation uses both lines and spaces, and the lines fall a third

---

[101] On Adémar's contributions to the representation of pitch in notation, see Grier, "Adémar de Chabannes (989–1034) and Musical Literacy," pp. 606–16.

[102] The first surviving musical source from Saint Martial not in Adémar's hand with accurate heighting is the proser Pa 1138/1338, probably from the second half of the 1030s. The first with a single horizontal line to guide the heighting is Pa 5240, which I date to the 1040s. See Grier, *The Musical World*, pp. 299–308. The earliest multi-line staves I have seen in Aquitanian sources occur in Pa 3549 (fols. 149–169) and the youngest portions of Pa 3719 (fols. 33–92), uersaria (collections of lyric song) that are roughly contemporary, and date from the middle of the twelfth century. See Fuller, "The Myth," p. 19.

[103] Guido, *Prologus in Antiphonarium* 46–76, ed. Smits van Waesberghe, pp. 67–81 (also edited and translated by Pesce in *Guido d'Arezzo's Regule rithmice*, pp. 418–35). See Smits van Waesberghe, "The Musical Notation"; Oesch, *Guido von Arezzo*, pp. 5–11; and Phillips, "Notationen und Notationslehren," pp. 581–85. On the date, see Palisca, "Introduction," in *Hucbald, Guido, and John*, trans. Babb, pp. 50–51; and Pesce, *Guido d'Arezzo's Regule rithmice*, pp. 1–3. For a different opinion on the date, see Oesch, *Guido von Arezzo*, pp. 15–16.

apart, just as in modern notation. Some scholars note the use of horizontal lines in some of the musical examples that illustrate the *Enchiriadis* treatises of the late ninth or early tenth centuries, together with the dasian symbols at the left edge of the lines, which serve as a clef to identify the pitches assigned to the lines. From these correspondences, they question Guido's originality in prescribing the staff.[104] These objections are baseless. First, the scribes who created the musical examples in this family of treatises did not invariably employ the system of horizontal lines; they sometimes wrote the symbols out horizontally directly above the text of the chant in the example. Second, when they do use lines, they are a second apart, not a third as in Guido's system. And third, the lines support the syllables of text, not the neumes.[105]

Nevertheless, we must ask whether Guido knew a system of notation that used accurate heighting, on which he then imposed the staff. Aquitanian notation certainly progressed in this way, from unheighted neumes to heighted neumes (showing the melodic intervals) without a line, to heighted neumes with a single-line staff, to finally a multi-line staff. But we need not suppose that Guido's experience or thought processes mirrored those developments. It is entirely possible that, working with unheighted neumes, Guido conceived of these two devices, accurate heighting and a staff of horizontal lines to regulate it, simultaneously. In any case, the staff functions to regulate heighting, either after its development or alongside it. And the clef, by which scribes fix the pitch of the notes, becomes a further refinement, although I hasten to note that Guido proposes the use of the staff and a clef system, by letter or colour, at the same time.[106]

Later Chant Notation

Although regional chant notations continued to be used throughout the Middle Ages, during the course of the thirteenth century, musicians in most of the Latin West adopted a single style of notation for copying chant,

---

[104] Haines, "The Origins of the Musical Staff," pp. 328–32 and 344–46; and Huglo, "Toward a Scientific Palaeography of Music," pp. 15–16.

[105] Smits van Waesberghe, "The Musical Notation," p. 53; Page, *The Christian West and Its Singers*, pp. 454–58; and Grier, "Adémar de Chabannes (989–1034) and Musical Literacy," p. 611.

[106] Cf. Duchez, "Des neumes à la portée," who proposes that Guido's invention of the staff proceeds directly from his theoretical conceptualization of tonal space.

called square notation because scribes wrote most of the notes with square noteheads. The history of square notation has yet to be written, and I do not attempt to accomplish that here.[107] Nevertheless, I believe it will be instructive to examine three manuscripts written for use at the abbey of Saint Denis near Paris between the eleventh and the thirteenth centuries. I do not thereby suggest that the notation originated there, nor that these three manuscripts possess any particular qualities that define the style. The most recent among them simply exemplifies it in a typical way, and its predecessors suggest some of the paths along which musicians and scribes may have experimented as they refined the features of the notation. They therefore allow us to sketch a tentative history of square notation.

The three manuscripts are PaM 384, a gradual for the Mass from the eleventh century, Pa 17296, a mid-twelfth-century antiphoner for the Divine Office, and Pa 1107, a noted missal written after A.D. 1259.[108] Codex PaM 384 contains unheighted French notation that in many respects resembles Saint Gall notation, certainly more than it does Messine or Breton.[109] (For comparison, Figure 2.9 presents the standard forms from the three Saint Denis sources in the same order as Figure 2.1 above, to which I add the ornamental neumes.)[110] In particular, the morphology of the *climacus* and the more common forms of the *porrectus* and *torculus* replicate the distinctive shapes of the Saint Gall notation, in contrast with the forms used by the other three early dialects. (The alternative and less common forms of the *porrectus* and *torculus* resemble neither the Messine nor Breton notation.) This French notation, therefore, also blends the symbolic and iconic forms typical of the Saint Gall notation, by using the iconic form of the *climacus*, for example, which begins with a *uirga* signifying the highest note of the three and continues with two *puncta* written descending to the right.

In other regards, the notation of PaM 384 shares features found in all four early dialects: it uses ligation and grouping to indicate the relationship

---

[107] See Helsen, "The Evolution of Neumes"; also Haines, "From Point to Square," which focuses on calligraphic developments. Huglo, "The Earliest Developments," pp. 168–69, and Cullin, "Notations in Carthusian Liturgical Books," attempt to place the origins of the style in Aquitanian notation, Cullin in a Carthusian context.

[108] Hesbert, ed., *Le graduel de Saint-Denis*, p. XI, dates PaM 384 to the eleventh century, Robertson, *The Service-Books*, p. 368, to the early eleventh century, with which Maître, ed., *Graduel de l'abbaye*, p. XIII, concurs. See further Robertson, *The Service-Books*, pp. 368–71. On Pa 17296, see ibid., pp. 393–99; on Pa 1107, ibid., pp. 381–83.

[109] On French notation, see Corbin, *Die Neumen*, pp. 100–31; and Klöckner, "Cod. H 159," especially pp. 80–85; on the relationship between East and West Frankish notations, Rankin, *Writing Sounds*, pp. 108–17, 194–228.

[110] For PaM 384, see the table in Hesbert, ed., *Le graduel de Saint-Denis*, p. XXXI.

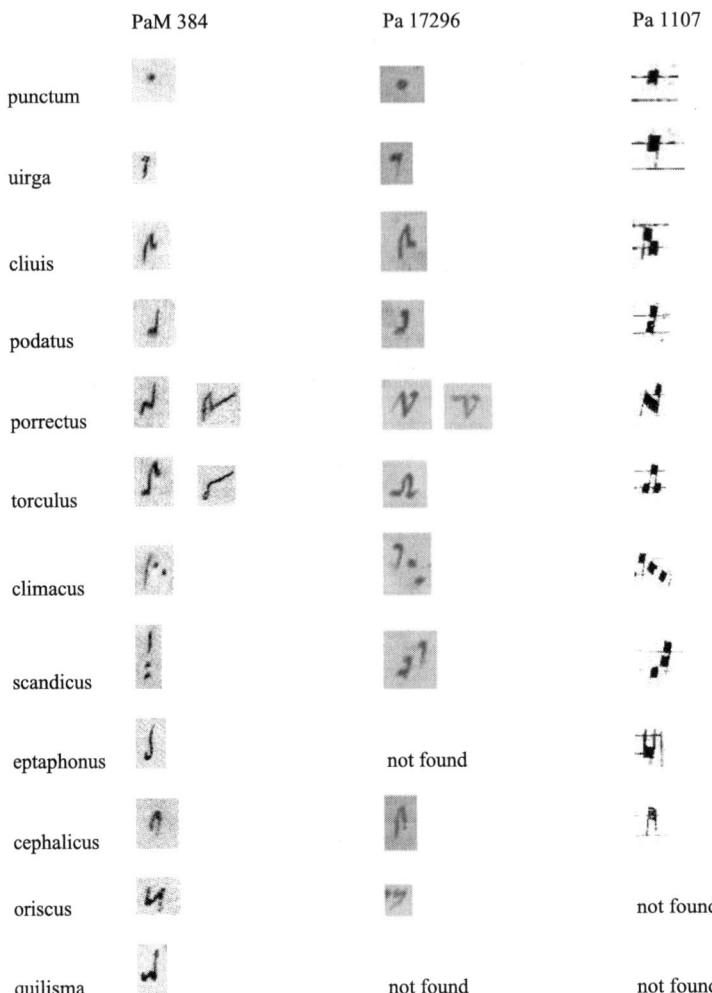

Figure 2.9 Neumes in PaM 384, Pa 17296 and Pa 1107
Courtesy of Paris, Bibliothèque Mazarine, Photo by Bibliothèque Mazarine; Paris, Bibliothèque nationale de France.

between text and music, and it employs the *quilisma* for ornamentation; the *oriscus* for repeated notes; liquescents, both ascending and descending; and a few instances of *litterae significatiuae*, those in use at Saint Gall.[111] Figure 2.10 gives *Alleluia* V *Video caelos* and shows the *eptaphonus* (above

---

[111.] They occur on fols. 33r and 143v–144r; for these and subsequent references, I use the foliation given in Maître, ed., *Graduel de l'abbaye*. See Robertson, *The Service-Books*, p. 343, who uses the older foliation.

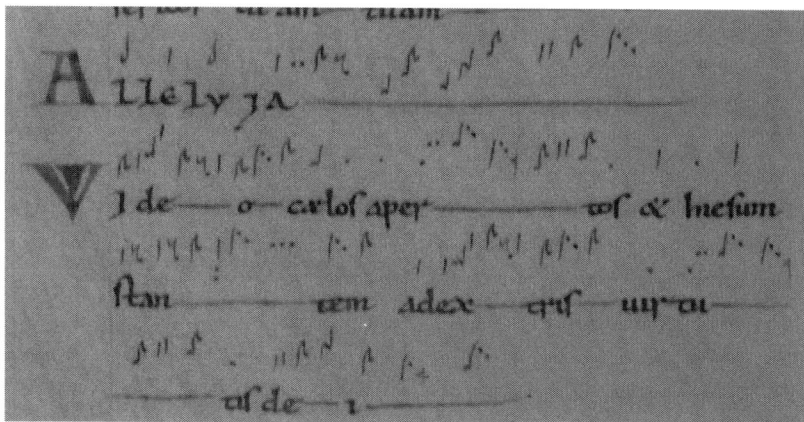

Figure 2.10 *Alleluia* V *Video caelos* PaM 384 fol. 4v

the first and third syllables of "Alleluia"), the *oriscus* (on the last syllable of "Alleluia" and first syllable of "dextris"), the *quilisma* (also the first syllable of "dextris") and the use of grouping and ligation to define the setting of individual syllables (e.g., "a dextris"). The *oriscus* and liquescents serve to clarify the manner in which singers ought to declaim the text in performance, precisely the same reason for their application in the four early notational dialects, and evidence that suggests that the French dialect too descended from the notation created at Metz during the Carolingian period.

Two features, however, suggest the path that subsequent scribes would take in crafting the square notation that came to dominate the Latin West by the fourteenth century. The *cliuis*, which appears in the Saint Gall notation as a curved line, ascending from left to right and then curving downward to the right, takes a similar form. The scribe of PaM 384, however, ends the stroke on the right with a notehead turned to the right, thus marking the second, lower note of the neume. He thereby creates a more concrete relationship between morphology and sound, and so increases the iconic content of the neume. Second, the *porrectus* in PaM 384 also closely resembles the Saint Gall form: an oblique line descending from left to right joins two vertical lines. But the scribe of PaM 384 draws the oblique line much thicker than in the Saint Gall form, and much thicker than the vertical lines it joins. This oblique line becomes one of the most distinctive traits of square notation, signifying two descending notes on the same syllable, as does the indication of individual notes within a ligated neume by discrete noteheads.

These features, particularly the latter, achieve greater prominence in Pa 17296, the antiphoner from the middle of the twelfth century. The *cliuis*, *torculus* and *climacus* look very much like those in PaM 384, while the scribe of Pa 17296 creates the *scandicus* by placing a *uirga* above a *podatus*, sometimes touching, sometimes not. Other ligated neumes, however, have acquired noteheads: the *uirga* now always possesses one, the *podatus* two, signifying each note. The *porrectus* takes two more or less interchangeable forms. One resembles that used in PaM 384, to which the scribe of Pa 17296 adds a notehead at the top of the right vertical stroke, turned to the left and representing the third note of the neume; he also makes the oblique line even thicker than that in PaM 384. The other form looks like that in the Messine and Breton dialects: it begins with a notehead from whose right edge a vertical line descends; an oblique line then ascends from left to right, ending in a notehead turned to the left.

The notation of Pa 17296, therefore, retains those iconic features found in PaM 384 and supplements them by adding to several neumes noteheads that signify individual notes within the neume. Two other aspects of the notation in this manuscript also indicate a desire to increase its specificity. The first, which regards neumatic morphology, exchanges some of the melodic nuances indicated in the early notational dialects for more precision in defining the melodic shape. To the best of my knowledge, the scribe of Pa 17296 uses neither the *eptaphonus*, the upwards liquescent, nor the *quilisma*. In places where one might expect the former, he simply writes a *podatus*. For some *quilismata*, he similarly writes ordinary ligated notes, while for others he indicates an upwards leap of a third, completely suppressing the decorative note.

Figure 2.11 shows the responsory *Missus est Gabriel*, in which earlier sources provide *quilismata* at, for example, the last syllable of "Gabriel" and the second of "angelus."[112] In the first case, the *quilisma* usually occurs as the third note of a four-note melisma, on B, but the scribe of Pa 17296 jumps over the embellished note with a leap of a third, A–C. Conversely, above the second syllable of "angelus," the scribe replaces the *quilisma* with a standard note on D, second of the melisma. Similarly, he substitutes a *podatus* for an *eptaphonus* on the first syllable of "apud" (the text scribe has written "adpud" incorrectly). He does, however, preserve the *cephalicus*, above "ad" in the phrase "ad Mariam" and the first syllable of "uirgo." The figure also illustrates the use of grouping and ligation (e.g., above "angelus").

[112.] E.g., the Hartker antiphoner, SG 390–91, SG 390 p. 16.

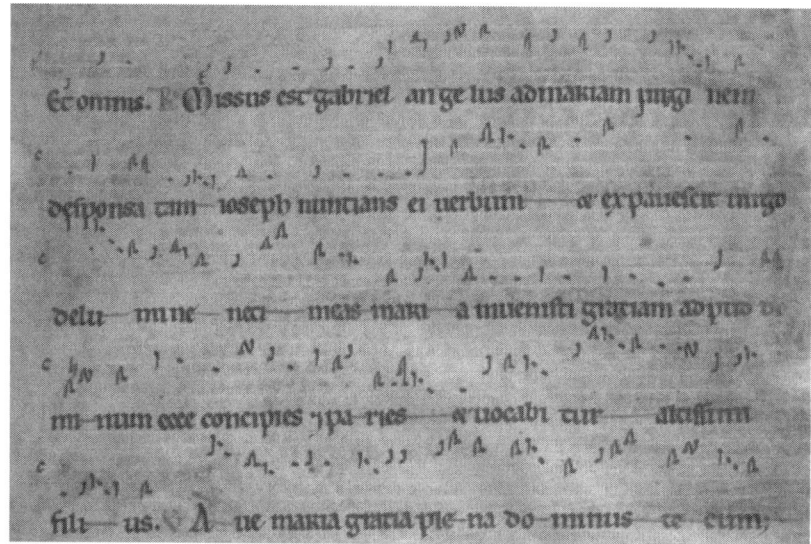

Figure 2.11 Responsory *Missus est Gabriel* Pa 17296 fol. 2v

The other feature concerns the more accurate inscription of pitch: the scribe of Pa 17296 imposes the music on a staff, generally of four lines, etched in the parchment with a drypoint stylus. He invariably writes a clef to identify the precise pitch of each melody, most often C, the equivalent of our middle C, and F, a fifth below, the same indicative pitches Guido d'Arezzo uses in his system. He also adds a flat on B, usually several notes before the indicated B♭ occurs, sometimes cancelled by the ♯, as in Figure 2.11 above the second syllable of "dominum". These symbols, then, accomplish two tasks: they signify the chromatic alteration of the note B, and they prepare it by warning the singer to apply the appropriate hexachord, soft where the flat occurs and hard with the natural.[113] Thus, this witness is the first we have encountered to which we might apply Treitler's category of literate notation; that is, a skilled musician can read it at sight without prior knowledge of the melody, as opposed to the written tradition that the earlier notational dialects represent, including the eleventh-century notation in PaM 384.[114]

In the notation of Pa 17296, therefore, we find a significant number of the traits that define the square notation of the thirteenth and subsequent

---

[113.] I defer a fuller discussion of the hexachord system and solmization to Interlude 1 below, on pitch.
[114.] Treitler, "Oral, Written, and Literate Process."

centuries. Many notes, whether the individual *puncta* or notes that form part of ligated neumes, take a decidedly square form, but all do not find representation as noteheads, the first note of the *cliuis*, for example, or the middle note of the *torculus* and *porrectus* (either form). These neumes derive their meaning from their older symbolic forms still familiar to the younger musicians who created and used Pa 17296 and manuscripts like it in the twelfth century. In particular, this notation preserves the care with which it communicates text–music relations, especially through grouping and ligation, even though some of the melodic nuances characteristic of the tenth- and eleventh-century dialects seem to have receded, at least from the notation if not from performance itself.

These older and more symbolic aspects of the neumatic forms found in Pa 17296 collided in the thirteenth century with the impetus to create an increasingly rational, systematized and ultimately precise form of notation. Codex Pa 1107, the noted missal written for Saint Denis in the middle of the thirteenth century, exhibits these characteristics. First, with the exception of the oblique stroke that typifies the *porrectus*, and the liquescent neumes, both of which I discuss below, all notes receive a discrete notehead. Second, the music scribe replicates the ligation and grouping found in PaM 384 and Pa 17296 to define the relationship between text and music. Third, the staff, now drawn with pigment, and clef appear throughout the codex, together with B♭ where necessary (see Figure 2.12). Anyone with modest musical literacy can read the pitch content of the chants inscribed in this codex.

Still, many connections remain with the notation of the two earlier codices, which might indicate a more likely descent of mature square notation from the French dialect than others, such as the Aquitanian, as some posit.[115] (I address this issue below.) For example, both the *cliuis* and *porrectus* begin with a vertical stroke descending from the left edge of the neume. This first note, then, might preserve some aspect of the *uirga* in its morphology, since, in both cases, the first note of the neume lies higher in pitch than the second. But already in PaM 384 and more definitely in Pa 17296, the *uirga*, as an independent note, exhibits a vertical stroke descending from its right edge, not its left, as is the case with the *cliuis* and *porrectus*. So, while the earlier form of these two neumes may in some way suggest that they begin with a *uirga*, by the time they arrive in Pa 17296, still more in Pa 1107, the stroke seems to represent a purely calligraphic reminiscence

---

[115.] See n. 107 above.

Figure 2.12 *Alleluia* V *Video caelos* Pa 1107 fol. XXIIra

of that relationship instead of a concrete reference to the *uirga* and its morphology.

A tendency already present in Pa 17296, namely, the suppression of some nuances of performance, extends a little wider in Pa 1107. The *quilisma*, absent from Pa 17296, is also lacking in Pa 1107; for example, PaM 384 (Figure 2.10) provides one on the first syllable of "dextris," second note, where Pa 1107 gives an ordinary note, the second note of a *podatus*. The *oriscus* also fails to appear in this codex, for example again on the first syllable of "dextris," where the scribe replaces the *oriscus* in PaM 384 with the first note of a *porrectus*. The *uirga*, nevertheless, appears to have taken over some of the responsibilities of the *oriscus*. For instance, it stands as the last of a series of repeated notes on the same pitch setting the same syllable of text, a position in which one would often see the *oriscus* in earlier notations.

Curiously, the *eptaphonus*, which I could not find in Pa 17296, reappears in Pa 1107 (e.g., Figure 2.12 on the third syllable of "Alleluia," in agreement with PaM 384), alongside the *cephalicus*. They both use vertical strokes on either side of the principal note, those on the *eptaphonus* ascending, as one might expect, those on the *cephalicus* descending. But the principal note of each differs slightly: that of the *cephalicus* a short, thick, oblique stroke, the *eptaphonus* more square. And the two vertical strokes on the *eptaphonus* are roughly equal in length, while the right stroke on the *cephalicus* is slightly shorter than the left one.

Finally, the music scribe of Pa 1107 uses another distinctive trait of this notation that holds importance for the subsequent development of rhythmic notation: for strings of more than two descending notes (he writes the *cliuis* for a group of two descending notes), he inscribes diamond shapes. These are most obvious in the *climacus*, which, as in PaM 384 and Pa 17296, consists of a *uirga* (always with tail descending from the left) and two *puncta* descending from left to right, but in Pa 1107, the *puncta* take the shape of diamonds, not squares. The scribe of Pa 17296 already wrote the last two notes of the *climacus* and longer strings of descending notes with noteheads drawn more on the oblique than the squarer ones of other neumes, but the scribe of Pa 1107 makes the difference much greater, appearing to have rotated the square noteheads through forty-five degrees to create the diamond-shaped notes. The morphology of these notes seems to have no semiotic weight beyond indicating descent (already clear from their relative position on the staff) and grouping on the same syllable.

I close this discussion with a couple of observations about the possible descent of square notation from the early French or Aquitanian dialects of chant notation. It is true that, by the end of the twelfth century, Aquitanian scribes had introduced a form of square notation, although I hasten to point out that Pa 17296, from the middle of that century, also exhibits notes that begin to resemble the squares of the next century. Most outstanding in my experience is the collection of sacred and secular song in Lo 36881, which consensus places at the end of the century, several decades later than Pa 17296.[116] In two respects, however, mature square notation resembles French notation more than it does Aquitanian: the manner of depicting ascent and descent, and the use of the oblique. For the latter, Aquitanian notation simply has no equivalent, but its mature form descends directly

---

[116]. On the date of Lo 36881, see Fuller, "The Myth," pp. 22–25; and Grier, "Some Codicological Observations," p. 52. For other examples, see Huglo, "The Earliest Developments," pp. 168–69, and Cullin, "Notations in Carthusian Liturgical Books."

from the morphology of the *porrectus* in French notation as exemplified by PaM 384.

Meanwhile, Aquitanian notation indicates ascending motion by placing the notes on an oblique plane, rising from left to right, while scribes using this dialect stack descending notes vertically. The same arrangement obtains in the twelfth-century manuscripts from Aquitaine with square noteheads. Precisely the opposite scheme characterizes French and square notation: pairs of ascending notes lie in vertical orientation, the higher note directly above the lower, and falling notes, distinguished by their shape (full diamonds in Pa 1107), descend obliquely from left to right. It would seem unlikely in the extreme that either of these features could have developed spontaneously from the Aquitanian square notation of the twelfth century. I present this evidence and these arguments not as a definitive history of square notation, but instead as a tentative sketch of how it might have come into existence in the thirteenth century.

More important than its historical precedents, however, is what square notation represents as a development in the semiotics of musical notation. Several features mark a preoccupation with creating visual precision in the presentation of pitch. First and most important is the use of discrete symbols for each note in place of the symbolic forms that appear in earlier dialects. The *cliuis* provides a good example. In PaM 384, a curved ascending line represents the first note, resembling the *uirga*, while a definite notehead indicates the presence and location of the second note at a lower pitch than the first. The scribe of Pa 17296 employs a similar form, but its place on the staff shows that the point at which the line turns to curve downwards marks the pitch of the upper note. In Pa 1107, however, the first note obtains its own notehead while the stem on its left side becomes the vestige of the curved line with which the earlier form begins.

It would not be fair to say that the morphology of the *cliuis* in Pa 17296, in combination with its position on the staff, left any doubt as to the pitch of the first note, but the form adopted in Pa 1107 provides a clear and discrete marker for its pitch that singers might more readily and speedily apprehend. Such considerations encouraged, in the earliest dialects, the use of grouping and ligation, a practice continued in square notation, to show the relationships between text and music. Ease of visual comprehension remains a motive throughout the history of Western notation, in part because of the complex nature of musical notation and in part because of the exigencies of performance. As musicians came to use written or printed music for reference during performance, it became increasingly important for the notation to communicate its information in such a way that musicians could grasp it in real time as they performed from it.

Two types of symbols in Pa 1107 do not conform to this ideal of a discrete sign for each note: the two liquescents and the oblique stroke with which the *porrectus* begins. These straddle the divide between iconic and symbolic representation as they all unequivocally indicate the direction of melodic motion, but readers of the notation must infer the presence of two notes in each symbol. The fact that thirteenth-century musicians would not find the correct interpretation of these neumes problematic does not obscure the contradiction they raise with respect to the consistency with which this notation embraces iconic modes of representation. Instead, it indicates to what degree skilled musicians internalize the processes needed to apprehend and understand the information encoded in the musical notation at hand, in whatever form it takes.

Second, the accurate heighting of the neumes and their constituent notes, regulated by the staff, governed by the clef and modified where necessary by B♭, enables the notation to specify unequivocally the pitch content of a chant. This system works in coordination with the first feature, the use of a discrete symbol for each note. The staff provides a means for locating a symbol with precision on the vertical axis of writing, but if the symbol itself does not assume a sufficiently discrete shape (e.g., it overlaps adjacent space and line or occupies two spaces and the intervening line), the reader cannot impose the information from the staff cogently. These two features, then, work together to provide a meaningful and easily comprehensible system for inscribing and reading precise pitch information.

Simultaneously, we observe that the music scribes of these documents from Saint Denis continue to reduce the amount of detail they provide with regard to performing nuances.[117] For example, the *quilisma* and the *oriscus* seem to have passed out of use by the production of Pa 1107. Does their absence from this manuscript suggest that the corresponding performance gestures too were no longer present in the chant as sung at Saint Denis? One theory about the origins of musical notation around A. D. 800, to which I subscribe, suggests that the Frankish singers devised

---

[117] On the loss of notational nuance as precision in pitch increases, see Duchez, "Des neumes à la portée," pp. 46–51.

notation in the first place to indicate where these nuances should occur and how to execute them, both tasks the Franks apparently found difficult to master. Had they sufficiently internalized these concepts by the twelfth or thirteenth century that they no longer needed the written indications? I would propose a different interpretation. I suspect that the performing techniques were never firmly established north of the Alps. As the political need to imitate Roman singing styles diminished with the collapse of the Carolingian Empire and its successor states, the style became obsolete and so the supporting indications in the notation disappeared.

* * *

Between the ninth and the fourteenth centuries, notation for chant underwent several metamorphoses. Most notably, musicians found devices for the increasingly precise indication of pitch, many of them innovations of Guido d'Arezzo. By the end of the Middle Ages, the system most common in modern Western notation was in wide use, namely the staff, regulating the vertical height at which scribes placed each note, with clef, which identified the specific pitches, and accidentals to modify notes with chromatic inflections. Simultaneously, the range of performing nuances characteristically indicated gradually diminished. Michel Huglo, in regard to Aquitanian notation, mentioned that as notation acquires greater specificity, it tends to lose its ability to communicate nuance.[118] This is not a necessary outcome. For example, the scribe of Pa 1107 invented or adopted a new symbol for the *oriscus*, and scribes could have replicated that achievement for other nuances, but for the most part, they did not.

From a semiotic point of view, the various styles of notation move from symbolic modes of representation to increasingly iconic ones. As the discussion of both the early dialects and mature square notation demonstrates, both modes of representation occur in all these styles of notation. Still, the diachronic development of these systems finds iconic modes replacing symbolic modes. I mention above changes to the form of the *cliuis* in the witnesses from Saint Denis that evince this development. The chief motivation for these changes would seem to lie in a desire for increased specificity, particularly in the precise indication of pitch. In what way do these developments reflect changes in the musical practices that lie behind the notation? Did musicians

---

[118.] Huglo, "La tradition musicale aquitaine," pp. 261–62 and 265.

require greater precision in the presentation of pitch because they had grown more distant from the oral practices that preceded notation? Does the reduction in the quantity of performing nuances suggest that they were fading from the living tradition?

First, it is difficult to believe that musicians of, say, the twelfth or thirteenth century who were part of a musical community that had been practising the liturgy continually since the Carolingian era would feel themselves in any way distant from the living tradition. In other words, there is no reason to believe that institutional memories had diminished at all by the time these communities adopted square notation and its more precise methods of identifying pitches. I would attribute the desire to adopt these more precise methods to the exigencies of pedagogy and the need to expedite the education of young singers in chant.[119]

Manuscripts like Pa 17296 and 1107 would permit young singers, once competent in the notation, to learn a great deal of the repertory from sight as opposed to learning by rote from hearing other singers perform the chant. Second, as I suggest above, the performing nuances may have become less important to an authoritative rendition of chant as the political necessity to incorporate them diminished. A recurrent theme throughout this book is that each phase of musical notation is sufficient for its purposes and contexts. Changes, such as we observe in chant notation, arise sometimes from concomitant changes in musical practices but also because of changes in the purposes for musical notation and the context in which musicians practise it.

[119.] See Grier, "Adémar de Chabannes (989–1034) and Musical Literacy," pp. 621–23; see also Duchez, "Des neumes à la portée," pp. 25–28.

Interlude 1: The Problem with Pitch

The notations used for chant from the ninth to the early eleventh century give very little information about pitch. As I discuss in Chapter 2, all the early dialects show melodic direction and the *littera significatiua* *e* indicates where two consecutive notes lie at a unison. But for the most part, pitch relations remain opaque. The fact that musicians knew three systems for the accurate presentation of pitch in the tenth and eleventh centuries places this situation in high relief: the palaeofrankish and dasian notations mentioned in Chapter 2, to which we can add the alphabetic notation advocated by Hucbald of Saint Amand derived from Boethius and that used in Norman manuscripts.[1] All three systems appear predominantly in theoretical sources to specify the pitch content of melodic passages in musical illustrations and, to a much lesser degree, in practical musical sources, particularly the alphabetic system that appears in Mo H. 159, where the music scribe combines it with neumatic notation of French origin.[2]

The question to be considered here, then, is why musicians of the ninth, tenth and, in some geographical regions, the eleventh centuries did not feel compelled to specify the pitch content of the melodies they were committing to writing despite the existence of these three techniques for doing so. Again, it would seem that prevailing musical practices and the concept of notational self-sufficiency lie behind this decision. Either the pitch sequences were firmly fixed in the memories of the singers and so presented less of a problem than other aspects of the melody, such as the relationship between the melody and the text, or the sequence of pitches was simply not fixed in the identity of each melody. Evidence supports the former explanation, as I show

---

[1.] Hucbald, *Musica* 44–55, ed. Chartier, pp. 194–212; trans. Babb, pp. 36–44. On letter notations in general, see Santosuosso, *Letter Notations*.

[2.] On illustrations in music theory treatises, see Treitler, "Reading and Singing," pp. 142–78. On Mo H. 159, see P. Wagner, *Neumenkunde*, pp. 251–57; Corbin, *Die Neumen*, pp. 102–7; Santosuosso, *Letter Notations*, pp. 69–81; and Klöckner, "Cod. H 159," pp. 79–80.

elsewhere in regard to the melodic tradition of the Aquitanian trope repertory.[3]

As I discuss in Chapter 2, the scribes who employed these early notational dialects placed a much higher priority on recording the performing nuances that seem to have vexed the Frankish singers so much and on depicting the manner in which singers were to set text to melody. But once we accept that ninth- and tenth-century singers retained the pitch sequences of the melodies in their memories, why did scribes of the next two centuries expend considerable effort to increase the visual specificity of their notations, particularly with regard to pitch? Were memories of those melodies fading, and so musicians needed better written records to retain them? Or were these notational developments part of a general trend toward a greater reliance on literacy in all aspects of life? It is difficult to believe that skilled musicians would be unable to recall the melodies they had been singing all their lives, and so I prefer the latter explanation.

In the first half of the eleventh century, Guido d'Arezzo emphasizes a second factor in his original exposition of the system of staff and clef, and that is pedagogy. With enhanced visual material at their disposal, student singers, no longer dependent solely on the oral tradition passed on to them by their elders, could expedite their acquisition of the professional repertory they needed to become soloists in their ecclesiastical institutions. We see the results of these efforts in Pa 17296, the twelfth-century antiphoner, and Pa 1107, the thirteenth-century noted missal, both written for the abbey of Saint Denis, discussed in Chapter 2. They give unequivocal and precise pitch information for the chants they preserve. Still, as in today's fully literate musical culture, younger singers would have done some of their learning by listening to their elders.

The elegance of Guido's system reinforces its pedagogical intent. In the first instance, he chose two significant notes to stand as identifiers, or in modern parlance, clefs on the staff: our middle C and the F below it. Each note forms the upper note of a minor second, E–F and B–C. (Guido only reluctantly recognized the practical necessity of admitting B♭ as a possible pitch on the gamut.)[4] In the prevailing

---

[3.] For an example of the stability of the tradition, see Grier, *The Musical World*, pp. 57–60; on variation, see *ibid.*, pp. 197–98; cf. Treitler, "Observations on the Transmission." See also Grier, "Adémar de Chabannes (989–1034) and Musical Literacy," pp. 623–26.

[4.] Guido, *Micrologus* 8, ed. Smits van Waesberghe, pp. 124–26; trans. Babb, p. 64. See also Guido, *Regulae rhythmicae* 67–71, ed. Smits van Waesberghe and Vetter, pp. 103–4 (also edited and

diatonic system, singers needed to know precisely where to place the semitone, and these two clefs reminded them of its position. Musicians subsequently used other notes for clefs, some without reference to the place of the semitone. First to come into use, of course, was G, a fifth above middle C, forming a symmetry with F a fifth below, also falling on a line. Other clefs less commonly encountered include D a seventh below middle C, and B♭ a second below; the former falls on a line in the system established by C and F, the latter on a space and functioning simultaneously as clef and solmization sign, eventually key signature.

A second feature of Guido's system, the alternation of line and space for adjacent notes on the diatonic gamut, benefits both its pedagogical utility and its practical application in musical literacy. By using both line and space as locations for discrete pitches, the system encourages the visual recognition of certain patterns that correspond to musical relations between notes. For example, notes a third apart fall on adjacent lines or spaces, leaving the intervening line or space empty, but notes a second apart occupy a line and the space immediately above or below. This feature first permits the student to grasp the relationship between musical and visual patterns more quickly, which then become fixed in the mind as the student progresses toward assuming responsibilities for solo singing.

At the same time as increased precision in pitch notation may have facilitated pedagogy, it is inescapable that this same development led, inevitably, to an increasingly fixed, perhaps even rigid, conception of the pitch content of the melodies in the chant repertory. The melodic variations that characterized the earliest phases of chant transmission, even if they were limited in scope, diminish in frequency as precise and accurate pitch notation becomes more common.[5] This situation stands in marked contrast to the way in which musicians recorded and transmitted non-liturgical repertories such as the twelfth-century Aquitanian *uersus* repertory. There, the scribes used notation to record substantive variants

---

translated by Pesce in *Guido d'Arezzo's* Regule rithmice, pp. 348–49), and *Epistola ad Michahelem*, ed. and trans. Pesce, pp. 510–17. For commentary, see Pesce, *The Affinities*, pp. 20–22; Atkinson, *The Critical Nexus*, pp. 223–24; and Blackburn, "The Lascivious Career," pp. 21–27.

[5.] For examples of the variations, see Treitler, "Oral, Written, and Literate Process," esp. pp. 476–91. For arguments and examples about the stability of the tradition, see D. Hughes, "Evidence for the Traditional View," and "From the Advent Project to the Late Middle Ages."

characteristic of individual versions.[6] Chant scribes, meanwhile, tended to preserve fixed versions of the melodies. To what degree the role of precise pitch notation in their pedagogy influenced this conception of melodic pitch content remains an open question, but it undoubtedly left some impression.

The development of pitch notation and its effect on patterns of transmission invite a consideration of Charles Seeger's categories of descriptive and prescriptive notation and their application to these early phases of the technology.[7] In his conception, the former type preserves music originally conceived in performance, while in the latter, writing precedes performance and therefore prescribes its particulars. The earliest chant notation records a written impression of how singers of the Carolingian era performed chant, and we could thus construe the relationship between the scribes, the notation and the music it purported to record as descriptive in the first instance. The cultural conditions under which musicians invented notation, however, suggest another way to understand its purpose. I observe in Chapter 2 that the Franks found the execution of certain performing nuances difficult.

The inventors of the notation therefore created special symbols to indicate where singers should perform these nuances and simultaneously devised methods for specifying relationships between text and music. With these techniques, the notation thus *described* how contemporary singers executed these aspects of chant performance. For readers of early notation, however, these indications *prescribed* how they should perform the chants. Thus, the perception of the function of the notation, as preserving the melodic tradition or as instructions for performance, depended on the perspective of the individual, scribe or singer who was using the notation, even when the same person was fulfilling both functions, and could in turn alter the relationship between the music and its notation as descriptive or prescriptive.

At the same time, the early witnesses of the tradition do not fully agree on where to place the performing nuances and, to a lesser degree, how text and music relate. Such variations show that scribes retained some discretion in applying the techniques and, by extension, singers in their execution. These circumstances mitigate the force of these indications as either descriptive or prescriptive, and suggest that, at least for some, they served

---

[6.] See Grier, "Scribal Practices," esp. pp. 400–20.
[7.] Seeger, "Prescriptive and Descriptive Music-Writing."

as guides instead of unequivocal instructions. The same considerations apply, whether the scribes were recording an actual performance they had experienced, as either singer or listener, or a potential performance they imagined cognitively, a condition I believe to be the usual mode in which scribes wrote music.[8]

This complex of relationships between scribes, singers, notation and music allows a further question. As notation becomes more specific in the way it records pitch and simultaneously loses nuances, does it become more prescriptive in nature? I would suggest that is certainly the outcome, whether intended or not.[9] Scribes would feel obligated to choose a specific sequence of pitches for each chant they were inscribing, even when they were aware, from their own performing and listening experience, of two or more versions of a given chant. The notation simply did not permit the indication of melodic variants. Those who were copying from a book with precise notation would have to make a conscious choice to alter the pitch sequence in the exemplar, barring scribal error of course.

Singers, too, even those who also acted as scribes of the very books from which they were singing, would be confronted with precisely noted pitches, in Pa 17296 for example. They would have learned the chants from such books, and when they turned back to them for reference in preparation for a performance, they would find the same precise record of the pitch sequence. These circumstances had to have had an impact on how they performed the chants, always tending in the direction of a fixed sequence of pitches. I suspect that Adémar, Guido and the others who contributed to the development of precise pitch notation did not intend in any specific way to limit the possibilities of performance, even though that became the eventual result. Rather, they were attempting to make the notation more efficient, particularly in pedagogy.

Alongside the regulation of accurate heighting through the staff, Guido proposed a complementary system to assist singers with accurate singing that also directly affected musical pedagogy, namely solmization.[10] As is

---

[8.] For discussion, see Grier, "Scribal Practices," pp. 412–14, and *The Musical World*, pp. 74–77, 162–82.

[9.] Grier, "Adémar de Chabannes (989–1034) and Musical Literacy," pp. 624–26.

[10.] Guido, *Epistola ad Michahelem*, ed. Pesce, pp. 464–71. For discussion and bibliography, see Adémar, *Opera liturgica et poetica*, ed. Grier, 1: pp. cxii–cxix; also Grier, "Adémar de Chabannes (989–1034) and Musical Literacy," pp. 620–21.

well known, Guido adapted a melody that, from its design, seems to have been composed for pedagogical purposes, to the first stanza of *Vt queant laxis*, an eighth-century hymn attributed to the historian and poet Paul the Deacon.[11] Each successive phrase of the melody begins on a note a second higher than the previous phrase, starting on C and rising through the hexachord. Guido assigns the first syllable of each line of the hymn text as a mnemonic for the note on which the syllable is sung. By memorizing the series of notes and their syllables, singers are able to produce musical intervals and sequences of pitches accurately: ut–mi for the major third, re–fa for the minor third, ut–re–mi for two ascending major seconds, re–mi–fa for a major second followed by a minor second, and so on.

As many scholars have pointed out, this system too, like Guido's choice of significative notes for the staff, exhibits elegance and stresses the central importance of the placement of the semitone in the successful rendering of chant. The hexachord divides into two symmetrical, disjunct trichords, each consisting of two major seconds, separated by the single semitone that occurs in the system, precisely in the middle of the hexachord, represented by the syllables mi and fa.[12] As a complement to musical notation, moreover, solmization works only with precise pitch notation. Unheighted notation depends on the memory of the singer for the accurate reconstruction of the pitch sequence, and so the application of the solmization syllables depends equally on that resource.

Solmization and precise pitch notation, however, operate in tandem to provide a firm visual and aural record of the chant and its pitches. Once singers recognize the first note or notes of the chant from its visual representation, they can apply the appropriate solmization syllables to create a precise aural image of the melody. Young singers who had already attained a familiarity with the chant repertory and who aspired to become soloists would benefit most from the combination of these two systems, precise pitch notation and solmization. Their application would greatly expedite the learning of new chants, particularly those a singer would need to perform alone, as a soloist, without the support of the rest of the musical community.

---

[11] Smits van Waesberghe, *De musico-paedagogico*, pp. 86–113.
[12] E.g., Wiora, "Zum Problem," p. 267.

In view of its utility in transmission and especially pedagogy, it seems surprising that Guido's technology of precisely representing pitch, that is, the staff with clef, took so long to achieve adoption across western Europe. I remark in Chapter 2 that Aquitanian scribes did not begin using the system until the middle of the twelfth century, at least a century after Guido had promulgated the system and they had adopted heighted notation, the precondition for the use of the staff. Joseph Smits van Waesberghe lists some 170 manuscripts that exhibit some form of Guido's notation, of which he dates only three unequivocally to the eleventh century.[13]

Smits van Waesberghe and Christopher Page propose various explanations for the delay in the adoption of the system, including the commitment of resources, human and material, for the production of new chant books; the resistance to a new technology, especially one that would require the rethinking of manuscript layout; and the reluctance of scribes who were accustomed to a flexible approach to the pitch content of a melody to fix it with the new notation.[14] The trajectory of the change in notational style at Saint Martial illustrates the reaction of one musical community to the situation. After Adémar introduced the technique of accurate heighting to the scriptorium while he was supplying the notation to Pa 1121 during the second half of A.D. 1027, the monks hastened to adopt it, failing to master it in the first layers of Pa 909 in early 1028, and then requesting that he teach it to them on his return in mid-1028. From that point on, music scribes at Saint Martial used the technology.

Almost as quickly, the monks implemented the single-line staff, first in Pa 5240, written in the 1040s, and so in the generation following Adémar, as I discuss in Chapter 2. Multi-line staves with clefs, however, became common a full century later, in the middle of the twelfth century. I conclude that musicians at Saint Martial found the combination of accurate heighting and the single-line staff adequate for their needs. The full system seems to have required some other impetus for its adoption, perhaps the acquisition of a manuscript from another house that used it or the reforming zeal of a single individual in the

---

[13.] Smits van Waesberghe, "The Musical Notation," pp. 20–28; the three eleventh-century manuscripts are nos. 1, 85 and 103 in his inventory.

[14.] Smits van Waesberghe, "The Musical Notation," pp. 43–48; and Page, *The Christian West and Its Singers*, pp. 397–99, 472–73.

scriptorium. But the monks at Saint Martial, whose pattern of acceptance may not parallel that of any other institution in the Latin West, show no resistance to the technology per se, and even some enthusiasm for it. It is only the refinement of the full system that took some time to gain approval.

3 | Polyphony and Rhythmic Notation

Beginning around A.D. 1000, musicians cultivated increasingly complex styles of polyphony. The earliest practical polyphony, from Winchester, Aquitaine and Paris, simply employed the prevailing style of plainsong notation.[1] By the middle of the twelfth century, that notation accurately specified the pitch content of a melody, as I discuss in Chapter 2 and Interlude 1, and so the pitch content of the simultaneously sounding voices became secure. Rhythmic coordination in the Winchester polyphony of the eleventh century caused no problems because it proceeds in strict note-against-note style, and so each note in the organal voice corresponds to a single note in the liturgical chant. Aquitanian polyphony of the next century, however, often sets more notes in the upper voice than in the lower, and so debates ensue as to how to orient the two voices. Bryan Gillingham and Theodore Karp have proposed controversial interpretations of the rhythmic structure of this polyphonic repertory.[2] Still, no convincing system for the regulation of the rhythmic relationship between the two voices has appeared.

Parisian musicians at the cathedral of Notre-Dame in the late twelfth and early thirteenth centuries created a repertory of liturgical polyphony, termed organum, for the most important feasts of the liturgical year, in which the lowest voice, or tenor (from the Latin *teneo* "I hold"), carried the appropriate chant.[3] The cathedral musicians composed polyphony in two, three or four voices, called, appropriately enough, organum duplum,

---

[1] Winchester: Cdg 473; see Holschneider, *Die Organa von Winchester*; and Rankin, "Winchester Polyphony"; on the notation of Cdg 473, see Rankin, ed., *The Winchester Troper*, pp. 22a–46b. Aquitaine: Pa 1139, 3719, 3549 and Lo 36881; see Fuller, "Aquitanian Polyphony"; Bonderup, *The Saint Martial Polyphony*; and Danckwardt, "Zur Notierung, klanglichen Anlage und Rhythmisierung." The principal witnesses of the Notre-Dame polyphony are W_1, F and W_2; see C. Wright, *Music and Ceremony*, p. 244.

[2] Gillingham, *Modal Rhythm*; Gillingham, ed., *Saint-Martial Mehrstimmigkeit*; commentary in Gillingham, "Saint-Martial Polyphony–A Catalogue Raisonné." Karp, *The Polyphony of Saint Martial and Santiago de Compostela*. For a detailed discussion of Karp's edition and a comparison with that of Hendrik van der Werf (*The Oldest Extant Part Music*), see Crocker, "Two Recent Editions." See also Stäblein, "Modale Rhythmen."

[3] The best general treatment of the repertory remains C. Wright, *Music and Ceremony*, pp. 235–72.

triplum or quadruplum; organum duplum also bears the name organum purum. The texture of the plainchant in the lowest voice determines the relationships between it and the upper voice or voices and, as a result, the use of rhythm in organum duplum. In all types of organum, where the plainchant moves syllabically or with short melismata, the tenor sustains long notes below florid motion in the upper voice or voices; scholars call this texture sustained-note organum. Where the chant uses a melismatic texture, however, the tenor accelerates; such passages are termed discant.

In three- and four-voice organum, the upper voices all move rhythmically throughout, in sustained-note organum and discant, chiefly to coordinate musical events in the entire texture, and so the rhythms become part of the compositional planning, as Leo Treitler points out.[4] Musicians treated rhythm in organum duplum, however, according to the texture of the chant. Controversy surrounds those passages where the tenor sustains the notes of the chant below the florid upper voice, but the consensus seems now to hold that the upper voice proceeds in free rhythm.[5] In discant passages, however, both voices move rhythmically. In addition, passages known as copula serve as transitional moments between the sustained-note sections and discant; here, the upper voice alone moves rhythmically while the tenor sustains long notes.[6]

Throughout the subgenres of Notre-Dame liturgical polyphony, the upper voices are melismatic in texture and therefore use ligatures predominantly, just as contemporary plainsong would in a melismatic context. The scribes of this repertory took advantage of the situation to create a notational system in which they assigned rhythmic patterns to patterns of successive ligatures. Each note, then, acquired a duration from its position

---

[4] Treitler, "Oral, Written, and Literate Process," pp. 490–91; see also C. Wright, *Music and Ceremony*, pp. 289–91.

[5] Durations based on modal rhythm: Waite, *The Rhythm of Twelfth-Century Polyphony*. Free rhythm: Yudkin, "The Rhythm of Organum Purum." See also Reckow, "Organum purum und Organumpurum-Verständnis im 13. und 14. Jahrhunderts," in *Der Musiktraktat des Anonymus 4*, ed. Reckow, 2:35–55; Treitler, "Regarding Meter and Rhythm"; Sanders, "Consonance and Rhythm"; Roesner, "Johannes de Garlandia on *organum in speciali*" and "The Emergence of *musica mensurabilis*"; and Atkinson, "Franco of Cologne." Mark Everist and Edward H. Roesner, in their editions of organa dupla in F and W$_1$, respectively, both adopt free rhythms for the sustained-note sections: Everist, ed., *Le Magnus liber organi*, 2: pp. lxxib–lxxiva; and Roesner, ed., *ibid.*, 7: pp. liva–lviib. Thomas B. Payne, however, applies measured durations to the corresponding passages of his edition of organa dupla in W$_2$: Payne, ed., *ibid.*, 6a: pp. lxxxa–xciiib. Hans Tischler prints rhythms throughout the dupla: Tischler, ed., *The Parisian Two-Part Organa*, 1:31b–32a.

[6] Reckow, *Die Copula*; Yudkin, "The *Copula* According to Johannes de Garlandia" and "The Anonymous of St. Emmeram and Anonymous IV on the *Copula*."

in a ligature within a pattern of ligatures, and so this aspect of the notation is entirely symbolic. This system became known as the rhythmic modes.

The Rhythmic Modes

The precise manner in which modal rhythms originated and came to function within the various Notre-Dame repertories remains shrouded in obscurity.[7] As many scholars have noted, the evidence on which we base our knowledge of these practices postdates the origins of the repertories themselves by decades. We know that musicians at Notre-Dame were singing polyphony in as many as four parts before the end of the twelfth century, and the career of the functionary at the cathedral whom Craig Wright identifies as Leoninus, to whom the late thirteenth-century theorist known as Anonymous IV (from the position of his treatise in the omnibus edition of Edmond de Coussemaker) attributes the compilation of the *Magnus liber organi*, spanned the period between 1179 and 1201.[8] In contrast, the earliest of the three principal manuscript sources, W_1 and F, scholars now date in the late 1230s (the former) and around 1250 (the latter), that is, several decades after the inception of the repertories.[9]

The theory treatises that describe these notational practices stand even more remote from the origins of the repertory than the practical sources. What most scholars consider the earliest treatise, the so-called *Discantus positio uulgaris*, survives as part of the compilation made by Jerome of Moravia at the end of the thirteenth century.[10] But it is entirely possible that Jerome revised it as he produced his composite text. He includes in the same chapter the treatise of Johannes de Garlandia, which survives in two other witnesses, from the state of whose texts we can deduce that Jerome either knew an alternative version of Garlandia's text or imposed the

---

[7.] See, e.g., Roesner, "The Emergence of *musica mensurabilis*."

[8.] The ordinance that Bishop Odo of Sully issued in 1198 specifies that two-, three- or four-voice organum could be sung at Vespers and at Mass; see C. Wright, *Music and Ceremony*, pp. 237–43, partial text, *ibid.*, Document no. 38, p. 369; translation, *ibid.*, p. 239. On Leoninus, see C. Wright, "Leoninus," esp. pp. 7–13; A.D. 1179 and 1201 are the dates of the earliest and latest documents that name him; see *ibid.*, pp. 32–35. Anonymous IV states, "magister Leoninus ... fecit magnum librum organi de gradali et antifonario" ("master Leoninus made the great book of organum from the gradual and the antiphoner"), ed. Reckow, 1:46 lines 6–7 (trans. Yudkin, p. 39). Coussemaker, *Scriptorum*, 1:327–64.

[9.] On W_1, see Everist, "From Paris to St. Andrews." On F, Haggh and Huglo, "*Magnus liber—Maius munus.*"

[10.] Hieronymus, *Tractatus de musica* 26, ed. C. Meyer and Lobrichon, pp. 176–81 (trans. Knapp in "Two XIII Century Treatises," pp. 203–7).

modifications himself.[11] Whatever the date of the original text of the *Discantus*, therefore, we have no guarantee that the version transmitted by Jerome agrees with it in every particular.

Scholarship is divided on the dates of the other three principal treatises that concern modal rhythm, those of Garlandia, the Anonymous of Saint Emmeram and Anonymous IV; I rely on Jeremy Yudkin's thorough and convincing account of their chrononology.[12] He begins with the secure date of 1279 for the treatise of the Saint Emmeram Anonymous, which derives from its colophon.[13] Because both this author and Anonymous IV model their treatises on that of Garlandia, the latter must date some years before; Yudkin suggests ca. 1260.[14] Furthermore, the Saint Emmeram Anonymous emphatically expresses disgust with the views and practices of Lambertus, whose treatise embraces certain principles equally enunciated by Franco of Cologne, and yet the Anonymous never mentions him by name.[15] Had Franco's treatise been available to him (Yudkin firmly establishes the Parisian milieu in which the Saint Emmeram Anonymous worked, and so it is impossible to argue that he might not have known of it had it existed), he would not have spared him the vitriol he expended on

---

[11] Jerome's text of Garlandia: Hieronymus, *Tractatus de musica* 26, ed. C. Meyer and Lobrichon, pp. 181–215 (trans. Birnbaum). On the witnesses of Garlandia, including Jerome, see Reimer, "Die Überlieferung des Traktats," in Garlandia, *De mensurabili musica*, ed. Reimer, 1:18–26. On the relationship between Jerome's text and the other witnesses, *ibid.*, 1:27–29; and Reimer, "Textkritischer Kommentar," in *ibid.*, 2:1–9 and 39–42.

[12] Yudkin, "Notre Dame Theory," pp. 232–38.

[13] Anonymous of Saint Emmeram, *De musica mensurata* 6, ed. and trans. Yudkin, p. 288 lines 32–37 (when I cite this work, I give the page and lines of the Latin text; in each case, Yudkin's translation appears on the facing page, here p. 289).

[14] The treatise of the Saint Emmeram Anonymous is a prosimetrum; i.e., it contains both verse and prose. But the author suggests that the principal text is the poetry, to which the surrounding prose acts as a running commentary; see Yudkin's introduction to Anonymous of Saint Emmeram, *De musica mensurata*, ed. and trans. Yudkin, pp. 1–10. He refers frequently to the *prosa* when he cites Garlandia's treatise, expanding it in the opening of the treatise to "prosa artis musicae mensurabilis" ("the prose of the art of mensural music"; *ibid.* Prologus, p. 64 line 1), and quotes or paraphrases it often; Yudkin provides a comprehensive list of sources used by the author, *ibid.*, pp. 291–325, in which Garlandia's treatise figures prominently; summarized at *ibid.*, p. 35 n. 69. Anonymous IV twice cites the incipit of Garlandia's treatise (ed. Reckow, 1:33 lines 8–9, 45, lines 15–16; trans. Yudkin, pp. 25 and 38, respectively) and names one Iohannes dictus Primarius (ed. Reckow, 1:46 lines 21–26, 50, lines 27–29; trans. Yudkin, pp. 40 and 44, respectively), both times in conjunction with Franco of Cologne; Reckow takes this Johannes to be Garlandia; see Reckow, "Personen-Register," in *ibid.*, pp. 97–98.

[15] On his reaction to Lambertus, see, e.g., Anonymous of Saint Emmeram, *De musica mensurata* Prologus, ed. and trans. Yudkin, p. 74 lines 3–4; for commentary, see Yudkin, introduction to *ibid.*, pp. 7–10, 34–36.

Lambertus.[16] Anonymous IV, however, mentions Franco by name, and so his treatise must postdate both Franco's and that of the Saint Emmeram Anonymous, probably in the early to mid-1280s.[17]

Therefore, both the principal treatises and the most important practical sources stand at some remove from the repertories' origins, and we must, consequently, classify them, in some respects at least, as retrospective on the practices they preserve and describe, rather than contemporary. Both the late date and the tone of the treatises authored by the Saint Emmeram Anonymous and Anonymous IV deserve more comment. The rejection of the innovations of Lambertus (and, by extension, those of Franco) by the former and the interest in historical issues on the part of the latter suggest that both anonymi were reflecting on, perhaps even yearning for, musical practices now waning in favour.[18] In fact, the two witnesses to the repertories that fall in the same period as the two anonymi illustrate precisely this trend.

Codices W_2 and Mo H. 196 both date from the last third of the thirteenth century, and both exhibit a shift in emphasis with regard to the repertories they preserve.[19] The second half of W_2 and virtually all of Mo H. 196 preserve motets and so attest the dominance of that genre among musicians in the latter part of the century.[20] As many scholars have pointed out, the motet requires a rhythmic notation that shows the durations of the individual notes that its syllabic style demands, exactly what Franco accomplished with his notational innovations, as opposed to the more melismatic texture of organum that normally employs the ligatures that permit the

---

[16.] On the Parisian context, see Yudkin, introduction to Anonymous of Saint Emmeram, *De musica mensurata*, ed. and trans. Yudkin, pp. 38–43; and Appendix II in *ibid.*, pp. 341–48; also Yudkin, "The Anonymous Music Treatise of 1279."

[17.] Anonymous IV names Franco twice (ed. Reckow, 1:46 lines 23–24, 50, lines 28–29; trans. Yudkin, pp. 40 and 44, respectively); see Reckow, "Personen-Register," in *ibid.*, pp. 95–96.

[18.] For the historical perspective of Anonymous IV, see the passages, ed. Reckow, 1:46 lines 1–26, and 1:50 lines 14–36 (trans. Yudkin, pp. 39–40 and 44–45, respectively); for a discussion of his retrospective attitude, see Wegman, "The World According to Anonymous IV," pp. 714–16. On the practice of organum at Paris, see Baltzer, "How Long was Notre-Dame Organum Performed?".

[19.] On W_2, see C. Wright, *Music and Ceremony*, p. 244, who places it in the second half of the century. If, however, F originated around 1250, as is the current consensus, a date soon after that seems too early for W_2, as Wright's own deductions about the repertorial differences between it and the other two principal sources allows one to infer, *ibid.*, pp. 268–72. On Mo H. 196, see Wolinski, "The Compilation of the Montpellier Codex"; and Stones, "Les manuscrits du Cardinal Jean Cholet," pp. 251a–57b, especially p. 253a.

[20.] W_2 fols. 123–253; see the inventories in Reaney, *Manuscripts of Polyphonic Music*, pp. 171–202 (W_2) and 272–369 (Mo H. 196).

Table 3.1 Rhythmic modes

Mode	Description	Ligatures	Modern Transcription
1	long, breve	one ternary, several binary	♩ ♪ ♩ ♪ ♩ ♪ ♩
2	breve, long	several binary, one ternary	♪ ♩ ♪ ♩ ♪ ♩ ♪
3	long, two breves	one longa, several ternary	♩. ♪ ♩ ♩. ♪ ♩ ♩.
4	two breves, long	several ternary, one binary	♪ ♩ ♩. ♪ ♩ ♩. ♪ ♩
5	all longs	several longae or several ternary	♩. ♩. ♩.
6	all breves	one quaternary, several ternary	♫♫ ♫♫ ♫♫ ♪

representation of the rhythmic modes.[21] The Saint Emmeram Anonymous and Anonymous IV, therefore, may have been resisting, each in his own way, the incursions of the motet and its style of notation on the organum practised at Notre-Dame since the twelfth century.

The four principal treatises all agree as to the number and content of the rhythmic modes (see Table 3.1) and further that a correct breve (*breuis recta*) has a length of one tempus, a correct long (*longa recta*) two tempora.[22] Further, Garlandia defines a tempus as the length of one "recta brevis," thus defining the terms by each other in a circular fashion, and, moreover, states that it is indivisible.[23] This, I believe, is the first of several missteps in coining and defining terminology for rhythmic practices in this early period. First, all four principal treatises, including Garlandia's, recognize the existence of the semibreve and so contradict his indivisible tempus.[24] Second, the semibreve, of course, does not always, especially in this early period, divide the breve in half, as its name suggests. The *Discantus positio uulgaris* allows us to infer

---

[21] E.g., Reckow, "Proprietas und perfectio," p. 130; Reimer, "Johannes de Garlandias Notationslehre und ihre geschichtliche Stellung im 13. Jahrhundert," in Garlandia, *De mensurabili musica*, ed. Reimer, 2:51–54; Tanay, *Noting Music, Marking Culture*, pp. 52–53; and A. Berger, *Medieval Music and the Art of Memory*, p. 177.

[22] *Discantus positio uulgaris*: Hieronymus, *Tractatus de musica* 26, ed. C. Meyer and Lobrichon, pp. 179–81 (trans. Knapp, pp. 206–7). Garlandia, *De mensurabili musica* 1.7–27 and 4, ed. Reimer, 1:36–38 and 52–56, respectively (trans. Birnbaum, pp. 1–2 and 8–10, respectively). Anonymous of Saint Emmeram, *De musica mensurata* 2, ed. and trans. Yudkin, pp. 190–212. Anonymous IV, ed. Reckow, 1:22–36 (trans. Yudkin, pp. 13–29).

[23] Garlandia, *De mensurabili musica* 1.20–22, ed. Reimer, 1:37–38 (trans. Birnbaum, p. 2); echoed by Anonymous of Saint Emmeram, *De musica mensurata* 1.1, ed. and trans. Yudkin, p. 102 lines 31–33.

[24] *Discantus positio uulgaris*: Hieronymus, *Tractatus de musica* 26, ed. C. Meyer and Lobrichon, p. 176 (trans. Knapp, p. 203), states, "Vltra mensuram sunt, que minori quam uno tempore … mensurantur ut semibreues" ("Beyond measure are those that are measured in less than one tempus, like the semibreves"), my translation; cf. Garlandia, *De mensurabili musica* 2.17 and 20, ed. Reimer, 1:46 (trans. Birnbaum, pp. 5–6), who names and describes how to write the semibreve, but does not define it.

that it partitions the breve into three equal parts, and the Saint Emmeram Anonymous unequivocally states, "if a correct breve or its equivalent is divided in two, it is necessary that they are unequal in measure," and later, "three semibreves placed in order without tails represent only one tempus."[25] Finally, later musicians introduce the minim, the shortest note, only to supersede it with yet shorter ones, as I discuss below.

Neither the *Discantus positio uulgaris* nor Garlandia specifies the ternary orientation of modes 3 and 4; they simply characterize them as consisting of a long and two breves (mode 3), or the opposite (mode 4). The Saint Emmeram Anonymous and Anonymous IV both indicate that these two modes use a long of three tempora together with one breve of one tempus and the second of two tempora.[26] First, the use of these values qualifies these modes as "beyond measure."[27] Second, the term for this second, longer breve has given much difficulty to modern scholars. The Saint Emmeram Anonymous calls the two breves "prior" and "illa" but then glosses the latter as "altera," while Anonymous IV uses the terms "prima" and "secunda."[28]

Since at least Franco, writers have taken the term "altera" as a pretext to characterize the process that doubles the length of the second of two

---

[25.] *Discantus positio uulgaris*: Hieronymus, *Tractatus de musica* 26, ed. C. Meyer and Lobrichon, p. 176 (trans. Knapp, p. 203), where the illustration gives three semibreves. Anonymous of Saint Emmeram, *De musica mensurata* 1.2, ed. and trans. Yudkin, p. 146 lines 42–45 ("si recta brevis vel suum aequippollens in duo frustra dividatur, necesse est illa esse inaequalia in mensura"), and p. 176 lines 1–8 ("tres semibreves suo ordine positae sine caudes unum tempus tantummodo repraesentant"); see also *ibid*. 1.1, p. 98 lines 5–8, and p. 108 lines 5–6. He may have derived the principle from Lambertus, *Musica mensurabilis* 25–26 and 80–84, ed. C. Meyer, trans. Desmond, pp. 64–67 and 76–77, respectively; and especially *ibid*. 114, pp. 82–83, which Anonymous of Saint Emmeram quotes, *De musica mensurata* 2, ed. and trans. Yudkin, p. 144 lines 12–15 (see *ibid*., p. 305).

[26.] Anonymous of Saint Emmeram, *De musica mensurata* 2, ed. and trans. Yudkin, p. 204 line 44– p. 206 line 20. Anonymous IV, ed. Reckow, 1:26 lines 5–9 (trans. Yudkin, p. 17).

[27.] *Discantus positio uulgaris*: Hieronymus, *Tractatus de musica* 26, ed. C. Meyer and Lobrichon, p. 176 (trans. Knapp, p. 203), "ultra mensuram." Garlandia, *De mensurabili musica* 1.9, ed. Reimer, 1:36 (trans. Birnbaum, p. 1); and Anonymous of Saint Emmeram, *De musica mensurata* 2, ed. and trans. Yudkin, p. 202 line 46–p. 204 line 23, "ultra mensurabiles."

[28.] Anonymous of Saint Emmeram, *De musica mensurata* 2, ed. and trans. Yudkin, p. 206 lines 8–20; see also p. 144 lines 12–15 (quoted from Lambertus, see n. 25 above), p. 148 lines 27–30 and p. 166 lines 36–40. He also uses the term *alter* to characterize the second and longer of two semibreves: Anonymous of Saint Emmeram, *De musica mensurata* 1.1, ed. and trans. Yudkin, p. 98 lines 7–8; and 1.2, ed. and trans. Yudkin, p. 150 lines 8–9. He may have borrowed the term from Lambertus, who customarily uses it for the second of two breves: e.g., Lambertus, *Musica mensurabilis* 24 and 60–63, ed. C. Meyer, trans. Desmond, pp. 64–65 and 70–73, respectively; in the second passage, Lambertus twice uses the term *secundus* as a synonym for *alter*. Anonymous IV, ed. Reckow, 1:26 lines 5–9 (trans. Yudkin, p. 17).

identical notes as alteration.[29] Franco does not mean "to alter" but rather "to make [the breve] a *breuis altera*."[30] Any other translation of *altero* in this context disguises the innocuous nature of the phrase *breuis altera* by distorting the meaning of the adjective *alter*, as Sandra Pinegar correctly points out.[31] The essential meaning in Latin is simply "the other" of two, the translation Yudkin uses for the gloss in the Saint Emmeram Anonymous. But it also carries the ordinal meaning of "the second," a synonym for *secundus*, the term used by Anonymous IV. None of this implies "alteration" of what is simply "the second" or "the other" note of two, which happened to be twice as long as "the first."

Similarly, scholars have assumed that the system of the rhythmic modes found its origins in classical quantitative metre.[32] Three pieces of evidence form the basis of this deduction: the similarities between the repetitive patterns of durations that define each of the modes and certain of the feet that make up some of the classical metres; the text of Saint Augustine's *De musica*, which describes the classical metres in detail; and a statement by Alexander de Villa-Dei that names the six metrical feet that correspond to the rhythmic modes. To take the last first, the passage in Villa-Dei concerns the use in poetry of a selection of the most commonly met feet in the classical metres that happens to coincide with the durational patterns that define the rhythmic modes, and any connection appears to be just that, coincidence.[33]

---

[29] Franco uses the verb *altero* twice, both times in the passive voice: *Ars cantus mensurabilis* 5.15 and 7.31, ed. Reaney and Gilles, pp. 36 and 51, respectively (trans. Strunk and McKinnon, pp. 232 and 235, respectively). See also Handlo, who uses it several times in the same sense, first instance, Handlo, *Regule* III.reg.III.max.3, ed. and trans. Lefferts, pp. 92–93.

[30] As Jean-Philippe Navarre translates these passages: Franco, *Ars cantus mensurabilis*, ed. and trans. Navarre, pp. 28–29 and 36–37, respectively. Strunk and McKinnon (see n. 29 above) simply translate, inappropriately, "altered." Franco uses the term *breuis altera* to mean the second and longer of two breves several times: e.g., *Ars cantus mensurabilis* 4.14 and 5.9–11, ed. Reaney and Gilles, pp. 30 and 33–34, respectively (trans. Strunk and McKinnon, pp. 229 and 231, respectively; always translated incorrectly as "altered" each time).

[31] Pinegar, "On Rhythmic Modes," p. 79 n. 14; and Handlo, *Regule*, ed. and trans. Lefferts, p. 93 n. 33 (note continues on p. 95); cf. the translation Desmond offers for Lambertus, *Musica mensurabilis* 24, ed. C. Meyer, trans. Desmond, pp. 64–65, "Quarta altera brevis appellatur, eo quod duas rectas breves tenet et quod semper alterum occupat locum" ("The fourth is called an *altera* breve, because it holds two *recta* breves and it always occupies an 'alternate' place"). In both places, the adjective *alter* should be translated "second": "it always occupies the second place."

[32] Waite, *The Rhythm of Twelfth-Century Polyphony*, pp. 26–55; Flotzinger, "Zur Frage der Modalrhythmik" and "Johannes de Garlandia und Anonymus IV"; Phillips and Huglo, "Le *De musica* de saint Augustin," esp. pp. 126–31; Tanay, *Noting Music, Marking Culture*, pp. 29–30; and A. Berger, *Medieval Music and the Art of Memory*, pp. 180–88.

[33] Alexander de Villa-Dei, *Doctrinale*, lines 1550–83, ed. Reichling, pp. 100–1.

The role of Augustine's *De musica* remains much more complex and controversial. The title of the work has caused much misapprehension of its contents, which concern, above all, time in the Christian understanding of the world, to which Augustine devotes Book 6, the last of the work.[34] The author identifies *musica* as one of the liberal arts, among the other mathematical fields that comprise the quadrivium, just as Boethius does in his treatise on the subject. In both Augustine's and Boethius' works, music governs the proportions. Augustine details, in his first five books, the ways in which humans measure time, for which he coopts the concept of quantity in classical poetic metre. As he shows, the Romans adopted the Greek practice of organizing metre according to the length of the syllable, assigning to all syllables one of two quantities, long and short, of which the latter is precisely half the length of the former. Metre, then, consists of various patterns of long and short syllables, organized into feet.

Augustine's distinction between rhythm and metre forms a central aspect of his theory: rhythm consists of an indefinite series of identical feet, extending without end; metre, on the other hand, embraces the variety of durations that result from the artful arrangement of feet and their constituent quantities in poetry.[35] These definitions, of course, reverse their usual modern meaning in music, where metre refers to the pattern of pulses and accents that underlie the music's varying surface rhythms. Augustine's conceptions of these phenomena, however, closely resemble the way musicians at Notre-Dame applied the rhythmic modes. The rhythmic pattern distinct to each mode, defined by its characteristic ligature pattern, underlies the surface rhythms of the music, which can vary as the ligature pattern varies. I do not believe, however, that the theorists who wrote about the rhythmic modes based their conception of them on Augustine's theories, because none of the principal treatises uses the language of poetic feet to describe the modes; they define them by simply naming the patterns of longs and shorts.[36]

Other difficulties obstruct a relationship between classical metre and the rhythmic modes. First, I know of no classical metres based on either the spondee or the tribrach, the feet that match the fifth and sixth modes,

---

[34] See Charru, "Temps et musique," pp. 171–80; Hentschel, "The Sensuous Music Aesthetics," pp. 3–13; and Formarier, *Entre rhétorique et musique*, pp. 28–30.

[35] Augustine, *De musica* books 3 and 4 discuss rhythm and metre; for the definitions of the two concepts, see *ibid.*, 3.1.1–2, ed. Bettetini, pp. 116–18 (trans. Taliaferro, pp. 237–39). Augustine bases his treatment on that of Quintilian, *Institutio oratoria* 9.4.45–57, ed. Winterbottom, 2:544–47 (trans. Russell, 4:187–93). In general, see Formarier, *Entre rhétorique et musique*, pp. 35–48; on Quintilian, pp. 36–38; Augustine, pp. 44–45.

[36] This is also the opinion of Apel, *The Notation of Polyphonic Music*, p. 222.

Table 3.2 Substitution in trochaic and iambic metres

Foot	Quantities	Musical Equivalent
trochee or	long-short	♩ ♪
iamb	short-long	♪ ♩
tribrach	short-short-short	♪♪♪
spondee	long-long	♩ ♩ or ♩. ♩.
dactyl	long-short-short	♩ ♪♪ or ♩. ♪ ♪
anapest	short-short-long	♪♪ ♩ or ♪ ♪ ♩.
proceleusmatic	short-short-short-short	♪♪♪♪ or ♪♪ ♪♪

respectively, and anapestic metres (the foot that parallels mode four) are rare.[37] Second, the dactyl and the anapest, matching modes three and four, respectively, contain four tempora, in the parlance of the thirteenth-century theorists, and so do not reflect the triple metre all theorists beginning with the Saint Emmeram Anonymous assign to them.

    dactyl,   long-short-short =   ♩ ♪♪
    anapest,   short-short-long =   ♪♪ ♩

Third, classical poets used as one of their most subtle means of creating metrical variety, substitution. That is, various feet could replace the prevailing foot of a particular metre. This practice underlies Augustine's distinction between rhythm, which uses only a single foot, and metre, which can use several in the same poetic line.

The dactylic metres offer perhaps the simplest example, as the dactyl (long-short-short) contracts its two short syllables into a single long to create the spondee (long-long) and preserves the duple nature of its constituent durations. The trochaic (long-short) and iambic (short-long) metres, however, as they appear in the lyric and dramatic genres, offer a much more complex range of possibilities (see Table 3.2). First, the long in either foot can resolve to two shorts and so become the tribrach (short-short-short). But second, and here any resemblance between poetic and musical practice vanishes, the short in either foot can become a long and so generate a spondee (long-long). Then, either long in the resulting spondee can resolve to two shorts, creating three further possibilities: dactyl (long-short-short), anapest (short-short-long) or proceleusmatic (short-short-

---

[37]. Among the many modern treatments of classical metres, see Raven, *Latin Metre*; and Halporn, et al., *The Meters*.

short-short). The mixture of units that contain three (trochee or iamb and tribrach) and four (spondee, dactyl, anapest and proceleusmatic) tempora certainly contradicts the prevailing triple subdivisions of the rhythmic modes.

One might object that the longs of these last four feet could contain three tempora each and pairs of breves become *breuis recta–breuis altera* combinations, but such a treatment would defeat the very purpose of substitution on three grounds: first, a single ternary unit (trochee or iamb) would become two; second, when the dactyl, anapest or proceleusmatic replaces an iamb, one would simply substitute like with like; and third, when any of these three replaces a trochee, one (with the dactyl or anapest) or two (with the proceleusmatic) iambs result, a substitution that violates the rules of classical metre and, if applied strictly to the Notre-Dame context, would cause the first rhythmic mode to transform into the second. As I show below, the rhythmic modes do countenance modifications of the prevailing rhythmic structure, through *fractio* and *collectio notarum*, but these changes do not in any way emulate the use of substitution in classical metre. And so, I believe we can unequivocally dismiss any connection between the classical quantitative metres and the rhythmic modes.

The Rhythmic Modes: *Proprietas et perfectio*

These two qualities occupy a significant amount of space in the treatises of Garlandia, the Saint Emmeram Anonymous and Anonymous IV without shedding a great deal of light on their precise meaning or effect in music of the thirteenth century and the notation used to record it.[38] Nevertheless, these two aspects of ligature formation remain important concepts not only for music theorists of the late thirteenth century, as Reckow points out, but also for the morphology and interpretation of ligatures in mensural notation.[39] First, however, we should consider the meaning of the two

---

[38] Garlandia, *De mensurabili musica* 2, ed. Reimer, 1:44–49 (trans. Birnbaum, pp. 5–7), describes the forms of the ligatures, while chapters 3–6, ed. Reimer, 1:50–63 (trans. Birnbaum, pp. 7–13), discuss their application. Similarly, Anonymous of Saint Emmeram, *De musica mensurata* 1.2, ed. and trans. Yudkin, pp. 118–82, describes the ligatures, while chapter 2, *ibid.*, pp. 184–240, discusses their application. See also Anonymous IV, ed. Reckow, 1:25 lines 20–31, and chapter 2, *ibid.*, 1:40–57 *passim* (trans. Yudkin, pp. 16–17 and 34–50, respectively). For commentary, see Reckow, "Proprietas und perfectio"; and Haines, "*Proprietas* and *Perfectio*"; on Garlandia, Reimer, "Johannes de Garlandias Notationslehre," in Garlandia, *De mensurabili musica*, ed. Reimer, 2:55–62.

[39] Reckow, "Proprietas und perfectio," p. 139.

terms. *Perfectio* seems less controversial as it appears to carry the meaning of completion, borrowed from its sense in grammar.[40] *Proprietas* presents greater difficulties. Reckow suggests that the most appropriate German translations ought to be *Eigenschaft* or perhaps *Eigenart*, meaning "characteristic" or "property," certainly the most common meaning of *proprietas* in classical and medieval Latin.[41]

But "property" means a distinctive characteristic of a thing, as the thirteenth-century encyclopaedist Bartholomaeus Anglicus shows: "Cum proprietates rerum sequantur substantias, secundum distinctionem et ordinem substantiarum erit ordo et distinctio proprietatum" ("Because the properties of things follow their substances, the order and distinction of the properties will accord with the distinction and order of their substances").[42] Thus, for Bartholomaeus and his contemporary Albert the Great, property is an abstract concept under which one classifies the defining characteristics of each thing, and both authors devote most of their respective works to just such classifications. Moreover, all three of the thirteenth-century theorists speak of ligatures that lack *proprietas* or that show the opposite *proprietas*. If we insist on taking *proprietas* as "property," these statements have no meaning in the sense that either Bartholomaeus or Albert would understand the term. What is an "opposite property"? To what is it opposed? An object without "property" has no characteristic that could allow us to classify or define it. Our three authors could not possibly have intended this meaning.

Garlandia may offer a tantalizing insight into the meaning of the term when he qualifies it with the adjective *proprius*.[43] Such a usage is tautologous, of course, in that *proprietas* derives from *proprius*, "appropriate appropriateness," as it were. In each case, however, Garlandia seems to mean more than just emphasis through repetition. The first passage (2.25) opposes ligatures that possess *proprietas* with those that do not, and the adjective *proprius* emphasizes this opposition. The second passage (6.9) treats the reduction of a single note and a following binary ligature to a ternary ligature "per aequipollentiam, et hoc est secundum propriam proprietatem, quia reducuntur ad aliquem modum proprium" ("through

---

[40.] See Reckow, "Proprietas und perfectio," p. 128.

[41.] Reckow, "Proprietas und perfectio," p. 128; see also Haines, "*Proprietas* and *Perfectio*," pp. 13–18, who does not acknowledge Reckow's priority.

[42.] Bartholomaeus, *De proprietatibus rerum*, "Prohemium," ed. H. Meyer, 1:51; for a conveniently available text of the complete work, see Bartholomaeus, *De genuinis rerum coelestium*. See also Bartholomaeus' contemporary, Albertus Magnus, *De causis proprietatum elementorum*.

[43.] Garlandia, *De mensurabili musica* 2.25 and 6.9, ed. Reimer, 1:47 and 63, respectively (trans. Birnbaum, pp. 6 and 13, respectively).

equivalent durations, and this is according to the proper *proprietas*, because they are reduced to some proper mode"). Garlandia expresses concern that the reduction to a ternary ligature will not affect the durations of the individual notes and uses three different terms to convey his concern: "aequipollentiam," "propriam proprietatem" and "modum proprium."

Proprietas, then, is itself a property that certain ligatures possess, others do not, and of which some possess a modified sort that is in some way the "opposite" of that possessed (or not) by the others. Garlandia's reinforcement of its meaning with the adjective *proprius* suggests that the noun must reflect, in some way, this sense of rectitude, that the ligature with propriety accords in some way with legitimate or orthodox rhythmic procedures within the context of prevailing practices in the rhythmic modes. And so we return to the translation "propriety," which I use in all renderings below. Still the precise meaning of perfection and propriety remain obscure because none of the three theorists defines either term, devoting, instead, most of their discussion to the appearance of the ligatures and their durations.

And Garlandia seems to contradict himself. He first says, "Figurarum ascendendo vel descendendo duae sunt species, quia quaedam dicitur cum proprietate a parte principii, quaedam a parte finis" ("There are two types of figures in ascent or descent, since one is with propriety with regard to the beginning, another with regard to the end").[44] He next describes the four types of propriety that ligatures exhibit at their beginning, a passage paraphrased by Anonymous IV.[45] But when he turns to the end of the ligature, he treats not propriety but perfection.[46] Hence, I suspect that the text at 2.24 is defective, that wording such as "cum perfectione" or "perfecta" has dropped out (i.e., "quia quaedam dicitur cum proprietate a parte principii, quaedam [**cum perfectione** *or* **perfecta**] a parte finis"). Such an emendation would create the parallel currently lacking in his text (propriety at the beginning of a ligature, perfection at its end) and that the discussions at 2.25 and 30 appear to require. Anonymous IV might well have harboured similar suspicions because after he paraphrased

---

[44.] Garlandia, *De mensurabili musica* 2.24, ed. Reimer, 1:47 (trans. Birnbaum, p. 6), my translation.

[45.] Garlandia, *De mensurabili musica* 2.25, ed. Reimer, 1:47–48 (trans. Birnbaum, p. 6); Anonymous IV, ed. Reckow, 1:45 lines 13–16 (trans. Yudkin, p. 38); on the paraphrase, see Reckow, 1:45 note a. Anonymous IV further removes another tautology of Garlandia's by suppressing his fourth classification, "sine opposite cum proprietate" ("without the opposite, with propriety"), which duplicates the first class, "cum proprietate" ("with propriety").

[46.] Garlandia, *De mensurabili musica* 2.30, ed. Reimer, 1:49 (trans. Birnbaum, pp. 6–7).

Garlandia's discussion of propriety at the beginning of the ligature, he did not return to the question of perfection (or propriety) at its end.

To extrapolate the meaning of these terms from their application in the treatises remains a challenge, despite Reckow's best efforts. For example, he states that Garlandia distinguishes ligatures with propriety from those without by situating the former within the norms of the rhythmic modes and the latter outside those norms.[47] Nowhere does Garlandia make such a statement, but he also stipulates that the final, ternary ligature of mode two lacks propriety, as does the single ternary ligature that occurs between rests in this mode.[48] This ternary ligature, then, ought to consist of breve-long-breve. Similarly, the last, binary ligature of mode four lacks perfection according to Garlandia.[49]

Still, he unequivocally defines the binary and ternary ligatures that possess both propriety and perfection. "Omnis figura ligata cum proprietate posita et perfecta paenultima dicitur esse brevis et ultima longa. Si sint ibi praecedentes vel praecedens, omnes ponuntur pro longa."[50] ("Every ligated figure placed with propriety and perfect is said to be in the penultimate short and the last long. If any note or notes precede, all are equivalent to a long.") The binary ligature consists of breve-long while the ternary, in which a single note precedes the final two, contains long-breve-long. The author of the *Discantus positio uulgaris* unequivocally describes these two neumes, without mentioning propriety or perfection, while both the Saint Emmeram Anonymous and Anonymous IV, the latter quoting Garlandia, agree in their definition (see Table 3.3).[51] The first rhythmic mode uses these two neumes, of course, and their privilege of place and the assignment of both propriety and perfection to them support arguments in favour of the historical priority of this mode, a point made, in fact, by Anonymous IV.[52]

[47.] Reckow, "Proprietas und perfectio," p. 128.
[48.] Garlandia, *De mensurabili musica* 4.4–5, ed. Reimer, 1:53 (trans. Birnbaum, p. 9); Anonymous IV, ed. Reckow, 1:51 line 30–1:52 line 4 (trans. Yudkin, p. 46).
[49.] Garlandia, *De mensurabili musica* 4.7, ed. Reimer, 1:54 (trans. Birnbaum, p. 9); Anonymous IV, ed. Reckow, 1:54 lines 12–21 (trans. Yudkin, p. 48).
[50.] Garlandia, *De mensurabili musica* 3.2–3, ed. Reimer, 1:50 (trans. Birnbaum, p. 9).
[51.] *Discantus positio uulgaris*: Hieronymus, *Tractatus de musica* 26, ed. C. Meyer and Lobrichon, p. 177 (trans. Knapp, p. 203); Anonymous of Saint Emmeram, *De musica mensurata* 1.2, ed. and trans. Yudkin, p. 122 line 38–p. 124 line 8, and p. 124 lines 22–33; and Anonymous IV, ed. Reckow, 1:45 lines 23–27 (trans. Yudkin, pp. 38–39). On Anonymous IV's quotation of Garlandia, see Reckow 1:45 n. d.
[52.] Anonymous IV, ed. Reckow, 1:46 lines 4–5 (trans. Yudkin, p. 39). Roesner, "The Emergence of *musica mensurabilis*," pp. 47–51, characterizes modes 1, 5 and 6 as "proto-modal."

Table 3.3 Propriety and perfection in binary and ternary ligatures

Sources	Binary	Ternary
Garlandia, Saint Emmeram Anon. and Anon. IV	perfect with propriety: breve-long	perfect with propriety: long-breve-long
Saint Emmeram Anon.	without propriety: long-breve	perfect without propriety: breve-long-breve
Saint Emmeram Anon.	imperfect with propriety: breve-breve (two tempora) or three tempora?	imperfect with propriety: breve-breve-breve
Saint Emmeram Anon.	imperfect without propriety: breve-breve	–

The Saint Emmeram Anonymous clarifies some details about individual ligatures while confusing others. He states that the binary neume without propriety contains long-breve while the perfect ternary neume without propriety consists of breve-long-breve;[53] that is, they exhibit precisely the opposite durations that the perfect binary and ternary ligatures, with propriety, possess according to Garlandia and the two anonymi. The Saint Emmeram Anonymous seems less sure about the treatment of imperfect ligatures. He first states that such a binary neume with propriety is equivalent to a long, without specifying whether it is a long of two or three tempora.[54] Later, he asserts that both the binary and ternary ligatures, imperfect with propriety, occupy three tempora, unless the binary ligature precedes a single breve or its equivalent, in which case its durations equal two tempora.[55] We can infer that the ternary neume consists of breve-breve-breve, and similarly that the binary neume of two tempora contains breve-breve.

But if the binary neume of three tempora contains breve-long, it is the same as a perfect binary ligature with propriety, and if long-breve, a binary without propriety. Such ambiguity seems problematic in an author who evinces such an Aristotelian zeal for classification.[56] His treatment of the imperfect binary neume without propriety gives equal cause for concern, as

---

[53.] Anonymous of Saint Emmeram, *De musica mensurata* 1.2, ed. and trans. Yudkin, p. 138 lines 4–15.

[54.] Anonymous of Saint Emmeram, *De musica mensurata* 1.2, ed. and trans. Yudkin, p. 160 lines 24–25.

[55.] Anonymous of Saint Emmeram, *De musica mensurata* 1.2, ed. and trans. Yudkin, p. 162 lines 18–23.

[56.] On the Aristotelian orientation of the treatise, see Yudkin, introduction to Anonymous of Saint Emmeram, *De musica mensurata*, ed. and trans. Yudkin, pp. 10–18.

he states that it is equivalent to the greater breve of two tempora, and so consists of breve-breve, precisely the value he assigns to the imperfect binary neume with propriety that contains two tempora.[57] Such ambiguities raise questions about the interpretation of ligatures in the Notre-Dame repertory. Anonymous IV seems just as uncertain about imperfection in that he eschews any treatment of the constituent durations and focuses instead on the fact that one cannot ligate consecutive notes at the unison, a condition that he identifies as the cause of imperfection.[58]

These three authors, then, agree on the value of only one set of ligatures, the perfect binary and ternary neumes with propriety. The confusion they exhibit over other combinations of these two properties does not inspire confidence as to their application in these early stages of rhythmic notation, and it stands in stark contrast to the precision with which they describe the graphic modifications to the ligatures that indicate whether the neume possesses either property. Scholars agree that the principal Notre-Dame musical sources do not use the notational nuances Garlandia and the two anonymi take such pains to define.[59] I deduce from the testimony of the three theorists and the music manuscripts themselves that Garlandia invented the system in an attempt to increase the precision of the notation, but that, other than the attendant morphology, he did not unequivocally define it, nor did it find rapid acceptance among musical scribes.

We must turn, therefore, to Franco of Cologne, whose innovations I treat in detail below, to elucidate the application and effect of these properties in late thirteenth-century notation. Writing around 1280 (after the Saint Emmeram Anonymous, whose date of 1279 is secure, and before Anonymous IV), he explains the system in his Chapter 7, entitled "De ligaturis et earum proprietatibus."[60] Here, the plural of *proprietas* can only mean "properties" in the sense in which Bartholomaeus Anglicus and Albert the Great would understand it. First, he specifies that the forms of ligatures that possess propriety and perfection agree with those used in plainsong:

---

[57]. Anonymous of Saint Emmeram, *De musica mensurata* 1.2, ed. and trans. Yudkin, p. 166 line 30–p. 168 line 3.

[58]. Anonymous IV, ed. Reckow, 1:47 line 5–1:48 line 14 (trans. Yudkin, pp. 40–41), a portion of which he paraphrases from Garlandia, *De mensurabili musica* 6.5–6, ed. Reimer, 1:63 (trans. Birnbaum, p. 13); see Reckow 1.47 n. h. Garlandia does not associate this phenomenon with imperfection.

[59]. Reckow, "Proprietas und perfectio," p. 123; and Pinegar, "On Rhythmic Modes" pp. 88–89.

[60]. Franco, *Ars cantus mensurabilis* 7, ed. Reaney and Gilles, pp. 43–51 (trans. Strunk and McKinnon, pp. 234–35).

Proprietas est nota primariae inventionis ligaturae a plana musica data in principio illius. Perfectio vero idem dicit, sed in fine ... Omnis ligatura descendens tractum habens a primo punctu descendentem a parte sinistra, cum proprietate dicitur, eo quod sic in plana musica figuratur.[61]

Propriety is the note of the primary invention of a ligature from plainsong given at the beginning [of the ligature]. Perfection is indeed the same, but at the end ... Every descending ligature having a line descending from the left side of its first note is said to be with propriety, just as it is written in plainsong.

Earlier, he stated that propriety concerns the beginning of the ligature, perfection the end.[62] Further, all internal notes carry the same duration, and "the position of those who hold that the middle note in some ternary ligatures is long and in others it will be short is patently false" ("patet positionem illorum esse falsam qui ponunt in ternaria aliqua mediam esse longam, in omnibus autem aliis fore brevem").[63] He is objecting, of course, to the perfect ternary ligature without propriety as described by the Saint Emmeram Anonymous, breve-long-breve.

After a detailed treatment of the morphology of the ligatures,[64] Franco specifies how the presence or absence of either property affects the durations:

Omnis ligatura cum proprietate primam facit brevem. Item omnis sine: longam. Item omnis perfectio longa, et omnis imperfectio brevis ... Item omnis media brevis.[65]

Every ligature with propriety makes its first note short. Likewise every ligature without propriety, a long. Likewise every perfection is long, every imperfection short ... Likewise, every middle note is short.

He could hardly be clearer, as he assigns specific durations to each note in a ligature, irrespective of its length, the first note according to whether the ligature possesses propriety, the last note, perfection, and all middle notes are short (see Table 3.4). He also treats ligatures with the opposite

---

[61.] Franco, *Ars cantus mensurabilis* 7.15–17, ed. Reaney and Gilles, p. 45 (trans. Strunk and McKinnon, p. 235); my translation. See Reckow, "Proprietas und perfectio," p. 118.
[62.] Franco, *Ars cantus mensurabilis* 7.6–8, ed. Reaney and Gilles, p. 44 (trans. Strunk and McKinnon, p. 234). See Reckow, "Proprietas und perfectio," p. 131.
[63.] Franco, *Ars cantus mensurabilis* 7.13, ed. Reaney and Gilles, p. 45 (trans. Strunk and McKinnon, p. 235); my translation.
[64.] Franco, *Ars cantus mensurabilis* 7.17–23, ed. Reaney and Gilles, pp. 45–50 (trans. Strunk and McKinnon, p. 235).
[65.] Franco, *Ars cantus mensurabilis* 7.26–30, ed. Reaney and Gilles, p. 50 (trans. Strunk and McKinnon, p. 235); my translation.

Table 3.4 Propriety and perfection according to Franco

First Note	Middle Notes	Last Note
with propriety: breve	all breves	with perfection: long
without propriety: long		without perfection: breve

propriety, a topic I address below. It remains to ask, however, whether Franco extracted order that was already present in Garlandia's system, or he imposed his own sense of order on an inchoate and imperfect system. The treatments of the three modal theorists, at least one of whom knew Franco's treatise (Anonymous IV), and the evidence of the music manuscripts lead me to prefer the second option.

The Rhythmic Modes: Opposite Propriety and the Plica, *Fractio et collectio*, Individual Notes and Rests

Modal theory offers three techniques for subdividing notes: opposite propriety and the plica involve the morphology of the neumes, while *fractio* and *collectio* modify the ligature patterns, thus introducing rhythms outside the prevailing patterns of the modes. Subdivision at the beginning of the neume, signalled by an ascending line from the left edge of the first note, occurs when the neume possesses the opposite propriety.[66] Garlandia states that the first two notes in a ligature with opposite propriety hold the same duration as a breve, and Anonymous IV quotes his definition.[67] Although the latter states that a semibreve can possess the value of one-third of a breve,[68] neither author specifies whether the two semibreves in such a ligature are equal. The Saint Emmeram Anonymous, however, asserts that pairs of semibreves are unequal, with the shorter always

---

[66.] Garlandia, *De mensurabili musica* 2.29, ed. Reimer, 1:48 (trans. Birnbaum, p. 6); Anonymous of Saint Emmeram, *De musica mensurata* 1.2, ed. and trans. Yudkin, p. 142 lines 21–28, and p. 148 line 42–p. 150 line 3.

[67.] Garlandia, *De mensurabili musica* 3.6, ed. Reimer, 1:50 (trans. Birnbaum, p. 7); Anonymous IV, ed. Reckow, 1:46 lines 29–30 (trans. Yudkin, p. 40); see Reckow, 1:46 n. f.

[68.] Anonymous IV, ed. Reckow, 1:45 lines 1–12 (trans. Yudkin, p. 38); also *Discantus positio uulgaris*: Hieronymus, *Tractatus de musica* 26, ed. C. Meyer and Lobrichon, p. 176 (trans. Knapp, p. 203).

preceding the longer.⁶⁹ We cannot know whether this statement reflects a practice known to Garlandia but left unexpressed by him, or an innovation of the later author.

Subdivision at the end of a ligature involves the addition of a plica to the last note. The physical appearance of the plica bears some relation to liquescence in plainsong as an appendage to the end of a neume, but the plica appears to carry only rhythmic meaning and no indication of a performance nuance like the liquescent.⁷⁰ Garlandia and the Saint Emmeram Anonymous agree that the plica divides the final note of a ligature, but Garlandia does not specify how. The Saint Emmeram Anonymous, however, gives detailed instructions as to the value of the plica that include specifying that if the plica divides a final breve of one tempus, its value is two-thirds of the breve, since the shorter always precedes the longer.⁷¹ This position coincides exactly with his treatment of the two semibreves in a ligature with opposite propriety.

Garlandia also notes that the usual notation of mode six employs the plica: it begins with a quaternary neume to which scribes add a plica, and a succession of binary neumes, each with a final plica; Anonymous IV concurs with this arrangement.⁷² Both allow that scribes could use a quaternary followed by a succession of ternaries, all without plica, although the former states, "non probatur per istam artem, sed bene probatur per exemplum" ("it is not approved according to this treatise, but it is well approved through example").⁷³ The Saint Emmeram Anonymous endorses this latter arrangement alone, although he characterizes the ligatures as imperfect with propriety, whereas Garlandia prescribes a quaternary with propriety and perfect ternaries with propriety, as does Anonymous IV, compounding the confusion regarding these properties.⁷⁴

[69.] Anonymous of Saint Emmeram, *De musica mensurata* 1.2, ed. and trans. Yudkin, p. 146 lines 42–45 and p. 150 line 4–42 (unequal semibreves), and p. 148 lines 27–31.

[70.] But see Lambertus, *Musica mensurabilis* 93, ed. C. Meyer, trans. Desmond, pp. 78–79: "Fit autem plica in voce per compositionem epygloti cum repercussione gutturis subtiliter inclusa" ("The plica, moreover, is made in the voice through the combination of the epiglottis with a repercussion of the throat subtly enclosed"), my translation. See McGee, *The Sound of Medieval Song*, pp. 50–52.

[71.] Garlandia, *De mensurabili musica* 3.9, ed. Reimer, 1:51 (trans. Birnbaum, p. 7); Anonymous of Saint Emmeram, *De musica mensurata* 1.2, ed. and trans. Yudkin, p. 96 line 41–p. 98 line 19; see also p. 158 lines 35–38.

[72.] Garlandia, *De mensurabili musica* 4.10, ed. Reimer, 1:56 (trans. Birnbaum, p. 10); Anonymous IV, ed. Reckow, 1:56 lines 5–8 (trans. Yudkin, p. 50); see Reckow, 1:56 n. d.

[73.] Garlandia, *De mensurabili musica* 4.11, ed. Reimer, 1:56 (trans. Birnbaum, p. 10); Anonymous IV, ed. Reckow, 1:56 lines 8–13 (trans. Yudkin, p. 50); see Reckow, 1:56 n. e.

[74.] Anonymous of Saint Emmeram, *De musica mensurata* 2, ed. and trans. Yudkin, p. 210 line 18–p. 212 line 20.

The terms *fractio et collectio [notarum]* appear to be inventions of Anonymous IV since they do not occur in Garlandia or the Saint Emmeram Anonymous.[75] They refer to the same procedure from opposite perspectives: *fractio* refers to the breaking of a longer note into shorter values; *collectio*, the collection of shorter notes to replace a longer one. Anonymous IV does not treat the opposite procedure, the replacement of several shorter notes by a longer one, although, as I discuss below, this practice seems to occur in the music manuscripts. He does, however, make it clear that *fractio* involves the use of individual notes and ligatures that interrupt the conventional ligature patterns of the modes. He frequently prescribes *currentes*, notes shaped like diamonds that he identifies as the semibreve, as the medium for invoking *fractio*.[76]

Finally, all three thirteenth-century authors offer detailed discussions of individual notes and the rest. They all describe the former in the same way: the long has a line descending from its right edge, the breve is square without lines, and the semibreve shaped like a diamond.[77] They also all concur on the physical appearance and significance of the rest.[78] The vertical length of the rest indicates its duration, and each space traversed by the rest equals one tempus. The Saint Emmeram Anonymous and Anonymous IV both admit the semibreve rest, indicating that it occupies half of a space. The latter specifies that it lasts one-third of a tempus, while the former states that it represents either the lesser or greater semibreve. Both authors, then, accept the triple subdivision of the breve. These discussions of individual notes and the rest signify two important developments in musical practice and the notation that represents it.

First, the articulation of the musical gesture has become an intrinsic part of musical language. The invention of the rest reflects the need for concrete indication of it. Second, although the duration of the rest precisely matches its physical form as measured by the number of spaces it traverses, the form

---

[75] Anonymous IV, ed. Reckow, 1:38 line 11 (trans. Yudkin, p. 30), uses the expression "in fractione et collectione brevis et longae"; I synthesize the two genitives into my own construction "notarum." Chapter 1.2, ed. Reckow, 1:37–40 (trans. Yudkin, pp. 29–33), concerns the application of this technique in the various modes.

[76] Anonymous IV also calls them "elmuahim," ed. Reckow, 1:41 lines 10–13, 1:43 lines 11–14, and 1:45 line 1 (trans. Yudkin, pp. 34–35, 37 and 38, respectively); see Haines, "Anonymous IV," pp. 397–411.

[77] Garlandia, *De mensurabili musica* 2.10–20, ed. Reimer, 1:45–46 (trans. Birnbaum, pp. 5–6); Anonymous of Saint Emmeram, *De musica mensurata* 1.1, ed. and trans. Yudkin, p. 90 lines 14–41; Anonymous IV, ed. Reckow, 1:41 lines 3–16 (trans. Yudkin, pp. 34–35).

[78] Garlandia, *De mensurabili musica* 7–8, ed. Reimer, 1:64–67 (trans. Birnbaum, pp. 13–15); Anonymous of Saint Emmeram, *De musica mensurata* 3, ed. and trans. Yudkin, pp. 242–56; Anonymous IV, chapter 3, ed. Reckow, 1:57–63 (trans. Yudkin, pp. 51–56).

of the individual notes does not permit singers to recognize their length. Any long could possess two or three tempora, any breve one tempus or two. Only context could allow singers to discern their precise duration. Scribes and singers would have found the iconic nature of the rest a material aid in the sea of symbolic representations that comprises modal rhythm. A long note, either alone or part of a ligature, could last either two or three tempora, depending on the context, and its morphology does not indicate which; but a rest that crosses three spaces occupies three tempora. In some ways, the rest, as an iconic symbol, becomes a metaphor for the more rational approach to notation adopted by Franco.

Six Modes or Two?

Anonymous IV, by introducing the concept of *fractio [notarum]*, which appears in the music sources alongside the opposite phenomenon, the replacement of several shorter notes with a single longer one, permits us to synthesize, to some degree, the rhythmic information encoded in the ligatures that define the rhythmic modes. Although the four thirteenth-century theory treatises clearly differentiate the six rhythmic modes, and each has its own identity, certainly in the minds of the theorists and possibly in those of the singers, the practical sources reveal that the limited stock of available ligatures leads inevitably to the combination of modes for practical purposes. That is, several of the modes share ligature forms and, more important, their rhythmic significance, to the point that we cannot assign certain passages unequivocally to one mode or another, and in fact, the choice of mode does not change the rhythmic shape of the passage.

For example, in modes two, three and four, the middle note of the ternary ligature has a duration of two tempora, whereas the middle note of the same ligature in modes one and six lasts for one tempus. (When ternary ligatures appear in mode five, all notes contain three tempora.) Thus, the musical texture can slip between mode three or four and mode two. The *Alleluia V Pascha nostrum* offers one such example. The refrain begins clearly in mode three, a single long followed by a succession of ternary neumes, the middle note of which lasts for two tempora. Soon, the scribe (or composer) begins to introduce binary neumes that suggest a shift to mode two, but when ternary neumes reappear, they indicate the same rhythmic shape as before, when the texture clearly embraced mode three.[79]

[79.] F fols. 23r–24v; see the transcription in Roesner, ed., *Le Magnus liber organi*, 1:96–103.

Mode four differs from mode three, of course, by starting with the ternary ligature instead of the single note, but its rhythmic shape is the same as that of mode three, and it is equally susceptible to the intervention of mode two.

Mode one, which may be the oldest of the modes, appears more frequently than any of the others, but it blends seamlessly with modes five and six.[80] When a single note interrupts the flow of binary neumes, it generates a long of three tempora (in place of the longs of two tempora that customarily occur in mode one), and so shifts the texture to mode five. When the last note of a ligature bears a plica, or a ternary neume appears among the prevailing binary ligatures, or a quaternary neume at the beginning of a phrase in place of the customary ternary neume, any of these three notational features breaks a long into two breves and so introduces mode six (see Example 3.1 and Figure 3.1).

Example 3.1 shows part of the verse from the organum triplum setting of *Alleluia* V *Pascha nostrum*.[81] First, the overall appearance of the notation strongly resembles that of Pa 1107, the gradual from Saint Denis examined in Chapter 2, that originated within a decade or so after the production of F. In particular, the ligatures in both manuscripts share morphology as we would expect from the testimony of Garlandia, the two anonymi and Franco: the ligatures used in mode one should possess both propriety and perfection, and Franco stated that such ligatures also occur in plainsong. So, the agreement between the notation in Pa 1107 and F supports Franco's position and does not surprise.

Second, the notation and its transcription show how modes one, five and six intermingle. The first ligature in the triplum, a quaternary, immediately introduces mode six, while the series of binary neumes that follows transforms the rhythm into that of mode one. In both voices, the plica (represented in Example 3.1 by a smaller note) breaks the final long of the ligature to which it appends into two breves. And in the duplum, individual notes lengthen the preceding note into a long of three tempora, the distinctive value of mode five. Thus, the three modes, one, five and six, exist together and move from one to another without disruption of the notation. In the ternary ligature, the middle note is always a breve of one tempus, whereas in the other three modes, two, three and four, the middle note is always a

---

[80]. Roesner, "The Emergence of *musica mensurabilis*," pp. 47–59, similarly groups modes 1, 5 and 6, and derives modes 3 and 4 from mode 2.

[81]. See n. 79 above. This passage occurs in F fol. 24r, and in Roesner, ed., *Le Magnus liber organi*, 1:101; see also Husmann, ed., *Die drei- und vierstimmigen Notre-Dame-Organa*, pp. 61–65, this passage p. 64. In Example 3.1, square brackets indicate ligatures and smaller notes those represented by the plica.

Polyphony and Rhythmic Notation 83

Example 3.1 *Alleluia* V *Pascha nostrum*, portion of verse, F fol. 24r

Figure 3.1 F fol. 24r
Firenze, Biblioteca Medicea Laurenziana, Ms. Plut. 29.1, fol. 24r
Su concessione del MiBACT
E' vietata ogni ulteriore reproduzione con qualsiasi mezzo.

long. And so, in practical terms, I understand these two groups as notationally unified.

Several other features of this example deserve comment. First, as the thirteenth-century theorists point out, ligatures cannot include consecutive notes at the unison. Immediately after the first ligature in the duplum, two consecutive notes on E occur that should, but cannot and do not, constitute a binary ligature. Two consecutive phrases in the triplum begin with consecutive notes on F, and the scribe has not ligated them. Still, this scribe had not assimilated all aspects of the modal notation as described by Garlandia. The individual notes just mentioned do not exhibit the differentiation between long and short that Garlandia and the other theorists describe. The two notes on E in the duplum, for example, are short followed by long, but the scribe has drawn them both the same. Perhaps most interesting of all, the rests do not accord with the practice explained by the theorists. All rests in this passage appear to contain a single tempus, but most occupy two spaces, and so, according to Garlandia, should last for two tempora.

It is clear from these disjunctions between the notation of F and the discussions of the theorists that throughout the thirteenth century the system continued to evolve in the interests of communicating with greater clarity and precision. But these disjunctions equally show that the system, although a brave attempt to bring rhythm into the realm of musical notation, contained far too many compromises and ambiguities to succeed, even with the innovations introduced by Garlandia and the two anonymi. The problem, and Franco recognized it, lay in the fact that the system relied too much on context and symbolic, as opposed to iconic, representation for the communication of durational values.

The rhythmic nuances of Example 3.1 illustrate the problem. The plicae that represent *fractio* and the individual notes that cause lengthening do so not out of their morphology but through context alone. Singers need to be aware of their signification in order to execute the rhythms they represent correctly. The two consecutive notes on E in the duplum suggest a possible solution, provided by the theorists beginning with Garlandia but unrealized by this scribe. A singer first needed to recognize that the two notes should be ligated, although their unison relation prevents them; then that if they were ligated, they would represent the pattern short-long, as all binary neumes do in this repertory. Had the scribe added a tail to the right edge of the second note, as the theorists recommend, he would have avoided the ambiguity. But he did not, illustrating that the innovations of Garlandia had not yet come into effect.

Mensural Notation: Lambertus and Franco

Lambertus and Franco, both writing after Garlandia but contemporary with the Saint Emmeram Anonymous and Anonymous IV, addressed some of these issues. Scholars usually describe the notational style that resulted from their innovations as Franconian and, as I suggest below, there remains good reason to retain the designation, although Franco borrows some key concepts from Lambertus and in some respects models his work after that of his predecessor. Yudkin dates both treatises within a narrow range.[82] Lambertus falls between Garlandia (ca. 1260) and the Saint Emmeram Anonymous (1279), because he clearly knows the former's treatise and the latter vilifies him.[83] Franco, whom the Saint Emmeram Anonymous does not mention but clearly would have had he known his treatise, wrote between the latter (1279) and Anonymous IV (ca. 1285), who does refer to him.[84]

The significance of these dates lies in their proximity to the music manuscripts, especially Mo H. 196, that exhibit the notations described by these two authors and also the repertory, the motet, whose musical characteristics elicited these notations. Above, I reflect that Garlandia and particularly the two anonymi were writing about a musical practice whose favour was clearly waning as the motet began to dominate progressive musical communities. In contrast, then, to the retrospective standpoint these theorists evince, Lambertus and Franco describe notational practices that pertained to, and perhaps originated from, a musical repertory that stood on the leading edge of contemporary musical practice during the last third of the century.

Lambertus and Franco share a number of important innovations concerning the notation they inherited from Garlandia and its signification. I begin with them because, in view of the chronological relationship between their respective treatises (Lambertus wrote before Franco), we must attribute their origin to Lambertus and not Franco, whose name modern scholars have associated with this style of notation. First and most important, both authors assign primacy of place to the perfect long of three tempora, Lambertus stating, "prima super omnes fons est et origo ipsius scientie atque finis" ("the first above all is the fount and origin of this very

---

[82.] See n. 12 above.

[83.] On his knowledge of Garlandia, see C. Meyer, introduction to Lambertus, *The 'Ars musica'*, ed. Meyer, trans. Desmond, pp. xxv–xxx. On Lambertus and the Anonymous of Saint Emmeram, see n. 15 above.

[84.] See n. 17 above.

science, and its end"), while Franco calls it "prima et principalis" ("first and principal").[85] As emerges from their subsequent discussion, both Lambertus and Franco conceive of the music as moving in multiples of this unit of three tempora, represented graphically by the perfect long.[86]

Their descriptions of the other types of notes, from the imperfect long of two tempora through *breuis recta* and *altera* (a term they both use consistently), to the semibreve, greater and lesser, all agree, including their treatment of the *duplex longa*.[87] These distinctions appear, of course, in the four treatises that deal with modal rhythm, but the treatment Lambertus and Franco offer indicates greater importance of the individual note, on the one hand, and, on the other, the stress on the idea that all music organizes itself into perfections three tempora in length. The two anonymi, in their treatment of the modes, allow us to infer that they conceived of music in this way, because each of the modes evinces groups of three tempora, but nowhere do they explicitly define this concept. Moreover, Franco designs his discussion of ligatures to allow singers to recognize the constituent notes of each figure on the basis of morphology instead of context, as required by modal theory. Again, the emphasis focuses on the individual note, whether written separately or as part of a ligature.[88]

Both authors give extensive rules for how to group notes of different duration into perfections of three tempora, and they largely agree.[89] Both begin with a principle that appears already in three of the modal treatises: a long before a long contains three tempora, or, in the parlance of Lambertus and Franco, a perfection.[90] They then offer guidelines for the solution of

---

[85.] Lambertus, *Musica mensurabilis* 17, ed. C. Meyer, trans. Desmond, pp. 64–65; Franco, *Ars cantus mensurabilis* 4.6, ed. Reaney and Gilles, p. 29 (trans. Strunk and McKinnon, p. 229); my translations.

[86.] Lambertus, *Musica mensurabilis* 27–36, ed. C. Meyer, trans. Desmond, pp. 66–67; Franco, *Ars cantus mensurabilis* 5.16 and 11.36, ed. Reaney and Gilles, pp. 36 and 75, respectively (trans. Strunk and McKinnon, pp. 232 and 242, respectively).

[87.] Lambertus, *Musica mensurabilis* 17–26, ed. C. Meyer, trans. Desmond, pp. 64–67; Franco, *Ars cantus mensurabilis* 4.6–15, ed. Reaney and Gilles, pp. 29–31 (trans. Strunk and McKinnon, p. 229). On the *duplex longa*, Lambertus, *Musica mensurabilis* 75–77, ed. C. Meyer, trans. Desmond, pp. 74–77; Franco, *Ars cantus mensurabilis* 4.13, ed. Reaney and Gilles, p. 30 (trans. Strunk and McKinnon, p. 229).

[88.] See Gallo, "Die Notationslehre im 14. und 15. Jahrhundert," p. 265.

[89.] Lambertus, *Musica mensurabilis* 44–84, ed. C. Meyer, trans. Desmond, pp. 68–77; Franco, *Ars cantus mensurabilis* 5.3–25, ed. Reaney and Gilles, pp. 31–40 (trans. Strunk and McKinnon, pp. 230–34).

[90.] Lambertus, *Musica mensurabilis* 44, ed. C. Meyer, trans. Desmond, pp. 68–69; Franco, *Ars cantus mensurabilis* 5.3, ed. Reaney and Gilles, p. 31 (trans. Strunk and McKinnon, p. 230). *Discantus positio uulgaris*: Hieronymus, *Tractatus de musica* 26, ed. C. Meyer and Lobrichon, p. 176 (trans. Knapp, p. 203); Garlandia, *De mensurabili musica* 1.29, ed. Reimer, 1:38 (trans.

various quantities of breves falling between two longs. Along the way, they propose a novelty of central importance to the resolution of potential ambiguities: a short vertical line between notes, called *divisio modorum seu perfectio* ("division of the modes, or a perfection," Lambertus), or *signum perfectionis* or *divisio modi* ("sign of perfection" or "division of the mode," Franco).[91] As follows from the discussion below, both authors recognized that even the rules they propose permit some variety of interpretation, and so the line that marks the end of a perfection provides a sure graphic sign of the limits of this key unit of three tempora.

The very first rule of discerning perfections illustrates the problem. Lambertus states that a long followed by a breve becomes imperfect and thus contains two tempora, but when a breve falls between two longs, it normally imperfects the preceding long, but sometimes the following one. Franco immediately seized upon this ambiguity and, recognizing that Lambertus and most musicians would impose imperfection on the preceding long in this case, asserted that the breve imperfects the following long only if the "signum perfectionis" appears after the preceding long, thus making it perfect and forcing the breve to imperfect the following one.[92] Lambertus only invokes the line of division when he discusses the case of four breves between two longs; three of the breves form a perfection, but the one left over could imperfect either the preceding long, the usual case, or the following one if the line appears after the first long.[93]

Franco's persistence in highlighting the idea that, when more than three breves separate two longs, the first breve imperfects the preceding long, creates another slight disagreement with Lambertus. The latter states that when five breves separate two longs, the first three form a perfection as do the next two by becoming a *recta–altera* pair. Franco's rule is more general: when more than three breves fall between two longs, the first breve imperfects the preceding long and the others form groups of three.[94] If two remain, they form a *breuis recta–altera* pair; a single breve would

---

Birnbaum, p. 2); Anonymous of Saint Emmeram, *De musica mensurata* 2, ed. and trans. Yudkin, p. 196 lines 29–31 and p. 198 lines 32–41.

[91] Lambertus, *Musica mensurabilis* 69–72, ed. C. Meyer, trans. Desmond, pp. 72–75; Franco, *Ars cantus mensurabilis* 5.6, ed. Reaney and Gilles, p. 32 (trans. Strunk and McKinnon, p. 230).

[92] Lambertus, *Musica mensurabilis* 45–51, ed. C. Meyer, trans. Desmond, pp. 68–71; Franco, *Ars cantus mensurabilis* 5.4–6, ed. Reaney and Gilles, p. 32 (trans. Strunk and McKinnon, p. 230).

[93] See n. 91 above.

[94] Lambertus, *Musica mensurabilis* 73, ed. C. Meyer, trans. Desmond, pp. 74–75; Franco, *Ars cantus mensurabilis* 5.17–20, ed. Reaney and Gilles, pp. 36–38 (trans. Strunk and McKinnon, p. 232).

imperfect the following long. So, in Franco's system, the rhythm would differ substantively from that of Lambertus for the same set of symbols.

Lambertus:

Franco:

Franco's rule generates three perfections, Lambertus' four because both longs in Lambertus are perfect and the final pair of breves occupies a full perfection. I deduce that Franco introduced his directive to facilitate reading. Singers, reading in the act of performance, do not need to count the breves between longs and then decide how to group them, as they do when following the system of Lambertus. Instead, after imperfecting the first long with the first breve, they would only need to read ahead three breves at a time, as opposed to reading the entire succession of breves, deciding which of Lambertus' rules to apply, and then imposing the solution.

They agree in their treatment of breves and semibreves. When two breves separate two longs, for example, they become a *breuis recta–altera* pair;[95] and semibreves occur in groups of two (unequal with the shorter first) or three (equal).[96] (Their views on pairs of semibreves reflect the position of the Saint Emmeram Anonymous, and, more important, duplicate the durations of the *breuis recta–altera* pair [shorter before longer], a point of great significance for developments in the fourteenth century.) In both cases, Franco gives more detail, covering more alternatives and reducing ambiguity, but without contradicting Lambertus' guidelines. Further, both authors describe the plica and its application in some detail.[97] A number of these ideas clearly originated with Lambertus, or at least he first described them; Franco then adopted them, clarified and adapted them to reduce ambiguity. His substantive contribution, however, came in his treatment of two aspects of mensural notation in which he disagrees fundamentally with Lambertus: rests and ligatures. These differences are

---

[95] Lambertus, *Musica mensurabilis* 60–65, ed. C. Meyer, trans. Desmond, pp. 70–73; Franco, *Ars cantus mensurabilis* 5.8–13, ed. Reaney and Gilles, pp. 33–34 (trans. Strunk and McKinnon, pp. 230–31).

[96] Lambertus, *Musica mensurabilis* 79–84, ed. C. Meyer, trans. Desmond, pp. 76–77; Franco, *Ars cantus mensurabilis* 5.21–25, ed. Reaney and Gilles, pp. 38–40 (trans. Strunk and McKinnon, pp. 232–34).

[97] Lambertus, *Musica mensurabilis* 88–97 and 156–60, ed. C. Meyer, trans. Desmond, pp. 78–81 and 94–97, respectively; Franco, *Ars cantus mensurabilis* 6 and 8, ed. Reaney and Gilles, pp. 41–43 and 51–54, respectively (trans. Strunk and McKinnon, pp. 234 and 236, respectively).

so great and Franco's achievement so important that I believe they fully justify the retention of his name to identify this style of notation.

Lambertus adapts the system of rests proposed by Garlandia and modifies it to provide rests of two different sizes for the greater and lesser semibreve and to avoid the imprecision of dividing a single space on the staff to indicate the two durations the semibreve could have: the greater occupies a full space, the lesser half a space.[98] This accommodation requires the rests of greater duration, breve and long, to occupy one space more than the number of tempora they contain. So, the perfect long covers four spaces in Lambertus instead of three in Garlandia. Franco responded to this counterintuitive arrangement by restoring Garlandia's system, in which the number of spaces spanned by the rest corresponds precisely to the number of tempora.[99] He also recognized (tacitly) that scribes did not need to distinguish the two semibreves because the context would always clarify when a semibreve would be greater or lesser: when two occur together, the second (whether note or rest) is always greater.

I introduce Franco's most significant accomplishment above when I discuss propriety and perfection in the treatises that explain modal rhythm. There, I show how Franco imposed order on a chaotic and imprecise system. Here, I would first indicate that Lambertus' treatment of what was already a confused system demonstrated the uncertainty around the application of these two properties. He does not discuss perfection in a ligature at all, and propriety for him seems to involve the presence of a stroke at the beginning of the ligature. He consistently differentiates between ligatures with and without propriety, and the witnesses illustrate the distinction by the presence or absence of a line descending from the left edge of the first note.[100] He also discusses ligatures with *proprietas non propria* (his term for ligatures with the opposite propriety) and shows that they all exhibit a stroke ascending from the left edge of the first note.[101]

Franco recognized the confusion in the system and realized that Lambertus only added to it. And so, he devised an orderly arrangement of the ligatures that acknowledged their origin in plainsong and provided

---

[98.] Lambertus, *Musica mensurabilis* 169–74, ed. C. Meyer, trans. Desmond, pp. 98–99.

[99.] Franco, *Ars cantus mensurabilis* 9.12–14, ed. Reaney and Gilles, p. 55 (trans. Strunk and McKinnon, p. 237).

[100.] Lambertus, *Musica mensurabilis* 98–99, 105–7, ed. C. Meyer, trans. Desmond, pp. 80–81; see also *ibid.* 108–12, 116–22, ed. Meyer, trans. Desmond, pp. 82–83, 84–85, respectively.

[101.] Lambertus, *Musica mensurabilis* 113–14, 124–25, ed. C. Meyer, trans. Desmond, pp. 82–83, 86–87, respectively.

Table 3.5 Morphology of ligatures to show propriety and perfection according to Franco

	Descending	Ascending
With Propriety	stroke descending from left edge of first note	no stroke
	FIRST NOTE BREVE	
Without Propriety	no stroke	stroke descending from left edge of first note
	FIRST NOTE LONG	
With Perfection	head of last note below and to the right of penultimate note	head of last note directly above penultimate note
	LAST NOTE LONG	
Without Perfection	last two notes of the ligature form an oblique bar	head of last note above and to the right of penultimate note, or last two notes of the ligature form an oblique bar
	LAST NOTE BREVE	
Opposite Propriety	stroke ascending from left edge of first note	stroke ascending from left edge of first note
	FIRST TWO NOTES SEMIBREVES	
	ALL INTERNAL NOTES BREVES, EXCEPT SECOND NOTE OF LIGATURE WITH OPPOSITE PROPRIETY, WHICH IS SEMIBREVE	

unequivocal rules about the morphology of each ligature that shows the presence or absence of propriety and perfection (see Table 3.5).[102]
As with the rule for the grouping of breves between longs, this practice greatly facilitates the rapid comprehension of ligatures in reading music while performing.

Et nota istas differentias essentiales esse et specificas ipsis ligaturis. Unde ligatura cum proprietate essentialiter differt ab illa quae est sine, ut rationale animal ab irrationali; similiter et in aliis differentiis prius dictis.[103]

And note that these differences are essential and specific to the ligatures themselves. Whence a ligature with propriety differs in essence from a ligature without propriety, just as a rational animal differs from an irrational one; similarly also in other differences mentioned above.

---

[102] Franco, *Ars cantus mensurabilis* 7.17–23, ed. Reaney and Gilles, pp. 43–50 (trans. Strunk and McKinnon, p. 235).
[103] Franco, *Ars cantus mensurabilis* 7.8–9, ed. Reaney and Gilles, p. 44 (trans. Strunk and McKinnon, p. 234); my translation.

He insists (by stating it twice) on the differences in essence these properties make because of the impact they have on musical literacy: the morphology of the ligatures unequivocally establishes the presence or absence of propriety and perfection, and those properties, or their absence, fix the identity of the constituent notes. All of these attributes promote efficient reading, and we can measure the success of his system by the fact that it remained in effect throughout the remaining life of ligatures, to the end of the sixteenth century. The clarification Franco introduced and his vigilance regarding ambiguity justify our continuing to call this system Franconian notation.

Example 3.2 gives the beginning of the motet *Se ie chante / Bien doi amer / Et sperabit* from Mo H. 196.[104] As Figure 3.2 shows, this manuscript presents polyphony not in score, as W_1, F and W_2 did for organum and conductus, but in parts: triplum and motetus in parallel columns, tenor across the bottom of the page.[105] This section of the manuscript, fascicle 8, which is probably coeval with the rest of the codex, uses Franconian notation extensively.[106] The present example exhibits most features of the dialect: distinct shapes for the three notes, and rests of distinct lengths to reflect the three values, longa, breve and semibreve; rests of the smallest value create a hocket between tenor and motetus in bar 11; ligatures of various types, including several with opposite propriety; and the plicated breve. Two forms do not appear, the perfect long of three tempora and the *breuis recta–altera* pair. The rhythm of the latter occurs in the combination of breve preceding and imperfecting a long, as in the tenor, bars 5, 8, 9 and 12.

---

[104] Mo H. 196 fols. 357v–359v; this passage fols. 357v–358r, using the older, ink foliation, top centre recto. See the edition in Tischler, ed., *The Montpellier Codex*, no. 311, 3:172–75; this passage pp. 172–73. In Example 3.2, square brackets indicate ligatures, slurs groups of semibreves and smaller notes those represented by the plica. The tenor has one additional note on the last beat of bar 13 that I have suppressed.

[105] Motets in F and W_2 use part notation; often the simultaneous voices occur on opposite sides of the same leaf. F fols. 381r–389v, 392v–398v, and W_2 fols. 123r–138v present three-voice conductus motets (both upper voices have the same text) with the top two voices in score and the tenor written separately at the end of the piece. F fols. 399v–414v, and W_2 fols. 145r–164v, 165v–167r, 168r–v, 173v–185v, 186v–192r, 208v, 216r–253v present two-voice motets with the voices each written as monophony. W_2 fols. 164v–165v, 186v–v, 193r–208v, 209r–v, 214v–215r also presents three-voice motets with each voice written successively; and fols. 209v–212r, a four-voice motet written in the same way. On the layout of Mo H. 196, see Huck, "Double Motet Layouts."

[106] Wolinski, "The Compilation of the Montpellier Codex," p. 299. See also the essays in Bradley and Desmond, eds., *The Montpellier Codex*. On the date, Curran, "A Palaeographical Analysis," esp. p. 41; Stones, "The Style and Iconography," esp. p.77; and Baltzer, "The Decoration of Montpellier 8," esp. p. 88.

Example 3.2 *Se ie chante / Bien doi amer / Et sperabit*, Mo H. 196 fols. 357v–359v

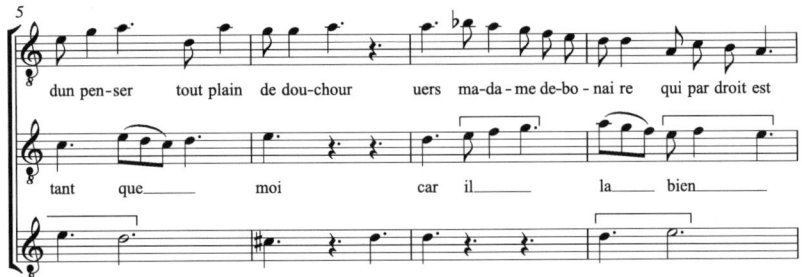

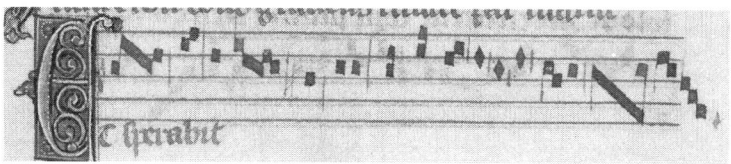

Figure 3.2 Mo H. 196 fols. 357v–358r
Bibliothèque interuniversitaire de Montpellier, BU historique de medicine
Copyright: BIU Montpellier/DIAMM, University of Oxford.

My interpretation of the semibreves corresponds precisely with the tenets of Lambertus, the Saint Emmeram Anonymous and Franco, who all advocate a triple subdivision of the breve by the semibreve: groups of three semibreves are treated as equal; in groups of two, the shorter precedes the longer. The music scribe conscientiously differentiates between the two types of groups by inserting a dot at the end of any group where ambiguity might arise. My transcription of the breve with plica derives from Lambertus' treatment of the perfect long with plica: he divides it into a principal note of two tempora and the plica of one.[107] I retain the same ratio in the case of the breve with plica, *mutatis mutandis*: two-thirds of a tempus for the principal note, and one-third to the plica, and so the opposite rhythm of a pair of semibreves.

The chief function of the plica would appear to lie in its ability to express this rhythm, as opposed to its role in chant, to facilitate the pronunciation of difficult combinations of letters; on both the second syllable of "amer" and the first of "ami" (bars 2 and 3, respectively), the duplum uses consecutive plicae, of which only the second would suffice to aid in pronunciation, if in fact that need existed. So the plica would appear to fill a gap in the possible rhythms of Franconian notation. Finally, still on the subject of text setting, the ligatures in the motetus (there are none in this portion of the triplum) all set a single syllable of the text, precisely the relationship that obtains between text and music in chant notation.

Franco, building on some of the innovations of Lambertus, as I detail above, significantly increased the efficiency of musical notation for fluid reading, principally through stressing the distinct morphology of each of the three note values. He further introduced a relatively simple system for inscribing those individual values in the ligatures still being used for the occasional melismatic passages in the motet, the genre whose prevailing syllabic style encouraged the development of Franconian notation. Although these aspects of his system move toward an iconic representation of relative duration (that is, the duration of one type of note in terms of another), the musician engaged in reading this notation must still derive the precise durations from context in order to distinguish the perfect from the imperfect long, the lesser from the greater semibreve, and to recognize a *breuis recta–altera* pair. Franco offers some assistance to this end by simplifying the system Lambertus introduced for determining whether a breve imperfects a long: in Franco's system, whenever four or more breves

---

[107] Lambertus, *Musica mensurabilis* 92, ed. C. Meyer, trans. Desmond, pp. 78–79.

separate two longs, the first breve always imperfects the first long, and the subsequent breves form groups of three.

Both Garlandia and Franco showed that they intuited the problem by proposing a system of rests that relies on the iconic representation of duration: the number of spaces the rest fills corresponds to the number of tempora it occupies. The other features of Franconian notation build on this relationship to fulfill a single goal, to facilitate and expedite the reading of music in real time, as the performance proceeds. Lambertus and especially Franco recognized that singers could not pause to determine how a succession of ligature shapes communicated first modal rhythms and then the actual durations of the musical lines they were reading and ultimately singing. They needed to be able to recognize the note values immediately on the basis of their morphology, whether as individual notes or within a ligature. Context still determined their precise duration, but these two musicians created the basis for modern durational notation.[108]

One refinement to the Franconian system arose from the idiosyncratic practice of a single presumably virtuosic singer, Petrus de Cruce, canon of the cathedral at Amiens. Several music theorists mention him by name and attribute to him a number of motets preserved in practical sources.[109] All the theorists agree that Petrus subdivided the breve into as many as seven equal semibreves, often with a different syllable of text on each note. Clearly, if the music moves at any speed, the singer would need to exercise great facility in enunciation to deliver the text in an intelligible way, hence my suggestion that Petrus must have evinced considerable virtuosity in his singing technique. Other singers do not seem to have emulated Petrus, as later motets do not employ this practice. But Petrus does anticipate an issue that subsequent developments in notation address, and that is a wider

---

[108] See Tanay, "The Transition," pp. 85–86.

[109] Jacques of Liège (Bent, *Magister Jacobus de Ispania*, pp. 63–65, incontrovertibly identifies the author as Jacobus de Ispania), *Speculum musicae* 7.17.7–10, ed. Bragard, 7:36–37; *Compendium musicae mensurabilis* 3.11, ed. Gallo, p. 69; and Handlo, *Regule* IV.reg.VIIIa, ed. and trans. Lefferts, pp. 106–7. Handlo also notes that Petrus introduces the technique of separating discrete groups of semibreves with a point, *ibid.*, *Regule* IV.reg.IV and VII, ed. and trans. Lefferts, pp. 100–5, precisely the practice in Mo H. 196 (see Example 3.2 and Figure 3.2 above). See also Gallo, "Die Notationslehre im 14. und 15. Jahrhundert," p. 268–72; Ristory, *Post-franconische Theorie*, pp. 43–85; Lersch, "Mensuralnotation"; and Desmond, *Music and the moderni*, pp. 126–30. Several of Petrus' motets occur in Mo H. 196; for a lucid account, see Sanders and Lefferts, "Petrus de Cruce"; also Bent, *Magister Jacobus de Ispania*, pp. 21–32. The two pieces that Jacobus de Ispania attributes to him, *S'amours eust* and *Aucun ont trouvé*, occur at Mo H. 196 fols. 270r–271r and 273r–275r, respectively; see Tischler, ed., *The Montpellier Codex*, nos. 253–54, 3:61–67. On the motets in Mo H. 196 that scholars attribute to him, see Everist, "Montpellier 8," pp. 20–21; and Maw, "*Je le temoin.*"

range of durations that in turn enables a more flexible rhythmic practice. This matter becomes a central concern of fourteenth-century musicians.

The *ars noua*

The period ca. 1300–1600 witnessed developments that led directly to the adoption of the modern system of rhythmic notation, beginning with the innovations grouped under the term *ars noua*. Scholars differ as to how Philippe de Vitry, cleric, administrator, composer and poet in the first half of the fourteenth century, contributed to these practices. Sarah Fuller, arguing from the differences between the texts that purport to transmit the views of Vitry, posits that those views circulated orally with greater or lesser certainty as to their connection with Vitry.[110] Karen Desmond begins with the critique offered by Jacobus de Ispania (Jacques of Liège) of a certain *doctor modernus* whose theories closely match those of the texts attributed to Vitry, and, from a close reading of the same texts investigated by Fuller, proposes that they may retain the traces of a written treatise authored by Vitry.[111]

Although Desmond admits that her case is not "watertight," she does make a convincing case that Jacobus may not have identified this *doctor modernus* as Vitry because of his caustic character.[112] More disturbing, and not mentioned by Desmond, is the fact that Johannes de Muris, author of our earliest detailed treatments of the rhythmic developments that distinguish the *ars noua*, does not name Vitry in any of the treatises in which he discusses these innovations, even though strong evidence exists for a close relationship between the two men.[113] Moreover, the earliest attributions to Vitry of writings on this subject date from around the middle of the fourteenth century, a quarter century or more after Muris' treatises.[114] In conjunction with the latter's silence about Vitry, is it possible that the

---

[110]. Fuller, "A Phantom Treatise."
[111]. Desmond, "Did Vitry Write an *Ars vetus et nova*?" and *Music and the moderni*, pp. 24–27.
[112]. Desmond, "Did Vitry Write an *Ars vetus et nova*?" pp. 486–87.
[113]. Wathey, "Philippe de Vitry's Books," p. 148 (Muris dedicates his *Quadripartitum numerorum* of 1343 to Vitry) and p. 150 (Vitry borrows books from Muris); on the latter, see also Gushee, "Jehan des Murs and His Milieu," p. 354; and Desmond, *Music and the moderni*, pp. 198–202.
[114]. Most scholars identify the colophon in Pa 7378A fol. 62rb as the earliest; Michels in Muris, *Notitia*, ed. Michels, pp. 24–25, dates the entire codex to A.D. 1362 on the basis of a colophon at the end of another work in the manuscript, fol. 14r. On the codex, see also Duhamel, "L'enseignement de la musique." On the colophons in general, see Fuller, "A Phantom Treatise," Table I, p. 25 and pp. 32–34; and Desmond, "Did Vitry Write an *Ars vetus et nova*?" p. 480.

connection between Vitry and the rhythmic innovations of the *ars noua* may be a late development?

In any case, the writings of Muris and the texts associated with Vitry agree in the two most important notational innovations of the fourteenth century, namely the establishment of duple division as equal in status to the triple division that characterizes thirteenth-century music, and the introduction of the minim as a value that subdivides the note previously regarded as the shortest, the semibreve. Both features facilitate the same desire, on the part of musicians, both performers and composers, to achieve greater rhythmic flexibility. The same motivation lies behind two other developments of the period, coloration and proportions. I construe these as less important because the former fell out of use during the fifteenth century and the application of the latter metamorphosed with the adoption of the modern notational system.[115]

Muris, like Jacobus de Ispania (both echo Lambertus and Franco in the previous century), asserts the primacy of ternary division through its association with Trinitarian doctrine.[116] A key passage of the *Notitia*, however, shows that Muris acknowledges the existence of imperfect time and therefore duple division in contemporary practice.

In fine huius opusculi notandum est, quod contingit fieri cantum ex perfectis notulis de tempore imperfecto ut tres breviores, et ex imperfectis de tempore perfecto ut duo breves. Adaequantur enim tres binarii et duo ternarii in 6, 12, 18, 24 et sic addendo 6. Sunt autem tres binarii perfecti de "tempore" imperfecto, sed duo ternarii imperfecti de perfecto, et ad invicem revolvuntur et aequa proportione finaliter adaequantur. Et ex perfectis de perfecto et imperfectis de imperfecto sicut convenit decantatur.[117]

At the end of this little work, it must be noted that a song happens to be made from perfect notes in imperfect time, that is three binary breves, and from imperfect

---

[115]. On Muris' rhythmic theories in general, see Michels, *Die Musiktraktate*; Gallo, "Die Notationslehre im 14. und 15. Jahrhundert," pp. 272–78; Tanay, "The Transition," pp. 90–104; and Ristory, *Denkmodelle zur französischen Mensuraltheorie*, 1:197–349, 2:68–106. The literature on Vitry is large; on his theoretical writings in general, see Fuller, "A Phantom Treatise"; Ristory, *Denkmodelle zur französischen Mensuraltheorie*, 1:515–50, 2:175–218; Desmond, "Texts in Play" and "Did Vitry Write an Ars vetus et nova?".

[116]. Muris, *Notitia* 2.1.7–2.3, ed. Michels, pp. 66–73 (trans. Strunk and McKinnon, pp. 262–64); see also Jacques of Liège, *Speculum musicae* 7.30, ed. Bragard, 7:60–62; and *Omni desideranti notitiam* 3 and 18, ed. and trans. Desmond, in "Texts in Play," pp. 116 and 132, respectively. Tanay, "The Transition," pp. 99–104, citing Michels, *Die Musiktraktate*, pp. 73–75, doubts that Muris authorized duple division as an independent rhythmic phenomenon.

[117]. Muris, *Notitia* 2.7.1–3, ed. Michels, p. 84 (trans. Strunk and McKinnon, pp. 267–68); my translation. See also Michels, *Die Musiktraktate*, pp. 75, 87–91.

notes in perfect time, that is two ternary breves. For three binary breves and two ternary breves become equivalent in groups of 6, 12, 18, 24 and other multiples of 6. There are, moreover, three perfect binary values in imperfect time, but two imperfect ternary values in perfect time, and they rotate in turn and finally, from their equal proportion, become equivalent. And from perfect notes in perfect time and imperfect notes in imperfect time just as it is appropriate, a song is performed.

This passage requires more unpacking than a simple translation permits. First, the phrases "ex perfectis notulis" and "ex imperfectis [notulis]" refer to the long: the perfect long contains three breves, the imperfect long two. But the expressions "de tempore imperfecto" and "perfecto" describe the division of the breve into two or three semibreves, respectively. Then Muris shows arithmetically that either system of subdivision results in a total of six semibreves for each long.

The next sentence appears to combine the levels of division, as the phrases "tres binarii perfecti" and "duo ternarii imperfecti" seem contradictory. How can a note be perfect and binary or ternary and imperfect simultaneously? The answer lies in the separation of the levels. The three binary breves are perfect because they combine to become equivalent to a single perfect long, and they belong to imperfect time because they are binary and therefore each contains two semibreves. *Mutatis mutandis*, the two ternary breves are imperfect because of their relationship to the imperfect long, but they participate in perfect time at the level of the semibreve. Muris then seems to imply that these two systems can occur in the same piece, perhaps concurrently in two (or more) voices or consecutively. The final sentence of the passage shows unequivocally that the two types of division, ternary and binary, share equal importance.[118]

If Muris only reluctantly accepted binary division, his contemporary Jacobus de Ispania outright rejected it, perhaps fighting the same kind of rearguard action as the Saint Emmeram Anonymous and Anonymous IV in the previous century.[119] Jacobus concludes Book 7 with a comparison of older and modern practices and a sharp critique of the latter,

---

[118]. The later treatise that purports to record Muris' teachings, *Ars practica mensurabilis cantus*, discusses all the combinations of triple and duple division at the three levels, long, breve and semibreve, chapter 2, ed. Berktold, pp. 9–10 and 98–99; and names the mensuration signs for all combinations, 6.1–4, *ibid.*, pp. 45–47 and 110–11.

[119]. On his rhythmic theories in general, see Gallo, "Die Notationslehre im 14. und 15. Jahrhundert," pp. 278–83; and Ristory, *Denkmodelle zur französischen Mensuraltheorie*, 1:125–68, 2:57–67. On his antipathy to modern practices, see Bragard, "Le Speculum musicae," *Musica Disciplina* 7:100–5; Smith, "Jacques de Liège," "Jacques de Liège's Criticism" and *Iacobi Leodiensis*, 1:19–31 and 3:18–64; and Desmond, *Music and the moderni*, pp. 36–40, 115–23, 138–41.

expressing regret that musicians no longer cultivated the full range of the older genres instead of just "motets and *chansons*" ("in solis motetis aut in cantilenis").[120] He stresses the priority of triple division by associating it with the Trinity (like Muris, as I note above), and also by quoting Lambertus in identifying the perfect long as the "fons ... et origo" ("fount and origin") of all notes.[121] He supplements his theological and numerological views with a historical one: thirteenth-century musicians (the ancients) used only triple divisions and never permitted imperfect time.[122] Imperfect values should always follow or precede a note of lesser value to create a perfection, even though the moderns sometimes use imperfect values independently.[123]

The theories Jacobus so vehemently opposed find their fullest unequivocal expression in the texts associated with Philippe de Vitry. Above, I state my reservations as to the authenticity of these attributions, but there remains no doubt regarding the nature of the innovations they disclose. I use as my principal reference the text in Pa 7378A, the oldest witness in the corpus, with references to other texts in the notes. It states that the long in perfect mode contains three tempora, in imperfect mode it is the equivalent of two, while the duplex long contains six and four, respectively.[124] A later passage, where the author discusses the possible combination of triple and duple divisions, the disposition of rests and examples of pieces that demonstrate these combinations, shows that the term "mode" (*modus*) refers to the relationship between long and breve.[125] So the author is describing two different instances of this relationship, a perfect one, where the long

---

[120.] Jacques of Liège, *Speculum musicae* 7.45–48, ed. Bragard, 7:86–95 (trans. Strunk and McKinnon, pp. 271–78); lament about older repertories, *ibid.* 7.46.9–11, ed. Bragard, 7:89 (trans. Strunk and McKinnon, pp. 273–74); quotation, *ibid.* 7.46.11, ed. Bragard, 7:89 (trans. Strunk and McKinnon, p. 274).

[121.] On the Trinity, see n. 116 above; quoting Lambertus: Jacques of Liège, *Speculum musicae* 7.21.2, ed. Bragard, 7:45.

[122.] Jacques of Liège, *Speculum musicae* 7.19.14 and 29.6–7, ed. Bragard, 7:42 and 59, respectively.

[123.] Jacques of Liège, *Speculum musicae* 7.21.3–4, 29.8 and 45.5–8 (trans. Strunk and McKinnon, p. 272), ed. Bragard, 7:45, 59 and 87, respectively. See Desmond, "Did Vitry Write an *Ars vetus et nova*?" pp. 457–59.

[124.] Pa 7378A fol. 61vb lines 17–18 and 23–26, ed. and trans. Gilles, "Un témoignage inédit," in Vitry, *Ars nova*, ed. Reaney *et al.*, p. 57. Also Vitry, *Ars nova* 17.5–9, ed. Reaney *et al.*, p. 25 (trans. Plantinga, p. 215); and *Omni desideranti notitiam* 3–5, ed. and trans. Desmond, in "Texts in Play," pp. 116–18.

[125.] Pa 7378A fol. 62rb lines 2–27, ed. and trans. Gilles, "Un témoignage inédit," in Vitry, *Ars nova*, ed. Reaney *et al.*, pp. 67–69. Also Vitry, *Ars nova* 17.2–3, ed. Reaney *et al.*, p. 25 (trans. Plantinga, p. 215). See also Jacques of Liège, *Speculum musicae* 7.18.4, ed. Bragard, 7:39–40. See Desmond, "Did Vitry Write an *Ars vetus et nova*?" pp. 461–62.

contains three breves, and an imperfect one, where it contains two, thus explicitly acknowledging duple division at the level of the mode.

He then extends the relationships just described between long and breve to the other smaller values, establishing that triple and duple divisions occur equally at all levels.[126] And, in the passage mentioned above, he summarizes all these developments.

Sciendum igitur quod sunt aliqui cantus perfecti modo et tempore, alii inperfecti, alii (perfecti) modo et non tempore, alii tempore et non modo, alii partim perfecti et partim inperfecti tam modo quam tempore. Igitur in modo perfecto longa ante longam tria valet tempora. In modo inperfecto longa vero non nisi duo, nec tria valet nisi punctus perfectionis apponatur.[127]

It must therefore be known that some songs are perfect in mode and time, some imperfect, others perfect in mode and not time, still others in time but not mode, and some are partly perfect and partly imperfect as much in mode as in time. In perfect mode, therefore, a long before a long is worth three tempora. In imperfect mode, a long is only worth two tempora and not three unless a point of perfection is placed.

Mode, then, refers to the relationship between long and breve, as mentioned above, and here tempus describes that between breve and semibreve. To these the author adds the next lower level, prolation, which applies to the relationship between semibreve and the new note below it, the minim.[128] Table 3.6 shows the resulting values. Further, he acknowledges, as does Muris, that different mensurations can occur together in the same piece, although again, he does not specify whether concurrently in different voices or consecutively. And finally, he calls the point that lengthens a note in duple division the point of perfection, without naming the point that marks the end of a perfection in triple division.[129]

---

[126] Pa 7378A fol. 62ra lines 24–46, ed. and trans. Gilles, "Un témoignage inédit," in Vitry, *Ars nova*, ed. Reaney et al., pp. 63–65. See Desmond, *Music and the moderni*, pp. 141–45.

[127] Pa 7378A fol. 62rb lines 2–7, ed. and trans. Gilles, "Un témoignage inédit," in Vitry, *Ars nova*, ed. Reaney et al., p. 67.

[128] Pa 7378A fol. 62ra lines 30–36 and fol. 62rb lines 33–45, ed. and trans. Gilles, "Un témoignage inédit," in Vitry, *Ars nova*, ed. Reaney et al., pp. 63 and 69, respectively. Also Vitry, *Ars nova* 20–24, ed. Reaney et al., pp. 29–31 (trans. Plantinga, pp. 218–20).

[129] On the point as the limit of a perfection in triple division, see Muris, *Notitia* 2.6.3 (trans. Strunk and McKinnon, p. 266) and 2.9.7–8, ed. Michels, pp. 80 and 90, respectively; Muris, *Ars practica mensurabilis cantus* 3.15–16, ed. Berktold, pp. 15–17 and 101; and Pa 7378A fol. 61vb lines 28–31, ed. and trans. Gilles, "Un témoignage inédit," in Vitry, *Ars nova*, ed. Reaney et al., pp. 57–59. On the ambiguities of the points, see Muris, *Notitia* 2.10.24–37, ed. Michels, pp. 97–100; Muris, *Ars practica mensurabilis cantus* 5, ed. Berktold, pp. 42–44 and 109–10; and *Omni desideranti notitiam* 19–22, ed. and trans. Desmond, in "Texts in Play," p. 134.

Table 3.6 Table of values in perfect and imperfect mensurations

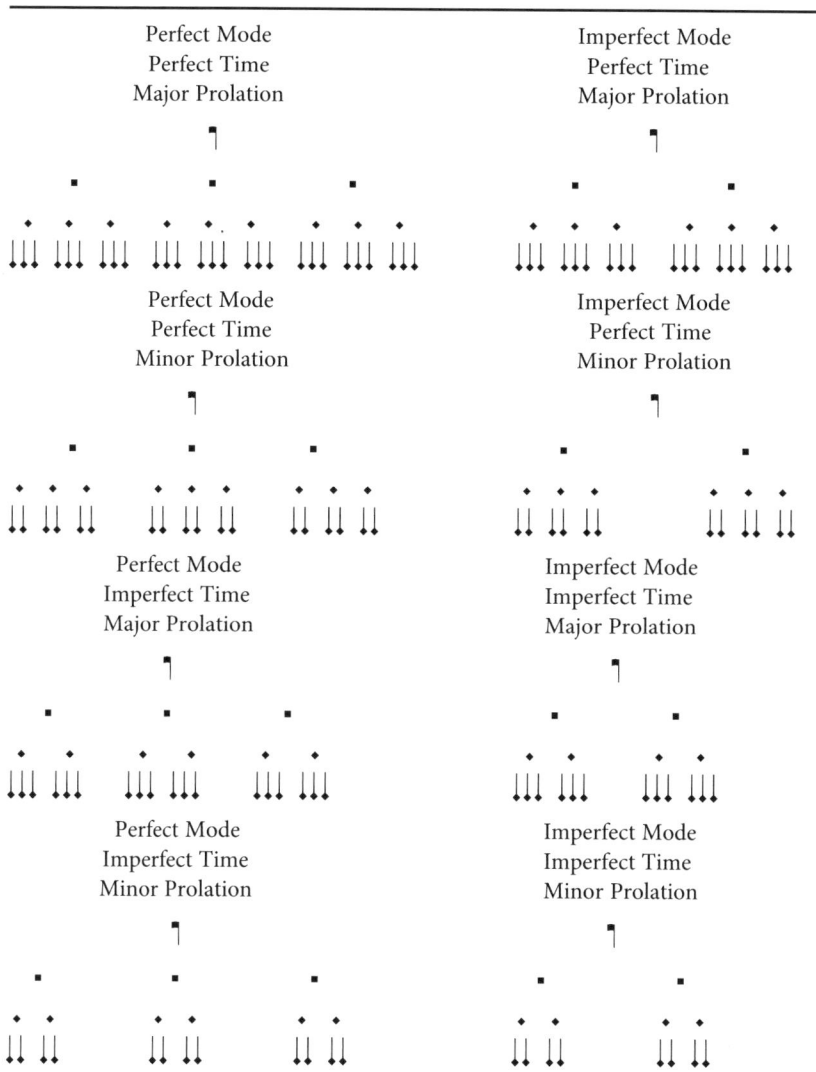

This last issue highlights the ambiguity that remained in the notation and clearly vexed fourteenth-century musicians, as it does modern scholars. Muris puts it succinctly, "perfectum et imperfectum figura similis repraesentat" ("the same symbol represents what is perfect and imperfect").[130] Franco already recognized the problem and accordingly

---

[130.] Muris, *Notitia* 2.6.2, ed. Michels, p. 80 (trans. Strunk and McKinnon, p. 266). See also Jacques of Liège, *Speculum musicae* 7.24.3–4 and 42.6–7, ed. Bragard, 7:51 and 82, respectively.

instituted a set of rules to help musicians identify the places where they should imperfect a long, to which he added the device of the point, apparently introduced by Petrus de Cruce but refined by Franco, to indicate the end of a perfection. The *ars noua* system of mensuration compounds the problem because, besides the issue of imperfection within the triple divisions (now applied to all levels of values, not just the relationship between long and breve as in Franco), entire pieces, sections or individual voices can move in duple time at one or more of the three levels, and the morphology of the notes, as Muris states, offers no guide.[131] For the first problem, our fourteenth-century authors offered extensive rules on how to recognize perfect and imperfect notes in the triple divisions, largely echoing Franco.[132]

The second issue required a more radical solution, a series of symbols that unequivocally indicate triple or duple division. The text in Pa 7378A provides a simple dichotomy between perfect time, indicated by either a full circle or three lines, and imperfect time, by a semicircle or two lines.[133] Muris concurs and additionally prescribes the inscription of two or three dots inside the circle or semicircle to indicate duple or triple subdivision of the semibreve.[134] All these innovations balance two competing desires on the part of fourteenth-century musicians. Against the wish to exploit a more flexible rhythmic palette, they needed to make these rhythmic subtleties and distinctions visually transparent to literate musicians so that they

---

[131.] On imperfection at various durational levels, see Desmond, *Music and the moderni*, pp. 147–55, and on the use of dots or points, pp. 199–233.

[132.] Muris, *Notitia* 2.6.3–5 (trans. Strunk and McKinnon, p. 266, omitting the table at 2.6.5) and 2.8–12, ed. Michels, pp. 80–81 and 87–103, respectively; Muris, *Compendium musicae practicae* 11, ed. Michels, pp. 143–44; and Muris, *Ars practica mensurabilis cantus* 3, ed. Berktold, pp. 11–35 and 99–107. Jacques de Liège, *Speculum musicae* 7.38–44, ed. Bragard, 7:75–86. Pa 7378A fol. 61vb lines 26–50, ed. and trans. Gilles, "Un témoignage inédit," in Vitry, *Ars nova*, ed. Reaney et al., pp. 57–59; curiously, this last text, lines 33–35 and 40–50, p. 59, follows Lambertus and not Franco in the treatment of more than three breves after a long by stating that the first three become a perfection, whereas Franco stipulates in this situation that the first breve always imperfects the preceding long, and then subsequent groups of three breves form perfections (see above). Also Vitry, *Ars nova* 17.10–13, ed. Reaney et al., p. 25 (trans. Plantinga, p. 216); and *Omni desideranti notitiam* 6–18, ed. and trans. Desmond, in "Texts in Play," pp. 118–32.

[133.] Pa 7378A fol. 62ra line 64–fol. 62rb line 2, ed. and trans. Gilles, "Un témoignage inédit," in Vitry, *Ars nova*, ed. Reaney et al., pp. 65–67. Also Vitry, *Ars nova* 16 and 18, ed. Reaney et al., pp. 24 and 27, respectively (trans. Plantinga, pp. 214–15 and 216–17, respectively). See A. Berger, *Mensuration and Proportion Signs*, pp. 13–14.

[134.] Muris, *Ars practica mensurabilis cantus* 6.1–4, ed. Berktold, pp. 45–47 and 110–11; see also *Omni desideranti notitiam* 23–25, ed. and trans. Desmond, in "Texts in Play," p. 136; and Jacques de Liège, *Speculum musicae* 7.47.4–15, ed. Bragard, 7:91–93 (trans. Strunk and McKinnon, pp. 275–76). See Desmond, "Did Vitry Write an *Ars vetus et nova*?" pp. 462–63.

could read and apprehend them in real time. The point of division strives to clarify rhythmic values, although not without some ambiguities, as I discuss above. More concrete, however, is the mensuration sign, which graphically defines the relationships between the various durational values.

These two devices, the point and the mensuration sign, further reveal the conflict between iconic and symbolic modes of representation. The point, when it divides perfections, borrows that function from its role as a punctuation mark in grammar, but in both environments, it operates symbolically. Moreover, in duple divisions, when it lengthens the duration of a note, it also does so symbolically, and context alone determines which role it fulfills, an issue that troubled Muris. The mensuration sign, however, combines symbolic and iconic modes. The logic behind the circle and semicircle representing, respectively, perfection and imperfection seems clear enough, but these symbols remain just that, symbolic, if logical, representations. The use of short lines or dots, though, two or three at a time, iconically shows when double or triple division applies. Still, the intent remains clear to indicate where and how to apply the new rhythmic subtleties introduced in the early fourteenth century.

An additional sign, the minim, strove to combine these aspirations of rhythmic flexibility and graphic clarity. To achieve the latter, it morphologically distinguishes itself from the next longer duration, the semibreve, by the addition of an ascending stem to the semibreve's diamond shape. And by adding one, if not two, levels of shorter durations to the range of values instituted by Franco, it widened the range of durations available.[135] Muris and Ispania both mention it in passing without defining it.[136] The text in Pa 7378A, however, makes it clear that the minim divides the semibreve, and that at this level too triple or duple division applies.[137] Moreover, the minim itself (despite its name, which ought to indicate that it cannot be divided) suffers division by a note commonly called the semiminim.[138] The fact that the semiminim divides the minim in two and not three equal parts

---

[135] See the table at Muris, *Notitia* 2.5.8, ed. Michels, p. 79 (trans. Strunk and McKinnon, p. 267).

[136] Muris, *Notitia* 2.5.5–8 (trans. Strunk and McKinnon, p. 266), 2.9, 2.11, ed. Michels, pp. 78–79, 89–92, 102, respectively; and Jacques of Liège, *Speculum musicae* 7.17.3, ed. Bragard, 7:36.

[137] Pa 7378A fol. 62ra lines 42–54 and fol. 62rb lines 33–45, ed. and trans. Gilles, "Un témoignage inédit," in Vitry, *Ars nova*, ed. Reaney et al., pp. 65 and 69, respectively. Also Vitry, *Ars nova* 15, ed. Reaney et al., pp. 23–24 (trans. Plantinga, pp. 213–14); and *Omni desideranti notitiam* 14–18, ed. and trans. Desmond, in "Texts in Play," pp. 128–32.

[138] Pa 7378A fol. 62ra lines 23–24, ed. and trans. Gilles, "Un témoignage inédit," in Vitry, *Ars nova*, ed. Reaney et al., p. 63, where the author notes the illogicality, "si dici possent semiminime" ("if they can be called semiminims"); see also *ibid.* lines 47–52, p. 65. Also Vitry, *Ars nova* 15.13–14 and 21.4, ed. Reaney et al., pp. 24 and 30, respectively (trans. Plantinga, pp. 214 and 219, respectively).

foreshadows subsequent developments. The physical description of this new smallest note in Pa 7378A ("illa vero que in oblicum versus dextrum latus caudata semiminima vocatur"; "that note indeed that bears an oblique tail toward the right side is called semiminim") seems to indicate the addition of the flag to the note's stem.[139]

Two final aspects of the notation known to these fourteenth-century authors deserve comment: syncopation and the use of red notes. Muris and the text in Pa 7378A describe a system whereby, in triple division, an isolated note between perfections can join other notes elsewhere in the piece to create a non-continuous perfection.[140] Perfections between these separated notes would thus begin at the place where the second of the group of three notes in a perfection would normally fall and continue through to the place of the first note, or, as the text in Pa 7378A puts it, "recta mensura syncopetur" ("the regular measure would be syncopated").[141] Muris' *Ars practica mensurabilis cantus* and the text *Omni desideranti notitiam* detail how the phenomenon can occur at all levels of mode, tempus and prolation, and provide examples.[142]

But as Ursula Günther points out, syncopation in triple divisions occurs rarely because of the difficulties presented by the notation.[143] The example in the *Ars practica mensurabilis cantus* that illustrates syncopation in perfect tempus demonstrates the problem (Line 1).[144]

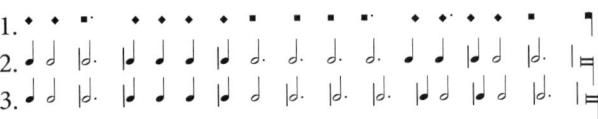

The group of four semibreves near the beginning of the example initiates

---

[139.] Pa 7378A fol. 62ra lines 47–49, ed. and trans. Gilles, "Un témoignage inédit," in Vitry, *Ars nova*, ed. Reaney et al., p. 65.

[140.] Muris, *Notitia* 2.7.4, ed. Michels, p. 84 (trans. Strunk and McKinnon, p. 268); and Pa 7378A fol. 62ra lines 59–63, ed. and trans. Gilles, "Un témoignage inédit," in Vitry, *Ars nova*, ed. Reaney et al., p. 65. See Günther, "Die Mensuralnotation," pp. 21–27; and Michels, *Die Musiktraktate*, pp. 88–89.

[141.] Pa 7378A fol. 62ra lines 62–63, ed. and trans. Gilles, "Un témoignage inédit," in Vitry, *Ars nova*, ed. Reaney et al., p. 65.

[142.] Muris, *Ars practica mensurabilis cantus* 9, ed. Berktold, pp. 65–72 and 117–18; and *Omni desideranti notitiam* 29–31, ed. and trans. Desmond, in "Texts in Play," pp. 140–42.

[143.] Günther, "Die Mensuralnotation," pp. 26–27. For other views on the application of syncopation to various levels of mensuration, see Dahlhaus, "Zur Geschichte der Synkope," pp. 385–87; and C. Berger, *Hexachord, Mensur und Textstruktur*, pp. 37–48.

[144.] Muris, *Ars practica mensurabilis cantus* 9.3, ed. Berktold, p. 68 (the example in Recensio B differs, p. 118; see also, for commentary, pp. 92 and 128). I render the ligatures as independent notes.

the syncopation: the first three form a perfection and the fourth stands as the isolated note that marks the syncopation (Line 2). The four breves that follow all become perfect because a note that precedes one of the same value remains perfect, while the point after the fourth breve prevents the following semibreve from imperfecting it.[145] These two semibreves, the second of which the scribe also marked with a point, then join with the isolated semibreve to form a perfection.[146]

Singers reading this notation in real time would need to look ahead in order to identify the syncopation and realize it successfully. First they have to recognize that the first of the four breves precedes another breve and so remains perfect. Consequently, the preceding semibreve cannot imperfect the first breve and so stands isolated. Second and subsequently, they must locate the values that will complement the isolated semibreve to form a full perfection; the requisite notes, the two semibreves set off by a point, stand five perfections distant. I believe this notation presents such difficulties of apprehension that it would be opaque to all but the most expert singers, and many of lesser achievement might well realize the rhythmic shape of the passage as in Line 3. Difficulties in the smooth apprehension of the notation such as these motivated Franco to simplify the rules of imperfection precisely to avoid the necessity of the singer's having to look ahead several notes to understand the rhythmic notation. The description of the practice in Pa 7378A, however, may indicate the solution for practical musicians: "et secundum aliquos deberent fieri rubee" ("and according to some, red notes ought to be used").[147]

The author of this text expands this statement to attribute three functions to the red note, each exemplified by the tenor of a motet: red notes are sung in the opposite measure to black notes (exemplified by *In arboris*) or they vary the mode or tempus (*Garison*); two breves between two longs remain equal in length, creating duple division (*In nova fert*); and the tenor should be sung an octave higher (*Quant amour*).[148] The discussion in *Ars nova* largely parallels

---

[145]. On the convention that a note preceding one of the same value remains perfect, see Muris, *Ars practica mensurabilis cantus* 3.14 (ed. Berktold, pp. 14–15 and 100–1) and 3.23 (pp. 22 and 102).

[146]. See the resolution provided by Christian Meyer in Muris, *Écrits sur la musique*, trans. Meyer, p. 217.

[147]. Pa 7378A fol. 62ra line 63, ed. and trans. Gilles, "Un témoignage inédit," in Vitry, *Ars nova*, ed. Reaney et al., p. 65.

[148]. Pa 7378A fol. 62rb lines 23–33, ed. and trans. Gilles, "Un témoignage inédit," in Vitry, *Ars nova*, ed. Reaney et al., p. 69. Also Vitry, *Ars nova* 19, ed. Reaney et al., pp. 28–29 (trans. Plantinga, pp. 217–18). *In arboris*, *Garison* and *In nova fert* are usually attributed to Vitry. See Sanders, "The Early Motets"; Leech-Wilkinson, "The Emergence"; and Kügle, *The Manuscript Ivrea, Biblioteca Capitolare 115*, pp. 89–119. *Quant amour* has apparently not survived.

this one but adds an important statement regarding the tenor of *Garison* that shapes subsequent theoretical treatments as well as practice: "In tenore enim illius moteti longae notulae nigrae tria tempora valent perfecta, rubeae vero duo tempora imperfecta" ("In the tenor of that motet, long black notes are worth three perfect tempora, red ones two imperfect tempora").[149] That is, red notes, irrespective of context, are imperfect. But the author then immediately continues, "Et aliquando e converso, ut in tenore moteti qui vocatur *Plures errores sunt*" ("And sometimes the opposite applies, as in the tenor of the motet that is called *Plures errores sunt*").[150]

Muris' *Ars practica mensurabilis cantus* adopts only the first half of this statement and, by ignoring the second half, creates a rigid dichotomy between black and red notes, a position that became the standard interpretation of red notes through the end of the fourteenth century and beyond.[151] Black notes, of course, continued to hold imperfect values either in duple or, when imperfected by shorter notes, triple divisions. But red notes forced the user to assign imperfect values when any ambiguity remained about the value of black notes in the same positions. This strategy addressed two issues. First, it facilitated the reading of complex rhythmic patterns in real time by unequivocally identifying imperfect values where the possibility of uncertainty lingered. In this way, it furthered Franco's goals in fostering notational practices that literate users could easily apprehend as they were reading in the act of performance. Second, it permits, again unequivocally, the use of syncopation in triple division.

Example 3.3 and Figure 3.3, Guillaume de Machaut's ballade *Biaute qui toutes autres pere*, illustrate the main features of fourteenth-century notation. I use the version in Pa 1584, the last of the surviving comprehensive Machaut manuscripts compiled during his lifetime, and I provide, for comparison, the tenor part in Pa 9221, a later manuscript.[152] We must first identify the mensuration that governs the rhythmic progression of the chanson. Codex Pa 1584 does not use mensuration signs, and so the notation itself must provide the evidence for this determination. The red

---

[149] Vitry, *Ars nova* 19, ed. Reaney *et al.*, pp. 28–29, quotation *ibid.* 19.12, p. 29 (trans. Plantinga, pp. 217–18).

[150] Vitry, *Ars nova* 19.12, ed. Reaney *et al.*, p. 29 (trans. Plantinga, p. 218). Also *Omni desideranti notitiam* 26–28, ed. and trans. Desmond, in "Texts in Play," pp. 138–40.

[151] Muris, *Ars practica mensurabilis cantus* 6.5–9 (Recensio A), ed. Berktold, pp. 48–51, and 6.7–11 (Recensio B), pp. 111–13.

[152] Pa 1584 fols. 455v; Pa 9221 fol. 152v. See Machaut, *The Works of Guillaume de Machaut*, ed. Schrade, 2:74–75. On the Machaut manuscripts, see Earp, "Machaut's Role." For bibliography on this chanson, see Earp, *Guillaume de Machaut*, pp. 295–96. I transcribe only the cantus and tenor; the contratenor occurs only in Pa 9221.

Example 3.3 Guillaume de Machaut, *Biaute qui toutes autres pere*, Pa 1584 fol. 455v

Figure 3.3a Pa 1584 fol. 455v

Figure 3.3b Pa 9221 fol. 152v
Courtesy of Paris, Bibliothèque nationale de France.

notes Machaut provides in the tenor (Example 3.3, bars 9–14, 22–23 and 31–36) indicate the tempus. (I indicate red ligatures with a broken bracket in Example 3.3, black ligatures with a solid bracket.) The red ligatures all consist of breves only, and because the red notation requires us to interpret them as imperfect values, we may deduce that black breves may be either perfect or imperfect, according to the context.

So the mensuration must include perfect time; that is, the perfect breve is divided into three equal parts by the semibreve, and the imperfect breve into two equal parts. The rules of perfection and imperfection dictate the relationship between breve and semibreve (imperfect breves in the cantus at bars 6, 9, 11, 13, 15, 25, 28, 31, 33 and 35; in the tenor bars 5, 6, 8, 19 and 24), and semibreves may form the *recta–altera* pair (cantus bar 30, tenor bars 25 and 29). The groups of six minims or equivalent (e.g., cantus bars 1–5), in conjunction with perfect time, as already determined, dictate minor prolation. Hence, the minim divides the semibreve into two equal parts, six minims equivalent to the perfect breve, four for the imperfect breve. The scribe of Pa 9221 confirms these relationships with the mensuration sign with which the tenor begins in that witness. So, this piece illustrates two distinctive features of fourteenth-century notation: duple division, here between semibreve and minim; and the application of imperfection and the use of the *recta–altera* pair to shorter durations, the breve and semibreve in this example.

Beyond serving as evidence for the presence of perfect time, as noted above, the red notation also permits the unequivocal use of syncopation within triple subdivisions, just as the text in Pa 7378A suggests.[153] This device, in conjunction with the use of duple division of the semibreve by the minim, increases the flexibility with which fourteenth-century musicians could shape rhythm. Conversely, this piece does not demonstrate that the addition of durations shorter than the semibreve necessarily contributes to the same goal. Example 3.2, the thirteenth-century motet *Se ie chante / Bien doi amer / Et sperabit*, employs three durations, long, breve and semibreve. *Biaute qui toutes autres pere*, however, employs the long sparingly, once as the first note of the tenor and once as the final note of the cantus. So, the main body of the chanson also uses only three durations, but at one level lower than those in the motet: breve, semibreve and minim. The range of durations, therefore, has not substantively increased.

Machaut's treatment of the long at the beginning of the tenor addresses a concern of the early fourteenth-century theorists. First, the counterpoint with the cantus shows that it must be imperfect in value. If it were perfect, the indicated E♭ would sound against the A in bar 4 of the cantus. Also, the tenor would be a full perfection longer than the cantus. But the value of the long receives further reduction from being imperfected by the semibreve that immediately follows. Johannes de Muris advocates this type of imperfection, but Jacobus de Ispania, while recognizing that modern musicians apply it, emphatically (and repeatedly) rejects it.[154] Machaut, by

---

[153]. See n. 147 above.

[154]. Muris, *Notitia* 2.10.9 and 2.10.19–21, ed. Michels, pp. 94 and 96, respectively; and Muris, *Ars practica mensurabilis cantus* 3.44, ed. Berktold, pp. 32 and 106. Jacques of Liège, *Speculum musicae* 7.21.3, 28.5, 38.9, 38.12 (the position of modern musicians), and 44.1–7, ed. Bragard,

Table 3.7 The commonly used mensuration signs, according to Prosdocimus de Beldemandis

⊙	Perfect Time, Major Prolation
○	Perfect Time, Minor Prolation
¢	Imperfect Time, Major Prolation
C	Imperfect Time, Minor Prolation

imperfecting an imperfect long in this way, along with his adoption of the other fourteenth-century innovations, reveals himself to be an advocate of the most modern notational devices.

We cannot say the same, however, with regard to mensuration signs, those indications that firmly identify the presence of triple or duple subdivision in tempus and prolation. The early fourteenth-century theorists describe a variety of such signs, as noted above, but, like Guido d'Arezzo's staff notation, musicians seem to have been slow to adopt them.[155] They do not, to the best of my knowledge, appear in any of the Machaut manuscripts that originated during the composer's lifetime, for example, and so we may question whether Machaut himself knew them. Nevertheless, the scribe of Pa 9221 did know them, in the form commonly used in the fifteenth and sixteenth centuries. Prosdocimus de Beldemandis, writing in the early fifteenth century, describes them, along with some of their competitors (see Table 3.7).[156] As Figure 3.3b shows, the scribe of Pa 9221, in the tenor of *Biaute qui toutes autres pere*, uses the mensuration signs for perfect and imperfect time, always with minor prolation, to replace the red notation found in Pa 1584. It would seem that he treats this voice as a special case because he does not mark the cantus with a mensuration sign (not shown in Figure 3.3b).

This example, then, demonstrates that Machaut, the leading composer of the fourteenth century, adopted most of the notational features that distinguish his century's musical practice from that of the previous century: duple division, the minim and syncopation (indicated by red notes). The one device he did not endorse is the mensuration sign. Perhaps he did not know of them, or possibly the diversity of practice discouraged him from adopting one or another system. As a result, Machaut's notational practices do not compare favourably with those of Franco in terms of transparency. The added complication of choosing between triple and duple division at two or three levels requires singers, in the absence of the mensuration signs, to analyze the notation to determine which

---

7:45, 58, 76, 77 and 84–85, respectively. See C. Berger, *Hexachord, Mensur und Textstruktur*, pp. 30–37.

[155] For a history and description of the theoretical discussions of the signs, see A. Berger, *Mensuration and Proportion Signs*, pp. 12–119.

[156] Prosdocimus de Beldemandis, *Tractatus practice*, ed. Coussemaker, pp. 214b-15a.

divisions govern the relationships between durations, a task only highly trained singers would be able to execute successfully. With the establishment of the mensuration signs endorsed by Prosdocimus in the fifteenth century, however, the transparent inscription of rhythm begins to approach that of pitch already achieved in the thirteenth century.

Parallel to these developments in France, fourteenth-century Italian musicians created a style of notation that used many of the same graphemes but a different system of organizing them into mensurations.[157] Semibreves occur in groups of four to twelve, each group equal to a breve. Groups of four and eight create duple divisions of the breve, groups of nine and twelve, triple; groups of six generate either two subgroups of three semibreves (equivalent to imperfect time, major prolation in the French system) or three subgroups of two semibreves (perfect time, minor prolation). Many sources indicate the groupings by a single letter: .q. = quaternaria, .i. = senaria imperfecta (two subgroups of three semibreves), .p. = senaria perfecta (three subgroups of two semibreves), .o. = octonaria, .n. = novenaria, and .d. = duodenaria. Because it is not possible to invoke syncopation across the unit of the breve, Italian composers, seeking more rhythmic flexibility, eventually abandoned their system for the French early in the fifteenth century. Simultaneously, of course, more musicians of French and Flemish origin and training were seeking professional employment in Italy, bringing their own style of notation with them.

Coloration and Proportion

We have seen that red notation began to appear in the fourteenth century, with a variety of meanings according to the early theorists, but in the course of the century, it came to indicate imperfect values, as Prosdocimus unequivocally states.[158] He makes it clear that red (or notes of another colour) or void notes (that is, notes without pigmentation in the note heads) invariably represent imperfect values, therefore creating a proportional relationship of two-thirds of the perfect value. Black notes, on the

---

[157]. The principal theoretical sources are Marchetto of Padua, *Pomerium*, esp. 1.7.4–6, ed. Vecchi, pp. 102–55; and Prosdocimus de Beldemandis, *Tractatus practice . . . ad modum ytalicorum*, ed. Sartori, esp. pp. 40–46. See also Sartori, *La notazione italiana*, pp. 73–158; K. von Fischer, *Studien zur italienischen Musik*, pp. 111–22, and "Zur Entwicklung"; Gallo, *La teoria della notazione* and "Die Notationslehre im 14. und 15. Jahrhundert," pp. 304–33; and Fellin, "The Notation Types."

[158]. Prosdocimus de Beldemandis, *Tractatus practice*, ed. Coussemaker, pp. 203b, 215a–216a and 227b.

other hand, can signify perfect or imperfect values at any rhythmic level, depending on the mensuration and the application of imperfection. Musicians of the late fourteenth and early fifteenth centuries expanded on this idea of imposing proportional relationships on durational values to realize greater rhythmic flexibility, with some composers, scribes and singers exploiting extremely complicated relations. A variety of practices arose whereby musicians indicated proportions by coloration, as mentioned, a simple vertical stroke through the mensuration sign, or numerical indications, culminating in complex fractions.[159]

Some of the most complex examples of such relationships occur in the Chantilly codex, Chan 564, the early fifteenth-century manuscript that transmits much of the repertory from the end of the previous century commonly known as *ars subtilior*, not least because of its rhythmic sophistication. Example 3.4 and Figure 3.4 present the anonymous ballade *Medee fu*.[160] It uses the mensuration signs ℂ, meaning imperfect time and major prolation, and ⊙, perfect time, minor prolation, and the proportions indicated by the numerals 2, 3 and 4. A canon (whose spelling I do not regularize) at the bottom of the page explains the three proportions.

Canon ad figuram 3 in preportione sexqualtera; a binariam in preporcione sexquiternia; ad quaterniam in proporcione dupla; cantentur relique prout iacent, et cetera.[161]

Rule: at the figure 3 in sesquialtera proportion; at the figure 2 in sesquiternia proportion; at the figure 4 in double proportion; the rest are to be as they appear, etc.

So, notes governed by the figure 3 stand in the proportion 3 to 2 against those that precede; by the figure 2, the proportion 4 to 3; and the figure 4, move at double the speed. The mensuration sign that occurs at the beginning of the tenor informs us how all three voices begin.

---

[159]. Koehler, *Pythagoreisch-platonische Proportionen*, especially 1:92–241, surveys the practical sources of the fourteenth and early fifteenth centuries; A. Berger, *Mensuration and Proportion Signs*, pp. 120–232, the theoretical sources. See also Bank, *Tactus, Tempo and Notation*, pp. 158–202; and Ham, "A Sense of Proportion."

[160]. Chan 564 fol. 24v. See Apel and Rosenberg, eds., *French Secular Compositions*, 2: no. 165, pp. 78–80; and Greene, ed., *French Secular Music*, 1: no. 26, pp. 74–76. On the date, see Plumley and Stone, introduction to *Codex Chantilly*, ed. Plumley and Stone, p. 127; in general, see Reaney, "The Manuscript Chantilly, Musée Condé 1047" and "A Postscript"; Scully, "French Songs in Aragon"; and Upton, "Inventing the Chantilly Codex." Like Apel and Greene, I follow the alignment of text and music in the manuscript as closely as possible to determine text underlay. For a critique of that procedure, see Upton, "Aligning Words and Music."

[161]. See Apel and Rosenberg, eds., *French Secular Compositions*, 2: ad no. 165, p. XIXa; and Greene, ed., *French Secular Music*, 1: ad no. 26, p. 154b.

Example 3.4 *Medee fu*, Chan 564 fol. 24v

Example 3.4 (cont.)

Such canons occur frequently in this codex and so underline a point made by Anna Maria Busse Berger, that in this period, the use of proportions followed a diversity of practices.[162] In *Medee fu*, the canon, in

---

[162] The theme of diversity of practice dominates A. Berger's treatment of proportions, *Mensuration and Proportion Signs*, pp. 120–232, but see especially her conclusion, pp. 227–32; see also Dal Maso, *Teoria e pratica*, pp. 131–88. For a survey of the canons, see Koehler, *Pythagoreisch-platonische Proportionen*, 1:180–213; and the critical notes in Apel and Rosenberg, eds., *French Secular Compositions*, and Greene, ed., *French Secular Music*.

Example 3.4 (cont.)

combination with the indications of mensuration and proportion signs, makes their solution relatively straightforward. For the most part, the scribe (or composer) clearly marks the end of a proportion with a mensuration sign. Only once, cantus bars 28–34, do two proportions follow in succession, but the context makes it clear that the second proportion applies not to that which immediately precedes it but to the prevailing mensuration. The equivalent of twelve minims follows the double proportion indicated at bar 34 by the numeral 4, and so they halve the duration of the minim under the previous mensuration. The singer therefore does not interpret the proportion signs cumulatively. The numerals also operate in a logical way, as higher numbers indicate shorter durations: the numeral 2 requires eight minims in the space of six; the numeral 3, nine in the same space; and the numeral 4, twelve.

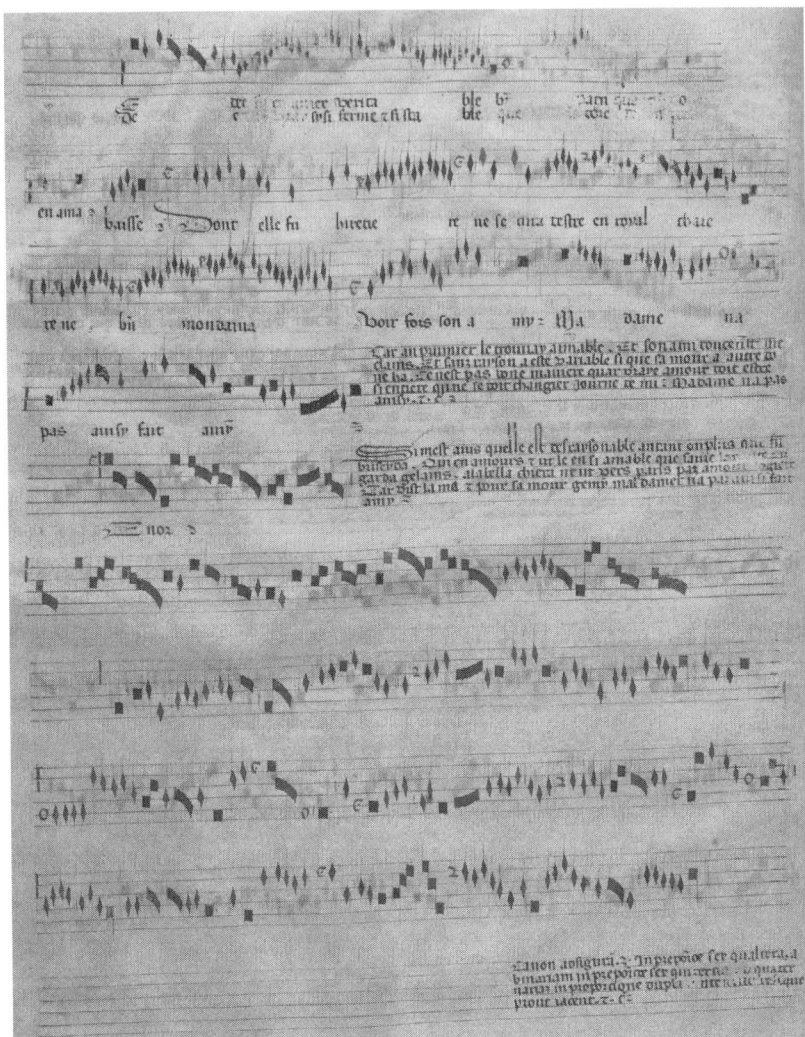

Figure 3.4 Chan 564 fol. 24v
Courtesy of Chantilly, Bibliothèque du château de Chantilly.

The proportions also create very sophisticated and complicated rhythms, both within the same line and in combination, particularly between cantus and contratenor. For example, the first proportion in the cantus, bars 6–11, requires a double adjustment on the part of the singer to execute it accurately. The minim up to this point moves in groups of threes according to the mensuration of imperfect time, major prolation. The numeral 3 dictates that three of the new minims, beginning bar 6, occupy the space of two of the old, the sesquialtera proportion, as the canon states. The singer must first reconsider the old minims (i.e., retaining their duration) in groups of two, in contrast to the grouping suggested by the mensuration, and then apply groups of three of the new minims to the time occupied by those groups of two.

♫♫ ♫♫ (♩ = ♪) → ♫♫♫ (♩ = ♫♫) → ♫♫♫ ♫♫♫

Similarly, the first proportion in the contratenor, bars 12–19 including both endings, requires four of the new minims to occupy the duration of three of the old ones.

Both new subdivisions would require extremely acute rhythmic accuracy in musicians of the fourteenth century or of today. And the successful execution of either proportion becomes all the more difficult because the initial flow of minims in neither voice securely establishes itself as a result of the complex syncopations that characterize the rhythms in each (e.g., cantus bars 2–4, contratenor bars 2, 6, 8 and 10). The proportions themselves do not simplify matters as those passages too evince a great deal of syncopation (e.g., cantus bar 9, contratenor bars 12–14). As problematic as the accurate performance of the individual lines might be, their combination generates even greater difficulties of coordination. In bars 13–14, for example, because cantus and contratenor operate under different proportions and because they both employ a good deal of syncopation, they sound together in only two places, the first two notes of each voice in bar 13. All the other notes in these two bars have unique points of attack. Clearly, this music, in conception as well as execution, demands musical virtuosity of a very high level.

This notation also uses several means to create syncopation in triple subdivisions, as both Muris and the text in Pa 7378A discuss.[163] The musicians who cultivated this repertory clearly coveted syncopation as a musical device in both duple and triple divisions, as *Medee fu* attests. The former presents no notational difficulties as a short note before a longer note that is duple in the mensuration forces the longer note into syncopation. For example, the cantus bars 13–14 operates in minor prolation, with the result that all semibreves are imperfect. The arrangement of minim notes and rests in this passage places the semibreves on F (across bars 13–14) and A (bar 14) in positions that bridge the division of the breve into three equal parts.

Because of the rules of imperfection and *recta–altera* pairs, syncopation in triple divisions requires more notational finesse. First, Chan 564 uses red

---

[163.] See n. 140 above.

notation, as suggested by the author of the text in Pa 7378A and as Machaut does in *Biaute qui toutes autres pere*. At bars 25–26, the cantus moves in imperfect time, major prolation, and so semibreves are perfect, divided in three equal minims. The red semibreves, therefore, marked with broken brackets in Example 3.4, are imperfect, equal to two minims, and create syncopation of the black, perfect semibreves that fall between them. Second, the scribe employs dots to prevent the application of imperfection. In the opening of the cantus (bars 2–4), syncopation begins with the isolated minim on B, followed by four dotted semibreves, each thus perfect, and then a single semibreve imperfected by the isolated minim in bar 2. The singer must look ahead five perfections to complete the perfection begun by the isolated minim, but the dots on the intervening semibreves facilitate the task.

Other instances do not announce themselves so readily. The contratenor opens with several syncopations each caused by an isolated short note or rest (bars 2, 6 and 10), with one additional case supplemented by a dot (bar 8). The figure in bar 6 combines the introductory short rest with the principle that like before like (semibreve before semibreve) is perfect; the minim rest, therefore, imperfects the second and not the first semibreve. The passages in bars 2 and 10 combine a preceding short value with the imperfection of the breve that follows, both at the beginning (by the introductory minim) and the end, even though the breve, in the prevailing mensuration, is already imperfect, equal in duration to two semibreves. Machaut uses precisely this form of imperfection in the opening of *Biaute qui toutes autres pere*, but at the next higher durational level, imperfect long being imperfected by the semibreve. The successful execution of these passages in *Medee fu* would require a great deal of anticipation on the part of the singer.

Finally, the complexities of the notation caused some difficulties for the scribe in at least three places that require emendation by the modern editor and would have caused the user of this manuscript grave consternation. At bars 25–26, the contratenor contains a ligature with three breves. Under the prevailing mensuration, imperfect time with major prolation, each breve is imperfect, equivalent to two perfect semibreves. The contratenor, then, would be longer than the other two voices by one perfection. Gordon K. Greene, perhaps reacting to a suggestion of Apel, implies that the mensuration changes to imperfect time with minor prolation, and thus shortens the breves so that they occupy two perfections in the other voices.[164]

---

[164] Greene, ed., *French Secular Music*, 1: no. 26, p. 75; see the alternative interpretation in Apel and Rosenberg, eds., *French Secular Compositions*, 2: no. 165, p. 79 and n. 1.

I find this interpretation unlikely because the scribe otherwise exercises great care to mark the mensuration changes, and duple division at the level of both breve and semibreve occurs nowhere else in the piece. One could generate the rhythm recommended by Greene if the former mensuration, perfect time minor prolation, were to be retained and the three breves written in red, forcing them, therefore, to be imperfect. More likely, I believe, is Apel's solution: the first two notes should be semibreves, and so the scribe would have drawn the stem that begins the ligature the wrong way, descending instead of ascending. The emendation gives us the requisite two perfections, keeping the contratenor coordinated with the other two voices.

In two other places, the editor needs to supplement the durations provided by the scribe. At bar 36, the last two notes in the contratenor, semibreve-minim, fall one minim short for the group. Greene dots the semibreve, again perhaps following a suggestion of Apel's, although the latter suggests a very complex chain of syncopations.[165] And in bar 37, both Apel and Greene print, as the last note in the cantus, the equivalent of a semibreve where the manuscript reads a minim. Again Apel proposes syncopation as an alternative.[166] I cite these examples not to impugn the work of this scribe but rather to point out that even one so accomplished as he can fall victim to the complexities of this notation, losing track, amid the shifting proportions and mensurations, as well as the levels of syncopation, of the precise number and duration of notes needed to fill out a particular unit of time. If a scribe could err during the deliberate act of copying, how much easier would it be for a singer to run afoul of the prescribed rhythms while reproducing their complexities in real time under the duress of performance?

The idiosyncratic nature of these practices, together with their manifest complexities, led musicians of the fifteenth century to standardize and systematize their application, with Johannes Tinctoris and his younger associate Franchinus Gaffurius in the forefront. Tinctoris, musician active at the court of Naples in the second half of the fifteenth century, provides a thorough treatment of the various proportions mathematically possible in the first two books of his work *Proportionale musices*, written in the 1470s.[167] Berger suggests two sources for his treatment, one negative, one

---

[165.] Greene, ed., *French Secular Music*, 1: no. 26, p. 75 and commentary p. 155a; and Apel and Rosenberg, eds., *French Secular Compositions*, 2: no. 165, p. 80.

[166.] Greene, ed., *French Secular Music*, 1: no. 26, p. 76; and Apel and Rosenberg, eds., *French Secular Compositions*, 2: no. 165, p. 80.

[167.] Tinctoris, *Proportionale musices* 1–2, in *Opera theoretica*, ed. Seay, 2a:12–41 (trans. Seay, pp. 3–30). Gaffurius provides a similar treatment in *Practica musice* 4.2–12, sig. ee vii verso-ll i verso (trans. Miller, pp. 156–233), on which see Miller, "Gaffurius' *Practica Musicae*," pp. 123–29.

positive. First, Tinctoris expresses disdain for what he considers imprecise and even incorrect practices embraced by composers of the fifteenth century.[168] Second, he was responding to recent developments in commercial arithmetic, particularly concerning proportions and how fractions accurately represent them, an interest Gaffurius also shared.[169] As a direct result of his connections with these innovations, Tinctoris specifies that arabic numerals, presented as a fraction, should identify all proportions, of which the numerator always refers to the following passage, the denominator to the preceding.[170]

Tinctoris also clarifies two further issues regarding the interpretation of proportions: how mensuration governs them and how musicians are to understand successive proportions. First, he stresses that all proportions function under the prevailing mensuration, with the corollary that proportions always compare like values with like.[171] This tenet standardizes the relationship between proportion and mensuration, particularly in those cases where composers or scribes used proportions as mensurations. And the corollary specifies that both numbers of the fraction that expresses the proportion refer to exactly the same value within the same mensuration. Second, Tinctoris establishes the practice that proportions operate cumulatively.[172] We have seen that the composer of *Medee fu* (or the scribe of Chan 564) did not treat proportions in this way. But Tinctoris (followed by Gaffurius) derived his practice as much from arithmetical principles as musical ones. Once he had established that numerals, expressed as a fraction, would identify the presence of a proportion, he felt obliged to treat them arithmetically as fractions.

Again, as with his treatment of the signs for proportions and the relationship between proportions and mensurations, Tinctoris, like Gaffurius after him, is attempting to impose order on a chaotic and wholly

---

[168]. See, e.g., the drubbing Petrus de Domarto receives, Tinctoris, *Proportionale musices* 3.3.2–8 and 3.5.8–19, ed. Seay, 2a:48–49 and 55–56, respectively (trans. Seay, pp. 36–37 and 43–44, respectively); for commentary, see A. Berger, *Mensuration and Proportion Signs*, pp. 156–62 and 177.

[169]. A. Berger, *Mensuration and Proportion Signs*, pp. 198–210.

[170]. Tinctoris, *Proportionale musices* 3.2.2–10, ed. Seay, 2a:42–43 (trans. Seay, pp. 30–31); see also Gaffurius, *Practica musice* 4.1, sig. ee vii verso (trans. Miller, p. 156).

[171]. Tinctoris, *Proportionale musices* 3.5–6, ed. Seay, 2a:53–58 (trans. Seay, pp. 41–46); see also Gaffurius, *Practica musice* 4.1, sig. ee vii recto (trans. Miller, pp. 155–56). For commentary, see A. Berger, *Mensuration and Proportion Signs*, pp. 187–98.

[172]. Tinctoris, *Proportionale musices* 1.3–8, ed. Seay, 2a:12–13 (trans. Seay, pp. 3–4); see also Gaffurius, *Practica musice* 4.13, sig. ll i recto–ll iii recto (trans. Miller, pp. 234–36). For commentary, see A. Berger, *Mensuration and Proportion Signs*, pp. 182–85.

idiosyncratic system. Ironically, as Berger points out, proportions had, by the time Tinctoris standardized the practice, become largely the province of theorists and held little interest any longer for practising composers.[173] Still, Tinctoris and Gaffurius strove to improve the transparency of an increasingly symbolic mode of representation. Morphology had come to dominate rhythmic notation in a completely arbitrary hierarchy of durational values. The imposition of a system of mensuration signs, along with a transparent arithmetical mode of identifying proportions (even if obsolete by the time of its promulgation by Tinctoris), helped to establish a context for their successful interpretation.

Developments of the Fifteenth and Sixteenth Centuries

Around 1400, possibly first in England, music scribes began to leave note heads void. Scholars propose the transition from parchment to paper for the preeminent writing surface as the probable cause, or transformations in the mensural system with the introduction of mensurations and proportions.[174] As Tinctoris and Gaffurius noted, musicians immediately seized upon this technique to create another, lower level of values by differentiating between notes with void heads and those with fully pigmented heads, a distinction that continues in practice today.[175]

Again, the difference between the note values emerges purely from morphology and remains relentlessly arbitrary, but it does advance the agenda of generating greater rhythmic flexibility by increasing the range of durational values, from shortest to longest, something musicians since at least the turn of the fourteenth century had been striving to achieve. Simultaneously, scribes began to add flags to the stem of the pigmented note to create yet another lower level of values.

Equally important for the regularization of notation was the application of the newly invented technology of printing from movable type to music, beginning with the publication of *Harmonice musices odhecaton* by

---

[173.] A. Berger, *Mensuration and Proportion Signs*, pp. 208–10.
[174.] Bukofzer, *Studies in Medieval and Renaissance Music*, pp. 92–96; and Vendrix, "La notation à la Renaissance," pp. 140–47.
[175.] Tinctoris, *Proportionale musices* 1.5.7, ed. Seay, 2a:16–17 (trans. Seay, p. 7); and Gaffurius, *Practica musice* 2.4, sig. aa iiii recto (trans. Miller, pp. 76–77).

Ottaviano Petrucci in 1501.[176] Of course, printed music has not replaced the manuscript transmission of music, in the sixteenth or the twenty-first century (although computer musicprocessing may well do so). The economy of printing, however, with its mechanisms for increased distribution of identical (or nearly identical) copies to a wider and more widespread audience (even if still specialized because of the need for musical literacy and therefore a degree of advanced musical ability), required a greater measure of standardization in the musical notation thereby disseminated.

Example 3.5 and Figure 3.5 present Petrucci's version of Loyset Compere's chanson *Garisses moy*.[177] The mensuration sign stipulates perfect time and minor prolation, and so the perfect breve would divide into three equal semibreves, but all breves in the piece are in fact imperfect. In addition to the long (which only occurs as the final note of all three voices), the piece uses five distinct values, of which the breve, semibreve and minim all exhibit void note heads. The two shortest values both have black note heads, differentiated by the addition of a flag to the stem of the shortest note. The mensuration's minor prolation divides the semibreve into two equal minims. In fact, as the context shows, all divisions below the semibreve are duple. I believe this practice extends the principle first enunciated in the text in Pa 7378A, which observes that the semiminim divides the minim in two equal parts.[178] Perhaps musicians, wary of the prospect of discerning and applying the principles of perfection, imperfection and the *recta–altera* pair at more than one level, were gravitating toward duple division as the default.

Like *Medee fu* in Chan 564, *Garisses moy* makes extensive use of syncopation, always, however, within the context of duple division. Compere consistently uses the isolated short note to generate syncopation (e.g., cantus bars 11–12), sometimes in conjunction with the dot (e.g., tenor bars 6–7). Compere's (and Petrucci's) application of the dot invites us to reconsider its function in the fourteenth and fifteenth centuries. As noted above, Muris in the early fourteenth century already remarked that the dot could have at least two different meanings, to lengthen a note in duple division and to indicate the end of a perfection in triple division.[179] Machaut uses the dot only once in *Biaute qui toutes autres pere* (tenor bar 3), where it shows that the preceding breve occupies the entire perfection.

[176.] On Petrucci, see Boorman, *Ottaviano Petrucci*; on this edition, no. 1, pp. 458–68.
[177.] *Harmonice musices*, fols. H 7v–8r; see Hewitt, ed., *Harmonice musices*, no. 58, pp. 343–44; and Compere, *Opera omnia*, ed. Finscher, 5:27.
[178.] See n. 137 above.   [179.] See n. 129 above.

Example 3.5 Loyset Compere, *Garisses moy*, *Harmonice musices odhecaton*, fols. H 7v–8r

Example 3.5 (cont.)

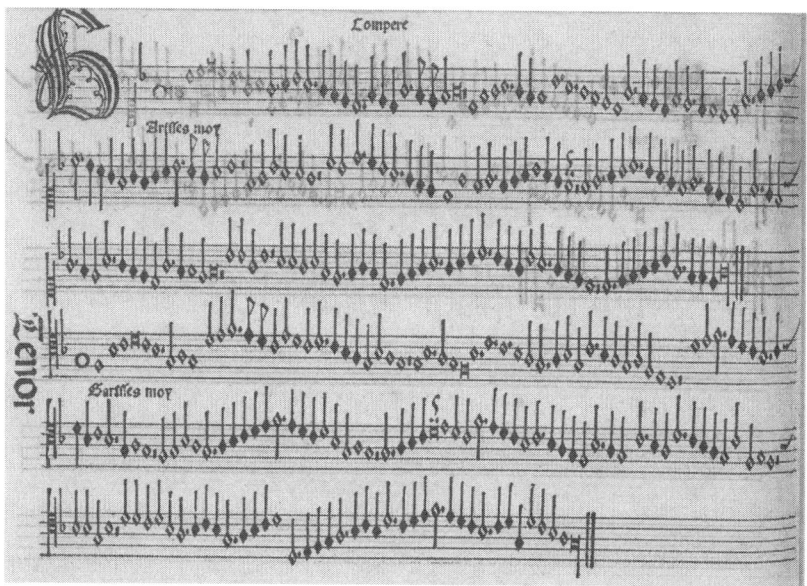

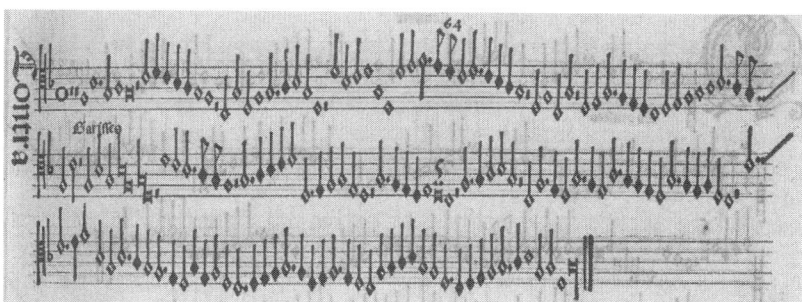

Figure 3.5 *Harmonice musices odhecaton* (1504 edition), fols. H 7v–8r
Courtesy of Paris, Bibliothèque nationale de France.

Medee fu exhibits a much more complex application of the dot. It still serves to indicate the end of a perfection (e.g., cantus bar 1, where it shows that the minim imperfects the imperfect breve, or tenor bar 50, where the dot after the semibreve prevents the following minim from imperfecting it). But more commonly, it lengthens the note by half, sometimes, as in the last example, by making the note perfect and therefore worth three of the next lower value, or in the cantus bars 2–4, by ensuring that the note, despite its position within the perfection, remains perfect, i.e., equal to three of the next lower value, and extends across the breve units. Similarly, in the contratenor bar 27, a dot after the breve in fact prevents a perfection from ending with the breve, and instead lengthens the breve to create a syncopation. In these last two cases, the scribe seems to assume that, without the dot, a singer would take the combination minim-semibreve (cantus bar 2) or semibreve-breve (contratenor bar 27) to constitute a perfection. The dot then lengthens while simultaneously creating syncopation.

Prosdocimus, writing at nearly the same time as the production of Chan 564, tries to clarify the situation by adopting the term *punctus perfectionis* used in the text in Pa 7378A and supplementing it with the phrase *punctus diuisionis*.[180] The latter clearly corresponds to the dot that in *Medee fu* marks the end of a perfection (e.g., cantus bar 1, tenor bar 50), while the former describes the dots (e.g., cantus bars 2–4, contratenor bar 27) that lengthen the note affected to three of the next lower values. Tinctoris adds a third type of dot, the *punctus augmentationis*.[181] His definition of the *punctus diuisionis* accords with that of Prosdocimus, but his treatment of the *punctus perfectionis* reveals confusion. He defines the latter in terms that essentially parallel the *punctus diuisionis*, including restricting the use of both to perfect mensurations only.[182] He thereby obscures the distinction Prosdocimus makes between them and fails to recognize that the dot could lengthen notes in perfect mensurations beyond the limit of the perfection, as it does in *Medee fu*. The *punctus augmentationis*, on the other hand, simply lengthens the note, just as Prosdocimus stipulates for the *punctus perfectionis*, but only in imperfect mensurations.

Gaffurius, however, returns to the twofold distinction, between the *puncti diuisionis* and *perfectionis*.[183] The former occurs only in perfect mensurations and does not lengthen a note, but defines the notes that constitute a perfection, either immediately (through immediately adjacent notes) or at a distance by indicating that notes at some remove join to create a perfection. The first statement is clear enough and accurately describes the dots in *Medee fu* in the cantus bar 1 and the tenor bar 50. The second statement also applies to the syncopations in the cantus bars 2–4 and the contratenor

---

[180]. Prosdocimus de Beldemandis, *Tractatus practice*, ed. Coussemaker, pp. 213b–214b.
[181]. Tinctoris, *Super punctis musicalibus* 2–4, in *Opera theoretica*, ed. Seay, 1:185–87.
[182]. The two definitions simply reverse the orientation of the division. The *punctus diuisionis* divides lesser notes from greater notes that they (the lesser notes) would imperfect, while the *punctus perfectionis* divides greater notes from lesser notes that would imperfect them (the greater notes). But the examples show precisely the same uses for both types of dot: Tinctoris, *Super punctis musicalibus* 2.2 and 4.3, ed. Seay, 1:185 and 186, respectively, with Examples 1 (1:186) and 2 (1:187). The subsequent discussion and examples, ibid. 7.2, 8.2, 9.2 and 11 (1:188, 189, 190 and 192, respectively), do not clarify the distinction.
[183]. Gaffurius, *Practica musice* 2.12, sig. bb viii recto–cc ii recto (trans. Miller, pp. 104–7).

bar 27, but the use of the dot differs. In Chan 564, the dot in both places follows the longer note, and so in effect lengthens it. In the example Gaffurius gives, the dot occurs before the short note that commences the syncopated sequence.[184] The equivalent places in Chan 564 would fall before the minim in the cantus bar 2 (where the scribe has already placed a dot to show that the minim in bar 1 imperfects the breve) and before the semibreve rest in the contratenor bar 27. The effect is the same, but the means differ.

The *punctus perfectionis*, on the other hand, does lengthen the note it affects, either by ensuring that a perfect note in a perfect mensuration retains its perfection when an adjacent shorter note could imperfect it or by lengthening an imperfect note in an imperfect mensuration so that it equals three of the next lower value. For the latter, he coopts Tinctoris' term *punctus augmentationis*. But in his last example, Gaffurius shows that, far from making the notation unambiguous, context can still determine the correct interpretation. He states that, in certain cases, a dot can simultaneously function as a *punctus diuisionis* and *augmentationis*.[185] His example, which he states verbally, requires that the sequence of note values he gives constitutes two perfections. Therefore, the dot after the first semibreve must lengthen it so that it, in combination with the shorter note values that follow, completes the second perfection.

Gaffurius compromises his own definition of the *punctus diuisionis* (it does not lengthen a note) because he also states that the *punctus augmentationis* only occurs in imperfect mensurations. Here is a note that has been lengthened in a perfect mensuration, and so he must combine both functions to maintain the legitimacy of the rhythmic gesture.

Gaffurius' sleight of hand disguises the fact that increasingly, the *punctus diuisionis* was becoming obsolete. Compere in *Garisses moy* (Example 3.5 above) uses perfect time, but every dot he supplies in every context functions as a *punctus augmentationis*. In the tenor bars 9–11, for example, three consecutive dotted semibreves occur after a breve. If we take the first as a *punctus diuisionis*, forcing the first semibreve to imperfect the breve, we arrive at the cadence in bar 21 one minim too soon. Had Compere omitted the dot, however, the singer would certainly imperfect the breve, just as the scribe of Chan 564 anticipated in *Medee fu* cantus bars 2–4 and contratenor

---

[184.] Gaffurius, *Practica musice* 2.12, sig. bb viii recto (trans. Miller, pp. 104–5).
[185.] Gaffurius, *Practica musice* 2.12, sig. cc i verso (trans. Miller, p. 107).

bar 27. So, despite the statements of so eminent a theorist as Franchinus Gaffurius, practice was superseding theory and making the dot a powerful signifier that carried a single meaning, lengthening a note by half its duration. In modern notation, of course, it represents the distinction between triple (perfect, as it were) and duple subdivision, as in all triple metres.

3/4	♩.	=	♩ ♩ ♩	=	♪♪♪
2/4	♩	=	♩ ♩	=	♪♪
6/8	♩.	=	♩. ♩.	=	♪♪♪ ♪♪♪

The Transition to Modern Rhythmic Notation in the Sixteenth and Seventeenth Centuries

The path to the system of rhythmic notation now commonly used seems to have begun with two innovations in early keyboard music. First, regular bar lines after every breve unit give the player visual cues. They appear in Faenza 117 (from the first half of the fifteenth century) and the earliest keyboard music printed in Italy, the *Frottole intabulate da sonare organi libro primo* published by Andrea Antico in 1517 (see Figure 3.6).[186] To indicate a sustained note beyond the limit of the breve unit, and therefore across a bar line, Antico introduces a second innovation, the tie. Two places in Figure 3.6a show a note sustained over a bar line (bars 5–6 and 10–11), and in a third instance, the tie joins two notes within a bar where Antico could have used a dot as a *punctus augmentationis* (bar 3). Figure 3.6a also exhibits the dot below (bar 2 last note top voice, bar 4 alto voice) or above a note (bar 5 first and third notes top voice) indicating the inflection of a sharp. He may have elected not to use the *punctus augmentationis* because of the possibility of confusion with these chromatic dots.

Figures 3.6b and c illustrate two other uses of the tie: to indicate a voice sustaining a note while another voice moves (Figure 3.6b, *Amor quando fioriva* bar 19), and to join a longer note to a note shorter than half the longer note's duration, i.e., to show a relationship that a *punctus augmentationis* could not achieve (Figure 3.6c, *Frena donna* bar 9). The invention of the tie, then, permits greater rhythmic flexibility by allowing the combination of

---

[186.] Faenza 117 fols. 35r–57r, 67r–96v. *Frottole intabulate*. On its status as the earliest printed Italian keyboard music, see Fenlon, *Music, Print and Culture*, p. 24. Figure 3.6a and b: *Amor quando fioriva* in *Frottole intabulate*, fols. 2v and 3r (detail). Figure 3.6c: *Frena donna* in ibid., fol. 6v (detail). See Antico, *Frottole intabulate*, ed. Sterzinger, pp. 4–5 (*Amor quando fioriva*) and 9 (*Frena donna*).

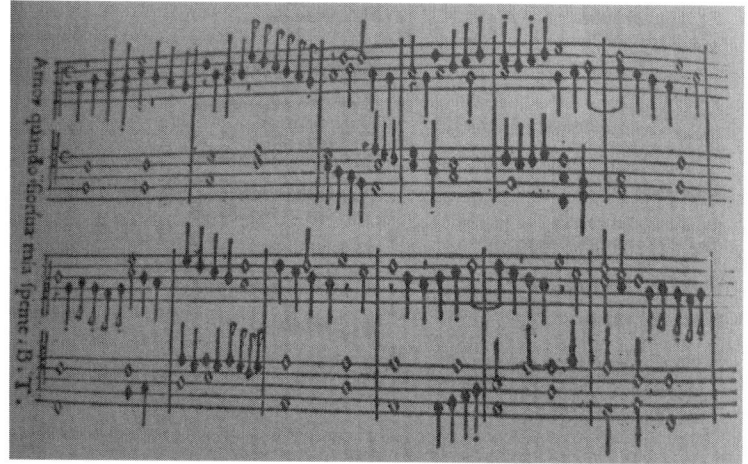

Figure 3.6 *Frottole intabulate* (1517)
Figure 3.6a *Amor quando fioriva*, fol. 2v
Collection of the National Museum, National Museum Library, gg 19, fols. 2v, 3r, 6v, Prague, Czech Republic.

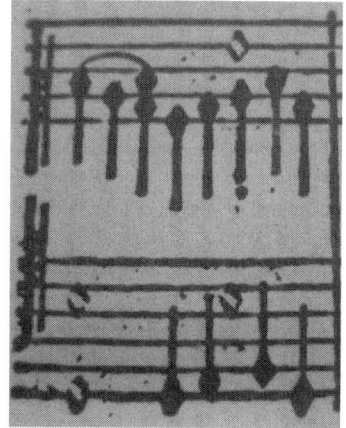

Figure 3.6b *Amor quando fioriva*, fol. 3r detail

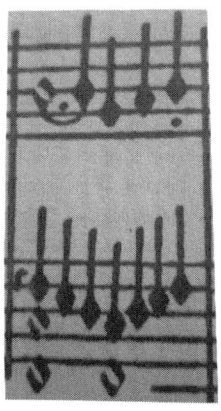

Figure 3.6c *Frena donna*, fol. 6v detail

Figure 3.7 Claudio Monteverdi, *Lamento della Ninfa*, bars 50–57, in *Madrigali guerrieri, et amorosi*, Basso continuo p. 57
Courtesy of Fondazione Claudio Monteverdi.

durations across visible barriers like the bar line and of durations that the dot cannot effect, but it can also clarify voice leading, as in Figure 3.6b.

The key development, however, that signalled the arrival of modern rhythmic notation is the hegemony of duple division at every durational level, irrespective of whether the prevailing rhythmic organizations created groups of three or two notes of the same duration, i.e., perfect or imperfect groupings. The late works of Claudio Monteverdi show that he retained an ambivalent attitude toward the notation of triple metre (see Figure 3.7). In the *Lamento della Ninfa* from his eighth book of madrigals (1638), he and the publisher Alessandro Vincenti consistently use dotted breves for triple values (e.g., basso continuo bars 50–57).[187] Since perfect time governs the passage, all the breves should be perfect, even if undotted. But for the sequence semibreve-breve, they print blackened notes (Canto bars 51, 54 and 56) to ensure that the breve functions as a duple value. For the opposite rhythm, breve-semibreve (Canto and Basso bar 55), they supply white notes, the semibreve imperfecting the breve.

[187.] Figure 3.7: Monteverdi, *Lamento della Ninfa*, bars 50–57, in *Madrigali guerrieri, et amorosi*, Basso continuo, p. 57; ed. Vacchelli, 1:185 (facsimile) and 2:528 (modern edition).

Figure 3.8 Francesco Cavalli, *Il novello Giasone*, Sinfonia Avanti il Prologo, Si L.V.33 fol. 3v
Courtesy of Siena, Biblioteca Communale degli Intronati di Siena.

Figure 3.9 Francesco Cavalli, *Scipione Africano*, act 1, scene 7, Ven 371 fol. 21r
Courtesy of Venice, Biblioteca nazionale Marciana.

A generation later, an analogous situation occurs in the opening sinfonia of Francesco Cavalli's *Il novello Giasone* (originally 1649; revival with revisions 1671) (see Figure 3.8). Here, at the next lower level, Cavalli writes blackened minim-semibreve (first violin, third bar) for the rhythm Monteverdi uses in *Lamento della Ninfa*, and three blackened semibreves (second bar) for equal imperfect values, equivalent to a perfect breve.[188] Again, the blackened notes force musicians to treat them as duple values, where they might understand white notes in this situation as perfect through the occurrence of like before like. Cavalli himself demonstrates the solution in a later work, *Scipione Africano* (1664) (see Figure 3.9). First, he moves the entire rhythmic structure to a still lower level, with three semiminims equal to a perfect minim.[189] Second, he dots all minims of

---

[188.] Cavalli, *Il novello Giasone*, Si L.V.33 fol. 3v.
[189.] Cavalli, *Scipione Africano*, act 1, scene 7, Ven 371 fol. 21r.

triple value (e.g., basso continuo last three bars) and leaves undotted all minims of duple value (e.g., violin I third bar). Blackened minims cannot serve for duple values at this level, because they automatically become semiminims. So, with this method, Cavalli unequivocally distinguishes between triple and duple values by adding a dot to the former, and thus ushers in the modern rhythmic system.

Almost immediately, musicians required a system to indicate subdivisions by other than two of the next lower value and, by the end of the seventeenth century, were placing a numeral above a group of notes to show these alternative subdivisions. Arcangelo Corelli, in the print of his Opus 5 sonatas for solo violin and continuo, and J. S. Bach, in the autograph of his sonatas and partitas for solo violin BWV 1001–6, both place the numeral 3 above groups of three eighth notes within a time signature that entails duple subdivision to indicate triple subdivision of the quarter note.[190] Eventually, musicians came to use virtually any number of subdivisions simply by placing the appropriate numeral above the groups.

Rests and Note Names

Above, I noted that Franco reestablished Garlandia's principle of determining the value of rests: that each space on the staff covered by a vertical line equals a tempus, or the value of a breve, irrespective of the prevailing mensuration, and the semibreve rest occupies a portion of the space. With the introduction of values shorter than the semibreve beginning in the fourteenth century with the minim and semiminim, musicians needed equivalent rests. Figure 3.6a, from Antico's 1517 publication of frottole, provides examples of the semibreve (bar 11 top voice, descending from the staff line), minim (bar 11 alto voice, resting on the staff line) and semiminim (bar 4 alto voice, right-angled hook facing right) rests. For the fusa rest, musicians simply used the semiminim rest facing left and added a flag for the semifusa rest.[191]

These symbols, much like their equivalent notes, became the ancestors of modern rests, including the semiminim rest, which remained in use in

---

[190.] Corelli, *Sonate a violino ... opera quinta*, Sonata 4, Allegro, pp. 26–27; Bach, *Sei solo*, Ber P 967, Partita 2, Corrente, fol. 12r. Further on triplet notation in this era, see Collins, "The Performance of Triplets."

[191.] See the tables at Apel, *The Notation of Polyphonic Music*, p. 87; and Vendrix, "La notation à la Renaissance," p. 144.

France through the end of the nineteenth century.[192] The modern semiminim or quarter rest seems to have originated as a graphological development of the mensural semiminim rest, much as the older sharp sign functioned as the ancestor of both the modern sharp and natural signs. First, musicians added a horizontal stroke to the bottom of the symbol, creating the reversed *z* form as seen in the Debussy print mentioned above. Then, they completed the transformation by adding a stroke to the top of the symbol. The modern form of this rest began to appear in Germany before 1840.[193] In both France and Germany, the transition appears to have been gradual, dependent on the practice of individual printers, and not driven by composers.[194]

Two equivalent systems of nomenclature for durations exist in English, one common in the British Isles, the other in North America. The first developed directly from the traditional Latin note names while the second descends from the German system that employs names based on arithmetic fractions (see Table 3.8). Thomas Morley uses the English names already in his *Plaine and Easie Introduction* of 1597, while the fractional system receives explications in the treatises of Johann Philipp Kirnberger and Johann Joachim Quantz, both published in the second half of the eighteenth century.[195]

* * *

By the end of the seventeenth century, therefore, musicians had developed all the main attributes of the modern system of rhythmic notation.

1. The morphology of the individual notes determines their relative durational values. Their differences are universally unequivocal so that literate musicians can instantly recognize each duration irrespective of context.

[192.] For example, the 1893 edition of Claude Debussy's *La demoiselle élue*, published by the Librairie de l'Art Indépendant uses the form derived from the mensural semiminim form, with an extra stroke added at the bottom that turns the symbol into something resembling a reversed *z*. The 1902 edition of the same piece, published by Durand, uses the modern symbol.

[193.] For example, Robert Schumann's *Carnaval*, Op. 9, published in 1837 by Breitkopf & Härtel, uses the mensural semiminim rest, whereas his *Fantasiestücke*, Op. 12, published the next year by the same publisher, incorporates the modern quarter rest. The older form persisted with some publishers, e.g., Pietro Mechetti, who used it in Schumann's *Humoreske*, Op. 20, published in 1839.

[194.] For example, Debussy continues to use the mensural form of the semiminim rest in his autographs; see *La mer*, Pa 967.

[195.] Morley, *A Plaine and Easie Introduction*, p. 9. Kirnberger, *Die Kunst des reinen Satzes*, 2, part 1, chapter 4, section 1, p. 107 (trans. Beach and Thym, p. 377); and Quantz, *Versuch einer Anweisung*, chapter 5, section 8, p. 54 (trans. Reilly, p. 62).

Table 3.8 Note names

Note Form	Latin	United Kingdom	North America
𝅝	semibreve	semibreve	whole note
𝅗𝅥	minim	minim	half note
♩	semiminim	crotchet	quarter note
♪	fusa	quaver	eighth note
𝅘𝅥𝅯	semifusa	semiquaver	sixteenth note

> The relationship between morphology and duration is arbitrary, but unequivocal. This attribute of the system is semiotically iconic.

2. All values divide equally into two of the next lower value; that is, duple subdivision is universal between immediately adjacent levels of the durational hierarchy. This aspect of the system is also arbitrary and unequivocal, as well as being iconic.
3. Triple subdivision is typically signalled by the addition of a dot to the higher of the two values, again an arbitrary, unequivocal and iconic attribute of the system.
4. Other subdivisions require the placement of a numeral above the notes affected, most commonly the triple subdivision of an undotted value but extending to subdivisions other than those implicit in the system (e.g., the prevailing duple subdivision, or the triple subdivision of dotted values). This aspect of the system is not arbitrary because the value of the numeral directly corresponds to the number of subdivisions required, but it is unequivocal and iconic.

Musicians embraced the goal of creating a system that they could apprehend in real time during performance by establishing unequivocal visual cues to differentiate the individual levels of the durational hierarchy and the pertinent subdivisions they needed to apply.

Interlude 2: Rhythm and Metre

The tension between surface rhythm and the organization of musical time into a regular succession of pulses existed from the beginning of rhythmic notation in the West. Johannes de Garlandia, writing about the rhythmic modes in the mid-thirteenth century, cites a rule ("Unde regula") that "every note that falls in an odd-numbered position ought to concord with each odd-numbered note" ("omne, quod fit impari, debet concordari omni illi, quod fit in impari").[1] This stipulation falls well short of constituting a comprehensive theory of musical metre, but it does seem to discourage us from perceiving rhythmic music of this period as consisting of a series of undifferentiated beats. Still, thirteenth-century notation makes no provision for indicating where stress should fall. The transition from modal to mensural notation in the second half of the century did not bring any further clarity to the situation. Even with the advent of mensuration signs in the following century, the question remains as to whether they signify real metrical organization in regular patterns of stress or just the collection of like notes into triple or duple groups. One piece of evidence may indicate the strength of these groups: syncopation.

As mentioned in Chapter 3, both Muris and the text in Pa 7378A describe a rhythmic practice whereby one portion of a group is separated from the rest of it.[2] The latter uses the verb *syncopo* to characterize the phenomenon: "recta mensura syncopetur" ("the regular measure would be syncopated").[3] This verb and its cognate noun *syncope/syncopa* derive from the Greek συγκόπτω and ἡ συγκοπή, which most frequently refer to cutting something up into pieces, whence the grammatical meaning of the omission of a letter. It is this literal meaning that the text in Pa 7378A is invoking and that Muris describes in his treatment of the phenomenon. A note or

---

[1] Garlandia, *De mensurabili musica* 11.13, ed. Reimer, 1:76 (trans. Birnbaum, pp. 20–21).

[2] Muris, *Notitia* 2.7.4, ed. Michels, p. 84 (trans. Strunk and McKinnon, p. 268); and Pa 7378A fol. 62ra lines 59–63, ed. and trans. Gilles, "Un témoignage inédit," in Vitry, *Ars nova*, ed. Reaney *et al.*, p. 65.

[3] Pa 7378A fol. 62ra lines 62–63, ed. and trans. Gilles, "Un témoignage inédit," in Vitry, *Ars nova*, ed. Reaney *et al.*, p. 65.

notes that belong to one group are separated by one or more perfections from the rest of the notes that constitute that group. We see precisely this arrangement in *Medee fu* from Chan 564 (Example 3.4 and Figure 3.4), which makes frequent use of syncopations.

This practice, then, depends upon the integrity of the group, even when it is "cut up," as the verb *syncopo* suggests, and separated by other whole and continuous groups. Again, the presence of stress does not seem to be explicit in this practice, but equally, the integrity of the groups, whether continuous or fragmented by syncopation, implies something stronger than an undifferentiated sequence of durations.[4] Recent research on music of the period 1300–1600, however, suggests that musicologists prefer the latter interpretation.[5] Many modern editions of music from this period use the *Mensurstrich* to indicate groups instead of the modern bar line.[6] This practice avoids the use of ties, which we see already in *Frottole* printed by Andrea Antico in 1517, and the implication of stress on the first note following a conventional bar line.

Metre began to emerge as an organizing principle in music around 1600. Two closely related developments in musical practice seem to have generated this phenomenon. First, performance in instrumental music became increasingly professionalized during the sixteenth century, and coincidentally, professional composers themselves more often had a background as instrumentalists, Monteverdi and Frescobaldi, for example, and composed more instrumental music for themselves and their newly professionalized colleagues. To a greater or lesser extent, texted vocal music, the predominant genre of composition before 1600, is always organized around the text: phrases, surface rhythm and patterns of stress. Instrumental music, however, in the absence of a literary text, requires a purely musical means of organization. One way to achieve this is through regular metrical patterns that allow the surface rhythms to move in and out of synchronization with them and coalesce into larger sections, such as phrases and periods.

Regularly occurring bar lines appear in instrumental music that uses score: already in the keyboard music contained in Faenza 117, from the first half of the fifteenth century, and in Antico's 1517 print of *Frottole*.[7] As I suggest in Chapter 3 regarding the Antico print, the bar lines in both early witnesses seem to serve as a visual guide, especially in the print, whose pieces typically use four voices, often moving independently. The creation

---

[4.] See C. Berger, *Hexachord, Mensur und Textstruktur*, pp. 25–30.
[5.] See, e.g., Dahlhaus, "Die Tactus- und Proportionenlehre," esp. pp. 345–49 and 360–61.
[6.] Grier, *The Critical Editing of Music*, pp. 165–66.
[7.] Faenza 117 fols. 35r–57r, 67r–96v; *Frottole intabulate*.

of visual units, for ease of reading and comprehension, especially in real time during performance, does not lead necessarily to the imposition of a system of metrical accents. Like the use of syncopation in vocal music of the fourteenth century, however, these bar lines do indicate that musicians were seeking means, either cognitively or visually, to group notes together. Similarly, Edward Lowinsky suggests that the regular bar lines he found in study scores from the sixteenth century facilitate reading and alignment of the voices but do not imply an accentual structure.[8]

The second source springs from the growing interest in instrumental music, and that is the influence of the dance, with its musical patterns that emulate the physical steps of the dance. Again, the question remains open as to whether those patterns coalesce into regular metrical accents, but the use of pickups in several examples, beginning in the thirteenth century, suggests that stress may play a role in the musical complexion. Three estampies in the *chansonnier du roi*, Pa 844, the fifth, sixth and eighth, begin with a single breve that introduces subsequent groups of three breves.[9] While the visual impact of the notation and its groupings may outweigh the musical effect, the latter carries some import. By starting with a pickup in all three estampies (as well as the other three examples I cite in the notes), the last note of each phrase falls on the first of a group. The distinction between the last note of a group, occurring as the first of the piece, and the first note of a group, always occupying the final position in each phrase, suggests that each note in the group differs qualitatively from the others.

All this evidence strongly suggests that musicians of the period 1200–1600 conceived of music in integral groups within which the notes differed in some qualitative aspect: the position of the consonances specified by Garlandia; the use of pickups in some dance pieces; syncopation as defined by Muris and the text in Pa 7378A; and the use of bar lines in keyboard music. Does this body of evidence unequivocally indicate that this qualitative difference entailed some form of accent or stress? Not unequivocal, I would aver, but this body of testimony undercuts, in my opinion, the prevailing opinion that music of this era moves continuously in an ongoing series of undifferentiated beats, and that the groups arise from the purely visual aspect of the notation.

[8.] Lowinsky, "Early Scores in Manuscript," pp. 156b–171b.
[9.] Pa 844 fol. 104v; see McGee, ed., *Medieval Instrumental Dances*, nos. 7, 8 and 10, pp. 64–65 and 67. See also *Dança amorosa* from F 17879 (around the turn of the fifteenth century), and *Trumpes* and *Bel fiore dança* in Faenza 117 fols. 52v–54r and 80v–81r, respectively; McGee, ed., *Medieval Instrumental Dances*, nos. 29, 45 and 47, pp. 119, 142–49 and 160–61, respectively.

Johann Philipp Kirnberger, writing in the second half of the eighteenth century, provides a definition and discussion of metre and its constituent patterns of accent that reflect the musical practice of his age.[10] He begins with the metaphor of a flowing stream, comparing its consistent flow to that of a melody in terms that remind the modern reader of the prevailing views about stress (or its lack) in early music.[11] But that consistent flow needs disruption, whose source in music is accent. "In the precise uniformity of the accents that are given to a few notes, and in the completely regular distribution of long and short syllables, measure exists in essence. That is, when these same heavier or lighter accents recur within the same period, so the song thereby contains a metre or a measure." ("In der genauen Einförmigkeit der Accente, die auf einige Töne gelegt werden, und der völlig regelmäßigen Vertheilung der langen und kurzen Sylben, bestehet eigentlich der Tackt. Wenn nemlich Eben dieselben schwereren oder leichteren Accente in gleichen Zeiten wiederkommen, so erhält der Gesang dadurch ein Metrum oder einen Tackte.")[12]

In the first instance, Kirnberger draws an analogy with the accent of poetic metre, but he then turns to the dance, how it consists in movement and the relationship between that movement and music. Noting that melodies depend on tempo and metre for their character, he states that nowhere does that dependency demonstrate itself more clearly than in dance melodies.[13] After presenting a schematic illustration of how accent defines the basic metres of two, three and four beats, Kirnberger devotes the rest of his discussion to the most common metres composers of the recent past and present employ and their character, with a brief epilogue on text setting.[14] Thus, he provides a detailed theory for the relationship between metre and accent, their importance for shaping melody, and prevailing practices in his own era.

---

[10] Kirnberger, *Die Kunst des reinen Satzes*, 2, part 1, chapter 4, section 2, pp. 113–36 (trans. Beach and Thym, pp. 381–403). For commentary, see Zenck, *Vom Takt*, pp. 156–83; Caplin, "Theories of Musical Rhythm," pp. 658–63 and especially 666–70; and Grant, "Epistemologies of Time."

[11] Kirnberger, *Die Kunst des reinen Satzes*, 2, part 1, chapter 4, section 2, p. 113 (trans. Beach and Thym, pp. 381–82).

[12] Kirnberger, *Die Kunst des reinen Satzes*, 2, part 1, chapter 4, section 2, p. 113 (trans. Beach and Thym, p. 382); my translation. I do not modernize spelling, but I do resolve the superscript *e* to the modern umlaut.

[13] Kirnberger, *Die Kunst des reinen Satzes*, 2, part 1, chapter 4, section 2, p. 114 (trans. Beach and Thym, p. 382).

[14] Kirnberger, *Die Kunst des reinen Satzes*, 2, part 1, chapter 4, section 2, pp. 114–16, schematic illustrations; pp. 118–34, character of metres; and pp. 134–36, text setting (trans. Beach and Thym, pp. 383–84, 386–400, 400–3, respectively).

How and when did these practices come about? Kirnberger focuses on poetic practice and the relationship between music and dance, the second of which I mention above. But he also notes in passing that cadences always fall on "the downbeat of the measure" ("den Niederschlag des Tackts").[15] Above, in my discussion of pickup openings in dances from the *chansonnier du roi* of the thirteenth century, I observed that these pickups result in placing the final note of each phrase on the first of a group, precisely what Kirnberger stipulates five centuries later. Karol Berger states that sixteenth-century theorists, including Nicola Vicentino and Gioseffo Zarlino, specify that the final sonority in a cadence must fall on the first note of a mensuration unit.[16] Inevitably, the placement of final cadential sonorities in this place, by whatever terminology we identify it, places some weight on the first note of a unit.

Similarly, as vertical sonorities, or harmonies, come to contribute actively to the musical complexion in polyphonic music, both vocal and instrumental, the moment when the harmony changes begins to assume importance. And that place, like the positioning of the final cadential sonority, frequently falls on the first note of a unit. For example, in the excerpt given in Chapter 3 as Figure 3.6a from *Amor quando fioriva* printed in Antico's 1517 *Frottole intabulate*, the four parts create harmonies that always change at the beginning of each breve group; often, they change more frequently, at the beginning of the intermediate semibreve halfway through the breve group, but in this passage, a harmony never carries over to the beginning of a new breve group. The ending of the Agnus dei from Josquin des Prez's *Missa De beata virgine* features strong harmonic progressions that lead to an emphatic cadence on C, the eventual final and tonal centre of the piece.[17] Each arrival on C, bars 121, 123 and 125, falls on the first note of a group.

And as a final example, I cite the passage given in Chapter 3 as Figure 3.7 from Claudio Monteverdi's *Lamento della Ninfa* in his eighth book of madrigals. The basso continuo part shows that Monteverdi changes harmony at the beginning of every dotted breve. All three examples, ranging from the early sixteenth to the early seventeenth century, show the arrival of important harmonic events on the first note of a group. Like final cadential sonorities, these events lend weight to these moments, perhaps not fully consistent with the kind of accent that Kirnberger describes, but

---

[15] Kirnberger, *Die Kunst des reinen Satzes*, 2, part 1, chapter 4, section 2, p. 122 (trans. Beach and Thym, p. 390).
[16] K. Berger, *Musica ficta*, pp. 132–38.
[17] Des Prez, *Missa De beata virgine*, Agnus dei, bars 119–126, ed. Elders, p. 83.

certainly differentiating the first note of a group from the others in it. Through the combination of these developments with the growing importance of dance forms in instrumental music, culminating with the sonata da camera of the late seventeenth century and the dance suites of J. S. Bach in the eighteenth, the accentual patterns described by Kirnberger permeated musical practice of the seventeenth and eighteenth centuries.

The notational manifestation musicians chose to convey the musical import of these phenomena was, of course, the time signature, with its dual significance in modern notation. First, like the mensuration signs of the fourteenth century and later, the time signature shows how many notes of which rhythmic level comprise the notational group and further indicates the predominant subdivisions within the group. So **3/4** signifies that three quarter notes make up the group but also that each quarter note subdivides into two eighth notes. In contrast, as I mention in Chapter 3, **6/8** stipulates that the group consists of six eighth notes but also that they group themselves into two subgroups of three eighth notes each. Second, the first note of each group receives an accent, as Kirnberger demonstrates. In **3/4**, therefore, every third quarter note receives the principal accent, whereas in **2/4**, the main accent falls on every second quarter note.

These conventions, familiar to every musician, have dominated musical practice from at least the end of the seventeenth century. Surface rhythm and metre remain in conflict, however, throughout this period. For example, G. F. Handel frequently combines two bars of triple metre into a single longer bar with three beats in a mannerism known as hemiola. The second of the longer beats extends across the bar line between the two bars of the prevailing metre.

3/4 ♩ ♩ ♩|♩ ♩ ♩

♩ ♩|♩ ♩

A typical example occurs at the final cadence of no. 12 in the *Water Music*.[18] Composers like Ludwig van Beethoven and Robert Schumann wrote long passages of syncopation that served to undermine metrical regularity. The passage in the development section of the first movement of the *Eroica* symphony combines syncopation and hemiola to suspend the sense of the prevailing triple metre for a period of some thirty-two bars.[19] Schumann

---

[18.] Händel, *Water Music*, HWV 349, no. 12, bars 37–38, ed. Best and Hogwood, p. 49.
[19.] Beethoven, Symphony no. 3 Op. 55, *Sinfonia Eroica*, movement 1, bars 248–79, ed. Churgin, pp. 16–17.

creates a melody that consistently avoids placing a note on the downbeat in *Kinderscenen* no. 10, and so fully defeats the sense of metrical accent even though the left-hand part plays just as consistently on the beat.[20]

Explorations in the combination of metrical patterns and surface rhythm continued into the last century. Igor Stravinsky, who famously decried the "tyranny of the bar," and Béla Bartók created works that compromised the regularity of metrical accent.[21] One of Bartók's characteristic strategies involved complex time signatures that generated irregular subdivisions of the bar so that the listener could not discern a regular periodic pattern of accents.[22] And Stravinsky, of course, frequently wrote melodic material that conflicted with the underlying metre.[23] Yet, in many ways, these devices all require that implicit regularity for their fullest effect. Handel's hemiola or the jagged rhythms in the opening of *Petrushka* would carry much less musical effect if their respective composers had not been able to depend on the listener's attempting to discern some regularity in the progression of musical time. And the time signature remains the musician's notational device of choice to convey that sense of regularity.

[20] Schumann, *Kinderscenen* Op. 15 no. 10, ed. Schumann, pp. 70–71.
[21] Stravinsky made the comment in reference to Nijinsky's choreography for *Le sacre du printemps*: "Interview with Stravinsky."
[22] E.g., Bartók, *Mikrokosmos*, 6, nos. 148 and 149, pp. 43–49.
[23] E.g., Strawinsky, *Petrushka*, beginning to 6 bars after rehearsal 1, p. 1.

4 | The Transition to the Modern Era: Instrumental Music and Performing Indications

The earliest written instrumental music uses contemporary vocal notation: the dances in Pa 844 (thirteenth century), Lo 28550 (the Robertsbridge codex, fourteenth century), Lo 29987 and Faenza 117 (both fifteenth century). The Robertsbridge codex contains a hybrid notation in which the upper voice or voices appear in conventional vocal notation and the lower voice is represented by the letter names of the notes. This system becomes the ancestor of German keyboard tablatures of the fifteenth century, which similarly use conventional and literal notation for the upper and lower voices, respectively. These developments signal independent and idiosyncratic approaches to notation that become specific for each instrument or group of instruments, which we today collect under the generic term tablature.[1]

The notations that musicians created for their instruments reflect the physical design of the instrument or technical issues that arise in playing it or both. As such, these notations accord closely with Peirce's semiotic classification of indexical signs: each sign prescribes a particular physical action on the instrument. In contrast, conventional vocal notation represents the duration and the pitch of each note in abstract means along the horizontal and vertical axes of writing, respectively. Duration, which depends on the arbitrary meaning of each rhythmic symbol, falls into Peirce's classification of symbolic representation, whereas pitch, with higher notes placed higher on the staff and lower notes lower, evinces iconic representation.

These tablatures occur in either music for solo performance or the accompaniment of a singer with a single instrument. Aspects of musical literacy, therefore, directly affected the development and dissemination of these notations. Learning to read tablature involved the cultivation of specialized tasks, idiosyncratic to each instrument, that did not readily

---

[1.] The best summaries of instrumental tablatures in English remain Apel, *The Notation of Polyphonic Music*, pp. 3–81; and Rastall, *The Notation of Western Music*, pp. 143–71. See also, on keyboard tablatures, Eppelsheim, "Buchstaben-Notation"; on lute tablatures, Coelho, *The Manuscript Sources of Seventeenth-Century Italian Lute Music*, pp. 27–32; and Fabris, "Lute Tablature."

transfer to other aspects of music making. Moreover, instrumentalists in various regions, as I discuss below, developed their own style of notation. So the cultivation of tablature, whether its design, modification, inscription or use, became highly individualized and a skill somewhat removed from the musical literacy required to read contemporary vocal music fluently. Simultaneously, instrumentalists in various regions continued to adapt vocal notation for their purposes. Some musicians, undoubtedly, acquired competence in both the specialized tablature for their own instrument and the more generally used vocal notation, implementing whichever the context demanded.

With the increasing professionalization of instrumentalists during the sixteenth century, musical literacy became a commensurately important skill. Simultaneously, composers such as Giovanni Gabrieli at the end of the century began writing music for ensembles that combined instruments and voices. These pieces required a single, uniform and standardized notation, equally applicable to all instruments as well as vocal music, and so the conventions of notation for vocal music came to serve as the basis for all notation, vocal and instrumental. Music for the lute formed the one exception to this standardization. Lutenists continued to use tablature throughout the instrument's active life into the nineteenth century because the instrument was usually used for solo music or the accompaniment of vocal music. Consequently, it did not need to be integrated into ensemble music that used other forms of notation. Moreover, a form of Italian lute tablature remains commonly used today for guitar and bass guitar in popular music.[2]

Keyboard Tablatures

The earliest tablatures appear in Germany during the fifteenth century in the realm of keyboard music. As noted above, they combine conventional vocal notation for the upper voices with letter notation for the lower voices, which, as indexical indications, specify to the player which key to depress. Perhaps the best example is the Buxheimer Orgelbuch, Mü 3725, from the mid-fifteenth century (see Figure 4.1).[3] The upper voice uses regular

---

[2.] For a remarkable example of tablature for guitar and bass guitar, see The Beatles, *Complete Scores*.
[3.] Figure 4.1, Mü 3725 fol. 87r, presents *Aue regina*; see Wallner, ed., *Das Buxheimer Orgelbuch*, no. 159, 2:214. On the notation of the Buxheimer Orgelbuch, see Southern, *The Buxheim Organ Book*, pp. 5–10; and Zöbeley, *Die Musik des Buxheimer Orgelbuchs*, pp. 20–77.

Figure 4.1 Buxheimer Orgelbuch, Mü 3725 fol. 87r
Bayerische Staatsbibliothek München, Mus.ms. 3725.

barring, like Faenza 117, and introduces beaming for consecutive notes at the value of the semiminim or lower. The lower voices vary in number between one and three, creating a free-voiced texture below the upper voice, and they cross frequently. These two features demonstrate the efficiencies of the system. The scribe has written each independent lower voice in a separate horizontal line.[4] Thus the player knows at each stage which voice is playing and which resting, all with notation that takes a minimum of space. To achieve such clarity with vocal notation, each voice would require a separate staff, an arrangement that would take four times as much space and frequently involve one or more empty staves.

The rhythmic values in the upper voice vary from the breve to the semifusa, with two beams, while the lower voices avoid the shortest of these, the semifusa. The scribe gives no symbol for the breve, and a dot for the semibreve. Notes to be sustained for more than a single semibreve receive two or three dots (the latter, of course, equivalent to the breve). The minim and semiminim become just the stem and stem with flag, respectively. The presentation of the pitch content in the lower voices is equally economical, as the scribe employs the Latin alphabet through G to represent the notes of the gamut. He indicates notes in the higher of two octaves by placing a curved horizontal line above the letters. Finally, a descending stem requires chromatic alteration, and one with a triangular loop signals an ornament. This scribe seems to have placed economical and compact presentation as his chief priorities, striving to facilitate the player's rapid apprehension of as many as four independent lines in real time during performance.

This zeal for economy expanded in the sixteenth century to encompass the upper voice, which German tablaturists now also wrote as a series of letters with rhythmic signs added above, like the lower voices in the Buxheimer Orgelbuch (see Figure 4.2).[5] Figure 4.2, from Elias Nikolaus Ammerbach's *Orgel oder Instrument Tabulaturbuch* of 1583, illustrates how a dense four-voice texture becomes elegantly economical in this style of notation. Each voice occupies a separate horizontal line, and the technique of beaming, found in the upper voice alone in earlier tablatures, now appears in any voice that presents consecutive notes of values smaller than the minim. Beaming allows the performer to perceive notes as a group, a strategy that expedites apprehension of the rhythmic content of a passage.

Spanish keyboard tablatures of the sixteenth century resemble their German counterparts by assigning to each voice a horizontal line of writing and placing the rhythmic values above. The Spanish notations, however, apply

---

[4.] See Zöbeley, *Die Musik des Buxheimer Orgelbuchs*, pp. 99–113.
[5.] Figure 4.2 presents *Sio canto*, Ammerbach, *Orgel oder Instrument Tabulaturbuch*, no. 28, p. 33; see Ammerbach, *Orgel oder Instrument Tabulaturbuch*, ed. Jacobs, no. 106, pp. 227–28. On Ammerbach's notation, see *ibid.*, pp. xviii–xxii.

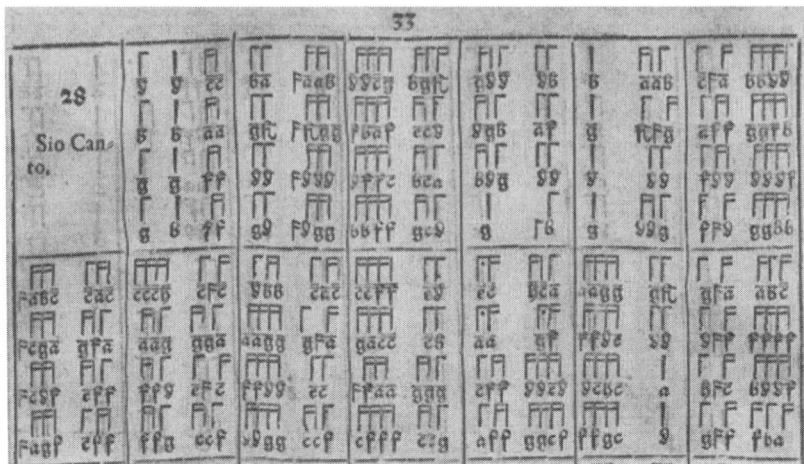

Figure 4.2 Elias Nikolaus Ammerbach, *Orgel oder Instrument Tabulaturbuch*, p. 33 Bayerische Staatsbibliothek München, 4 Mus.pr. 130.

a further level of abstraction to the task of instructing the player which key to depress. Instead of the letter name of the note with the appropriate octave designation as in German practice, Spanish tablaturists assign an arabic numeral to each note on the keyboard, starting at the bottom. Several features of the instruments used in Spain and of the notation itself ensured that each form of tablature preserved idiosyncrasies. First, many Spanish keyboard instruments of the era use an incomplete lowest octave, and so the numbering of that portion of the gamut remains unique for each instrument. Second, different tablatures treat chromatic inflections in different ways, and third, similarly, they designate the octave placement of notes by idiosyncratic means. Hence, each tablature requires independent assessment.

Two printed examples from the late sixteenth century show some of the differences and commonalities between competing tablatures (see Figures 4.3 and 4.4).[6] Antonio Valente's *Intavolatura de cimbalo* (1576) and Antonio de Cabezón's *Obras de música* (1578) both place independent voices on separate

---

[6.] Figure 4.3 presents the beginning of *Pisne, disminuita*, Valente, *Intavolatura de cimbalo*, p. XXXIIII; see Valente, *Intavolatura de cimbalo*, ed. Jacobs, no. 9, pp. 57–67, bars 1–12, p. 57. Valente describes his tablature, *Intavolatura de cimbalo*, ed. Jacobs, pp. xi–xvi; see also Tonda, "Nuove osservazioni." Figure 4.4 presents the seventh arrangement of the verse for the Magnificat in mode 7, Cabezón, *Obras de música*, fol. 39r; see Cabezón, *Obras de música*, ed. Anglés, 2: no. XLVIII, VII, p. 36; Cabezón, *Collected Works*, ed. Jacobs, 3: no. 15(g), p. 32; and Cabezón, *Obras de música*, ed. Artigas Pina, *et al.*, 2:64–65. Cabezón describes his notation, *Obras de música*, fols. VIIIr–Xv, printed in Cabezón, *Obras de música*, ed. Anglés, 1:25a–28a, followed by commentary through 28b; see also Griffiths, "¿Fantasía o realidad?"

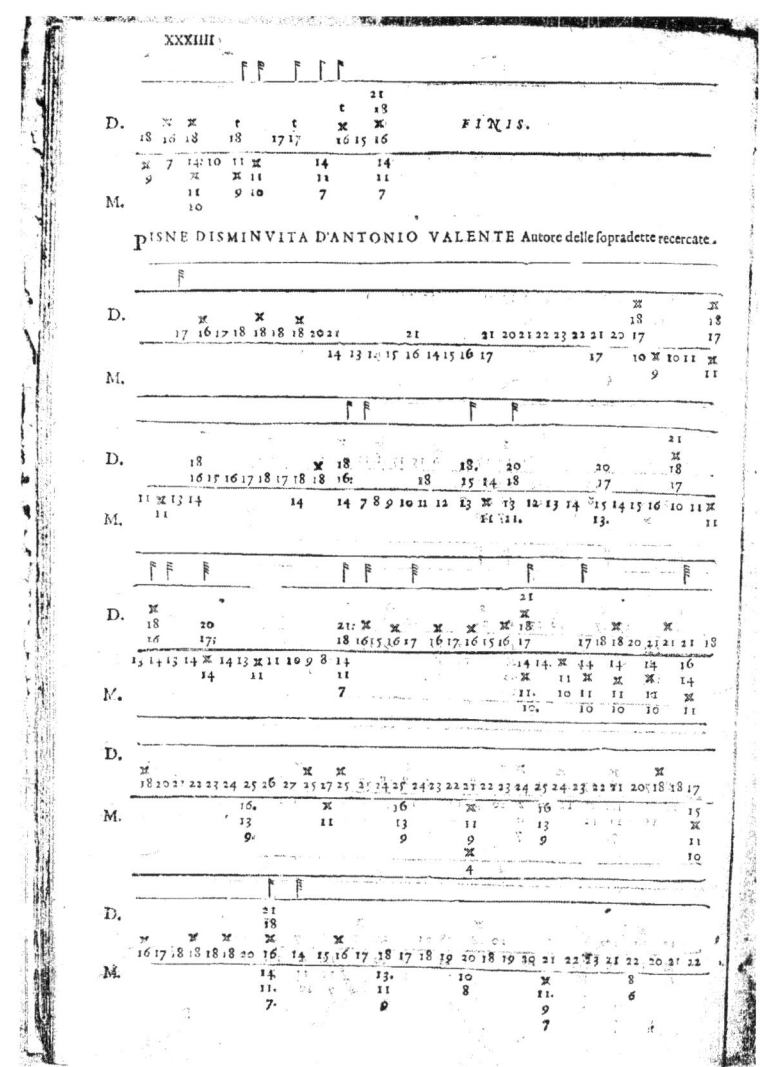

Figure 4.3 Antonio Valente, *Intavolatura de cimbalo*, p. xxxiiii
Courtesy of Naples, Biblioteca nazionale.

horizontal lines and print rhythmic values on a separate line above the voices. Cabezón visually reinforces the independence of the voices by printing a horizontal line for each voice on which the numerals representing the pitches appear. Valente also prints horizontal lines, but they visually separate elements of the presentation: they distinguish musical systems, they separate the line of rhythmic values from the notes they affect (printed below the line), and they divide the voices he assigns to each of the player's hands.

Figure 4.4 Antonio de Cabezón, *Obras de música*, fol. 39r
Courtesy of Madrid, Biblioteca Nacional de España.

The treatment of rhythmic values differs from that adopted in the German tablatures, as both Spanish notations give a single note that remains in effect for all consecutive notes until superseded by another value. For example, Valente's *Pisne, disminuita* (Figure 4.3) begins with running thirty-second notes (transcribed by Jacobs as sixteenths), alternating between the right- and left-hand parts, until midway through the second system, where first a single sixteenth note and, in the next group of thirty-seconds, two further sixteenth notes interrupt the flow (bars 6 and 7, respectively). Longer notes in other voices derive their duration from their placement within the running thirty-seconds, as in the first system, second group (first in the left hand, bar 2) where the notation instructs the right hand to strike the note D (represented by the numeral 21) twice, simultaneously with the first and fifth thirty-seconds of the group. Thus each of the notes in the right-hand part becomes an eighth note, equivalent in value to four thirty-seconds.

Cabezón supplements the rhythmic information in his tablature by providing mensuration signs and bar lines. His Magnificat verse in mode 7 (Figure 4.4) begins in triple mensuration, with three semibreves or whole notes to the bar (transcribed by Anglés and Jacobs as half notes), changing to duple five bars before the end (bar 16). The penultimate bar (19) shows that the duple section uses a single whole note for the bar (unreduced by Anglés and Jacobs). Like Valente's notation, Cabezón's also uses spacing to indicate duration. So, in bar 2, for example, the half note written above the music applies to the lowest voice, but the even spacing of the numerals in the second lowest voice shows that its three notes are all equal, or whole notes. Consequently, the spacing of the notes in the lowest voice indicates that only the first is a half note, followed by a whole note, another half note and then ends with a whole note, as the duration above the music dictates.

As in Valente's tablature, the position of notes relative to those defined by the values above generates their duration. The half note printed above the beginning of bar 3 affects the first five notes of the lowest voice, while the quarter note applies to the last two. The position of the notes in the second lowest voice shows that they are, respectively, breve and whole note. Cabezón uses two further signs, the oblique slash (/) and the comma (,); the former indicates a rest, the latter the extension of the previous note. In both cases, context dictates the value. In bar 7, for example, the rest in the second lowest voice occupies a breve; that in the lowest voice, the entire bar. The comma in the third lowest voice doubles the length of the preceding note. Both tablatures evince an elegant economy in the way they depict duration, combining the rhythmic values printed above with spacing and positioning relative to the moving part to generate a visual image that the knowledgeable reader can readily apprehend during real time in performance.

The differences between the tablatures emerge from the manner in which each indicates pitch, using numerals to stipulate which key on the keyboard the player strikes. Valente employs numerals from 1 to 27 for the white keys between C two octaves below middle C through C two octaves above. An "x," which resembles the modern double sharp, calls on the player to strike the black key above (i.e., to the right of) the white key designated by the numeral.

Example 4.1 Pitch values in the tablatures of Valente and Cabezón

This system results in some counterintuitive formations, such as the numeral 11, signifying A, with an "x" that generates B♭, or 7, D, with the "x" to indicate E♭. Also, the short bottom octave uses black keys for notes that are not chromatically inflected, namely D and E (see Example 4.1).

The mechanical nature of the assignment of numerals to pitches from lowest to highest in Valente's notation finds a marked contrast in the system devised by Cabezón, who consciously organizes the numerals to correspond with musical organization. He predicates the system of numerals on a central octave between F a fifth below middle C and F a fourth above. (See Example 4.1.) To this octave, he assigns the numerals 1 through 7. The octave below this one receives the same sequence of numerals, but to each one, he attaches a single stroke to the bottom of the numeral, with the exception of 6, on which the stroke appears at the top. He indicates the notes C, D and E below this octave with the numerals 5 through 7, each with a double stroke, at the bottom of 5 and 7, as in the octave above, and the top of 6. The octave above the central octave uses the same series of numerals again, this time with a dot after each, and then the final sequence of pitches above that octave, F through C, receives the numerals 1 through 5, distinguished by the addition of an apostrophe after the numeral.

Thus, each pitch uses the same numeral irrespective of the octave in which it lies, which Cabezón indicates by inflecting the numeral with an additional sign. He applies similar logic to the indication of chromatic inflections, using flats for B♭ and E♭, sharps for F♯, C♯ and G♯, and further to the short octave at the bottom of the keyboard, where the notes D and E, even though they correspond to black notes, appear as numerals without any supplementary indication. So, the musical identity of the note determines how Cabezón has devised his system of stipulating which pitch to sound, as opposed to Valente's system, which depends entirely upon the physical position of the key he requires the player to strike. Consequently, Valente's notation forces the player to memorize the entire sequence of numerals and the pitches to which they correspond, together with the notion that the added "x" stipulates that the player strike the black key to the right of the white key indicated by the numeral to which he adds the "x," irrespective of the actual chromatic inflection, sharp or flat, or even if the note is uninflected, as in the short octave.

Lute Tablatures

Like keyboard tablatures, lute intabulations evince an indexical mode of signification by indicating at which fret and on which string the player stops the string. And also parallel to the history of keyboard tablatures, national schools developed that employed different strategies for conveying this information, principally in the way in which they specify at which fret to stop the string. In all cases, however, the information takes a purely mechanical form and so resembles Valente's keyboard tablature more than Cabezón's. Moreover, most tablatures use the same visual means to represent the neck of the lute by drawing horizontal lines, resembling the staff, that correspond to the strings or, if some are doubled at the octave or unison, courses. The number of lines, therefore, equals the number of strings or courses on the instrument envisaged for the notation. But the national schools divide on the order of the strings. Italian tablaturists place the highest sounding string lowest in the diagram and most Spanish notations adopt this arrangement. French musicians, however, reversed the order, situating the highest sounding string highest, and at least one Spanish lutenist, Luis de Milán, favoured this system.

Of course, the Italian arrangement replicates the actual physical construction of the instrument, with the highest sounding string sitting lowest, but the French system captures the visual image the player sees when looking down at the neck of the instrument while playing it. A player can perceive the Italian arrangement only by watching another player or by seeing her- or himself in the mirror. The French system, then, corresponds more closely to the player's actual experiences and perceptions while playing. Second, the position of the highest sounding string highest in

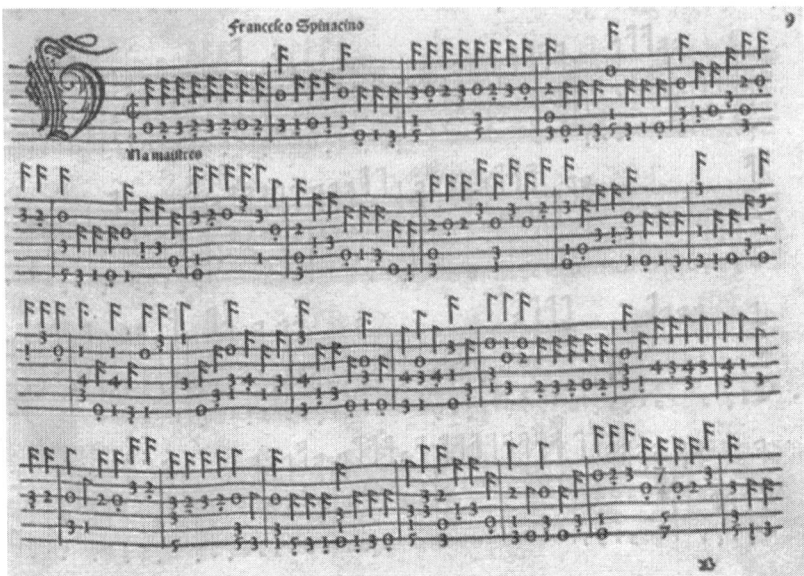

Figure 4.5 *Intabulatura de lauto libro primo*, fol. 9r
Courtesy of Paris, Bibliothèque nationale de France.

the diagram accords with the organization of the staff in vocal music, with higher sounding notes placed toward the top of the staff, and lutenists who were literate in this form of notation might feel more comfortable with this arrangement. These factors may have contributed to the modern adaptation of Italian tablature for the guitar, which situates the highest sounding string at the top of the diagram, in the French manner.

I begin with Italian tablature because it enjoyed widespread popularity beyond Italy in southern Europe. Among the earliest witnesses to this style of notation stand two prints by Petrucci produced in 1507 that present intabulations by Francesco Spinacino.[7] Both volumes begin with a brief synopsis of the notation that introduces its conventions to the reader.[8] The tablature borrows its rhythmic notation from German keyboard tablatures, with a duration recorded for each note in the moving voice (see

---

[7] *Intabulatura de lauto libro primo, libro secondo*. See Boorman, *Ottaviano Petrucci*, nos. 33–34, pp. 645–54. On Petrucci's early involvement in printing lute music, see *ibid.*, pp. 294–96; Fabris, "Lute Tablature," pp. 17–23; Minamino, "Production and Reception"; and Coelho and Polk, *Instrumentalists*, pp. 78–85.

[8] *Intabulatura de lauto libro primo*, fol. 2r; *Intabulatura de lauto libro secondo*, fol. 1v; printed in Boorman, *Ottaviano Petrucci*, pp. 645–46. See also Fabris, "Lute Tablature," pp. 17–23; and Minamino, "Production and Reception," pp. 46–47.

Figure 4.5).[9] In bar 2, for example, Spinacino marks all notes as sixteenths, but clearly the notes in the lower voice, both on an open string, ring while the upper voice continues to move and so become the equivalent of quarter notes. He achieves the same effect in the next bar with two upper voices although, sounding on stopped strings, these notes likely do not ring to the same extent as the open string in the lower voice, previous bar. Spinacino regulates the rhythmic information given by the durations through a mensuration sign and regular bar lines.

He indicates at which fret to stop the string by arabic numerals up to 9 (0 designates an open string, 1 the first fret, and so on) and the roman numeral X for the tenth fret, above which he adds one and two dots to denote, respectively, the eleventh and twelfth frets. This system, then, uses purely mechanical means to guide the player's fingers in much the same way as Valente, in his keyboard tablature, indicates which key to strike, irrespective of the musical structure to which the note belongs. Because the notes are divided across the strings of the lute, however, the player does not need to memorize the significance of each numeral in the same manner as keyboardists playing from Valente's notation must, and so Spinacino and Petrucci have devised a system that permits efficient apprehension and application by the lutenist.

The dots added below some of the numerals reflect a developing aspect of lute technique that also affects the treatment of independent voices. The dot requires the player to pluck the string with the index finger, while its absence designates the thumb (i and p, respectively, in modern guitar notation). They alternate in running passages, but no dot occurs when two or more notes sound simultaneously, e.g., in bars 2–3. As the prefatory instructions indicate, the player must pluck the strings with individual fingers.[10] The three-note combination that begins bar 6, for example, stipulates a silent string between each pair of sounding strings. To avoid striking the silent strings, the player must pluck each note with a different finger, presumably the thumb for the lowest note and the index and middle finger (m) for the other two.

Although this technique permits several notes to sound simultaneously, the realization of real polyphony remains difficult because the player can execute only a limited number of notes with the four fingers of the left hand. The instrument more properly suits the execution of melody with

---

[9.] Figure 4.5 presents the opening of Antoine Brumel's *Una maitresse*, *Intabulatura de lauto libro primo*, fol. 9r; modern edition of the chanson, Brumel, *Opera omnia*, ed. Hudson, 6:102–3.

[10.] See Heartz, "Les premières 'Instructions'," pp. 83–85; and Coelho and Polk, *Instrumentalists*, p. 82.

sparse accompaniment in a free-voiced texture. And Spinacino's adaptation of Brumel's chanson reflects that function. For example, the lute frequently sounds three notes together throughout bars 3–17, but each time, only one voice moves while the others provide accompanying harmony without counterpoint. The tablature presents this information in an efficient and compact manner, providing the specific indexical and mechanical instructions for the player in a clear and unequivocal way.

Spanish tablaturists for the most part adopted Italian conventions.[11] Among the most distinguished early Spanish collections of lute music is Alonso Mudarra's *Tres libros de musica en cifra para vihuela*.[12] Mudarra imitates the Italian notation by using numerals (including the roman numeral X) to indicate the fret, but his notation departs from it in two ways. First, like the Spanish keyboard tablatures of Valente and Cabezón, each durational symbol applies to all notes until a new duration occurs. And like Cabezón, Mudarra prints the full note instead of just the stem, as Valente and Spinacino do. Second, he does not use dots to indicate the alternation of thumb and index finger. As Mudarra explains in his preface, he occasionally stipulates the use of two fingers (presumably thumb and index) by printing below the music *dosde* (as one word, meaning *dos dedos*), as distinct from a single finger, *dedi* (*dedillo*).[13] A singular exception to the Italian practices among the Spanish tablaturists is Luis de Milán, whose collection *El maestro* reverses the order of the strings, with the highest sounding string represented by the highest line; in all other respects, however, he follows the Italian tablature of Spinacino and Petrucci.[14]

French tablature for the lute also resembles Italian in the disposition of the horizontal lines, representing the courses of the instrument, and rhythmic signs. Pierre Attaingnant's first publication for the lute contains a brief preface that describes the instrument and the notation he employs for it.[15] The lute has eleven strings arranged in six courses, of which the lowest five are doubled, and eight frets, although occasionally one requires

---

[11] Griffiths, "La producción de libros."
[12] Mudarra, *Tres libros de musica*. See Coelho and Polk, *Instrumentalists*, pp. 97–100.
[13] Mudarra, *Tres libros de musica*, fol. A iii r; printed in Mudarra, *Tres libros de musica*, ed. Pujol, p. 40; see also Griffiths, "The Vihuela," pp. 176–78; and Coelho and Polk, *Instrumentalists*, p. 99.
[14] Milán, *Libro de musica*. Milán notes the order of the strings in his preface, *ibid.*, fol. iiii v; printed in Milán, *El maestro*, ed. Jacobs, p. 19.
[15] Attaingnant, *Tres breue et familiere introduction*, fols. i v–ii r. On the volume in general, see Heartz, *Pierre Attaingnant*, no. 13, pp. 225–26.

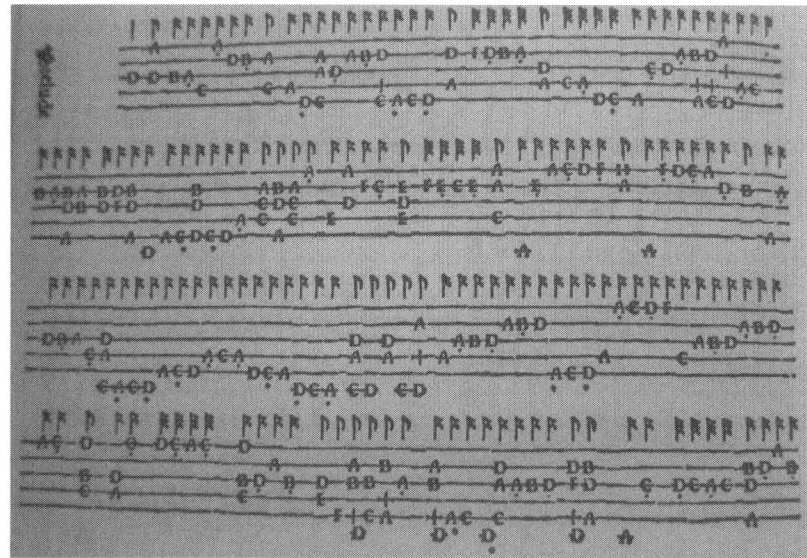

Figure 4.6 Pierre Attaingnant, *Tres breue et familiere introduction*, fol. v v
Courtesy of Berlin, Staatsbibliothek Preußischer Kulturbesitz.

a ninth. His method for stipulating at which fret to stop the string differs from Italian practice by using letters instead of numerals: *b* through *i*, with *k* reserved for the ninth fret; although he does not specify it, the letter *a* clearly signifies the open string. The notation uses five horizontal lines below which he prints the letters that represent the notes played on the sixth and lowest sounding string. From this arrangement, we may deduce that the other five lines signify the five highest strings, with the highest sounding on top, like Milán's idiosyncratic system, and the opposite of Italian and most Spanish practice.

Attaingnant further discusses the rhythmic symbols in some detail, showing that duple division regulates all durational relationships. His avoidance of triple subdivision, then, obviates the need for mensuration signs, and he dispenses with most bar lines. He employs for durational values only the stems and provides one for every note, like Spinacino and Petrucci. The opening of the book's fourth prelude exhibits these features (see Figure 4.6).[16] When Attaingnant invokes the lowest sounding string, as in the third system, bars 6–7, he prints a line through the letters that

---

[16.] Attaingnant, *Tres breue et familiere introduction*, fol. v v; modern edition, Heartz, ed., *Preludes, Chansons and Dances*, no. 4, pp. 8–9.

represent the frets, making a kind of leger line. He also uses the dots printed below the letters to indicate the alternation of thumb and index finger in precisely the same way as Spinacino and Petrucci.

Modifications to the structure of the lute in the seventeenth century, namely the addition of bass strings that did not lie on the fingerboard and thus could not be stopped, required an accommodation in the notation. Tablaturists wrote the letter *a*, signifying the open string, below the lowest horizontal line in the diagram, and because luthiers eventually added several such strings, then wrote oblique or horizontal strokes for each lower sounding string, one stroke for the second highest, two for the third highest, and so on. (By the end of the sixteenth century, French notation was now using six lines, instead of the five printed by Attaingnant, for the six courses of the lute that the player could stop, an expansion that became obligatory with the addition of the bass strings.) Perhaps the best example of this notation is the famous manuscript from the mid-seventeenth century that contains the works of Denis Gaultier, *La rhétorique des dieux*.[17] The repertory in this collection requires a lute with five additional bass strings, tuned C, D, E, F and G, occasionally retuned to suit the tonal fabric of the piece, which Gaultier notes sometimes with the letter *b* on the second highest string to indicate a retuning to F♯.[18]

German lute tablature departs significantly from the conventions of Italian and French tablatures: first, it does not use a diagram of the strings to show which string to pluck, and second, it employs a completely different manner of stipulating at which fret to stop the string. Instead, it encodes both pieces of information in a single symbol that simultaneously maps string and fret. To each intersection of string and fret, then, the German tablaturists assign a single symbol, so that each symbol indicates unequivocally precisely where to place the finger of the left hand. Controversy surrounds the invention of the system. Sebastian Virdung, writing in 1511, attributes it to the blind organist Konrad Paumann (1410–73), but already in the next decade, Martin Agricola cast aspersions on Virdung's claim.[19] But, as modern scholars show, the system would work satisfactorily for oral communication between blind and sighted lutenists, and would permit precise

---

[17.] Ber 78 C 12.
[18.] E.g., *La Gaillarde*, bar 6, Ber 78 C 12, p. 230; see Gaultier, *La rhétorique des dieux*, ed. Buch, no. [47], p. 62; and Gautier (*sic*), *Oeuvres*, ed. Rollin and Goy, no. 90, p. 162.
[19.] Virdung, *Musica getutscht*, fol. K iii v; trans. Bullard, pp. 156–57. Agricola, *Musica instrumentalis deudsch*, fol. xxix r–v; trans. Hettrick, pp. 29b–30b.

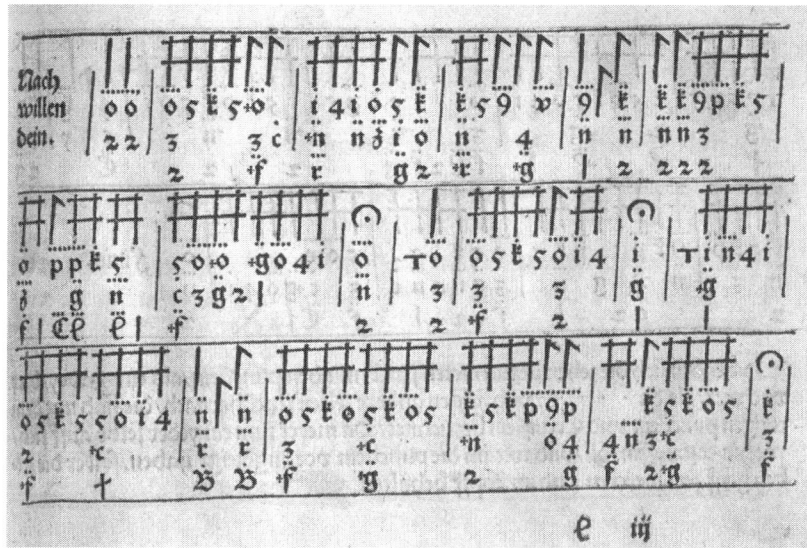

Figure 4.7 Hans Newsidler, *Ein newgeordent küntslich Lautenbuch*, fol. l iii r
Bayerische Staatsbibliothek München, 4 Mus.pr. 439.

dictation from a blind musician to her or his amanuensis.[20] So some consensus exists regarding the ascription to Paumann.

If Paumann did in fact invent the system, then it would be at least as old as any Italian or French tablature, and probably predates most of them. The structure of the system itself suggests its age, because it envisages an instrument of five courses, not the six in the notations of Petrucci and Attaingnant. The tablature designates each of the five strings with an arabic numeral 1 through 5, beginning with the lowest sounding string. These numerals also represent the open strings. The letters of the alphabet then apply to the frets, *a–e* for the first fret on each of the five strings, *f–h* for the second fret, and so on through the end of the German alphabet, *z*, which represents the fifth fret on the third string. Additional symbols, which resemble arabic 7 and 9, but which are actually Latin abbreviation signs for *et* and the prefix *con-*, respectively, complete the fifth fret, and then the alphabet begins again, each letter now with a superscript stroke, for the subsequent

---

[20] Oral communication: Dorfmüller, "La tablature de luth allemande," pp. 246–47; dictation: Hemming, "German Lute Tablature," p. 9. See also Minamino, "Conrad Paumann," esp. pp. 299–301.

frets 6 through 9.[21] Like the keyboard tablature of Antonio Valente, this system functions in an entirely mechanical way to indicate where to stop the string.

By the time German music publishers were beginning to issue books of lute tablature in the early sixteenth century, luthiers had added a sixth string to the instrument, with the result that several systems arose to supply symbols for the notes sounded on that string. This complication, in conjunction with the fact that, unlike the Italian and French systems, it does not use a visual representation of the fingerboard, may have shortened its useful life, as it appears to have fallen out of favour by the end of the sixteenth century. Still, as Kurt Dorfmüller points out, and as the opening of *Nach willen dein* shows (see Figure 4.7), from Hans Newsidler's *Ein newgeordent küntslich Lautenbuch*, the system evinces some advantages, particularly in the designation of independent voices. In this regard, it closely resembles German keyboard tablatures.[22]

For example, this passage moves freely among textures that involve one, two or three voices, to each of which Newsidler dedicates a single horizontal register. Sometimes, voices change strings, as in bar 3, where the top voice begins on the fourth string (*i*, 4, *i*, *o*), and the middle voice on the third (*n*, *n*, *z*). As the top voice ascends, it switches to the fifth string (5, *k*), while the middle voice, also ascending, moves to the fourth (*i*, *o*). The register denotes the voice within the musical texture, not the string, and voices share strings as needed, the fourth string in this instance. Like the Italian lute music discussed above, the German idiom exploits a free-voiced texture as opposed to a full polyphonic one, but the German notation stresses the identity of the individual voices more than does the Italian.

Figure 4.7 also exhibits the manner in which this notation indicates rhythms, left-hand fingerings and a special sign for sustaining one voice while the others move. The rhythmic symbols resemble those used by Ammerbach in his keyboard tablature, particularly in regard to the use of beaming to connect consecutive notes of the same duration.[23] For the fingerings of the left hand, Newsidler has apparently devised a new system

---

[21.] For a typical contemporary account, see Newsidler, *Ein newgeordent küntslich Lautenbuch*, fols. a iii v–a iiii r; trans. Southard and Cooper, pp. 9–10. For modern commentary, see Dorfmüller, "La tablature de luth allemande," pp. 245–46; and Minamino, "Conrad Paumann," pp. 299–301.

[22.] Newsidler, *Ein newgeordent küntslich Lautenbuch*, fol. l iii r. Dorfmüller, "La tablature de luth allemande," pp. 247–52; and *Studien zur Lautenmusik*, pp. 68–113; see also Minamino, "Conrad Paumann," pp. 300–1.

[23.] Newsidler, *Ein newgeordent küntslich Lautenbuch*, fols. b iii v–b iiii v; trans. Southard and Cooper, pp. 15–16. See Dry, "Instructions allemandes," p. 114.

that consists of a series of dots, one for the index finger, two for the middle finger, and so on, that he prints above the symbol for the note.[24] For example, in the first two bars, he specifies that the player use the fourth finger for the note F (indicated by the letter *o*), and the second finger, first for the note A (*k*) and then for D in the lowest voice (*f*). Finally, he prints a little cross beside this last note to indicate that the player sustains it to the beginning of the next bar and the note A (*r*) while the middle voice moves A–B♭–C (3–*c*–*n*).[25] The player then sustains this last C while the top voice moves.

Lute tablature satisfied the demand for a notation unique to the instrument that offered indexical indications for the player to play a specific string, stopped at a specific fret. The three national varieties accomplish the task each in a unique way. The Italian and French systems use a graphic representation of the instrument's fingerboard but stipulate the frets differently, with numerals and letters, respectively. The former seems easier to intuit because, in the French notation, one might readily confuse the letters of the tablature with the letter names of the notes, whereas that confusion simply does not arise in the Italian system. The avoidance of this ambiguity in the Italian tablature may have encouraged its adoption for modern guitar notations, modified to use the organization shared by the French systems and Luis de Milán, with the highest sounding string at the top of the diagram. Most idiosyncratic and shortest lived is the German tablature, which exhibited a purely mechanical means of specifying where to place the fingers of the left hand. Its ability to stipulate the independent voices of the musical texture did not hold sufficient importance for an instrument unsuited to complex polyphony.

Similarly, keyboard tablatures addressed a specific audience of players who needed an idiosyncratic notation that stipulated specific actions at the keyboard. Again, musicians adopted a variety of strategies to map the keyboard into alphanumeric characters. The German tablatures and that adopted by Antonio de Cabezón both organized their systems for identifying the keys the player is to strike around the musical structure of the octave, the Germans by using the letter names of the notes, Cabezón by assigning the same numeral to a note irrespective of the octave. In contrast, Antonio Valente arbitrarily allocated to each key on the instrument a numeral that consequently did not correspond to any aspect of musical organization.

[24.] Newsidler, *Ein newgeordent küntslich Lautenbuch*, fols. b v–b ii v; trans. Southard and Cooper, pp. 13–14. See Dry, "Instructions allemandes," pp. 113–14. On German lute technique in general, see Radke, "Zur Spieltechnik."

[25.] Newsidler, *Ein newgeordent küntslich Lautenbuch*, fols. b ii v–b iii r; trans. Southard and Cooper, p. 14.

The Adoption of Vocal Notation by Instrumentalists

During the sixteenth century, musicians developed tablatures for other instruments, and simultaneously adopted vocal notation for a variety of instruments.[26] For example, Italian music for keyboard used a form of contemporary vocal notation already in Faenza 117 and in Andrea Antico's *Frottole* of 1517. By the end of the century, the practice had become more common, first in publications, such as Giovanni Gabrieli's *Sacrae symphoniae* of 1597, that combined vocal and instrumental pieces, then in works like Claudio Monteverdi's *L'Orfeo* (1607) that united vocal and instrumental performing forces in the same ensemble. The continuing professionalization of instrumentalists and the increasing integration of vocalists and instrumentalists in performance stimulated the need for a single system of notation that all could read.

The twelve partbooks that constitute Gabrieli's *Sacrae symphoniae* all contain both vocal and instrumental items, although no piece calls for both vocal and instrumental performers.[27] We readily recognize the vocal music because of the text under the music. Music that lacks text, therefore, we might suspect is instrumental.[28] But Gabrieli offers more specific indications by using generic titles such as *Canzon* (sometimes expanded with *per sonar*) and of course the famous *Sonata pian e forte* for the instrumental works.[29] Moreover, in several items, he stipulates an instrument for each part, for example in the *Sonata pian e forte*, which requires a cornetto, a violino (which occupies the same range as the modern viola) and six trombones, divided into two groups, the first with cornetto in the highest sounding voice, the second with the violino in that part, and three trombones in each group on the three lowest sounding voices.[30]

Both vocal and instrumental pieces use precisely the same notation, that familiar from vocal music of the fifteenth and sixteenth centuries. What

---

[26.] On tablatures for other instruments, see Rastall, *The Notation of Western Music*, pp. 164–71.
[27.] Gabrieli, *Sacrae symphoniae*.
[28.] See, for example, Cantus, fol. D iii r, which contains the end of the *Magnificat, Anima mea*, no. 28, and the beginning of the *Canzon primi toni*, no. 29; reproduced at Gabrieli, *Opera Omnia*, 10: *Instrumental Ensemble Works*, ed. Charteris, Plate IV, p. LXVII.
[29.] Items 30–35, 44–49, 57–59 and 62 in Gabrieli's index of *Sacrae symphoniae*. See, e.g, Cantus partbook, fol. [I ii v]; also Gabrieli, *Opera Omnia*, 10: *Instrumental Ensemble Works*, ed. Charteris, p. IX.
[30.] Gabrieli, *Sacrae symphoniae*, no. 35, Cantus, fol. E iii v; Altus, fol. E iii v; Tenor, fol. E iii v; Sextus, fol. E iii v; Septimus, fol. D iiii v; Quintus, fol. E iii v; Octavus, fol. E ii v (*sic*; in error; actually fol. D ii v); and Bassus, fol. E iii v. See Gabrieli, *Opera Omnia*, 10: *Instrumental Ensemble Works*, ed. Charteris, no. 6, p. 49, commentary pp. XXXVI–XXXVIII.

significance does the appearance of both types of music in the same partbooks carry? The answer depends upon the circumstances under which musicians used them. It is clear, for example, that San Marco in Venice, where Gabrieli served as organist from 1585, employed during his tenure separate groups of vocalists and instrumentalists.[31] It seems unlikely, therefore, that musicians performing under Gabrieli's direction would double as vocalists and instrumentalists. But the print enjoyed dissemination beyond Venice and San Marco.[32] Musicians elsewhere at institutions that did not possess the same resources as San Marco may have required the same individual to sing or play according to the scoring of the piece. The greater significance of the combination of vocal and instrumental music in the same partbooks, however, beyond particular performing exigencies, is that both singers and instrumentalists were reading from the same notation and, even more important, that instrumentalists by the end of the sixteenth century needed to be able to read vocal notation in order to execute their professional duties successfully.

A decade after the publication of Gabrieli's *Sacrae symphoniae*, Claudio Monteverdi, in 1607, premiered his opera *L'Orfeo* in Mantua, and published the score two years later.[33] He calls for an orchestra of significant size and diversity, including wind, keyboard and string (bowed and plucked) instruments.[34] The 1609 score provides the same notation for all performers, vocalists and instrumentalists: vocal notation of the sixteenth and early seventeenth centuries. I assume that the instrumentalists would have performed from parts (undoubtedly prepared in manuscript for the first performances in Mantua and never in Monteverdi's lifetime printed), not from the score. To the best of my knowledge, no parts have survived.[35] It is always difficult to argue from silence, but it seems most likely that any parts Monteverdi had prepared for the Mantua performances would have replicated the notation presented in the score. Again, as in the case of Gabrieli's

---

[31] On the personnel at San Marco, see Selfridge-Field, *Venetian Instrumental Music*, pp. 13–25 and the individuals listed in Appendix F, pp. 297–308; and D. Arnold, *Giovanni Gabrieli*, pp. 32–34, 137–40 and 157–58. On the general musical environment of Venice during this period, see Ongaro, "All Work and No Play?".

[32] Charteris, *Giovanni Gabrieli*, p. 384a–b, records surviving copies of the print in Austria, Germany, Spain, the United Kingdom, Italy, Poland and Slovenia (as well as the United States).

[33] Monteverdi, *L'Orfeo*.

[34] Given at Monteverdi, *L'Orfeo*, fol. [A 2r]; for discussion, see Vacchelli, "Introduzione," in Monteverdi, *L'Orfeo*, ed. Vacchelli, pp. 25–34. Monteverdi supplements this list with instructions given at the beginning of each instrumental piece; conveniently gathered by Glover, "A List of Monteverdi's Instrumental Specifications."

[35] Vacchelli records as witnesses for the piece only the printed scores of 1609 and the reprint of 1615: "Introduzione," pp. 18–19, and "Apparato critico," p. 55, both in Monteverdi, *L'Orfeo*, ed. Vacchelli.

Sacrae symphoniae, it would seem that the instrumentalists who participated in the early presentations of *L'Orfeo*, including keyboardists and players of the chitarrone, read vocal notation and not the tablatures tailored to their particular instruments.

From around 1600, then, the musical notation that practitioners had developed for vocal music became a kind of *lingua franca* for all professional musicians, singers or instrumentalists. As the score for Monteverdi's *L'Orfeo* shows, the use of mixed ensembles played a significant role in this development. Performers may have needed to consult parts other than their own to prepare for the challenges of ensemble playing, or composers, like Monteverdi who was himself an organist, may have wanted to standardize the notation for the entire ensemble, irrespective of the scoring. Eventually, conductors would require a uniformly noted score. In any case, the development of a standard notation to all performers carried significant benefits for musical literacy, as our brief survey of specialized tablature demonstrates. Each tablature, while sharing some attributes with the other systems, nevertheless presents enough idiosyncracies to make mastering several of them a prohibitively difficult enterprise. The existence of a uniform system of notation streamlines the requirements of musical literacy and renders transparent music for all manner of performance demands.

Figured Bass Notation

Three publications, all from 1600, contain keyboard parts that consist of the bass line alone and figures to indicate what harmonies to play in the higher parts: Peri's *Euridice*, Caccini's *Euridice* and Cavalieri's *Rappresentatione di Anima e di Corpo*.[36] Numerals represent the interval to be played above the bass note and accidentals printed alone usually apply to the note a third above the bass; accidentals placed beside numerals indicate that the note represented by the numeral is affected by the accidental. The actual realization of the higher voices, beyond the specification of the notes through figures and accidentals, remains the province of the player. This circumstance led almost immediately to the production of guides and manuals for the player, already in Peri's Preface to his published score of *Euridice*.[37] The

---

[36] Peri, *Le musiche sopra l'Euridice*; Caccini, *L'Euridice*; and Cavalieri, *Rappresentatione di Anima e di Corpo*. See also F. T. Arnold, *The Art of Accompaniment*, pp. 33–65.

[37] Peri, *Le musiche sopra l'Euridice*, "Avvertimento."

debates continue to the present and show no sign of waning.[38] The system itself, however, began to wane in the eighteenth century. Already J. S. Bach, in some of his flute sonatas, was writing for obbligato keyboard accompaniment.[39] By the end of the century, the custom of using figured bass had virtually disappeared as composers sought to assert their control over all aspects of their keyboard accompaniments.

Idiosyncratic Notation for Instruments

In the process of adapting the notation of vocal music to the needs of instrumental music, the differences in technique used by the performing media required several accommodations. First, common symbols acquired specialized meaning for individual instruments. For example, the slur in vocal music joins notes sung to the same syllable; in keyboard music, it signifies legato playing effected without lifting the hands; in bowed strings, it defines the notes played without a bow change; in plucked strings, notes played on a single plucking of the string; and in wind instruments, notes played in a single breath without tonguing. In each case, the meaning of the same symbol changes to accommodate the techniques used on each class of instruments.

Second, specialized instructions for individual instruments came into use for particular techniques, and these took two forms: symbols and verbal instructions, often in Italian. As examples of the former, I cite the designation for the depression and subsequent articulation of the damper pedal in music for the piano, and the symbols for upbow and downbow in string music. These often take iconic form. For example, the symbol for the damper pedal begins with the cursive abbreviation ℘ed, standing for *pedale*, and then continues with a horizontal line denoting the continued depression of the pedal, punctuated by inverted Vs that indicate where the player releases and then again depresses the pedal. These inverted Vs graphically resemble the motion the player's foot makes as it lifts and then depresses the pedal. So too, the symbols for upbow and downbow in string music assume the appearance of the relevant parts of the bow: a *V*

[38.] For a survey of guides, see F. T. Arnold, *The Art of Accompaniment*, pp. 242–323; and Campagne, *Simone Verovio*, pp. 187–234. See also Bach, *Precepts and Principles*.

[39.] Bach, Sonatas for Flute and Harpsichord, BWV 1030 and 1032, in *Werke für Flöte*, ed. Schmitz, pp. 33–53 and 54–68, respectively; BWV 1031, in *Verschiedene Kammermusikwerke*, ed. Hofmann, pp. 13–24. On the controversies surrounding the attributions of these works, and a defence of the authenticity of BWV 1031, see Marshall, "J. S. Bach's Compositions."

for the tip, where the upbow starts, and a square bracket for the frog V ⊓, respectively.

The verbal instructions tend to take on a self-explanatory form: for example, *con* and *senza sord.* (= *sordino*), with and without the mute; *sul pont.* (= *ponticello*) or *sul tasto*, on the bridge or fingerboard; *ord.* (= *ordinario*), a return to playing without special techniques; *pizz.* (= *pizzicato*) or *arco*, plucked or bowed; *una corda* or *tre corde*, depress or lift the *una corda* pedal on the piano. The growth of increasingly specialized techniques in instrumental playing has led to the development of equally specialized notational devices, such as the Bartók pizzicato for string instruments, which calls for the player to lift the string vertically and then release it so that it strikes the fingerboard. Even within the context of a standardized notation, therefore, based on the system used for vocal music, each class of instruments developed its own idiosyncratic notational language, whether through the specialized meaning of commonly used symbols or the creation of new ones specific to the instrument. All musicians were attempting to communicate efficiently the particular playing techniques required for a specific passage or context. I append a list of publications that explain and exemplify these techniques for individual instruments.[40]

Bibliography of Notational Techniques

Flute

On twentieth- and twenty-first-century notations:
Levine, Carin, and Christina Mitropoulos-Bott. *The Techniques of Flute Playing*. Kassel: Bärenreiter, 2002.
Toff, Nancy. *The Development of the Modern Flute*. New York: Taplinger, 1979, pp. 230–39.

French Horn

On notations for muting and hand stopping:
Gregory, Robin. *The Horn: A Comprehensive Guide to the Modern Instrument & Its Music*. 2nd ed. London: Faber and Faber, 1969, pp. 56–59.

[40.] In general, see Read, *Contemporary Instrumental Techniques* and *Compendium of Modern Instrumental Techniques*.

Harp

Inglefield, Ruth K., and Lou Anne Neill. *Writing for the Pedal Harp: A Standardized Manual for Composers and Harpists.* The New Instrumentation, 6. Berkeley, Los Angeles and London: University of California Press, 1985.

Rensch, Roslyn. *The Harp: Its History, Technique and Repertoire.* New York and Washington: Praeger Publishers, 1969, pp. 173–80.

Salzedo, Carlos. *Modern Study of the Harp.* New York: G. Schirmer, 1921, pp. 7–25.

Tournier, Marcel. *The Harp.* Paris: Henry Lemoine & Cie., 1959, pp. 43–92.

Guitar

Schneider, John. *The Contemporary Guitar.* The New Instrumentation, 5. Berkeley, Los Angeles and London: University of California Press, 1985, pp. 105–94.

Percussion

Smith Brindle, Reginald. *Contemporary Percussion.* London: Oxford University Press, 1970, pp. 5–17.

Solomon, Samuel Z. *How to Write for Percussion: A Comprehensive Guide to Percussion Composition.* 2nd ed. New York: Oxford University Press, 2016, pp. 55–84.

Piano

On notation for pedalling:

Faricy, Katherine. *Artistic Pedal Technique: Lessons for Intermediate and Advanced Pianists.* Mississauga, ON: Frederick Harris Music, 2004, p. 99.

Raucher, Walter L. *The Art of Pedalling.* N.p.: Raucher Music, 1972.

Organ

On notation for pedalling:

Ritchie, George, and George Stauffer. *Organ Technique: Modern and Early.* Englewood Cliffs, NJ: Prentice Hall, 1992, p. 75.

Strings

On twentieth-century notations:
Penesco, Anne. *Les instruments à archet dans les musiques du XXe siècle.* Musique—Musicologie, 21–22. Paris: Librairie Honoré Champion, 1992.

Violin

On twentieth- and twenty-first-century notations:
Strange, Patricia, and Alen Strange. *The Contemporary Violin: Extended Performance Techniques.* The New Instrumentation, 7. Berkeley, Los Angeles and London: University of California Press, 2001, pp. 1–140.

Accidentals, Mode, Key and Signatures

The earliest indications of chromatic inflection arise from theoretical expositions of the medieval gamut that recognize the existence of B♭, situated a second below and a seventh above our middle C, perhaps derived from the synemmenon tetrachord of ancient Greek music theory, as Hucbald of Saint Amand acknowledges.[41] Transposition slightly broadened the medieval chromatic palette to include low B♭, a ninth below our middle C, and E♭, written as F and B♭, respectively, in chants ending on D that have been transposed to A. Likewise, the transposition of a chant ending on E to A permits the use of a note a major second above the final, noted B♮, the equivalent of F♯. These chromatic inflections affect the immediate intervallic content of the melody and carry no significance for the ecclesiastical modal system, because that system does not define the individual modes on the basis of octave species.

Simultaneously, the system of hexachords first proposed by Guido d'Arezzo creates a practical means for positively locating the semitone at three different positions in the gamut, each designated by the solmization syllables mi–fa: B–C in the hard, E–F in the natural and A–B♭ in the soft hexachord. Singers trained in the system could identify which hexachord to apply according to the melodic situation and therefore where to sing B♭ or B♮. Not all melodies, however, permit the unequivocal application of

---

[41.] Hucbald, *Musica* 34–39, ed. Chartier, pp. 178–87; trans. Babb, pp. 29–34.

solmization, and so musicians rapidly developed symbols that specified where to flat the B and where not. Already in the mid-eleventh century, the scribe of Mo H. 159 distinguished between B♭ and B♮ in his alphabetic notation by writing the letter *i* either inclined clockwise at forty-five degrees (B♭) or upright (B♮).

Following the adoption of accurate heighting for the communication of relative pitch, scribes began to employ the flat sign, derived from the round *b* (*rotundus*) with which music theorists distinguished B♭ from square *b* (*quadratus*), B♮.[42] The scribe of Tol 44.2, an antiphoner written around the end of the eleventh century and eventually used in Spain, entered the round *b* several times to designate B♭; he also wrote a symbol that resembles the letter *h* of the text hand in the manuscript.[43] It is not clear that he intended this symbol to mean B♮, but my assessment of the palaeographic and melodic environment suggests this is precisely its meaning.

Christian Berger proposes that accidentals carry an indexical semiotic function in that they unequivocally require the musician to adjust the marked note chromatically; he also posits that they could function iconically.[44] I argue above that instrumental tablatures fall into the category of indexical signs because each symbol requires the instrumentalist to take a specific physical action, but staff notation, including accidentals, represents musical materials on a symbolic basis because no part of the sign intrinsically matches or represents the equivalent musical events. Indications for higher and lower pitch, by the placement of the notes on the vertical axis of writing, as I discuss in Chapter 2, become fixed by convention, just as the signs for chromatic inflection, and so they move to the iconic class of symbols.

Composers of polyphonic music in the later Middle Ages expanded the tonal system by transposing the hexachord system to other portions of the gamut. They adopted three symbols, two of them synonymous, to designate these transpositions: the flat, already in use in plainsong, to indicate fa, and either the sharp or the natural, both derived from the theorists' *b quadratus*, for mi. These symbols do not stipulate chromatic inflection per se but instead fix the application of a particular hexachord through the assignment of either mi or fa to a particular note; chromatic inflection

---

[42] Pseudo-Odo, *Dialogus* 2, ed. Gerbert, p. 253a–b; and Guido, *Micrologus* 2–3, ed. Smits van Waesberghe, pp. 93–102; trans Babb, pp. 59–61.

[43] See, e.g., Tol 44.2 fol. 115r, the responsory *Benedicat nos deus* in the Office of the Trinity. On the manuscript in general and its provenance, see CANTUS, *An Aquitanian Antiphoner*, pp. vii–viii; and Collamore, "Aquitanian Collections," pp. 57–63.

[44] C. Berger, *Hexachord, Mensur und Textstruktur*, pp. 92 and 136.

ensues from the application of the hexachord.[45] The placement of these accidentals in the practical sources demonstrates their function as solmization signs first and indications of chromatic inflection second. Scribes often entered the accidentals several notes before the note whose inflection was affected and thereby indicated where the new hexachord should begin.[46]

Machaut's *Biaute qui toutes autres pere* (Figure 3.3 and Example 3.3 in Chapter 3) presents several instances of this strategy. The scribe of Pa 1584, working during Machaut's lifetime under his supervision, enters an E♭ at the beginning of the tenor. Its first note is G, and the E does not occur until the third note. As a result, the flat stipulates that G, the first note, be sung as la, with the result that E becomes fa and therefore E♭. Similarly, in the cantus, the scribe places a sharp on F just before the first G in the voice. As a result, that note becomes fa and the Fs that follow mi, F♯. The situation does not always present a clearcut solution. The cantus, for example, clearly begins in the natural hexachord; after four notes, the scribe enters B♭. But the next note is E, and unless we suggest that the B♭ designates ut (with the result that E becomes fa and E♭, thus invoking the same hexachord as the tenor), we must continue with the natural hexachord and not mutate until the next note, D re = la, to bring us to fa on B♭.

These chromatic inflections suggest that Machaut was working with a flexible melodic idiom that requires frequent mutation between hexachords. The accidentals in the cantus, for example, generate first a melodic augmented fourth between the E in the continuing natural hexachord and the B♭ stipulated by the accidental and the resulting soft hexachord; then a mutation to the *ficta* hexachord on D, designated by the next accidental, produces a diminished fourth between that B♭ and the F♯. The rest of the chanson exploits similar inflections, none of which affects the overall tonal structure of the piece; it resides solidly on D, as each principal cadence reinforces, both at the end of the A section (bars 18 and 19, first and second endings) and the final cadence (bar 39). Machaut adjusts the intervallic structure above D to

---

[45] See A. Hughes, *Manuscript Accidentals*, pp. 44–51; and C. Berger, *Hexachord, Mensur und Textstruktur*, pp. 134–37.
[46] See A. Hughes, *Manuscript Accidentals*, pp. 59–69.

create melodic and harmonic colour, but these adjustments do not alter the tonal identity of the piece.[47]

Scribes of the thirteenth century began to place the solmization sign as a signature at the beginning of a piece, often assigning different signatures to different voices in the same piece, a usage modern scholars have designated partial or conflicting signatures.[48] In the first instance, the signature would seem to suggest which hexachord would dominate the voice, and because different voices in the same piece could use different hexachords simultaneously or serially, scribes differentiated them with their signatures. But these signatures only conflict in so far as they denote the application of different hexachords to different voices. Consequently, like the presence or absence of B♭ in plainsong, these signatures, conflicting or otherwise, carry no significance for the modal identity of the piece.

Several pieces in Bam 115 evince different signatures in different voices, and they reveal a variety of practices. For example, the short motet *O Maria / Audi pater / Alleluya* has a signature of one flat in the tenor and none in the motetus or triplum.[49] In fact, the whole of the tenor falls in the soft hexachord, and so signature and melodic disposition agree entirely. So too the upper voices require only the natural and hard hexachords, precisely those suggested by the signature, for their entirety. Longer pieces present more complex situations, as we see in the very next piece in Bam 115, *Amours vaint / Autens d'esté / Et gaudebit*, which uses the same signature.[50] The melodic disposition of the tenor resembles that in *O Maria / Audi pater / Alleluya*, as it uses either the soft or natural hexachords throughout, and so again signature and melody agree.

The upper voices, however, exhibit a more flexible practice and present some problems. Up to bar 14, both motetus and triplum move in either the natural or hard hexachord, just as the signature would suggest. But at bar 15, the motetus twice sings B and the

---

[47.] On Machaut's tonal language, see Brothers, *Chromatic Beauty*, pp. 88–135, especially on *Biaute qui toutes autres pere*, pp. 108–13; Bain, "Tonal Structure" and "'Messy Structure'?"; and Jackson, "Guillaume de Machaut and Dissonance."

[48.] Apel, "The Partial Signatures"; Lowinsky, "The Function of Conflicting Signatures" and "Conflicting Views"; Hoppin, "Partial Signatures" and "Conflicting Signatures Reviewed"; A. Hughes, *Manuscript Accidentals*, pp. 51–54; and K. Berger, *Musica ficta*, pp. 65–69.

[49.] Bam 115 fol. 5v. See Aubry, ed., *Cent motets*, 2: no. IX, p. 20; and Anderson, ed., *Compositions of the Bamberg Manuscript*, no. 9, p. 13.

[50.] Bam 115 fols. 5v-6v. See Aubry, ed., *Cent motets*, 2: no. X, pp. 21–24; and Anderson, ed., *Compositions of the Bamberg Manuscript*, no. 10, pp. 13–15.

triplum once, against a sustained F in the tenor; Aubry recommends a shift to the soft hexachord in both upper voices to avoid the tritone, while Anderson retains the hard hexachord, for which he offers no explanation. Perhaps he wishes to maintain the integrity of the signature. The manuscript itself, however, frustrates that logic because, beginning in bar 19, frequent B♭s in the motetus force that voice into the soft hexachord, and for the most part, Aubry and Anderson agree in editorially flatting the rest of the Bs.[51] And B♭ occurs in the triplum at bar 42. In short, the scribe of Bam 115 does not shrink from invoking a hexachord in conflict with those implied by the signature.

Perhaps the most problematic passage occurs at bars 29–31. The tenor and motetus fall unequivocally in the soft and natural hexachord, respectively. The triplum sings B twice, in bar 29 against F in tenor and motetus, and again in bar 30 against an E in the motetus. The triplum begins the phrase, in bar 28, on the natural hexachord and could mutate to either hard or soft hexachord in the next bar to facilitate the descent below C. But the hard hexachord creates a tritone against both motetus and tenor in bar 29, while the soft hexachord clashes in the same way with the motetus in bar 30. Both Aubry and Anderson retain the hard hexachord here, but other possibilities could arise in performance, not without the difficulties I note above.

In several places, the manuscript accidentals reflect real musical choice, either by the composer of the motet or by the scribe in its inscription. The melodic line descends in each case by conjunct motion to the marked B♭ from E, and so the scribe has provided the accidental to prevent the singer who would prefer to avoid a direct melodic tritone from singing B♮. Some of these descents begin from F or G, but all pass through E and so create a melodic augmented fourth with the marked B♭.[52] So, these accidentals occur not just to invoke the soft hexachord but also to insist on a particular melodic formulation that involves dissonant intervals.

In contrast with the motetus, the triplum for the most part remains in the hexachords proposed by the (lack of a) signature: natural and hard. At only one point in the piece does the scribe invoke the soft hexachord in this

---

[51.] Anderson suggests the hard hexachord at bars 26–27 to avoid a tritone against the E in the triplum, bar 26. Bars 49–51 probably use the hard hexachord. In both places, Aubry invokes the soft hexachord with editorial accidentals.

[52.] Descents from G: motetus, bars 24–25, 38–39. From F: motetus 29–32, 53–54, 64, 66–67. From E: triplum, bar 42.

voice via an accidental, bar 42, where, as I suggest above, the accidental functions on a purely melodic basis to require the singer to sing B♭ at the end of a conjunct descent from E. In one other passage, bars 51–55, the triplum might use the soft hexachord, as Aubry suggests. The entire passage falls in this hexachord without mutation, the motetus unequivocally moves to the soft hexachord at bar 54 as the marked B♭ requires, and F dominates the tenor and motetus bars 52–53. Anderson retains the hard hexachord throughout.

These three voices, then, evince three different relationships between signature and the melodic fabric of the voice. The tenor uses only those hexachords suggested by its signature, while the triplum falls predominately in those proposed by its signature, definitely moving to the soft hexachord at only one place, and perhaps using it at a second. The motetus fits neither description as, from bar 19, it frequently employs the soft hexachord as stipulated by accidentals on B♭. Perhaps the best way to describe how the motetus relates to its signature is to state that it opens, bars 1–18, with those hexachords the signature suggests, natural and hard. After that, the scribe, or composer, employs accidentals to show the singer where to invoke the soft hexachord.

A much more complex melodic and harmonic idiom confronts us in Guillaume Du Fay's *Flos florum*, even leaving aside the dramatic harmonization of the text's final stanza (bars 60–65).[53] Tenor and contratenor share a signature of one flat, while the superius has none. As in *Amours vaint / Autens d'esté / Et gaudebit* from Bam 115, the tenor of *Flos florum* evinces the most straightforward relationship with its signature, remaining in either natural or soft hexachord for most of its duration; the hard hexachord appears at two places through an accidental B♮, bars 11 and 59. It replicates the relationship the triplum of *Amours vaint / Autens d'esté / Et gaudebit* maintained with its signature: the two hexachords suggested by the signature dominate the voice but not to the exclusion of the hard hexachord. Similarly, the contratenor uses for the most part the soft and natural hexachords proposed by the signature. Its one accidental, a C♯ at bar 29, moves the voice temporarily to the *ficta* hexachord built on A. It serves a melodic and harmonic function, as it forces the contratenor to sing an augmented fourth G–C♯, and it creates a perfect fourth with the F♯ in the cantus.[54]

[53.] Bol Q.15 new fols. 267v–268r. See Du Fay, *Opera omnia*, ed. Besseler, 1: no. 2, pp. 6–7.
[54.] Besseler suggests several editorial accidentals in the contratenor that may or may not be necessary: F♯ in bar 9 to avoid a tritone with the B in the cantus; hard hexachord in bars 19 and 43 to create a double leading-tone cadence.

The superius stands in a more complex relationship with its signature, beginning with its first phrase, bars 1–4, which falls in the soft hexachord, as Besseler suggests, in contradiction to the signature and without an accidental in the manuscript. Moreover, at several places, the superius sings an uninflected B against F in either tenor, contratenor or both (bars 5, 9, 14, 19, 25, 31, 37, 38, 46 and 55). At least some of these would seem to stand as good candidates for the soft hexachord and the resulting B♭, as Besseler suggests.[55] And, as in the other two voices, accidentals invoke hexachords not envisaged by the signature. At bar 12, E♭ suggests the *ficta* hexachord built on B♭, although neither the scribe of Bol Q.15 nor Besseler flats the B at the end of the bar, probably to retain the leading tone for the cadence on C, bars 12–13.

The sequence F♯–B♭ at bar 29 forces the superius to sing first the *ficta* hexachord built on D, perhaps beginning in the previous bar, and then the soft hexachord, although the singer must mutate to the natural hexachord almost immediately to accommodate the E at the end of the bar. The accidentals also require the cantus to sing an interval of a diminished fourth. Finally, a B♭ at bar 42 introduces the soft hexachord but leaves us wondering about the Bs that directly precede in bars 41 and the first half of 42, which Besseler leaves uninflected. The superius, then, does not relate to its signature with the same transparency as the other two voices. They focus on the two hexachords prescribed by their signature and only move away unequivocally via accidentals imposed by composer or scribe. The superius uses accidentals in precisely the same way, but throughout it vacillates between all three of the common hexachords, soft, natural and hard, and in fact almost certainly begins in the soft, despite the signature and lack of accidentals.

These two pieces, *Amours vaint / Autens d'esté / Et gaudebit* and Du Fay's *Flos florum*, allow us to deduce several principles regarding the use of conflicting signatures. First, the signature can prescriptively fix the selection of hexachords, and therefore pitches, available to the voice, as in the tenor of *Amours vaint / Autens d'esté / Et gaudebit*. Second, it can define the hexachords the voice will principally use, except where accidentals invoke foreign hexachords: the triplum of *Amours vaint / Autens d'esté / Et gaudebit*, and the tenor and contratenor of *Flos florum*. The motetus of *Amours vaint / Autens d'esté / Et gaudebit* and the superius of *Flos florum* present the gravest problems. The former begins with the two hexachords stipulated by its signature,

---

[55.] Bars 14, 19, 31, 37, and 55.

but moves to the soft hexachord soon after and frequently returns to it. The latter, however, appears to open on the soft hexachord and then uses all three hexachords. Perhaps the scribes of Bam 115 and Bol Q.15 (or the composers of the two pieces) felt more comfortable leaving the signature blank and imposing accidentals when they required the soft hexachord than providing a flat in the signature that they then had to cancel for the hard hexachord.

In the sixteenth century, signatures, invariably consisting of flats, became associated with transpositions of the octave species. In conjunction with contemporary modal theory, which revived the ancient Greek concept of the Ptolemaic τόνοι, composers and scribes identified the octave species with mode.[56] Heinrich Glarean provides a full definition of the octave species and a detailed discussion of the relationship between them and the modes identified by their Greek names.[57] In his examples, Glarean demonstrates the relationship between mode, signature and octave. Two that exemplify the dorian mode, one from Obrecht, the other by Adam of Fulda, use different signatures, Obrecht none, Fulda one flat in each voice.[58] Aside from sharing the same mode, just the point Glarean is making by citing these pieces, they also use the same octave species: Obrecht's piece ends on A, while Fulda's ends on D; the flat in the latter creates the same octave species above the tonal centre as in Obrecht's piece.

Modern scholars note that the order of the pieces in Cipriano de Rore's *Il primo libro de madrigali a quattro voci* (1550) follows that of the eight ecclesiastical modes.[59] Nevertheless, his use of signatures and accidentals indicates that the octave species affects his definition of tonal space. First, all voices in every piece agree in signature, no signature for the first group

---

[56] Ptolemy, *The Harmonics* 2.8–11, trans. Barker, pp. 333–40. See also Mathiesen, *Apollo's Lyre*, pp. 458–66; and Barker, *Scientific Method*, pp. 169–91.

[57] Glarean, *Dodecachordon* 2.1–7 and 15–37, pp. 65–83 and 101–74, respectively; trans. Miller, 1:103–21 and 139–205, respectively. See Fuller, "Defending the *Dodecachordon*"; Judd, "Renaissance Modal Theory," pp. 383–89; Loesch, "Musica," pp. 188–93; C. Meyer, "Zur 'Konstruktion'"; and Werbeck, "Glareans Vorstellung." Gioseffo Zarlino also associates the modes with species of the octave: *Le istitutioni harmoniche* 4.10–17, pp. 309–20; trans. Cohen, pp. 37–54; see Palisca, "Die Jahrzehnte um 1600 in Italien," pp. 260–62; and Judd, "Renaissance Modal Theory," pp. 389–98. In general, see Meier, *Die Tonarten*, pp. 32–35.

[58] Glarean, *Dodecachordon* 3.13, pp. 260–63; trans. Miller, 2:327–30. On his examples in general, see Judd, *Reading Renaissance Music Theory*, pp. 138–76.

[59] Rore, *Il primo libro de madrigali a quattro voci*; modern edition by Meier, Rore, *Opera omnia* 4. On its modal order, see Powers, "Monteverdi's Model," pp. 194–95; Owens, "Mode in the Madrigals," especially pp. 3–4; and Lloyd, "Ordering and Reordering," especially pp. 3–7 and 11–12. For analyses of individual pieces by Rore that show his modal orientation, see Meier, *Die Tonarten*, pp. 104–9, 161–64, 264–65, 292–93, 295–97, 358–63, 375–76. See also McClary, *Modal Subjectivities*, pp. 101–21.

of pieces and one flat for the second, beginning *Se'l mio sempre*. Second, accidentals, supplied either by Rore himself or his publisher, tend to modify the modal structure in two ways: flats invoke the octave species one step around the cycle of fifths on the flat side, while sharps, or naturals that cancel flats, create cadences in which the seventh degree of the octave species (raised by the sharp or cancelling natural) ascends by semitone to the governing pitch of the cadence (what musicians would later call the root).

A single passage from *Signor mio caro* illustrates his method.[60] The piece carries no signature and exhibits a clearly defined tonal centre of G, with strong cadences on that pitch throughout, many of which Rore reinforces with F♯ (e.g., bars 3, 5–6 and 7). Owens assigns the piece to mode 8, on the basis of the piece's final, the range of the cantus (rising a fifth above the final and falling a fourth below, as is usual in mode 8), and the low cleffing (C-clef on the first line for the cantus, and F-clef on the fourth line for bass, the modern soprano and bass clefs, respectively).[61] Rore balances the F♯ with which he inflects the cadences with the frequent use of F♮ (e.g., bars 8–9 and 14–19) to solidify the octave species indicated by the signature.

In the passage bars 26–35, chromatic inflections invoke passing changes of octave species and tonal centre. Rore frames the passage with cadences on G that feature the leading tone F♯ (bars 27 and 34). At bars 29–32, F♯ gives way to F♮ so that first the octave species defined by the signature returns and then, as B♭ enters in the lower voices (bar 31), he shifts the tonal fabric to the octave species that uses one additional flat.[62] The C♯ at bar 32, however, signals a cadence on D, but that pitch immediately yields to G as the tonal centre with the cadence at bars 34–35. The signature and established tonal centre define the octave species while, in this passage, the chromatic inflection B♭ invokes a new octave species, the C♯ a change in tonal centre, both modifications temporary. It is clear, therefore, from his use of signature and accidentals, that Rore's conception of tonal space reflects contemporary thinking about octave species.

As the modal system yielded, in the seventeenth and eighteenth centuries, to the major/minor dichotomy of the common practice period, musicians identified key signatures with specific major and minor keys, and key signatures consisting of sharps appeared alongside those with flats. Several treatises, published between 1701 and 1713, by Tomáš Janovka, Francesco

---

[60.] Rore, *Il primo libro de madrigali a quattro voci*, all part books, pp. 5–6; ed. Meier, 4:15–18.
[61.] Owens, "Mode in the Madrigals," p. 4.
[62.] The turn to the original octave species might begin already at bar 28, with the pitch F in the alto that Meier editorially sharps.

Gasparini, Johann Heinichen and Johann Mattheson, locate the pairs of scales on each degree.[63] Perhaps the crowning acknowledgement of the system's new hegemony resides in J. S. Bach's *Well-Tempered Clavier*, the first part of which he published in 1722, containing twenty-four preludes and fugues, one in each of the twelve major and minor keys, ascending chromatically from C.[64] Still, Bach sometimes uses for minor keys a signature with one flat fewer than what became standard, implying a dorian orientation, as for example in the Toccata and Fugue in D minor, BWV 538, which uses no signature.[65] Nevertheless, he applies many B♭s as accidentals and at such striking places (e.g., the subject and the concluding passage of the fugue, bars 1–7 and 204–22, respectively) that one can hardly assert that the dorian mode dominates the piece.

The system remained in general use throughout the nineteenth century and, in some idioms, up to the present. The broadening tonal spectrum employed by art music composers in the twentieth century led many to abandon key signatures as their music explored tonal formulations beyond the modal and common practice systems, Arnold Schoenberg, for example, in *Das Buch der hängenden Gärten*, published in 1914.[66] Experiments with microtonal divisions of the semitone led composers to create symbols that indicated inflections of a quarter-tone or other size. Charles Ives uses square notes to indicate quarter-tones in his Fourth Symphony, composed over the period 1912–25.[67] These experiments provide a logical extension to the attempts by musicians of the Middle Ages to obtain greater tonal variety by invoking the soft hexachord and the semitone A–B♭ that resulted.

---

[63]. Janovka, *Clavis ad thesaurum*, s.v. "Cantus," pp. 7–10; and s.v. "TONUS," pp. 287–304; trans. Lester, *Between Modes and Keys*, pp. 163–73. Gasparini, *L'armonico pratico*, pp. 72–89, esp. 84–87; trans. Stillings, pp. 64–77, esp. 74–75. Heinichen, *Neu erfundene und gründliche Anweisung*, part 1, chapter 4, §4, and part 2, chapter 1, §§38–44 and 54–55, pp. 104, 199–204 and 211–12, respectively; trans. Brilmayer and Mongoven, pp. 69, 129–33 and 137–39, respectively. Mattheson, *Das neu-eröffnete Orchestre*, part 1, chapter 4, §§17–20, pp. 60–63; partial translation, Lester, *Between Modes and Keys*, pp. 114–15. On seventeenth-century predecessors, see Lester, *Between Modes and Keys*, pp. 97–104; on Janovka, Heinichen and Mattheson, *ibid.*, pp. 105–17; also Lester, *Compositional Theory*, pp. 169–71; see also Powers, "From Psalmody to Tonality," especially, on Mattheson, pp. 278–81.
[64]. Bach, *Das Wohltemperierte Klavier*, ed. Dürr.
[65]. Bach, Toccata and Fugue in D minor, ed. Kilian.
[66]. Schönberg, *Das Buch der hängenden Gärten*, Op. 15, ed. Rufer.
[67]. Ives, Symphony no. 4, movement 2, rehearsal no. 35, strings, p. 78; see "Conductor's Note," pp. 12b–13a.

Dynamics, Tempo and Expression

The earliest notations in the medieval West offered guidance in the expressive delivery of plainsong as well as the relative speed at which the music should proceed. A number of special neumes, such as the *quilisma*, require particular vocal nuances. Some scholars, myself included, believe that Carolingian musicians developed notation for the principal purpose of indicating where singers ought to use these distinctive vocal techniques, as I discuss in Chapter 2. Musicians in different regions of the post-Carolingian West developed supplementary systems of significative letters that offered a variety of additional information on pitch, tempo and mode of delivery. Scribes wrote these near the neumes they affected and so modified or amplified the information explicit in the neume. These notational nuances disappeared as medieval musicians concentrated their attention on the specifics of pitch and rhythm.

Composers moved beyond considerations of pitch and rhythm in the sixteenth century. At the end of the century, Giovanni Gabrieli and other composers began to add dynamic marks in instrumental music, most famously in Gabrieli's *Sonata pian e forte*.[68] The system of verbal indications he and his contemporaries devised, *piano* and *forte*, remains in effect today with only two modifications since then: the addition of indications for gradual changes in dynamics and the expansion of the system with further gradations. The former first took purely verbal form, *cresc.* and *dim.* or *descresc.* (*crescendo* and *diminuendo* or *descrescendo*), and later adopted iconic symbols in the form of the so-called "hairpin" signs. Musicians expanded the system by multiplying the symbols ***p*** and ***f*** and the addition of ***mp*** and ***mf*** (*mezzo piano* and *mezzo forte*) in the middle. Many might ask what significance ***ppp*** and ***fff*** might carry, never mind four or more of the symbols, if ***pp*** and ***ff*** mean, respectively, *pianissimo* and *fortissimo*, and the superlative degree preserves its literal meaning.

We find a more complex historical situation, however, in another development that occurred around the middle of the sixteenth century, and that is the set of conventions Vicentino records within the system of durational notation that indicated tempo.[69] Longer durations imply slower

---

[68.] Gabrieli, *Sacrae symphoniae*, no. 35, Cantus, fol. E iii v; Altus, fol. E iii v; Tenor, fol. E iii v; Sextus, fol. E iii v; Septimus, fol. D iiii v; Quintus, fol. E iii v; Octavus, fol. E ii v (*sic*; in error; actually fol. D ii v); and Bassus, fol. E iii v. See Gabrieli, *Opera Omnia*, 10: *Instrumental Ensemble Works*, ed. Charteris, no. 6, p. 49, commentary pp. XXXVI–XXXVIII.

[69.] Vicentino, *L'antica musica* 2.31, fol. 42r–v; trans. Maniates, p. 135.

tempi, shorter durations faster, as is common, for example, in Arcangelo Corelli's sonatas. In the Trio Sonata, Op. 1, no. 3, the two middle movements, marked Allegro and Adagio, respectively, demonstrate the convention: the former moves predominantly in eighths and sixteenths, while the latter uses whole and half notes for the most part.[70] G. F. Handel exhibits much more equivocation in his sonatas for flute and continuo. For example, of the last two movements of the G minor Sonata (HWV 360), marked Adagio and Presto, respectively, the first exhibits motion in half notes, while the finale moves consistently in eighths. The sonata's first movement, however, marked Larghetto, uses rhythms at the level of the sixteenth note.[71]

J. S. Bach further subverts these conventions. In the opening movement of his Sonata for flute and harpsichord in B minor, BWV 1030, marked Andante, the rhythms consist largely of sixteenths, both duple and triple, while eighths predominate in the middle movement, Largo e dolce, with melodic decorations in thirty-second notes. The opening of the Presto finale, in 2/2 metre, moves in eighth notes, followed by a second section in 12/16 dominated by sixteenths.[72] Bach does not endorse Vicentino's system, particularly in the last two movements, which share durations despite occupying opposite ends of the spectrum in terms of their respective tempi. Beethoven, on the other hand, completely inverted the system by writing faster pieces in longer durations and slow movements in shorter values. For example, in the opening of the *Pathétique* Sonata, Op. 13, passages marked Grave alternate with Allegro molto e con brio.[73] The former adopts a dotted sixteenth/thirty-second rhythm that breaks into passagework with even shorter values, down to a series of one hundred and twenty-eighth notes in bar 10. The Allegro molto e con brio, however, moves consistently in quarters and eighths, and so the two contrasting sections unequivocally contradict Vicentino and his system.

By Beethoven's era, of course, musicians had long been supplementing the system of tempi that Vicentino suggested with character designations (Adagio, Allegro and others) that eventually became an independent system of tempo indications. These seem to have begun appearing in the early seventeenth century, in Adriano Banchieri's second edition of his *L'organo suonarino* (1611), for example. *La battaglia*, a programmatic piece for organ, includes the character designations Adagio, Presto, Allegro and

---

[70.] Corelli, Trio Sonata, Op. 1, no. 3, in *Sonate de chiesa*, ed. Lütolf, pp. 48–51.
[71.] Händel, Sonata for Flute and Continuo in G minor, HWV 360, ed. Schmitz, pp. 16–20.
[72.] Bach, Sonata for Flute and Harpsichord, BWV 1030, ed. Schmitz, pp. 33–53.
[73.] Beethoven, Sonata for Pianoforte, Op. 13, ed. Schmidt, pp. 142–49.

Veloce.[74] And in the glossary at the end of the second edition of his treatise on the Italian manner of singing (1658), Johann-Andreas Herbst defines Adagio, Lento, Largo, Tardo and Presto.[75]

The invention of the metronome in the early nineteenth century provided a mechanical means to fix tempi.[76] Although Beethoven, who worked directly with the device's inventor, Johann Nepomuk Mälzel, adopted it with enthusiasm, other composers viewed it as a mixed blessing at best.[77] Wagner, for example, recounts an incident that occurred during a rehearsal of *Tannhäuser*, the score of which he amply provided with metronome indications. When he objected to what seemed to be an incorrect tempo, the conductor demonstrated that it accorded exactly with Wagner's own metronome marks.[78] In reaction, he stopped using metronome marks in his scores, and in *About Conducting*, he specifies that the correct tempo arises from the character of the piece alone.[79] Stravinsky also had a vexed relationship with tempo, and used at least two means in addition to metronome markings to attempt to fix it.

First, in collaboration with Columbia Records beginning in 1927, he undertook a project to record his complete catalogue, which continued up to 1966.[80] Stravinsky wished to specify his interpretation, particularly in regard to tempo, about which he chides other performers, referring them to his own recordings in order to learn the correct tempi.[81] Second, he insisted that durations, determined by his playing the piece through at the piano, be printed in several of his published scores.[82] His motivation was partly practical, as durations helped in the planning of concert programmes,

---

[74.] Banchieri, *L'organo suonarino* (1611), ed. Cattin, pp. 38–39.
[75.] Herbst, *Musica moderna*, pp. 75–76.
[76.] Harding, *The Metronome*; and Kolisch, *Tempo und Charakter*.
[77.] On Beethoven's favourable reaction to it, see Kolisch, *Tempo und Charakter*, pp. 3–12. Cf. the partially facetious complaints of Schoenberg regarding conductors and interpretation, "About Metronome Markings."
[78.] Wagner, *Über das Dirigieren*, in *Sämtliche Schriften*, 8:275; trans. Ellis, 4:304–5.
[79.] Wagner, *Über das Dirigieren*, in *Sämtliche Schriften*, 8:275–76, 285; trans. Ellis, 4:305, 314. See also Wagner, *Über die Aufführung des "Tannhäuser"*, in *Sämtliche Schriften*, 5:144; trans. Ellis, 3:190.
[80.] Strawinsky, *Chroniques de ma vie*, pp. 161–63. See Hamilton, "Igor Stravinsky: A Discography." For a critical overview of the recordings, see Lipman, "Stravinsky: Rerecording History."
[81.] See Stravinsky's letter to Robert Craft of 7 October 1947, printed in Craft, "'Dear Bob[sky]'," pp. 396–97.
[82.] On the method of determining the durations, see Craft, "'Dear Bob[sky]'," p. 415 n. 44. On the timings of the *Mass* and the negotiations with Boosey & Hawkes over their being printed correctly in the published score, see the letters of Stravinsky to Craft of 3 and 9 November and 14 December 1948, *ibid.*, pp. 415, 416, 419–20, respectively.

and he constructed at least one piece, the *Mass*, so that its individual movements would each fill one side of a 78-r.p.m. disc.[83]

But he also desired to impose his will on performances by others, a control that did not always extend to his own performances, as Craft notes and the composer himself acknowledges. When Stravinsky found that his own later performance differed from an earlier estimate of the duration, as Craft reports, Stravinsky would write in his own copy of the score, "'Today I do it in …' and give his latest timing, as if the discrepancy required an explanation."[84] Wagner and Stravinsky were responding to their own music as any performer would, adjusting tempo according to any number of criteria that they did not take into consideration when they entered the metronome mark, and in the case of Stravinsky, the timings, into their scores.

Questions of control seem to have affected the development of two other notational nuances, ornaments, beginning in the seventeenth century, and articulation in the eighteenth. Instrumentalists adopted a series of stenographic signs to designate specific ornaments. Some involve abbreviations of verbal instructions, like **tr** for *trillo*. Others use special symbols such as the mordent ∿ or turn ∞. Practices varied across instruments, national schools and eras.[85] The application of these symbols seems to be related to the actual durational values of the notes that constitute the ornament. For example, not every musician is able to trill at the same speed. The instruction simply requires one to alternate between the two notes of the trill as quickly as possible. Writing out specified durations would compromise its execution and potentially make it impossible for some musicians. Eighteenth-century composers added dots for staccato, slurs for legato (discussed above), tenuto marks, accents and sforzandi to stipulate how performers should deliver individual notes and groups of notes. All these nuances increase the range of sounds available to musicians, and rapidly became standard musical effects.

What might have caused composers of the early modern period to assume more control over these aspects of performance is debatable. Before the advent of music printing early in the sixteenth century, many performances of music would have directly involved the composer.

---

[83] On the use of the timings in programming, see Craft, "'Dear Bob[sky]'," p. 415 n. 44; on the relationship between the duration of the movements of the *Mass* and their recorded format, ibid., p. 422.

[84] Craft, "'Dear Bob[sky]'," p. 415 n. 44.

[85] See the table in Kreitner *et al.*, "Ornaments," pp. 738–41. See also the table given by J. S. Bach in the *Klavierbüchlein für Wilhelm Friedemann Bach*, ed. Plath, p. 3.

Manuscript witnesses did travel beyond their place of origin and take with them repertories now outside the immediate realm of the composer. But printing created an entirely new paradigm of dissemination, actively encouraging performance in circumstances that composers could no longer directly control. Possibly, they sought to assure greater fidelity in performance by giving in writing more detailed instructions that they might have communicated to the performers orally when they directed the performances themselves.

A second reason might be the exploration of notational indications of tempo, dynamics and other modes of expression as new compositional resources. By assuming greater notational control of these aspects of the music, composers could employ them for strictly musical reasons to help shape their pieces. Much of the effect of Gabrieli's *Sonata pian e forte*, which was, of course, disseminated in print as part of his *Sacrae symphoniae*, derives from the contrast between the soft and loud passages, aided by the largely antiphonal writing for the two groups of instruments. Nevertheless, Gabrieli would not have been able to achieve the effect without the notational device, and so we confront the issue of whether the musical effect generated the need for the notation, or the notation made possible the musical effect.

Interlude 3: The Score

Western art music distinguishes itself from the music of many other cultures by the use of polyphony. The need to show the simultaneous progression of two or more lines of music has generated a number of novel solutions over the millennium or so that Western musicians have practised polyphonic music. Monophony, of course, poses no particular problems of layout. Medieval scribes of monophonic music chose to write the music from left to right, borrowing the conventions from writing text, largely because monophony was texted. They inscribed the music either all the way across the page or in columns, but that choice did not materially affect the presentation of the music or its apprehension in reading or copying. The earliest practical sources for polyphony, the Winchester tropers of the early eleventh century, write the voices separately as monophony, in distinct sections of the book or even in two books.

The earliest polyphonic sources from Aquitaine, written around 1100, also separate the two constituent voices, but normally write them consecutively one immediately after the other, a convention that Sarah Fuller calls successive notation.[1] All such pieces employ forms, either stanzaic or the double cursus form, that use the same music for successive stanzas. Because such texts exhibit the same metrical form in all (stanzaic) or consecutive (double cursus) stanzas, the literary text assures the coordination of the voices. Still, issues remain that prevent the books from being used in performance. In places, music to be sung simultaneously appears on opposite sides of the same folio, and so singers would be unable to read that music during performance. Such evidence suggests to me that singers used the books for study and memorization, which then became the basis for performance.[2]

Precisely at the same time that Aquitanian scribes were using successive notation for polyphony, they were also writing the voices to be sung together, one above the other, in what we would call score notation.[3] The only piece written in score in the oldest portion of Pa 1139, *Iubilemus*

[1.] Fuller, "Hidden Polyphony." [2.] Grier, "Some Codicological Observations," pp. 20–21.
[3.] Grier, "Some Codicological Observations," pp. 22–23, and on the dates, 52.

exultemus (fol. 41r), cannot be written in successive notation because its musical setting does not exhibit repetition. But score notation rapidly replaced successive notation in Aquitaine, even for those pieces for which it was suitable. The two oldest sections of Pa 3719 (fols. 15–22 and 23–32) are roughly coeval (I date them ca. 1100), but they differ in their notation for polyphony, folios 23–32 with successive notation, folios 15–22 score.[4] Yet the pieces in score do use repetitive forms and so could have been written in successive notation.

The scribe of this early portion of Pa 3719, therefore, and subsequent Aquitanian scribes, saw a clear advantage in using score notation, despite the fact that it does not solve all problems of alignment, however, because the rhythms in Aquitanian polyphony, and other twelfth-century repertories, such as that of the Codex Calixtinus, were not fixed. As Marianne Danckwardt points out, many of the details of alignment in twelfth-century polyphony, from Aquitaine or elsewhere, can only be realized in the act of performance.[5] Nevertheless, score notation does offer the advantage of providing to singers a rapid, general orientation of the relationship between the two voices, something that successive notation simply does not afford.[6]

The real advantages of score notation emerge in the polyphony associated with Notre-Dame in the next century.[7] In the organa and conductus, up to four voices move at more or less the same rhythmic pace, with, therefore, the same density of musical symbols. (Most passages of organum, of course, include one voice, the tenor, that moves significantly slower.) As in polyphony of the twelfth century, the arrangement in score helps to orient the singers at a glance to the way in which the voices relate to one another. The more voices in a polyphonic texture, the more effective score notation is for this type of visual orientation. Modal notation, in the conductus as well as three- and four-voice organum, helps to determine the alignment of the voices, but is not definitive, as I discuss in Chapter 3. Motets in the Notre-Dame sources also use score notation, but by the end of the century, scribes were breaking down polyphony into its constituent voices and writing them as monophony, in Mo H. 196, for example.

One might suggest that scribes were attempting to save space by writing the voices as monophony, but the motet and chanson repertory of the late

---

[4] Grier, "Some Codicological Observations," pp. 38–45 and 52.
[5] Danckwardt, "Zur Notierung," pp. 31. 38–39.
[6] On the difficulties of coordinating the voices in successive notation, see Fuller, "Hidden Polyphony," p. 174; and Danckwardt, "Zur Notierung," p. 59.
[7] The sources are W_1, F and W_2.

thirteenth century offers relatively few opportunities for such savings. Typically, the upper voices move at more or less the same speed and therefore take up the same amount of room, while the tenor moves somewhat slower. The exception to this rule of thumb is the corpus of motets attributed to Petrus de Cruce, in which the three voices create a decidedly stratified rhythmic texture, and their mise-en-page in Mo H. 196 graphically demonstrates this arrangement: the two upper voices appear in parallel columns, with that for the faster top voice wider, to accommodate more symbols, and that for the middle voice narrower; the tenor runs across the bottom of the page.[8] Much greater savings could be realized in the Notre-Dame organum, where the tenor often holds a note for an entire system or even longer. Score notation is obligatory for these pieces, however, to guarantee the alignment of the moving voice or voices with the sustaining tenor.

To return to the writing of late thirteenth-century polyphony in parts, then, it seems that the saving of space does not play an important role. Much of that music, however, exploits the mensural notation of Franco of Cologne and his successors. This system, as I discuss in Chapter 3, incorporates features that facilitate its reading in real time during performance. Is it possible that singers felt more comfortable reading their individual lines as monophony and then relying on their ears and sense of ensemble to fit their parts into the polyphonic texture? Modern players from parts develop precisely these skills to achieve the same goal. Were musicians of the thirteenth century any less capable? In any case, the presentation of polyphony, sometimes very complex polyphony, in parts remained the standard practice in manuscript and, after 1501, in print, into the seventeenth century. In a related development, sixteenth-century scribes and printers began to create partbooks in which they collected the music for the individual parts of polyphonic pieces instead of placing them in the same book.

Musicians turned again to score format during the sixteenth century to study complex contrapuntal textures or to read them at the keyboard.[9] Typically, they use vertical lines drawn through the entire system at regular durational intervals (usually the breve or the semibreve) to assist with the alignment of the parts and to facilitate reading. As ensembles became more complex at the end of the century, however, and increasingly involved both

---

[8.] Mo H. 196 fols. 270r–271r and 273r–275r.
[9.] Lowinsky, "On the Use of Scores" and "Early Scores in Manuscript"; and Owens, "The Milan Partbooks," pp. 293–97.

instruments and voices, composers, scribes and engravers adopted score notation for the finished product. The mixture of performing forces seems to have been the principal motivating factor for the move to score. As I discuss in Chapter 4, Gabrieli published his *Sacrae symphoniae*, with separate pieces for voices and instruments, in parts, while Monteverdi's *L'Orfeo*, which employs mixed performing forces of voices and instruments together, appeared in score. Around 1600, then, as around 1100, the complexity of simultaneous musical events required the use of score notation for their efficient presentation and to ensure their coordination.

The conventions that govern the presentation of score notation, however, only gradually evolved from 1600, as the score for *L'Orfeo* (1609) reveals. Voices and instruments occur, for example, in order of their range, the highest sounding at the top, the lowest at the bottom, as in the overture and the first chorus.[10] And obbligato instruments appear above the vocal line and the bass.[11] But Monteverdi offers a variety of strategies for specifying which instruments play which lines.[12] Most specific are the directions for the famous piece "Possente spirto," in which the composer first identifies the continuo resources ("Orfeo al suono del Organo di legno, & vn Chitarrone") and then assigns the top two lines first to violins, then harps and finally violins again.[13] He offers less particular instructions elsewhere, but the texture allows us to conclude the disposition of the instruments. For example, before a trio texture in act 2 following a recitative by Orfeo, when Monteverdi states, "Questo Ritornello fu suonato di dentro da vn Clauicembano, duoi Chitaroni, & duoi Violini piccioli alla Francese," it is clear that the two violins play the two top parts while all the other instruments provide the continuo realization.[14]

[10.] Monteverdi, *L'Orfeo*, fol. [A 2v] and p. 8, respectively.
[11.] This is the arrangement in "Possente spirto," discussed below; Monteverdi, *L'Orfeo*, pp. 52–64.
[12.] See Glover, "A List of Monteverdi's Instrumental Specifications."
[13.] Monteverdi, *L'Orfeo*, pp. 52 (continuo and violins), 58 (harps) and 63 (violins); Glover, "A List of Monteverdi's Instrumental Specifications," p. 183.
[14.] Monteverdi, *L'Orfeo*, p. 27; see also p. 28 ("Questo Ritornello fu sonato da duoi Violini ordinarij da braccio, vn Basso de Viola da braccio, vn Clauicembano, & duoi Chittaroni"), where the two violins play the treble parts, and p. 30 ("Fu sonato di dentro da duoi Chitaroni vn Clauicembano, & duoi Flautini"), where the two flutes perform the same function; also the conclusion of "Possente spirto," p. 64 ("Furno sonate le altre parti da tre Viole da braccio, & vn contrabasso de Viola tocchi pian piano") before a four-part texture, and immediately following, p. [67] before a Sinfonia in five parts ("Questa Sinfo. si sonò pian piano, con Viole da braccio, vn Org. di leg. & vn contrabasso de Viola da gamba"); in both cases, the viole da braccio play the three or four upper parts, respectively. Glover, "A List of Monteverdi's Instrumental Specifications," pp. 182 and 183, respectively.

Other instructions offer significantly less precision. Monteverdi calls on all instruments to play the overture, but above the five voices, he prints "Clarino, Quinta, Alto e basso, Vulgano, Basso," without specifying which instruments, other than the clarino, play each line.[15] Even more problematic is the chorus in act 1 immediately following a recitative by Ninfa: "Questo Balletto fu cantato al suono di cinque Viole da braccio, tre Chittaroni, duoi Clauicembani, vn'Arpia doppia, un contrabasso de Viola, & un Flautino alla vigesima seconda."[16] Presumably, the five viole da braccio double the five vocal lines, and so must all differ in size, except the top two, which occupy the same range; the chitarroni, clauicembani, arpia doppia and contrabasso de viola all perform the continuo; I cannot imagine what instrument Monteverdi means by a flautino doubling one of the lines three octaves above. Many pieces have no indications whatsoever, the Sinfonia A 7 that concludes "Possente spirto," for example.[17]

The composer's instructions for the continuo instrumentation also create a certain amount of frustration. For example, in the act 2 dialogue between Pastore, Messaggiera and Orfeo, he offers some clarity that inevitably leads to confusion. Pastore begins the dialogue without any indication as to the makeup of the continuo, but before Messaggiera's first entry, Monteverdi specifies, "Vn organo di legno & vn Chit."; when Pastore replies, he is accompanied by "Vn Clauic. Chitar. & Viola da bracio."[18] The dialogue continues and soon Orfeo joins it, but the composer gives no further instructions for the continuo. Are we to infer that the two contrasting continuo groups persist in differentiating the speeches of Pastore and Messaggiera, even though Monteverdi does not provide that specific instruction? And what of Orfeo's contribution to the conversation? The composer is silent until Orfeo's concluding speech, when he states, "Vn organo di legno & vn Chitarone," the same group he required for Messaggiera.[19] Do we simply take his instructions literally and assume that the group specified for Pastore's reply continues to play through all the speeches until Orfeo's final remarks?

Similar questions persist regarding the continuo part for "Possente spirto." As I mention above, Monteverdi specifies the continuo

---

[15.] Monteverdi, L'Orfeo, fol. [A 2v].
[16.] Monteverdi, L'Orfeo, pp. [10]–13; Glover, "A List of Monteverdi's Instrumental Specifications," p. 182.
[17.] Monteverdi, L'Orfeo, pp. 68–69.
[18.] Monteverdi, L'Orfeo, pp. 35–40; Messaggiera and Pastore, p. 36. Glover, "A List of Monteverdi's Instrumental Specifications," p. 183.
[19.] Monteverdi, L'Orfeo, p. 39; Glover, "A List of Monteverdi's Instrumental Specifications," p. 183.

instruments at the beginning. This texture presumably continues through all the passages in which the two treble parts (violins alternating with harps) accompany Orfeo. When they give way to a four-part texture in which viole da braccio play the three upper parts (as noted above), a contrabass replaces the continuo group. In the Sinfonia that follows, in five parts with the four upper parts played by viole da braccio (also noted above), an organ joins the contrabass.[20] Monteverdi provides two further instructions for Orfeo's closing remarks, first "Orfeo canta al suono del Organo di legno solamente," and then "Qui entra nella barca e passa cantando al suono del Organo di legno."[21] This last incorporates a stage direction, something that occurs in other instrumental rubrics in the score.[22]

It is clear that Monteverdi and his publisher, Amadino, were struggling with the problem of what information to provide in the score, particularly regarding the instrumental forces to be employed. But why should such instructions be necessary? In Chapter 3, I suggested, in discussing Monteverdi's use of vocal notation in the score for all the instrumental parts, that the players probably performed from parts, like the performers of Gabrieli's *Sacrae symphoniae*. Those parts would presumably obviate the necessity for exact instrumental instructions in the score. The individual players would know precisely when to play because the requisite music appeared in their parts and no other. The question then arises as to who Monteverdi envisaged would use the score. Both the original 1609 print and its reissue in 1615 present themselves as offerings to Monteverdi's patron, Francesco Gonzaga, who, we must assume, is the principal audience of the score, and not music directors of possible future productions. Nevertheless, the composer, by introducing these limited and occasionally confusing specifications regarding the instrumentation, is clearly feeling the tension between providing a dedicatory score and one that would provide sufficient information for the successful performance of the piece.

Pieces with less complex instrumental ensembles created less ambiguity. For example, Francesco Cavalli conventionally required a uniform string ensemble. In *Il novello Giasone*, he stipulates five parts, two with treble clef, presumably first and second violin, two with alto clef, first and second viola,

---

[20] On these last two instrumental instructions, see n. 14 above.
[21] Monteverdi, *L'Orfeo*, pp. [67] and 68, respectively; Glover, "A List of Monteverdi's Instrumental Specifications," p. 183.
[22] Monteverdi, *L'Orfeo*, pp. 80 and 89; Glover, "A List of Monteverdi's Instrumental Specifications," p. 184.

and the lowest with bass clef for cellos, basses and continuo.[23] Scores that employ a broader instrumental palette provide specific indications at the beginning of each section, as J. S. Bach does in the B Minor Mass, BWV 232: at the opening of the Kyrie, he groups woodwinds together (first flute and oboe on the top staff, then second flute and oboe) above the higher strings (first and second violin, viola); voices lie between them and the continuo part on the lowest staff.[24] When he introduces brass and percussion, at the opening of the Gloria, they occupy the top of the system, above the woodwinds.[25]

W. A. Mozart also groups instruments by families for the most part, but arranges them in a different order. The score for *Don Giovanni* places the higher strings (first and second violin, viola) at the top of the system, followed by the woodwinds (flutes, oboes, clarinets and bassoons) above the brass (horns and trumpets) and percussion. The lowest staff carries, as has become conventional, the bass, consisting of cellos and basses.[26] The voices lie immediately above the bass.[27] Beethoven arranges his instruments in what was to become the conventional order: woodwinds at the top, above brass and percussion, with strings occupying the lowest staves.[28] The voices in the finale of the Ninth Symphony, however, appear at the bottom of the page, below the cello and bass, unlike the scores of Bach and Mozart.[29] Schott's contemporary print places the initial entry of the baritone soloist at the bottom of the page, in agreement with the autograph, but when the full complement of soloists and chorus enter, they appear above cello and bass, in the conventional place, where they remain for the rest of the piece.[30]

A number of conventions emerge from this sample of scores. First, as we see already in the score of Monteverdi's *L'Orfeo*, composers and publishers order instruments and voices by their range, higher sounding generally appearing above lower sounding. By the early eighteenth century, composers such as J. S. Bach were grouping instruments by families, woodwinds, brass and strings, but the order in which the families appeared had not become conventional by the late eighteenth century, as Mozart's score of *Don Giovanni* shows. I believe personal preference caused Bach to place the

---

[23]. Cavalli, *Il novello Giasone*.   [24.] The autograph is Ber P 180; opening of the Kyrie, p. [1].
[25]. Ber P 180, p. 20.   [26.] The autograph is Pa 1548 (1–8); see the overture, Pa 1548 (1), fol. 1r.
[27]. Pa 1548 (2), fol. 1r.
[28]. See the autograph of Symphony no. 9, Opus 125, Ber 2/204; opening of the first movement, Ber 2, fol. 1r.
[29]. Entry of the baritone soloist, Ber 204, p. 41; soloists and chorus, p. 47.
[30]. Baritone soloist: Beethoven, *Sinfonie mit Schluß-Chor*, pp. 111–12; soloists and chorus, p. 113.

Table Interlude 3.1 Placement of solo piano in scores for concerti

Composer	Work	Date	Source	Placement of Solo Piano
Mozart	KV 467	1785	autograph	between timpani and bass
Beethoven	Op. 37	1803	autograph	below bass
Beethoven	Op. 73	1809	autograph	below timpani, above cello and bass
Schumann	Op. 54	1862	print	between timpani and strings
Brahms	Op. 15	1875	print	below bass
Brahms	Op. 83	1882	print	between viola and cello

brass at the top of the system and Mozart the higher strings. Placing the woodwinds at the top of the score, the convention that eventually prevailed, results just as surely from an arbitrary procedure. One might argue that flutes generally play higher than horns, but one cannot make the same argument about violins, which, in the current convention, appear very close to the bottom of the system.

More interesting, I believe, is the placement of the voices when they are combined with an orchestra. Bach and Mozart illustrate the convention of placing them immediately above the bass. I suspect that initially the continuo player and then later the conductor found it convenient to see the precise relationship between the bass line (and the harmonies it implies) and the vocal parts. Beethoven's apparently idiosyncratic placement of the voice parts in his autograph for the Ninth Symphony may have resulted from the fact that he had already set up the page for the orchestra with four empty staves at the bottom. It was simply easier to add first the baritone solo and then the rest of the vocal resources at the bottom of the page instead of diverting the cello and bass to a lower staff to accommodate the singers above them. The publisher Schott certainly felt that Beethoven's arrangement was unusual because after setting the baritone solo in the same place as Beethoven had, he moved the voices to the conventional position, above the bass line, for the rest of the movement.

Even less stable is the placement of the solo instrument in the solo concerto during this period, as Table Interlude 3.1 shows.[31] This selection of piano concerti shows that composers of the eighteenth and nineteenth centuries adopted various placements for the solo instrument, Beethoven

---

[31] Sources cited in the table: Mozart, Piano Concerto, KV 467, NY 266; Beethoven, Piano Concerto, Opus 37, Ber 14; Beethoven, Piano Concerto, Opus 73, Ber 15; Schumann, Piano Concerto, Opus 54, *Concert für das Pianoforte*; Brahms, Piano Concerto, Opus 15, *Concert für das Pianoforte Op. 15*; Brahms, Piano Concerto, Opus 83, *Concert für das Pianoforte Op. 83*.

and Brahms choosing different locations in different pieces. Like voices accompanied by the orchestra, the piano often lies immediately above the bass, as in the case of Mozart's KV 467, Beethoven's Op. 73 and Brahms's Op. 83 (in the latter two of which, both composers construe cello and bass as jointly constituting the bass line). Elsewhere, Beethoven (in Op. 37) and Brahms (Op. 15) both place the solo piano at the bottom of the system, below the bass. Within this sample, only Schumann's publisher, Breitkopf und Härtel, uses what was to become the conventional position, between percussion and strings, for his Op. 54. This practice only came into common use around the turn of the twentieth century, about the same time that composers and publishers began to place voices within orchestral textures in the same position.

Other conventions have evolved over the years. Before the early twentieth century, composers and publishers presented the music for transposing instruments in transposition, both parts and score. Since then, musicians have adopted the convention to write that music at sounding pitch in the score, although the parts are usually transposed. Performing materials vary with performing medium: singers in ensembles normally perform from score, instrumentalists from parts, with the exception of the pianist in chamber music or accompanying voices, who usually uses a score. These conventions do not necessarily reflect the optimum means for presentation. For example, cues from other parts of the texture are entered into parts to facilitate tracking long rests. Such cues would not be necessary if all performers played from score, but that strategy, too, is cumbersome, as not all performers need access to the entire score. As in many circumstances, here too form follows function. Musicians use the performing materials that balance clarity of presentation with efficiency to create the means with which to generate a satisfactory performance.

5 | Notational Nuance in the Twentieth Century and the Motives for Notational Innovation

Over the last century, composers have exercised increasing control over every aspect of performance. They have adopted several strategies, including Stravinsky's programme of recording performances of every piece he composed with himself as pianist or conductor in order to provide templates for all other performances.[1] The principal means for achieving this control, however, lay in the density and specificity of notational instructions. Composers were already using notation to assume control over aspects of performance before the end of the sixteenth century, perhaps beginning with the dynamic marks Giovanni Gabrieli introduced in his *Sacrae symphoniae* of 1597. A significant increase in the specificity of notation occurs in the works of Beethoven, who, because of the physical infirmity of his deafness, was the first major composer unable to participate effectively in performances of his own compositions.[2]

In the slow movement of the *Hammerklavier* Sonata, Op. 106, for example, Beethoven provides many detailed performance indications, including gradations of tempo and dynamics, imprecations for expressivity and especially instructions for pedalling.[3] In several places, he specifies "ritardando" followed by "a tempo" (e.g., bars 44–45) and frequently supplements the conventional dynamic signs with "cresc." (e.g., bars 8–15, where he also uses the "hairpin" signs, bars 11–12 and 14–15) and "dimin." (e.g., bar 44); the verbal instructions "mezza voce" (bar 2) and "smorzando" (bar 86, following "dim." bar 85) suggest further nuances in the dynamics.[4] These indications combine with numerous rejoinders for expressive playing, "espressivo" (e.g., bar 26), "con grand espression" (e.g., bar 28) and "molto espressivo" (e.g., bar 91) to suggest the range of performing nuances that Beethoven himself might have introduced in a concert.[5]

---

[1] Strawinsky, *Chroniques de ma vie*, pp. 161–63. I discuss this project in Chapter 4, where I observe that one of the issues Stravinsky attempted to solve with these recordings was tempo.
[2] On his withdrawal from public performance, see Solomon, *Beethoven*, pp. 230 and 268.
[3] Beethoven, *Grande sonate pour le piano-forte*, pp. 25–38.
[4] Beethoven, *Grande sonate pour le piano-forte*, "ritardando ... a tempo," p. 27; "cresc.", p. 25; "dimin.", p. 27; "mezza voce," p. 25; "smorzando," p. 30.
[5] Beethoven, *Grande sonate pour le piano-forte*, pp. 26 and 30.

Furthermore, Beethoven controls the player's application of both damper and *una corda* pedals with dense commands, starting with a detailed footnote at the opening of the movement: "Una Corda (:U:C:) bedeutet Eine Saite, Tutte Corde (:T:C:) bedeutet Drey Saiten, poi a poi tre Corde nach und nach 2. Und 3. Saiten" ("*una corda* (U.C.) signifies one string, *tutte corde* (T.C.) signifies three strings, little by little three strings gradually the second and third strings").[6] The piece opens with the player depressing the *una corda* pedal from the beginning (bars 1–26), to which Beethoven adds the instruction "mezza voce," as I observe above.[7] The long crescendo (bars 8–15) occurs while the *una corda* pedal is engaged. The composer also invokes the damper pedal, although more sparingly than the *una corda*, beginning bars 5–6.[8] Finally, as the opening footnote suggests, Beethoven twice requires the player to release the *una corda* pedal gradually, striking first two and then all three strings, "poco a poco due e lora T:C:" (bars 76–79 and 87).[9]

With these instructions, Beethoven is attempting to control the colour the player may produce from the instrument with the modulation of the two pedals. Again, these nuances would emerge in performance were Beethoven able to perform in public. In the absence of his personal engagement, then, he strives to provide the player with as much instruction as the notation will allow. The density of those instructions in this movement comes into stark relief when one compares them with the notation Mozart uses in his late sonatas (e.g., KV 570 and 576, both from 1789), or even Beethoven's early sonatas (e.g., Op. 2, published in 1796).[10] Beethoven's intimidating stature among succeeding generations of composers caused them to imitate his notational proclivities.[11] All these practices rapidly paled, however, before the intensity of notational innovation in the twentieth century.

Some of this zeal was purely fetishistic: composers, influenced by the views of Wagner and Stravinsky, who decried the act of interpretation, felt that performers could not be trusted to produce reliable or authentic

---

[6.] Beethoven, *Grande sonate pour le piano-forte*, p. 25.

[7.] Beethoven, *Grande sonate pour le piano-forte*, pp. 25–26.

[8.] Beethoven, *Grande sonate pour le piano-forte*, p. 25; the Artaria print uses the abbreviation "Ped.," printed thus in roman, with the coda sign ⊕ to indicate the release of the pedal.

[9.] Beethoven, *Grande sonate pour le piano-forte*, pp. 29 and 30, respectively.

[10.] Mozart, Sonatas for Pianoforte, KV 570 and 576, in *Klaviersonaten*, ed. Plath and Rehm, 2:132–63. Beethoven, *Trois Sonates pour le Clavecin ou Piano-Forte*.

[11.] Many have made this observation, none in a pithier way than Stockhausen, "Musik und Graphik," p. 13.

performances.[12] Notation proved an imperfect tool to assure the reproducibility of performance, and so composers redoubled their efforts to fix performance instruction with ever greater notational detail. A second impulse driving composers toward notational innovation was the fascination with creating new sounds through manipulations of timbre and performance effects, such as the harmonics glissandi Stravinsky introduced in the *Firebird*. At one extreme, musicians invented new instruments, such as the theremin or the flexatone, to widen the timbral palette at their disposal. Most, however, restricted themselves to inventing new techniques on conventional instruments. Composers also experimented with complex rhythmic formulations that moved beyond conventional rhythmic organization, and with manipulations of pitch that involved divisions of the semitone.

All these techniques required innovative notations to communicate them effectively to performers, and many twentieth-century compositions include tables of newly invented symbols accompanied by explanations for their implementation and interpretation. Few of these new symbols have entered standard usage. Already in 1927, avant-garde composer Henry Cowell complained that, because conventional modern notation could not convey all the nuances himself and his contemporaries wished to incorporate in their new compositions, composers felt obliged to invent new symbols and systems of symbols, with very little liaison between them and no attempt at standardization.

> The result of all this is that each composer devises his own improvements which enable him to express his ideas more or less well, but as nothing is standardized a good deal of confusion arises. Many similar effects are notated in an entirely different manner by different composers, while totally separate effects are indicated by the same symbols; and in each instance copious footnotes are offered to the puzzled performer.[13]

The situation Cowell laments continued to deteriorate, particularly in regard to competing notational systems, a theme Karlheinz Stockhausen addresses in his wide-ranging essay entitled "Musik und Graphik."[14] Published in 1960, it critiques contemporary notational developments

---

[12.] See Grier, "Authority of the Composer," pp. 17–22.
[13.] Cowell, "Our Inadequate Notation," p. 31.
[14.] Stockhausen, "Musik und Graphik," p. 13; see also the essays by Carl Dahlhaus, György Ligeti, Roman Haubenstock-Ramati, Mauricio Kagel, Earle Brown, Siegfried Palm, Aloys Kontarsky and Christoph Caskel in *Darmstadter Beiträge zur neuen Musik* 9 (1965).

that have led to a division between notation, composition and performance, as I discuss below.

Performing Techniques

Performing techniques comprise by far the largest quantity of innovative notational devices, as composers demand that singers and players explore novel means of creating sounds. Two examples from Luciano Berio's *Sequenza* series provide typical illustrations of the range of possibilities: *Sequenza III per voce femminile* and *Sequenza VII per oboe solo*.[15] Berio gives the singer of *Sequenza III* instructions that specify (1) different modes of sound production, indicated by distinctive noteheads; (2) rhythmic delivery, represented by different types of beaming, always within the framework of the proportional notation that Berio explains in the instructions and uses in the score; (3) the inscription of relative and precise pitch; (4) the delivery of the text; and (5) other types of sound production, mostly with the voice but including fingersnaps. To these, he adds a lengthy list of instructions that suggest the manner in which the singer deliver the text. With the exception of the pitch and rhythmic notations, which modify and adapt traditional symbols, and the last group of signs, which are all literal, the indications Berio adopts fall in the category of symbolic indications. They are thus applicable to this piece, but possibly no other.

Most of the notational symbols the composer provides in *Sequenza VII* for oboe invoke special fingerings that affect the sound quality in various ways: modifications to the timbre of individual notes, harmonics, multiphonics, double trills (i.e., one of the two notes of the trill employs two distinct fingerings), trills with microtones, and effects that involve overblowing. Again, the signs are symbolic, such as that for overblowing, or arbitrary, as in the case of the alternative fingerings for timbral modifications, which use a simple system of arabic numerals keyed to the instructions. Similarly, Krzysztof Penderecki requires the string ensemble that performs his *Threnody* to execute various techniques of sound production, some conventional, some not, each marked with symbols of his invention.[16] Attempts to catalogue such lists remain noble and useful but doomed to immediate obsolescence because of the continuing initiatives of

---

[15] Berio, *Sequenza III and VII*.   [16] Penderecki, *For the Victims of Hiroshima*.

composers and performers to invent new techniques and their corresponding notations.[17]

Rhythm

In addition to exploring new sounds, and inventing the symbols that might represent them, composers also experimented with techniques that would break musicians free from the constraints of conventional rhythmic patterns, with their predominant duple (by default in music from the end of the seventeenth century) and triple subdivisions.[18] Berio, in several pieces in the *Sequenza* series, uses proportional notation to suggest the surface rhythms.[19] Instead of bar lines, he marks distances on the horizontal plane with timings. In *Sequenza III*, he uses equidistant divisions noted as ten seconds in length, although he adds the qualification "ca" (*circa*) to the first one to indicate that he does not expect the performer to observe the timeframe rigorously. The performer then executes the notes as they appear on the horizontal plane, notes further to the left occurring earlier in the ten-second window, and those on the right later, according to their proportional placement in the space. As Berio allows us to infer from his stipulation of *circa*, he anticipates that different performers will vary the execution of the rhythms he implies.

Berio employs a more complex system in *Sequenza VII*. As in *Sequenza III*, he sets up the page to regulate each system in precisely the same way. But instead of equidistant segments, he varies the durations of the segments across the page, but each segment in vertical alignment shares the same duration. So, each system in the score begins with a segment three seconds long, followed by one 2.7 seconds long, and so on. The durations vary from one to three seconds. But Berio, or his publisher, Universal Editions, does not use a consistent scale across these divisions of variable length and so compounds the problems of accurately perceiving the relationship between horizontal space and time. For example, Berio marks segments 3 through 6 at two seconds long each, but they occupy between fifty-two and fifty-five millimetres in length, and only two, the last two, are the same length. The

---

[17.] See Chapter 4 for the list of secondary sources that document idiosyncratic notations for individual instruments or families, where I mark those that specifically treat notations of the twentieth century and later. In general, see also Karkoschka, *Das Schriftbild der neuen Musik*; Cole, *Sounds and Signs*; Risatti, *New Music Vocabulary*; Boretz and Cone, eds., *Perspectives on Notation and Performance*; Lombardi, *Scrittura e suono*; Stone, *Music Notation in the Twentieth Century*; Read, *Source Book of Proposed Music Notation Reforms* and *Pictographic Score Notation*. For bibliography, see Warfield, *Writings on Contemporary Music Notation*.

[18.] See Read, *Modern Rhythmic Notation*.   [19.] See, e.g., Berio, *Sequenza III* and *VII*.

differences are, admittedly, not great, but they could cause some variation, already implicit in this notation as I argue above, in the mind of the performer as to where to situate each note.

Some composers use variable beaming to indicate accelerando or ritardando. In the former, the group begins with a single beam that then widens out to two or more beams, while the opposite designates the latter. The first movement of Elliott Carter's *Eight Pieces for Four Timpani* provides a good example.[20] The first two instances occur in passages marked *ad lib.*, but the second is immediately followed by a bar of 6/8. Here, he stipulates that a group of seven notes, beginning with thirty-second notes but slowing to sixteenths, occupies the time of the first three eighths of the bar, followed by a group of four notes (consisting of one sixteenth, two dotted sixteenths and one eighth), all required to slow further, that occupies the second group of eighths in the bar. One might think that the successful execution of this bar in strict 6/8 metre would pose problems, but Carter adds the designation *molto rit.* above it, thus compounding the written out ritardando via the variable beaming with the written instruction.

Carter also employs the technique of metrical modulation in this piece.[21] This method permits the smooth transition from one metre to another via the equivalence of note values. For example, in the first movement, Carter presents a passage dominated by steady eighth notes in bars ranging from 5/8 to 10/8, ending with several bars of 5/8. In the last of these, the composer divides the bar evenly in half with the value of a quarter note tied to a sixteenth. This composite value then becomes equal, in the next bar, to a single quarter note in 4/4 metre. The equivalence of the two values thus produces a smooth transition from the running eighths, in various metres, to the quarter notes of the ensuing passage.[22] Carter reinforces the relationship between the two tempi and metrical organizations with metronome markings: dotted quarter at 50 during the running eighths (equal to eighth note at 150) and quarter note at 60 in the following passage.

A transition in the fourth movement entails a purely visual manipulation of subdivisions in various metres.[23] The composer imposes nine thirty-second notes in the space of eight first in 4/4 then in 2/4 metre. With the shift to 18/32,

---

[20.] Carter, *Eight Pieces for Four Timpani*, movement I Saëta, pp. 3 and 5; see also *ibid.*, movements III Adagio, p. 8; and VI Canto, pp. 16–17.

[21.] The term was coined by Richard F. Goldman; see "Current Chronicle," pp. 87–88; see also J. Bernard, "The Evolution of Elliott Carter's Rhythmic Practice," pp. 167–82, who modifies it to "metric modulation." Also Carter, "The Time Dimension in Music," esp. pp. 29b–30c, and "Music and the Time Screen," pp. 70–71 and 77–83.

[22.] Carter, *Eight Pieces for Four Timpani*, movement I Saëta, p. 3; repeated p. 5.

[23.] Carter, *Eight Pieces for Four Timpani*, movement IV Recitative, pp. 11–12.

the quarter note of 2/4 becomes equivalent to the dotted eighth tied to a dotted sixteenth in the new metre. The surface rhythm continues at the level of the thirty-second note, in groups of nine, but without the designation "9" above the beams. Consequently, the surface rhythm continues at precisely the same pace. A single bar of 9/32 interrupts the running thirty-second notes, followed by a bar of 14/32 in which the thirty-seconds, now in groups of seven, continue at the same tempo. The final transition moves the metre to 2/4, with the double dotted eighth (equivalent to a single group of seven thirty-seconds) of the earlier metre becoming equal to a quarter note in the new metre. The surface rhythm again proceeds with running thirty-seconds, now designated with a "7" to indicate that seven of them occupy the space of eight in 2/4, or a single quarter note. Throughout this passage, all notes written as thirty-seconds share exactly the same duration.

All these techniques reveal a more flexible approach to rhythmic organization than one finds in the immediately preceding common practice period. Composers sought to avoid rigorous subdivisions through proportional notation and variable beaming, and move beyond the conventional duple and triple subdivisions of earlier music. Carter, with his metrical modulation, imposes a rigid logic on the relations between metres and the surface rhythms that articulate them while simultaneously making clear and unambiguous how one complex pattern of subdivisions moves precisely into another. All these techniques also require the performer to embrace new methods of conceptualizing musical time and present challenges in the precise realization of these relationships during performance.

Pitch

As I note above, composers from the early part of the twentieth century were exploring methods of dividing the semitone into smaller units, e.g., Charles Ives. Such experiments continued, as Penderecki's *Threnody* illustrates.[24] In his list of symbols at the beginning of the score, he gives signs that represent quarter-tones below and above a conventional pitch.[25] These differ from those used by Ives in his Fourth Symphony, as I indicate above. Penderecki also creates textures that depend on glissandi.[26] He specifies a beginning and ending pitch, and the rate at which the player

---

[24] See Read, *20th-Century Microtonal Notation*.
[25] Penderecki, *For the Victims of Hiroshima*, [p. 3].
[26] Penderecki, *For the Victims of Hiroshima*, e.g., bars 10–14, pp. 8–9.

should move from one to the other, via the proportional notation he uses and the timings he indicates for each bar at the bottom of the score. But the essence of the texture he is creating depends on the constantly moving pitches each player executes.

Aleatoric Notation

Composers devised new notations to incorporate into their compositions chance or improvisatory elements left to the discretion of the performer.[27] In *Available Forms 1*, Earle Brown combines conventional pitch notation with proportional notation to present the basic sonic materials of the piece to the players.[28] Brown cedes control of the content of the piece to the performers on two levels. First, he divides the piece into twenty-seven discrete sonic events over six pages. The conductor may ask the orchestra to play any of the events in any order. Second, although the composer indicates relative duration through the proportional notation, the actual rhythmic execution of the notes remains at the discretion of the player. Similarly, in event 5 on page 4, Brown specifies the melodic contour that three of the instruments are to execute, but not the precise pitches or rhythm, as he stipulates in his "Performance Note": "*Page 4, event 5, Trombone, Viola, Bass:* Relative contours through the respective registers. Pitch, duration, and timbre are the choice of the performers."[29]

Morton Feldman employs a more abstract form of notation in *Intersection 2*.[30] In place of conventional pitch or rhythmic notation, he presents a grid representing high, middle and low registers of the piano on the vertical axis and temporal units on the horizontal, 158 of which occupy one minute. Within each box, he stipulates the number of keys the performer should depress and indicates duration by the number of boxes linked together; many events last a single box. Pitch, rhythm and dynamics remain at the discretion of the performer. The composer alone, however, determines the order of the events, unlike Brown in *Available Forms 1*.

Karlheinz Stockhausen abandons all conventions in the complex notation he invented for *Plus Minus*.[31] He provides seven pairs of pages for up to seven players, and so the performance consists of up to seven layers, as

---

[27] See the essays published in Brinkmann, ed., *Improvisation und neue Musik*; and Sbordoni and Rostagno, eds., *Free Improvisation*; also Bailey, *Improvisation*, pp. 59–85; Feisst, *Der Begriff 'Improvisation'* and "Negotiating Freedom"; and Fox, "Opening Offer or Contractual Obligation?" pp. 11–19.
[28] E. Brown, *Available Forms 1*.   [29] E. Brown, *Available Forms 1*, inside back cover.
[30] Feldman, *Intersection 2*.   [31] Stockhausen, *Nr. 14: Plus Minus*.

he puts it, decided by the players.[32] Each pair of pages consists of one on which he has imposed a series of squares, each of which prescribes aspects of a single musical event, and a second on which appear two series of note complexes, the first numbered I–VII, thus in roman numerals, the second 1–6 in arabic numerals. The squares on the first page of each pair are to be executed in order.[33] Each square consists of a *Zentralklang*, to which the performer adds one or more *Akzidentien* in the same register as the *Zentralklang* but of indeterminate pitch, and *Nebennoten*.

Stockhausen stipulates seven combinations of *Akzidentien* and *Zentralklang* that each correspond to one of the seven note complexes identified by roman numerals on the note page.[34] He does not, however, specify which note complex corresponds to which combination, and so one infers that the performers make that decision. He does identify the *Nebennoten* by arabic numerals, and so they correspond to one of the note complexes thus identified on the note page. These features specify the pitch content of each musical event. The composer uses two methods to stipulate the rhythmic delivery: the duration of the *Akzidentien* through the shape of the sign assigned and the speed of the *Nebennoten* by a line or arrow drawn through the symbol.[35]

Performers modify the number of *Akzidentien* and *Zentralklänge* in an event according to positive and negative quantities indicated in a flag attached to the symbol for the *Zentralklang*.[36] The reckoning is cumulative; i.e., subsequent flags modify the number of *Akzidentien* and *Zentralklänge* already established. Other symbols affect changes in register, dynamics and duration; rests; methods of sound production; substitution of individual musical events; coordination of the layers, if the performers undertake more than one; and the substitution of pitches from another layer. The extraordinary complexity of the notation required the composer to supply detailed instructions, running to more than five pages.[37]

Any performance that would respect all the nuances Stockhausen supplies would demand an enormous amount of study and rehearsal on the part of the performers (or, as Christopher Fox puts it, "the days needed to convert the Stockhausen [i.e., *Plus Minus*] into notations from which the musicians can actually play").[38] And that amount of preparation would restrict the degree of

---

[32.] Stockhausen, *Nr. 14: Plus Minus*, score p. 11 no. 2.
[33.] Stockhausen, *Nr. 14: Plus Minus*, score p. 11 no. 5.
[34.] Stockhausen, *Nr. 14: Plus Minus*, score p. 11 nos. 6–7.
[35.] Stockhausen, *Nr. 14: Plus Minus*, score p. 11 no. 5.
[36.] Stockhausen, *Nr. 14: Plus Minus*, score pp. 11–12 nos. 8–16.
[37.] Stockhausen, *Nr. 14: Plus Minus*, score pp. 5–10 (German), 11–16 (English).
[38.] Fox, "Opening Offer or Contractual Obligation?" p. 12.

spontaneity the performers might be able to lend the performance. I find these circumstances ironic in view of a statement Stockhausen made just a few years before the publication of *Plus Minus* regarding improvisation and spontaneity: "was man heute noch—zum Beispiel im Jazz—Improvisation nennt, ist kaum noch spontane Erfindung musikalischer Gedanken, vielmehr Reproduktion auswendig gelernter Klischees" ("what one even today calls improvisation – in jazz, for example – is hardly still spontaneous invention of musical ideas, but rather the reproduction of clichés learned by rote").[39] Musicians undertaking a performance of *Plus Minus* might not engage in the reproduction of clichés, but they would certainly find it difficult to instill any sense of spontaneity in their reactions to Stockhausen's complex notation.

Stockhausen significantly simplifies the notation for *Spiral*, a later piece that also invites performers to improvise but leaves to them much more discretion.[40] Each system in the score presents four horizontal lines of symbols, assigned to duration, register, dynamics and rhythmic segmentation as decided by the performer; i.e., the performer could choose to assign the top line to any of the four aspects.[41] Stockhausen provides a limited range of symbols and most concern increasing the particular aspect of performance, decreasing it, or keeping it the same, indicated by plus, minus and equal signs.[42] By using fewer and much less complex symbols, Stockhausen materially cedes control of much of the musical substance, especially pitch and rhythm, to the discretion of the performer, who in turn plays a much greater role in determining the specific musical events that constitute it.

These four pieces by Brown, Feldman and especially the two by Stockhausen provide a metaphor for the interaction between the composer and notation in the twentieth century. All four composers struggle with creating the correct balance between determining the course of the piece themselves and leaving it to the discretion of the performers, and notation is the plane on which the contest takes place. A major site of contestation lies in the question of whether to use conventional forms of notation, which the composers then adapt, as in the case of Brown, or to invent new symbols or systems of symbols, as Feldman and Stockhausen do.

Conventional notation, of course, brings with it a good deal of semiotic baggage, no matter how the composer attempts to adapt it, and new symbols, besides whatever semiotic codes they invoke, present the

---

[39] Stockhausen, "Musik und Graphik," p. 5; see also pp. 18–22 for the interaction between notation and improvisation and the resulting "ambiguous" notations ("vieldeutig"), p. 19.
[40] Stockhausen, *Nr. 27: Spiral*. [41] Stockhausen, *Nr. 27: Spiral*, p. 11.
[42] Stockhausen, *Nr. 27: Spiral*, pp. 11–12.

disadvantage of unfamiliarity to the performer, hence necessitating the extensive instructions Berio, Penderecki and Stockhausen supply. And although they allow the composer to explore new techniques and sounds, the study they require on the part of the performers challenges the quality of spontaneity they might be able to apply especially when the piece envisages improvisation, as in Stockhausen's *Plus Minus*. And so composers always run the risk that by trying to impose yet more control on the performance, they might jeopardize that control through issues that arise in the notation.

The Tension between Composition and Performance, and Notational Innovation

The Tyranny of the Composer

> The fact that art-music has been written down instead of improvised has divided musical creators and executants into two quite separate classes; the former autocratic and the latter comparatively slavish. It has grown to be an important part of the office of the modern composer to leave as few loopholes as possible in his works for the idiosyncrasies of the performer. The considerable increase of exactness in our modes of notation and tempo and expression marks has all been directed toward this end, and though the state of things obtaining among trained musicians for several centuries has been productive of isolated geniuses of an exceptional greatness unthinkable under primitive conditions, it seems to me that it has done so at the expense of the artistry of millions of performers, and to the destruction of natural sympathy and understanding between them and the creative giants.[43]

So wrote Percy Grainger a century ago in the first volume of *The Musical Quarterly*. Apart from any other aspect of this striking passage, I find it remarkable that he uses the term "executant" to classify the person we would normally call "performer," precisely the linguistic turn Igor Stravinsky employed several decades later in his *Poetics*.[44] But Grainger, already in the second decade of the last century, was diagnosing a circumstance that increasingly defined the relationship between

---

[43] Grainger, "The Impress of Personality," p. 428.
[44] The last of the Charles Eliot Norton Lectures, which Stravinsky delivered at Harvard University in 1939–40, is entitled "Performance," Strawinsky, *Poétique musicale*, pp. 82–92; tellingly, he uses the French "exécutant" in place of the usual word, "interprète"; see Grier, "Authority of the Composer," p. 21.

composer, performer and notation, a circumstance that I address above.[45] Notation, however, is not a neutral force in this relationship, a simple conduit to facilitate communication between composer and performer. By its very existence, it stimulates composers to seek ways to create meanings through writing and its constituent symbols. Some of those meanings reflect the realities of performance; others, the composers' zeal for innovation.

The history of musical notation in the West presents a complex narrative that reflects the ongoing interaction between performance and composition. Musicians needed to communicate performing nuances already in use, but composers felt compelled to seek control over aspects of performance as part of their compositional resource and to supplement that resource by devising and demanding new techniques that required new symbols to represent them. The original impulse to record music in writing arose from the perceived need by Carolingian musicians to specify precisely where performance nuances should occur, as I discuss in Chapter 2. The Frankish singers whom the three successive rulers Pippin, Charlemagne and Louis the Pious required to learn the Roman repertories of chant and the performing nuances that characterized them, instead of the Gallican chants then in use, had difficulty in executing those nuances. The notation they invented at least told them where the nuances should occur.

Subsequently, performers and scribes collaborated to devise conventions that accurately recorded pitch and rhythm. Their purpose was largely the preservation of existing repertories, but already two of the early innovators in pitch notation were simultaneously composers. In the early tenth century, Hucbald of Saint Amand, who composed an Office for Saint Peter and other works, advocated the complementary use of neumes for performing nuances, and literal notation for accurate pitch information. A century later, Adémar de Chabannes inscribed the earliest surviving practical sources with accurate relative pitch information, and used the technique to record his new compositions for the liturgies of Saint Martial and his companions. In many ways, these notational developments reflect the simple fact that during much of the Middle Ages, the church and its clergy controlled the technology of writing. By attempting to fix in notation at least some aspects of the music that formed such an integral part of their

---

[45.] See also Stockhausen, "Musik und Graphik," pp. 5–13; Fox, "Opening Offer or Contractual Obligation?", offers a more collegial and collaborative view of this relationship.

liturgical ceremonies, they were extending this control to notational representations of musical sound.

Secure rhythmic notation first occurs in works of the late twelfth and early thirteenth centuries from the cathedral of Notre-Dame in Paris, whose composers included Leoninus and Perotinus. Fixed rhythms occur in two contexts. First, in two-voice organum, both voices move rhythmically where the tenor, singing the plainchant on which the piece is based, encounters melismatic writing. This practice might have arisen in the extemporaneous performance of these pieces, whence it may have entered the musical vocabulary of composers working in the genre. Second, the upper voices of three- and four-voice organum needed rhythmic coordination for their successful performance. This circumstance places the implementation of rhythmic notation squarely in the purview of the composer as part of the compositional planning of the piece.

Franco of Cologne, who records the shift from modal to mensural notation toward the end of the thirteenth century, may have simply been acknowledging innovations introduced by contemporary composers of the motet. In contrast to the melismatic upper voices of liturgical organa, motets evince a largely syllabic texture. Consequently, the ligatures that scribes use for melismatic textures and on which modal notation depends cannot serve for syllabic writing. Composers and scribes, then, needed to confer rhythmic meaning on the individual symbols used for the new motet textures. Franco codifies these developments in his treatise. Still, throughout this period, the barrier between singing and composing remains permeable, as in the example of Petrus de Cruce, whose subtle rhythmic notation may reflect his own virtuosic vocal technique.

To this point, the end of the thirteenth century, I detect a delicate relationship between performance and composition as the motivating factor for introducing notational innovations. Some seem to arise from the practice of performance; others, from compositional initiative. A change in the balance seems to take place, however, around the turn of the fourteenth century, and a new group of musicians, the theorists, make a material contribution to the debate. We ought to remember at this point that all three of these activities, performing, composing and writing music theory, could very well have been practised by the same individual, although it would seem that those respective tasks were becoming increasingly differentiated.

We know that composers of this era were becoming more conscious of their position in musical society and indeed society in general as creative artists. I adduce as evidence of this awareness the manuscripts in which first Adam de la Halle around the turn of the fourteenth century and then later, at the mid-point of the century, Guillaume de Machaut collected their works, musical and poetic, in manuscripts produced under their personal direction.[46] Those who commissioned or received manuscripts of Machaut's work included members of the French royal family and aristocracy. I would aver that composers such as Adam and Machaut, by preparing these manuscripts, were asserting their place in the decision-making process and, by extension, control over the notation that would define the sequence of musical events that constitute a piece. In Charles Seeger's term, they were reaching the point of imposing prescriptive notation on those who would perform (or read) their musical works.

One aspect of that control resided in the rhythmic organization of the music. The system, with its logical arrangement of two or three strata in each of which one could employ duple or triple division, suggests a level of control that emerges from the notation itself, from the system of symbols devised to communicate it. When those symbols are combined with the refinements that syncopation, coloration and proportion provide, the entire system offers a range of flexibility characteristic of detached compositional planning instead of the spontaneity of performance. Simultaneously, we must not underestimate the contributions of the music theorists to these developments, on whose writings, as I show in Chapter 3, we depend for our knowledge of the system. As in the case of Franco of Cologne, I suspect that Johannes de Muris and the author or authors of the texts associated with Philippe de Vitry codified the practices they saw in operation among contemporary composers, including Vitry himself.

As composers came to assume increasing control over notation as part of the process of composing, the imposition of musical notation on the page came to be identified with the act of composition, and notational innovation became, for many, a central part of the creative act. But control flowed by no means in one direction only, although the discernible trend, from ca. 1300 to the present, demonstrates that composers gradually abrogated more of it to themselves. Performers took, or were granted, greater or lesser discretion over a number of aspects of the musical work over time. For example, throughout the seventeenth and eighteenth centuries, composers tended to give simple

---

[46] Adam de la Halle, Pa 25566; see Everist, "The Polyphonic *Rondeau c.* 1300." Several manuscripts that contain Machaut's collected works were produced during his lifetime, of which I cite Pa 1584 in Chapter 3; see Earp, "Machaut's Role"; and Leach, "Machaut's First Single-Author Compilation."

dynamic instructions without indicating any nuances. No performer would deliver every note of a phrase marked f, say, at precisely the same dynamic level, but the composers gave no instructions for modulating the dynamic in the course of the phrase, leaving it to convention and the discretion of the performer.

Similarly, during the same period, aspects of an accompanying part played on a chording instrument remained at the discretion of the performer, as the composer sketched out the part with figured bass notation. And equally, soloists took the initiative to ornament their parts on the basis of the melodic material provided by the composer. In a more formal sense, some composers ceded control over aspects of the performance to the performer by means of aleatoric elements in the notation, as I discuss above, although sometimes the opportunity for spontaneity in the act of performance encountered barriers in the very nature of the notation. Although the balance has consistently tipped in favour of the composer in Western music over the last centuries, a degree of tension between composer and performer exists, even when the same person fulfills both roles. Stravinsky, as I discuss above, in performing some of his own works, ignored the very specific instructions he included in his scores because of the exigencies of performance, the clearest possible indication of the separation of the two acts in modernist musical practice despite the best efforts of Stravinsky himself to limit the options of performers, or executants, as he preferred.

The realities and limitations of notation in the most recent times are perhaps coming to a head in the widespread use of computer-based notational programs, their benefits and their restrictions as they increasingly dominate written manifestations of music. Christopher Fox outlines some of the problems in the concluding paragraph of his challenging essay on the function of notation in the modern era.

Yet the widespread availability of composer notation packages has made composers today, and perhaps young composers especially, far less likely to practise notational innovation and far more likely to believe that there is a simple equivalence between the score and the music. Programs like Finale and Sibelius have had an insidious influence on composers' imaginations: why try to imagine music that will be awkward to notate on the computer? Why think about the sounds of real instruments or the behaviour of real musicians when a key stroke will start and stop the playback of the notes on the screen? It is a paradox of contemporary musical life that computer typeset scores are legible but do not read well. The conservatism imposed by the default settings of notation software is probably only temporary, however, and I remain optimistic that the resurgence of interest in different ways of thinking about notation which is so evident in the work of younger composers like Molitor and Lely and the musicians of Apartment House will continue and flourish.[47]

The technology Fox describes is new, but the problems he enunciates are not. Musical notation is a technology itself that has developed and continues to develop in response to the push and pull of communication between composer and performer. The dynamic Fox describes in respect to the use of computer technology differs not at all from the professional and cultural striving that resulted in the invention of neumatic notation in the ninth century. Musical sounds and their translation to and from writing continually pose challenges to musicians who in turn refuse to yield to them but always seek new solutions in response that in turn inspire new musical challenges.

---

[47]. Fox, "Opening Offer or Contractual Obligation?" p. 19.

Coda: The Meaning of Musical Literacy

From its inception in the medieval West, musical notation constituted a complex system of visual communication that required extensive and specialized knowledge of the musical practices it attempted to depict along with a fine visual discrimination and apprehension of the symbols, to translate them from symbol to sound. Consequently, musical literacy has remained, since its introduction, the exclusive product of professional training at a high level, and, in some areas of musical practice, an indispensable credential for achieving professional status. Yet, this system simultaneously exerts enabling and limiting forces on musical practice. Obviously, a musician separated by distance and time from the creation of a musical work is able to read, study and perform it through the efficacy of notation and literacy. The ability to execute these tasks depends on the musician's competency in musical literacy as well as her or his knowledge of the notation and musical style of the work, strictly historical considerations.

At the same time, Western notation imposes limits on musical practice. First, it establishes a relatively rigid grid of temporal and pitch events in comparison with musical practices in many other cultures. The customary duple and triple divisions and subdivisions of durations in combination with conventional metrical shapes create a rhythmic framework that privileges regularity over flexibility, Stravinsky's "tyranny of the bar." Modifications to that framework, such as tempo rubato, accelerando and ritardando, or Elliott Carter's metrical modulations, provide some variability, but always through violation of the standard, regular progression of rhythm and metre. Proportional notation, a twentieth-century innovation, seeks to avoid this tyranny, but it usually fails precisely because it contradicts the prevailing practice.

Pitch, too, is relatively fixed, in part because of the widespread use of keyboard and pre-tuned percussion instruments that depend on equal temperament for their practical employment. But the limits in flexibility are not restricted to such matters as the tuning of the ostensibly enharmonic equivalents G♯ and A♭ when used as tendency tones in a tonal context. These limits include the alteration in pitch for expressive effect, as

Gershwin attempts in the clarinet passage with which *Rhapsody in Blue* opens. Some twentieth-century composers have experimented with microtonal notations, but, as in the case of proportional notation, these processes operate in opposition to well-established conventions in Western musical practice, some of which are predicated on the very nature of the notation.

A more significant problem, I believe, is the limitations that notation imposes on the extemporaneous determination of many aspects of performance in the act and at the time of performance, what some might call expressivity. I would locate an acceleration of those limits in the period since 1900, largely under the influence of first Wagner's posthumous impact on aspects of performance and interpretation and afterwards Stravinsky's approach to the same two acts.[1] That their attitudes came to dominate much of the thinking about the distinction between composition and performance led directly to the exponential increase in notational complexity over the last century without, on the one hand, making an appreciable difference in the precision with which composers communicate their instructions to performers, while at the same time, on the other hand, significantly limiting the performer's freedom to express.

Karlheinz Stockhausen places this acceleration in notational complexity in the context of the separation of performing, reading and listening.[2] In response to contemporary attitudes among musicians, both composers and performers, regarding the use of notation, he observes that the division between notation and the sounds it is intended to represent has led to the development of "read" music ("*gelesene Musik*").[3] The artistic use of graphemes that are not directly connected to sound has facilitated this development, which in turn, constitutes a completely different musical experience from listening. For example, the eye is free to move backward and forward through a score, free of the temporal restraints of the unfolding of successive musical events in a performance taking place in real time. Stockhausen remains confident, however, that, as the meaning of new symbols obtains clarification, reading and hearing will continue to work together collaboratively, what music psychologists have defined as audiation.[4]

The investigation of the mechanics and function of musical literacy is essentially historical in nature. The musicians and scribes who devised and used these notations worked in a particular historical, artistic, cultural,

---

[1.] For a summary of their approach, see Grier, "Authority of the Composer."
[2.] Stockhausen, "Musik und Graphik," pp. 13–25.
[3.] Stockhausen, "Musik und Graphik," p. 13 (Stockhausen's italics).
[4.] Stockhausen, "Musik und Graphik," pp. 22–24.

political and economic context that profoundly affected the way they practised music and the role that notation fulfilled in those musical practices. Second, notation provides a powerful tool for the recording, preservation and communication of music. Although some of these systems have become quite complex, they never completely replace the oral/aural communication of music, which supplies its own powerful systems and processes for these purposes that work alongside written and literate processes in a potentially powerful symbiosis. Many musicians take the complexity of notation for granted. Typically, they have expended so much time and effort acquiring facility in musical literacy that they have internalized the multiple, complex and multiply complex processes, visual, cognitive and aural, that occur when they read a score or part. Happily, music psychologists, in the most recent literature, have adopted a sophisticated view of music reading that begins to take into account some of these complexities.

Unhappily, a large gulf still exists between those who view musical literacy as a *sine qua non* of musical ability, and those who recognize that oral/aural processes contribute meaningfully to the equation. I cite only one example to illustrate the lack of sympathy between these two views. The debate regarding oral and written processes in early plainsong that occupied a good deal of space in such places as the *Journal of the American Musicological Society* and *Early Music History* in the 1980s and 90s revealed quite inflexible positions on both sides. I summarize the most important contributions to that debate in Chapter 2. Those who advocated written transmission seemed to believe that, once musical notation appeared in the medieval West, whenever that occurred, oral/aural processes ceased to have any significant function, while the supporters of oral transmission seemed to underestimate, by a significant margin, the visual, written and literate processes that contributed to the creation of the musical documents on which they based their arguments.

In my own studies of this matrix of processes in Aquitanian music of the eleventh and twelfth centuries, I have attempted to isolate the ways in which visual and oral/aural processes participate in the copying procedures by which musicians/scribes create musical documents, and how they interact in cognition to generate the readings transmitted in those documents. I show, for example, how Adémar de Chabannes possessed an extraordinarily acute aural memory of the endless streams of untexted neumes that comprise the sequentia, the untexted sequence.[5] That memory allowed him to correct errors of pitch he had made in his first copy

---

[5.] Grier, *The Musical World*, pp. 182–200.

(written between mid-1027 and early 1028) when he came to write out all this music a second time, between mid-1028 and 3 August 1029. Still, he succumbed in both copies to a number of rather banal errors generated by visual confusion. Visual and oral processes therefore operate, sometimes in conflict, sometimes in collaboration, but always simultaneously in the course of copying music.

The following discussion considers musical literacy in its historical context. By musical literacy, I mean the visual comprehension of the musical document and its translation into sound, actual or internalized. I do not differentiate between sight-reading and the kind of music reading that occurs in study and practice, because I believe the same visual, cognitive and aural processes occur in both kinds of reading; where they differ, they do so in degree and not qualitatively. Similarly, reading that directly generates performance, that is, the direct translation from notation to sound, employs the same processes as internal reading or audiation. On the issue of historical context, it is true that musicians engaged in the performance of early music increasingly employ original performing materials and so replicate, in practical terms, the processes musicians of earlier eras may have employed in music reading, but I am aware of no overreaching discussion of how musical literacy operates on a theoretical or cognitive basis in history.

Psychologists of music who have studied the reading of modern notation all agree that efficient readers of music tend to group notes according to patterns, and the more familiar the patterns and the greater the number of patterns that the readers recognized quickly, the more efficient the reading.[6] I can think of no reason why skilled musicians of earlier eras, reading the typical notations of their day, would not have applied this elementary concept; in fact, many of the notational conventions practised in various eras and notational systems, such as ligation and grouping in medieval notations, and barring and beaming in modern, seem designed to exploit that very phenomenon.[7] Some might see circularity in the argument

---

[6.] For an overview of the phenomenon and its literature, see Sloboda, "Experimental Studies of Music Reading." Among the many more specialized studies, I found the following the most useful: Bean, "An Experimental Approach to the Reading of Music"; Lowery, "On Reading Music," esp. pp. 82–84; Sloboda, "The Eye-Hand Span," "Phrase Units" and "The Psychology of Music Reading"; Wolf, "A Cognitive Model"; Halpern and Bower, "Musical Expertise and Melodic Structure"; Waters, Townsend and Underwood, "Expertise in Musical Sight Reading"; Drai-Zerbib and Baccino, "L'expertise dans la lecture musicale"; and Zhukov, "Evaluating New Approaches."

[7.] For bar lines as a help or hindrance in reading, see Penttinen and Huovinen, "The Early Development of Sight-Reading Skills"; and Byo, "Effects of Barlines." On beaming, Sheldon, "Visual Representation of Music."

because becoming a skilled musician requires, in large part, the ability to recognize more musical patterns and more complex ones. Still, not all skilled musicians are efficient readers, and it is on that particular quality and the possible reasons for more efficient visual apprehension that this research focuses.

Further evidence emerges from the study of eye movements during music reading.[8] Physiologists classify eye movements as saccades, when the eyes move (progressions when they move left to right and regressions when right to left, according to the direction of reading in the West), or fixations, when they remain fixed on a point. The brain receives visual information only during fixations. Experiments show that skilled readers tend to use fewer fixations than the quantity of notes in a given passage, and that many of the fixations fall on the empty space between notes. Both these findings suggest that efficient readers apprehend more than one note in a single fixation, a result that complements that regarding musical perception to reinforce the idea that musicians group notes into patterns, first during visual processing and then cognitively.

Aural imagining of the music, or audiation, also contributes to efficient reading, as any musician would suspect.[9] Research in the brain functions stimulated by reading music indicates that those areas of the brain associated with visual processes are activated first, as one might anticipate, but those linked with auditory processes rapidly follow.[10] By forming an accurate aural image of the music in the mind, a skilled musician anticipates the upcoming phrase and the physical actions necessary for its

---

[8.] Recent research on the subject uses more sophisticated and less invasive technology, with the result that it provides more precise findings. For overviews, see Dunford, "Optometry and Music"; and Madell and Hébert, "Eye Movements and Music Reading." Among the specialized studies, see Goolsby, "Eye Movement in Music Reading" and "Profiles of Processing"; Truitt, Clifton, Pollatsek and Rayner, "The Perceptual Span"; Waters and Underwood, "Eye Movements"; Servant and Baccino, "Lire Beethoven"; Gilman and Underwood, "Restricting the Field of View"; and Drai-Zerbib, Baccino and Bigand, "Sight-Reading Expertise."

[9.] Lowery, "On Reading Music," pp. 84–85; Kornicke, "An Exploratory Study"; Waters et al., "Expertise in Musical Sight Reading"; Gillman [sic], Underwood and Morehen, "Recognition of Visually Presented Musical Intervals"; Brodsky, Henik, Rubinstein and Zorman, "Auditory Imagery"; Highben and Palmer, "Effects of Auditory and Motor Mental Practice"; Schön and Besson, "Visually Induced Auditory Expectancy"; Lee, "The Role of Inner Hearing"; Fine, Berry and Rosner, "The Effect of Pattern Recognition"; and Brodsky, Kessler, Rubinstein, Ginsborg and Henik, "The Mental Representation of Music Notation."

[10.] Sergent, Zuck, Terriah and MacDonald, "Distributed Neural Network"; Sergent, "Music, the Brain and Ravel," pp. 169a–170a; Nakada, Fujii, Suzuki and Kwee, "'Musical Brain'"; Schürmann, Raij, Fujiki and Hari, "Mind's Ear in a Musician"; Gunter, Schmidt and Besson, "Let's Face the Music"; Stewart, Walsh and Frith, "Reading Music"; and Yumoto, Matsuda, Itoh, Uno, Karino, Saitoh, Kaneko, Yatomi and Kaga, "Auditory Imagery."

successful execution. Again, more experienced and capable musicians command a greater repertory of patterns, which then facilitates accurate audiation.[11] And again, the circle of logic fractures at the intersection of musical ability and the reading faculty, which do not coincide in all individuals. All skilled musicians do not possess equal ability in audiation, and therefore familiarity alone with patterns does not lead inevitably to successful, accurate application of the skill. That requires the ability to translate the data from notation into sound, which equally depends on a well-trained ear. Three factors, therefore, contribute to efficient reading: the recognition of musical patterns, eye movements that grasp several notes in a single fixation and accurate audiation.

Let me now address issues in the complexity of musical notation, illustrated by a couple of examples to remind ourselves of some of the matters we take for granted. Figure Coda.1 shows the opening of the flute part of the finale of Poulenc's Sonata for Flute and Piano.[12] Most would agree that this is not the most complex example of notation available: single line of music (no multiphonics); title that gives the Italian character designation, from which we infer a tempo, reinforced by the metronome marking; clef and time signature without key signature as in much music of this period; and notation that consists of notes (providing pitch and rhythm), dynamics, articulation and the occasional ornament. Perhaps only the quantity of leger lines distinguishes this page from most other music, although no self-respecting flute player would admit it.

Still, the page presents a considerable amount of information that the player must process visually, cognitively and aurally in order to translate it into sound. Pitch information dictates fingerings and octave placement regulated by ear and lip; rhythms require the coordination of the durational values of note and rest; articulations translate into slurring and differing qualities of tonguing (percussive for the accents, short and crisp on the staccato notes); and dynamic differentiation as indicated, although the dynamics on this page remain unsubtle. Much of this occurs at a subconscious level. No experienced flute player, and no beginner would attempt this piece, needs to instruct her or his fingers to employ the appropriate fingering or embouchure to secure the correct octave placement for any of these notes.

[11.] Gordon, *Learning Sequences in Music*, pp. 3–25, presents a theory of audiation in which the recognition of patterns plays a central role.

[12.] Poulenc, *Sonata, Flute and Piano*, flute part, p. 6.

Figure Coda.1 Francis Poulenc, Sonata for Flute and Piano, third movement, p. 6 Sonata For Flute and Piano Composed by Francis Poulenc © Copyright 1958, 1992 Chester Music Limited. All Rights Reserved. International Copyright Secured. Used by Permission of Hal Leonard Europe Limited.

Moreover, an issue on which music psychologists all agree applies here, namely that experienced musicians, in reading, perceive structurally defined groups of notes as "chunks" of information instead of processing them one note at a time, and that they do so cognitively. The psychologists see analogies with reading text in that the individual notes and groups of notes form parallels with letters and words, respectively, and in the detection of patterns. So, despite the absence of a key signature, a knowledgeable flute player recognizes the melodic patterns of A major in the first line and a half, with a passing modulation to its dominant in the second half of line 2, and A major again, the movement's tonic, in line 3, leading to the firm cadence in A at rehearsal number 2. The psychologists would argue, and I would agree, that the cognitive recognition of these patterns facilitates the execution of some aspects of the performance at a more subconscious level, such as the employment of correct fingerings, familiar not just from long practice but also from long practice of A major and E major scales. So the notes function not as simple instructions for particular finger movements, but rather recognizable patterns of musical events that trigger the subconscious to place the fingers correctly.

Similarly, rhythms coalesce into patterns, particularly as this page does not present any special rhythmic complexities. And the repetition of patterns, melodic and rhythmic, further promotes the apprehension of groups. So, most experienced players would capitalize on the nearly exact repetition from the pickup to bar 5 in the first line, through bar 8 to perceive this passage as a single unit. The lack of repetition in the next four bars suggests that the player would perceptually and cognitively group in two-bar units, bars 9–10 (aided by the melodic sequence in these bars) and 11–12. These three groups, from the pickup to bar 5 through bar 12, define themselves musically through melodic and rhythmic gesture, and these structural limits find reinforcement in the physical limits of rests and bar lines.

Thomas Goolsby, in a sophisticated study of eye movement during music reading, shows that more competent readers habitually look beyond certain physical limits, such as the end of a line.[13] Thus, experienced flutists, having apprehended bars 5–8 as a single unit, probably look ahead to the new passage in bars 9–10 before they finish playing bar 8. Moreover, they use rests to look ahead.[14] During the three-plus bars of rest

---

[13] Goolsby, "Profiles of Processing," esp. p. 116.
[14] Goolsby, "Profiles of Processing," employed examples that did not include any rests during or between phrases, but his examples did feature some long notes, and his more experienced

from the end of line 2 to the beginning of line 3, our proficient flute player has probably absorbed the passage up to rehearsal number 2. Goolsby also suggests that experienced players use their peripheral vision for certain notational features. He could not detect a fixation of the eye on dynamic indications, for example, although his subjects implemented them in their performances and therefore clearly saw them.[15]

So, we see that even a single line of music like this one poses certain visual and cognitive problems that move music reading significantly beyond reading text in complexity because the musician must coordinate several different types of visual information simultaneously for a successful performance. Of course, skilled musicians regulate all the information they receive visually and process cognitively with their sense of hearing to ascertain they are performing pitches, rhythms, dynamics, articulation and expression correctly. These problems become more complex when we consider vocal music, which adds the sung, literary text to the visual stimulus; potentially polyphonic instruments like plucked or bowed string instruments; and keyboard instruments, which conventionally play polyphony written on two or three staves. Reading an ensemble score further increases the problems of apprehension but, because the principal purpose of such a score is either study or in the case of a large ensemble, reference for a conductor, the reader in neither case directly translates the music into sound by singing or playing an instrument.

The conductor in performance does engage in physical gestures to lead the ensemble, gestures in direct response to the visual information presented in the score and the cognitive processes she or he employs to interpret it. This type of reading, therefore, differs only in degree and not in substance from the kind of reading a singer or player uses. A skilled conductor follows several lines of music simultaneously, reading a variety of clefs and parts for transposing instruments, as well as dynamics, articulations, expressive marks and other indications. There are limits, however, on the number of lines even the most prodigious conductor can follow, and some composers feel obliged to call the conductor's attention to specific parts within the score.

On this page from the second of Schoenberg's *Five Pieces for Orchestra*, Opus 16, the composer or printer has added majuscule *H* or *N* with a square bracket to designate, respectively, *Hauptstimme* or *Nebenstimme*, principal or secondary voice.[16] Such signs occur frequently in Schoenberg, although

---

subjects used the long notes to look ahead, pp. 113–15 and 121, just as I am suggesting that readers of the Poulenc flute part might use rests for this purpose.

[15] Goolsby, "Profiles of Processing," pp. 115–16.

[16] Schoenberg, *Five Pieces for Orchestra*, p. 26.

these ones appear to be second thoughts. In the first printed edition, 1912, a few brackets occur in the fifth piece only, without the *H* or *N*.[17] Those on this page were added to this edition, revised by the composer for reduced orchestra in 1949 and first printed in 1952. A note by Richard Hoffmann, dated June 1952, explains: "Metronome markings, numbered measures, and principal and secondary voice indications were likewise added so that rehearsal time might be reduced considerably and the actual performance be as faithful a realization of the composer's intentions as possible."[18] I would also note that, although the instruction at the beginning of the third piece reads in part, "There are no motivs in this piece which have to be brought to the fore," passages throughout are marked *Hauptstimme*.[19]

The application of the procedure from the perspective of the conductor is simple enough. For example, the *Hauptstimme* continues in the first violins from the previous page, although it never receives a closing bracket either on this page or subsequently. Schoenberg then marks the doubling in the second violins and the oboes. To this point, then, with the exception of omitting the closing bracket in the first violins, the procedure is clear. Schoenberg's treatment of the *Nebenstimmen*, however, requires some discussion. First, he designates the contrapuntal use of motivic material from the *Hauptstimme* in second bassoon and second, third and fourth horns as *Nebenstimme*, to which he adds the English horn in the next bar. Again, because of the motivic relations between this voice and the *Hauptstimme*, Schoenberg's reasoning seems quite clear.

Simultaneously, Schoenberg also marks the long-note gesture doubled in first piccolo, flute and clarinet as *Nebenstimme*, but not, curiously enough, its further doubling in the xylophone. The rhythmic diminution of this idea then appears in first and second trombones, also designated *Nebenstimme* and overlapping with the other two *Nebenstimmen* just mentioned. Again, a doubling, this time in the third trombone at the octave below, is not marked. So, whereas Schoenberg meticulously indicates all the doublings of the *Hauptstimme* as they enter and depart, he has omitted, either by oversight or design, at least two doublings of designated *Nebenstimmen*. If we are to understand the latter interpretation, then these voices should form part of the background accompaniment, and simply provide support for the marked voices they double, but the inconsistency is remarkable.

[17.] Schönberg, *Fünf Orchesterstücke, Opus 16*.
[18.] Schoenberg, "Explanatory Notes," *Five Pieces for Orchestra*, unnumbered page.
[19.] Schoenberg, *Five Pieces for Orchestra*, p. 31.

Figure Coda.2 Arnold Schoenberg, *Five Pieces for Orchestra*, Opus 16, no. 2, p. 26
Five Pieces for Orchestra, Opus 16 by Arnold Schoenberg © Copyright 1952 by Henmar Press Inc. Used by permission C.F. Peters Corporation. All Rights Reserved.

What remains in this dense contrapuntal texture to comprise the background? Quite a bit, actually, such as the active inner voice in second piccolo and flute, the motivic interchange between second clarinet and first bassoon, also rhythmically active, and another active inner voice in the violas and cellos, as well as the figuration in the harp and celeste. Some conductors would welcome the guidance Schoenberg offers through this dense and complex score, to expedite and facilitate their own literate consumption of it as well as to reduce rehearsal time as Hoffmann advocates. Others will find Schoenberg's designations arbitrary, particularly those of the *Nebenstimmen*, and wonder why some voices merit it and others do not. These ambiguities, then, might impede the musical literacy of those conductors.

Other composers, or their publishers, simplify the visual layout of the score by deleting the staves of instruments that rest, even within the system. Figure Coda.3 reproduces a page from Stravinsky's Huxley Variations, showing how he or Boosey & Hawkes has treated rests.[20] I chose this page because the printer interrupts the oboe, horn, harp, piano and string parts instead of showing three bars' rest in the conventional manner. Stravinsky and Schoenberg, by adopting these strategies of presentation, acknowledge the complexity of their scores, and therefore use enhanced visual information to guide the conductor. To be sure, Schoenberg has intervened more actively to designate those lines of the first and second importance, while Stravinsky, perhaps atypically for him, has assumed a more passive posture, uncluttering the score by removing silent parts, but each directs the conductor's eye.

These examples remind us of the complex range of processes that comprise the action of reading music, even when confronted by a relatively straightforward passage like the page from Poulenc's Flute Sonata. Eye, mind and ear interact to process and interpret the visual inputs and translate them into sound. These considerations will serve to illuminate issues of literacy that musicians of other eras may have faced when they tackled the musical notations most familiar to them. I close with one example of early medieval neumatic notation to illustrate what kind of reaction from literate musicians that style of notation would evoke.

This page from SG 359, the tenth-century chant manuscript, shows the end of the Mass for the First Sunday of Advent and the beginning of the Mass for Saint Lucy. The Alleluia for Advent Sunday, with verse *Ostende nobis*, illustrates the challenges that await the musically literate reader. As I discuss in Chapter 2, the morphology of the neumes indicates melodic direction and the number of notes. The *uirga* and *punctum* designate a single note, the former a note higher than the preceding note, the latter lower. Ligatures, like the *cliuis* and *podatus*, both binary neumes, and the *porrectus*, which designates three notes of which the middle note is the lowest, indicate that their constituent notes set a single syllable of text. This

---

[20] Stravinsky, *Variations, Aldous Huxley in Memoriam*, p. 16.

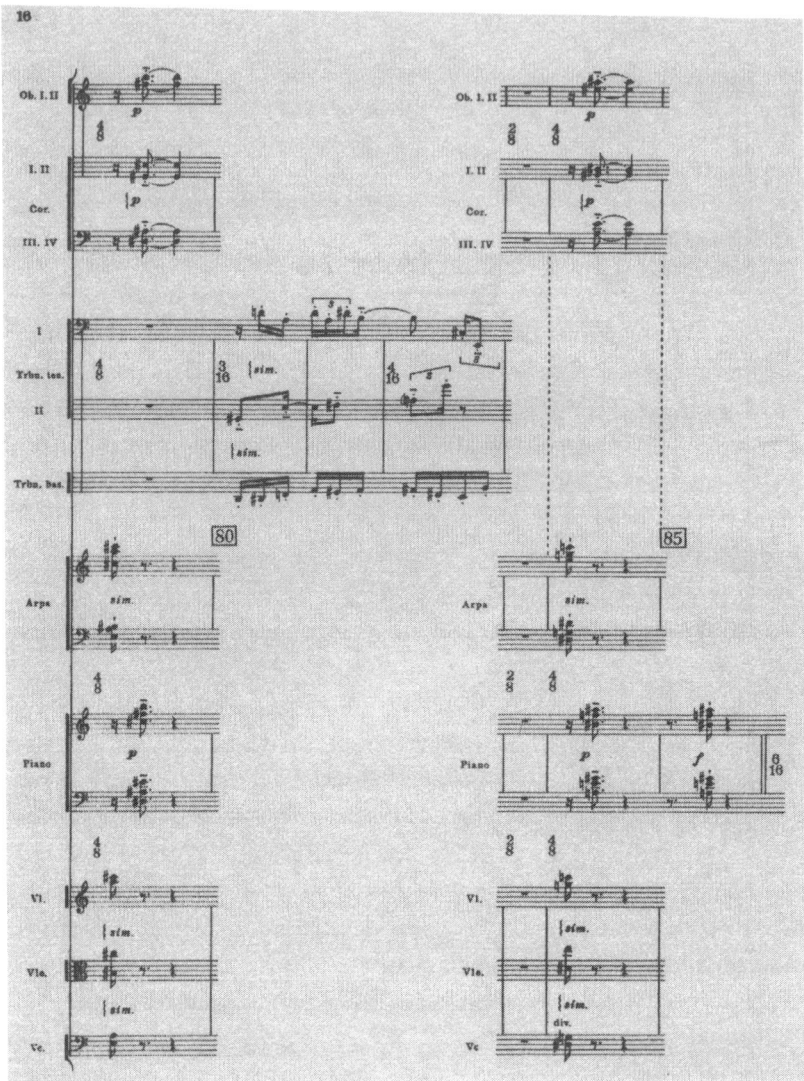

Figure Coda.3 Igor Stravinsky, *Variations, Aldous Huxley in Memoriam*, p. 16
"Variations: Aldous Huxley in Memoriam" by Igor Stravinsky © 1965 by Boosey & Hawkes Music Publishers Limited. All Rights Reserved. Used With Permission.

dialect also combines neumes to create longer groups, such as the *uirga* with two *puncta* or the *podatus* with two *puncta* to form groups of three and four notes, respectively.

So, these formations use ligation and grouping to show the singer which notes are to be sung for each syllable of text. The setting of the phrase "et

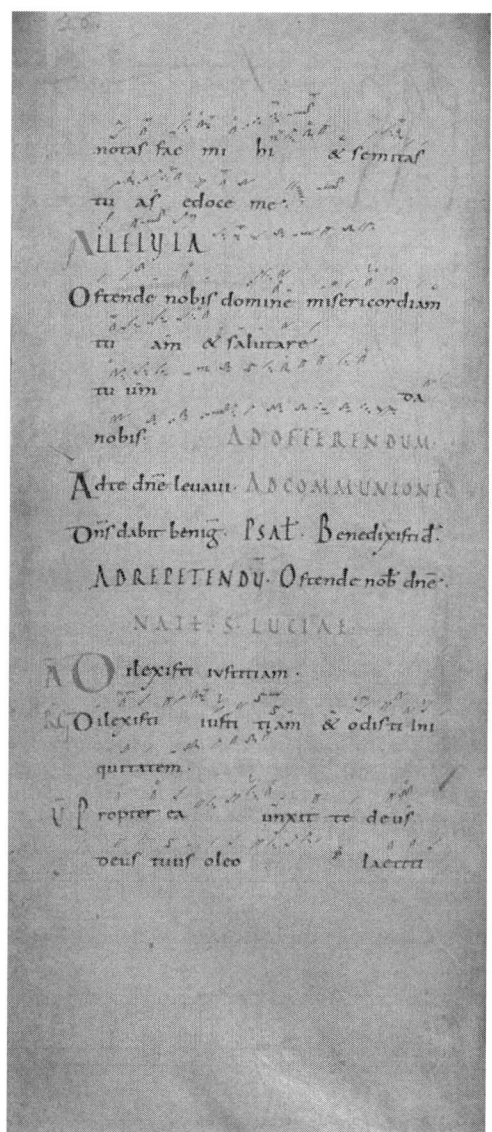

Figure Coda.4 SG 359, p. 26
Courtesy of Saint Gall, Stiftsbibliothek.

salutare" illustrates the technique, as the monosyllabic "et" and the first two and final syllables of "salutare" each receive a single note, while the accented penultimate syllable has three, as the ligated *porrectus* unequivocally shows. In three places, the text scribe, who worked first and wrote in a darker ink than the music scribe, has left insufficient horizontal space for the melody: "domine," "tuam" and "tuum." He shares this tendency with the scribe of Char 47, as I discuss in Chapter 2. In each case, the music scribe has continued the music upwards and to the right, creating space below the line of neumes for the musical setting of the subsequent syllables or syllable. He has thus used the two-dimensional space in a creative way to maintain the integrity of this aspect of the musical notation, namely the clear designation of the musical setting for each syllable of text.

The scribe also provides supplementary information about the execution of the melody in the form of ornaments, aids for declamation, and some details about the speed and duration of notes. Among the most common ornaments in plainsong is the *quilisma*, defined by medieval music theorists as a turning or tremulous movement, and so a purely melodic decoration. Three examples occur in the Alleluia: above the second syllable of "Alleluia," in the melisma on the final syllable of the same word, and in the verse on the final syllable of "nobis," all clearly marked by its distinctive neume. Scribes and singers employed liquescents, comprising two notes, the first sung full voice on the vowel and the second as a semi-vocal note, to assist in the declamation of certain combinations of letters. A descending liquescent, or *cephalicus*, occurs on the first syllable of "Alleluia" to facilitate the pronunciation of the double consonant between the first two vowels, while an ascending one, an *eptaphonus*, appears on the final syllable of "misericordiam" to aid the enunciation of the final consonant *m* before the next word, "tuam."

Two devices indicate speed and duration. The *tractulus*, a short horizontal line added to a neume, indicates that the singer should lengthen the note. Several examples occur in this Alleluia; those in the refrain appear on the *cliuis* and the *quilisma* above the second syllable of "Alleluia" and again on a *cliuis* on its final syllable. The scribe has also added *litterae significatiuae* or significative letters, which affect virtually every aspect of the performance. Most common here are the letters *t* (on the final syllable of "Alleluia" and the first of "tuam") and *c* (on the first syllable of "nobis," and three times on the first of "tuum"), which mean "tenere" or "trahere" (to hold or to draw out) and "celeriter" (quickly), and so longer and shorter notes, respectively. Modern palaeographers remain uncertain about the precise significance of these symbols. For example, do they pertain to the entire neume or a single note within the neume? And does the *tractulus* differ in nature from the *littera significatiua t*, for example, when either is applied to a *cliuis*? Knowledgeable tenth-century singers did not share our uncertainties, of course, and would use these indications for guidance in the execution of the chant.

We turn now to the information these neumes communicate to us regarding the pitch or intervallic content of the chant, and it is slim. As I mention above, they do show melodic direction, but principally within the neume itself, and not between neumes. For example, the verse begins with two *uirgae*, the first of which shows that it is higher than the last note of refrain. But what is the relationship between the first and second notes? On the basis of the neumes alone, the second note could either lie above the first note or stand in unison with it; if the former, there is no indication of how large an interval separates them. But the problems continue with the very next neume, completing the setting of the second syllable of "Ostende." The neume's shape identifies it as a *torculus*, a ternary neume in which the middle note is the highest. But, not only do we not know the neume's constituent intervals, we also do not know whether its first note lies above, below or at the same pitch as the preceding *uirga*, never mind what the interval might be if not a unison.

In one place, the notation does give specific relative pitch information, between the first and second syllables of "misericordiam," where the music scribe has written the *littera significatiua e*, meaning "equaliter" or unison, signifying that the *punctum* on the first syllable and the *uirga* on the second indicate the same pitch, counterintuitively, of course, because a *uirga* ought to mean that its note stands higher than the preceding note. On the next neume, the *cliuis* on the third syllable of "misericordiam," beside the letter *c* for "celeriter," the scribe has written the letter *l*, meaning "leuare," raise. Some scholars believe that this refers to pitch, and so the first note of the *cliuis* should be higher than the preceding *uirga*. Scribes more often use the letter *a* or the abbreviation "alt," meaning "altius" or higher, to indicate pitch, and the letter *l* here may well mean raise in the sense of emphasize, perhaps by accent or volume.

So, the notation provides firm indication of melodic direction only within the neume and not between neumes, and the scribe supplies a single *littera significatiua* that specifies a relative pitch relationship. A very thin harvest, indeed. Scribes of this era had at their disposal two means of showing pitch relationships with greater accuracy: palaeofrankish notation can (but sometimes does not) indicate intervallic or relative pitch information accurately by their placement on the vertical axis of writing, while dasian notation provides firm absolute pitch information through its distinctive symbols. The scribe of this manuscript, therefore, used neumatic, non-pitched notation by choice, probably driven by convention.

How did a knowledgeable tenth-century singer go about reading this notation? We can assume that he possessed unambiguous knowledge of two aspects of the piece: the pitch content from long exposure to the melody as an observer and participant in the liturgy, and the text, which is psalmodic, from long study of the Bible, particularly the psalter. The text scribe has provided a full text to show unequivocally what part of the psalm functions as the text of the chant. Beyond that indication, this notation specifies two other aspects of the piece in more detail than any other: the relationship between text and music, and the application of melodic ornaments and nuances. The first, in conjunction with the information about melodic direction, serves as a mnemonic to remind the singer of the precise course of the chant. The second, the indications of ornaments and nuances, responds to a perceived difficulty Frankish singers encountered in adopting Roman chant and, more important, Roman styles of singing, as I discuss in Chapter 2. The solution, I believe, involved the invention of notation principally to indicate where the nuances, so difficult for the Frankish singers to execute, should occur.

So, the singer would begin by identifying a reasonable "chunk" of music for visual apprehension. In the first instance, the text, where present, would define the chunk. Some chunks would consist of a group of words, perhaps "Ostende nobis" at the beginning of the verse or "et salutare" at the end of the second line; some would comprise a single word, such as "domine" or "da," isolated between two lengthy melismata. This particular chant provides no good example of an instance where the singer might proceed one syllable at a time, but there are four obvious places, the melismata at the end of "Alleluia," on the first syllables of "tuam" and "tuum," and the final syllable of "nobis," where he would break the melisma into its constituent musical components. The music scribe suggests where some of those breaks might occur through the horizontal spacing of the neumes.

Once the singer has visually absorbed the chunk of information, the cognitive processes that ensue differ slightly from those of the flute player reading the Poulenc Sonata because the notation does not specify pitches. The singer, therefore, coordinates the neumatic information regarding the distribution of the music above the text with the directional indications to match those data with the aural image of the melody retained in memory. Our flute player may have memorized large sections of the Poulenc Sonata, but the presence of pitch information in the score permits a precise matching of memory with visual data and confirmation of the version stored in memory. The singer of this chant, on the other hand, must supply the pitch information from memory and coordinate it with the much less precise notation. Instead of seeking patterns like the A major and E major pitch collections found in the Poulenc, the singer must recall the exact pitch sequence of this chant. Even the role of the ears differs, as the singers must regulate what they are singing against their memory of the chant instead of the visual information supplied by the notation, which does not offer sufficient detail.

Along the way, the singer absorbs the special signs that indicate ornaments, like the *quilisma* and the liquescents, and sees, perhaps in peripheral vision as happens with dynamics in reading conventional notation, the performing nuances suggested by the *litterae significatiuae* and applies them. His sense of hearing regulates the whole, but here, memory plays a much bigger role because of the nature of the notation. So, the visual, cognitive and aural processes in which the singer of plainchant engages closely resemble those of the modern flute player working with the score of the Poulenc Sonata, and where they differ, they do so because the singer must accommodate the qualitatively different type of information the notation provides.

Different styles of notation, then, require different strategies of reading in the coordination of visual, cognitive and aural processes. Sometimes practice and convention determine the combination, as in our tenth-century example from Saint Gall, where the music scribe has deliberately chosen a notation that shows pitch information poorly but clearly defines the distribution of music over the text and the placement of vocal nuances, each decision reflecting his perception of the singer's needs. At the other extreme, composers of the twentieth century create new notational symbols as a means of exploring the creation of new sounds. Both notations generate special challenges in reading, challenges that we often underestimate because those of us who are musically literate in the conventional sense take so much for granted when we consume a musical score as a direct result of our having risen to the challenge of musical literacy and internalizing the processes we undertake.

Bibliography

Manuscripts

Albi 44 Albi, Bibliothèque municipale Rochegude, MS 44 (reproduced at archives-numeriques.mediatheques.grand-albigeois.fr).

Bam 115 Bamberg, Staatsbibliothek, MS Lit. 115 (*olim* Ed. IV. 6) (facsimile ed. Aubry; reproduced at www.nbn-resolving.de/urn:nbn:de:bvb:22-dtl-0000002752).

Ber 2/204 Berlin, Staatsbibliothek Preußischer Kulturbesitz, Mus. ms. Autogr., L. v. Beethoven, 2, and Artaria 204 (facsimile ed. Lockwood *et al.*; reproduced at https://bit.ly/30DZ5M6).

Ber 14 Berlin, Staatsbibliothek Preußischer Kulturbesitz, Mus. ms. Autogr., L. v. Beethoven, 14 (reproduced at https://bit.ly/2PesWo0).

Ber 15 Berlin, Staatsbibliothek Preußischer Kulturbesitz, Mus. ms. Autogr., L. v. Beethoven, 15 (reproduced at https://bit.ly/2DvjMkA).

Ber 78 C 12 Berlin, Staatliche Museen Preußischer Kulturbesitz, Kupferstichkabinett, MS 78 C 12 (facsimile ed. Lesure).

Ber P 180 Berlin, Staatsbibliothek Preußischer Kulturbesitz, Mus. ms. Bach P 180 (facsimile ed. Dürr; Wolff; reproduced at https://bit.ly/3fhuFU1).

Ber P 967 Berlin, Staatsbibliothek Preußischer Kulturbesitz, Mus. ms. Bach P 967 (facsimiles, see below under Bach, Johann Sebastian, *Sei solo a violino senza basso accompagnato*; reproduced at https://bit.ly/3ksIN0F).

Bol Q.15 Bologna, Museo Internazionale et Biblioteca della Musica di Bologna, MS Q.15 (facsimile ed. Bent).

Cdg 473 Cambridge, Corpus Christi College, MS 473 (facsimile ed. Rankin).

Chan 564 Chantilly, Bibliothèque du château de Chantilly, MS 564 (facsimile ed. Plumley and Stone).

Char 47 Chartres, Bibliothèque municipale, MS 47 (facsimile *PalMus* 11).

F Florence, Biblioteca Medicea Laurenziana, MS Pluteo 29,1 (facsimile ed. Dittmer; Roesner; reproduced at https://bit.ly/3ikeGGO and at imspl).

F 17879 Florence, Archivio di Stato, Notarile Antecosimiano, No. 17879 (facsimile ed. McGee, "*Dança amorosa*").

Faenza 117 Faenza, Biblioteca comunale, MS 117 (facsimile ed. Carapetyan; Memelsdorff; reproduced at https://bit.ly/2F5uGOF).

Laon 239 Laon, Bibliothèque municipale, MS 239 (facsimile *PalMus* 10; reproduced at manuscrit.ville-laon.fr).

Lo 28550 London, British Library, Additional MS 28550 (facsimile ed. Wooldridge and H. Hughes, 1: plates 42–45).

Lo 29987 London, British Library, Additional MS 29987 (facsimile ed. Reaney; reproduced at https://bit.ly/3ifPwJk).

Lo 36881 London, British Library, Additional MS 36881 (facsimile ed. Gillingham; reproduced at https://bit.ly/2XHTFxN).

Mo H. 159 Montpellier, Bibliothèque Interuniversitaire Médecine, MS H. 159 (facsimile *PalMus* 8).

Mo H. 196 Montpellier, Bibliothèque Interuniversitaire Médecine, MS H. 196 (facsimile ed. Rokseth; reproduced at https://bit.ly/3gGsM4Z and at imspl).

Mü 3725 Munich, Bayerische Staatsbibliothek, Mus. ms. 3725 (facsimile ed. Wallner; reproduced at https://bit.ly/3ffW8FO).

NY 266 New York, Pierpont Morgan Library, MS Heineman 266 (facsimile ed. LaRue).

Pa 844 Paris, Bibliothèque nationale de France, MS français 844 (facsimile ed. Beck; reproduced at gallica.bnf.fr).

Pa 909 Paris, Bibliothèque nationale de France, MS latin 909 (reproduced at gallica.bnf.fr).

Pa 967 Paris, Bibliothèque nationale de France, département Musique, MS 967 (reproduced at gallica.bnf.fr).

Pa 1107 Paris, Bibliothèque nationale de France, MS latin 1107 (reproduced at gallica.bnf.fr).

Pa 1121 Paris, Bibliothèque nationale de France, MS latin 1121 (reproduced at gallica.bnf.fr).

Pa 1138 Paris, Bibliothèque nationale de France, MS latin 1138 (reproduced at gallica.bnf.fr).

Pa 1139 Paris, Bibliothèque nationale de France, MS latin 1139 (facsimile ed. Gillingham; reproduced at gallica.bnf.fr).

Pa 1338 Paris, Bibliothèque nationale de France, MS latin 1338 (reproduced at gallica.bnf.fr).

Pa 1548 (1–8) Paris, Bibliothèque nationale de France, département Musique, MS 1548 (1–8) (facsimile ed. Richard *et al.*; reproduced at gallica.bnf.fr).

Pa 1584 Paris, Bibliothèque nationale de France, MS français 1584 (reproduced at gallica.bnf.fr).

Pa 3549 Paris, Bibliothèque nationale de France, MS latin 3549 (facsimile ed. Gillingham; reproduced at gallica.bnf.fr).

Pa 3719 Paris, Bibliothèque nationale de France, MS latin 3719 (facsimile ed. Gillingham; reproduced at gallica.bnf.fr).

Pa 5240 Paris, Bibliothèque nationale de France, MS latin 5240 (reproduced at gallica.bnf.fr).

Pa 7378A Paris, Bibliothèque nationale de France, MS latin 7378A (reproduced at gallica.bnf.fr).

Pa 9221 Paris, Bibliothèque nationale de France, MS français 9221 (reproduced at gallica.bnf.fr).

Pa 17296 Paris, Bibliothèque nationale de France, MS latin 17296 (reproduced at gallica.bnf.fr).

Pa 17436 Paris, Bibliothèque nationale de France, MS latin 17436 (reproduced at gallica.bnf.fr).

Pa 25566 Paris, Bibliothèque nationale de France, MS français 25566 (reproduced at gallica.bnf.fr).

PaM 384 Paris, Bibliothèque Mazarine, MS 384 (facsimile ed. Hesbert; Maître).

SG 359 Saint Gall, Stiftsbibliothek, MS 359 (facsimile *PalMus* ser. 2, 2; MPG 3; reproduced at www.cesg.unifr.ch).

SG 390–91 Saint Gall, Stiftsbibliothek, MSS 390–91 (facsimile *PalMus* ser. 2, 1; MPG 4; reproduced at www.cesg.unifr.ch).

Si L.V.33 Siena, Biblioteca Communale degli Intronati di Siena, MS L.V.33 (facsimile ed. Usula).

Tol 44.2 Toledo, Biblioteca Capitular, MS 44.2.

Ven 371 Venice, Biblioteca nazionale Marciana, MS It. IV, 371 (facsimile ed. Brown).

W_1 Wolfenbüttel, Herzog August Bibliothek, MS Helmstedt 628 (facsimile ed. Baxter; Staehelin; reproduced at diglib.hab.de/?db=mss&list=ms&id=628-helmst).

W_2 Wolfenbüttel, Herzog August Bibliothek, MS Helmstedt 1099 (facsimile ed. Dittmer; reproduced at diglib.hab.de/?db=mss&list=ms&id=1099-helmst).

Editions of Music

Adémar de Chabannes. *Opera liturgica et poetica: Musica cum textibus*, ed. James Grier. 2 vols. *Ademari Cabanensis Opera Omnia Pars II*. Corpus Christianorum Continuatio Mediaevalis, 245, 245A. Turnhout: Brepols, 2012.

Ammerbach, Elias Nikolaus. *Orgel oder Instrument Tabulaturbuch*. Nürnberg: Gerlach, 1583 (reproduced at books.google.ca/books?id=7 K-PGwXyKR8 C&printsec=frontcover& source=gbs_ViewAPI&redir_esc=y#v=onepage&q&f=false).

———. *Orgel oder Instrument Tabulaturbuch (1571/83)*, ed. Charles Jacobs. Oxford: Oxford University Press, 1984.

Anderson, Gordon A., ed. *Compositions of the Bamberg Manuscript: Bamberg, Staatsbibliothek, Lit. 115 (olim Ed. IV. 6)*. Corpus Mensurabilis Musicae, 75. Neuhausen-Stuttgart: American Institute of Musicology, 1977.

Apel, Willi, and Samuel N. Rosenberg, eds. *French Secular Compositions of the Fourteenth Century*. 3 vols. Corpus Mensurabilis Musicae, 53. N.p.: American Institute of Musicology, 1970–72.

Attaingnant, Pierre. *Tres breue et familiere introduction*. Paris: Pierre Attaingnant, 1529 (facsimile ed. François Lesure [Geneva: Éditions Minkoff, 1988]).

Aubry, Pierre, ed. *Cent motets du XIIIe siècle*. 3 vols. Publications de la Société Internationale de Musique, Section de Paris. Paris: U. Rouart, Lerolle & Co. and Paul Geuthner, 1908.

Bach, Johann Sebastian. *Klavierbüchlein für Wilhelm Friedemann Bach*, ed. Wolfgang Plath. Neue Ausgabe Sämtlicher Werke, ser. 5, 5. Kassel: Bärenreiter, 1962.

Messe in H-moll, BWV 232: Faksimile-Lichtdruck des Autographs mit einem Nachwort, ed. Alfred Dürr. Kassel: Bärenreiter, 1965; repr. in Documenta Musicologica, ser. 2: Handschriften-Faksimiles, 12 (Kassel: Bärenreiter, 1983).

Messe in H-moll, BWV 232 mit Sanctus in D-Dur (1724), BWV 232^{III}, ed. Christoph Wolff. Documenta Musicologica, ser. 2: Handschriften-Faksimiles, 35. Kassel: Bärenreiter, 2007.

Sei solo a violino senza basso accompagnato. 2nd ed. Kassel: Bärenreiter, 1958.

Sei solo a violino senza basso accompagnato. Monumenta Musicae Revocata, 2. Florence: Studio per Edizioni Scelte, 1985.

Sei solo a violino senza basso accompagnato, ed. Georg von Dadelsen. Faksimile-Reihe Bachscher Werke und Schriftstücke, 22. Leipzig: Deutscher Verlag für Musik, 1988.

Sei solo a violino senza basso accompagnato, ed. Sven Hiemke. Meisterwerke der Musik im Faksimile, 8. Laaber: Laaber-Verlag, 2006.

Toccata and Fugue in D minor, in *Präludien, Toccaten, Fantasien und Fugen I*, ed. Dietrich Kilian. Neue Ausgabe Sämtlicher Werke, ser. 4, 5. Kassel: Bärenreiter, 1972, pp. 76–89.

Verschiedene Kammermusikwerke, ed. Klaus Hofmann. Neue Ausgabe Sämtlicher Werke, ser. 6, 5. Kassel: Bärenreiter, 2006.

Werke für Flöte, ed. Hans-Peter Schmitz. Neue Ausgabe Sämtlicher Werke, ser. 6, 3. Kassel: Bärenreiter, 1963.

Das Wohltemperierte Klavier, 2 vols., ed. Alfred Dürr. Neue Ausgabe Sämtlicher Werke, ser. 5, 6.1 and 6.2. Kassel: Bärenreiter, 1989–95.

Banchieri, Adriano. *L'organo suonarino*. Venice: Ricciardo Amadino, 1611; partial repr. ed. Giulio Cattin, Bibliotheca Organologica, 27 (Amsterdam: Frits Knuf, 1969); also in Bibliotheca Musica Bononiensis, sezione 2, no. 31 (Bologna: Forni Editore, 1969).

Bartók, Béla. *Mikrokosmos*. 6 vols. London: Boosey & Hawkes, 1987.

Baxter, J. H., ed. *An Old St. Andrews Music Book (Cod. Helmst. 628)*. St. Andrews University Publications, 30. London: Oxford University Press, 1931; repr. New York, 1973.

Beatles, The. *Complete Scores*, ed. Tetsuya Fujita, Yuji Hagino, Hajime Kubo and Goro Sato. Milwaukee: Hal Leonard, 1993.

Beck, Jean, ed. *Le manuscrit du roi: Fond français de la Bibliothèque nationale*. 2 vols. Corpus Cantilenarum Medii Aevi, 1: Les Chansonniers des Troubadours et des Trouvères, 2. Philadelphia: University of Pennsylvania Press, 1938; repr. New York, 1970.

Beethoven, Ludwig van. *Grande sonate pour le piano-forte*. Vienna: Artaria et Compag, 1819 (reproduced at https://bit.ly/2DtST02).

Klaviersonaten, 1, ed. Hans Schmidt. Beethoven Werke, ser. 7, vol. 2. Munich-Duisburg: G. Henle Verlag, 1971.

Sinfonie mit Schluß-Chor über Schillers Ode "An die Freude". Mainz: B. Schotts Sohnen, n.d. (reproduced at https://bit.ly/2Xmn14J).

Sinfonie no. 9, Op. 125: Autograph, Staatsbibliothek zu Berlin, Preussischer Kulturbesitz, Beethoven-Haus Bonn, Bibliothèque nationale de France, ed. Lewis Lockwood, Jonathan Del Mar and Martina Rebmann. Documenta Musicologica, ser. 2: Handschriften-Faksimiles, 42. Kassel: Bärenreiter, 2010.

Symphony no. 3 Opus 55 Eroica, ed. Bathia Churgin. Beethoven Werke, ser. 1, vol. 2. Munich: G. Henle Verlag, 2013.

Trois Sonates pour le Clavecin ou Piano-Forte. Vienna: Artaria, n.d.

Bent, Margaret, ed. *Bologna Q15, The Making and Remaking of a Musical Manuscript: Introductory Study and Facsimile Edition*. 2 vols. Ars Nova, nuova serie, 2. Lucca: Libreria Musicale Italiana, 2008.

Berio, Luciano. *Sequenza III per voce femminile*. London: Universal Edition, 1968.

Sequenza VII per oboe solo. London: Universal Edition, 1971.

Brahms, Johannes. *Concert für das Pianoforte mit Begleitung des Orchesters, Op. 15*. Leipzig: J. Rieter-Bidermann, 1875.

Concert für das Pianoforte mit Begleitung des Orchesters, Op. 83. Berlin: Simrock, 1882.

Brown, Earle. *Available Forms 1*. New York: Associated Music Publishers, 1962.

Brown, Howard, ed. See Cavalli, Francesco.

Brumel, Antoine. *Opera omnia*, ed. Barton Hudson. 6 vols. Corpus Mensurabilis Musicae, 5. N. p.: American Institute of Musicology, 1969–72.

Cabezón, Antonio de. *Collected Works*, 3: *Versos & Fugas*, ed. Charles Jacobs. Gesamtausgaben, 4/3. Brooklyn: Institute of Medieval Music, 1976.

Obras de música para tecla arpa y vihuela. Madrid: Francisco Sanchez, 1578 (reproduced at bdh-rd.bne.es/viewer.vm?id=0000037786).

Obras de música para tecla arpa y vihuela, ed. Higinio Anglés. 3 vols. Monumentos de la Música Española, 27–29. Barcelona: Consejo Superior de Investigaciones Científicas, 1966.

Obras de música para tecla arpa y vihuela, ed. Javier Artigas Pina, Gustavo Delgado Parra, Antonio Ezquerro Esteban, Luis Antonio González Marín, José Luis González Uriol and José Vicente González Valle. 4 vols. Zaragoza: Consejo Superior de Investigaciones Científicas, Instituición «Fernando el Católico», 2010.

Caccini, Giulio. *L'Euridice*. Florence: G. Marescotti, 1600; repr. ed. Piero Mioli, Archivum Musicum, Musica Drammatica, 5 (Florence, 2000).

Carapetyan, Armen, ed. *An Early Fifteenth-Century Italian Source of Keyboard Music: The Codex Faenza Biblioteca comunale, 117*. Musicological Studies and Documents, 10. N.p.: American Institute of Musicology, 1961.

Carter, Elliott. *Eight Pieces for Four Timpani (one player)*. New York: Associated Music Publishers, 1968.

Cavalieri, Emilio del. *Rappresentatione di Anima e di Corpo*. Rome: Nicolo Mutii, 1600; repr. Fransborough, 1967; and in Bibliotheca Musica Bononiensis, sezione 4, 1 (Bologna, 1987).

Cavalli, Francesco. *Il novello Giasone*, ed. Nicola Usula. 2 vols. Drammaturgia Musicale Veneta, 3. Milan: Ricordi, 2013.

Scipione Africano, ed. Howard Mayer Brown. Italian Opera 1640–1770. New York: Garland, 1978.

Compere, Loyset. *Opera omnia*, ed. Ludwig Finscher. 5 vols. Corpus Mensurabilis Musicae, 15. N.p.: American Institute of Musicology, 1958–72.

Corelli, Arcangelo. *Sonate a violino e violone o cimbalo opera quinta*. [Rome]: Incisa da Gasparo Pietra Santa, [1700] (facsimile London: Schott, 1987; reproduced at stimmbuecher.digitale-sammlungen.de/view?id=bsb00087066).

Sonate da chiesa, Opus I und III, ed. Max Lütolf. Arcangelo Corelli, Historisch-kritische Gesamtausgabe der musikalischen Werke, 1. Laaber: Laaber-Verlag, 1987.

Debussy, Claude. *La demoiselle élue*. Paris: Librairie de l'Art Indépendant, 1893 (reproduced at gallica.bnf.fr).

La demoiselle élue. Paris: A. Durand & Fils, 1902 (reproduced at gallica.bnf.fr).

des Prez, Josquin. *Missa De beata virgine*, in *The Collected Works of Josquin des Prez*, 3: *Masses Based on Gregorian Chants*, 1, ed. Willem Elders. Utrecht: Koninklije Vereniging voor Nederlandse Muziekgeschiednis, 2003, pp. 32–83.

Dittmer, Luther, ed. *Firenze, Biblioteca Mediceo-Laurenziana, Pluteo 29,1*. 2 vols. Veröffentlichung Mittelalterlicher Musikhandschriften, 10–11. Brooklyn: Institute of Mediaeval Music, n.d.

ed. *Wolfenbüttel 1099 Helmst*. Veröffentlichung Mittelalterlicher Musikhandschriften, 2. Brooklyn: Institute of Mediaeval Music, 1960.

Du Fay, Guillaume. *Opera Omnia*, ed. Heinrich Besseler. 6 vols. Corpus Mensurabilis Musicae, 1. Rome: American Institute of Musicology, 1951–66.

Everist, Mark, ed. *Le Magnus liber organi de Notre-Dame de Paris*, 2: *Les organa à deux voix pour l'office du manuscrit de Florence, Biblioteca Medicea Laurenziana, plut. 29.1*. Les Remparts, Monaco: Éditions de l'Oiseau-Lyre, 2003.

Feldman, Morton. *Intersection 2 for Piano Solo*. New York: C. F. Peters, 1962.

Frottole intabulate da sonare organi libro primo. Rome: Andrea Antico, 1517 (facsimile ed. Giuseppe Radole, Bibliotheca Musica Bononiensis, sezione 4, 51B [Bologna: Forni Editore, 1970]).

Gabrieli, Giovanni. *Opera Omnia*, 10: *Instrumental Ensemble Works in 'Sacrae symphoniae' (Venice, 1597), Printed Anthologies and Manuscript Sources*, ed. Richard Charteris. Corpus Mensurabilis Musicae, 12, no. 10. Neuhausen: Hänssler-Verlag, 1998.

Sacrae symphoniae. 12 vols. Venice: Angelus Gardanus, 1597 (reproduced at http://data.onb.ac.at/rec/A09917003).

Gaultier, Denis. *La rhétorique des dieux*, ed. François Lesure. Geneva: Éditions Minkoff, 1991.

La rhétorique des dieux, ed. David J. Buch. Recent Researches in the Music of the Baroque Era, 62. Madison, WI: A-R Editions, 1990.

Gautier [sic], Denis. *Oeuvres de Denis Gautier*, ed. Monique Rollin and François-Pierre Goy. Corpus des Luthistes Français. Paris: CNRS-Éditions, 1996.

Gillingham, Bryan, ed. *Paris Bibliothèque Nationale, fonds latin 1139*. Veröffentlichungen Mittelalterlicher Musikhandschriften, 14. Ottawa: Institute of Mediaeval Music, 1987.

ed. *Paris Bibliothèque Nationale, fonds latin 3719*. Veröffentlichungen Mittelalterlicher Musikhandschriften, 15. Ottawa: Institute of Mediaeval Music, 1987.

ed. *Paris Bibliothèque Nationale, fonds latin 3549 and London, B.L. Add. 36,881*. Veröffentlichungen Mittelalterlicher Musikhandschriften, 16. Ottawa: Institute of Mediaeval Music, 1987.

ed. *Saint-Martial Mehrstimmigkeit*. Wissenschaftliche Abhandlungen, 44. Henryville, Ottawa and Binningen: Institute of Mediaeval Music, 1984.

Greene, Gordon K., ed. *French Secular Music: Manuscript Chantilly, Musée Condé 564*. 2 vols. Polyphonic Music of the Fourteenth Century, 18–19. Les Remparts, Monaco: Éditions de l'Oiseau-Lyre, 1981–82.

Händel, Georg Friedrich. *Elf Sonaten für Flöte und bezifferten Bass*, ed. Hans-Peter Schmitz. Hallische Händel-Ausgabe, ser. IV, vol. 3. Kassel: Bärenreiter, 2007.

Water Music, ed. Terence Best and Christopher Hogwood. Hallische Händel-Ausgabe, ser. IV, vol. 13. Kassel: Bärenreiter, 2007, pp. 3–62.

Harmonice musices odhecaton. Venice: Ottaviano Petrucci, 1501 (facsimile of 1504 edition in Collezione di Trattati e Musiche Edite in Fac-Simile [Milan: Bollettino Bibliografico Musicale, 1932]; 1504 edition reproduced at gallica.bnf.fr).

Heartz, Daniel, ed. *Preludes, Chansons and Dances Published by Pierre Attaingnant, Paris (1529–1530)*. Publications de la Société de Musique d'Autrefois, Textes Musicaux, 2. Neuilly-sur-Seine: Société de Musique d'Autrefois, 1964.

Hesbert, René-Jean, ed. *Le graduel de Saint-Denis: Manuscrit 384 de la Bibliothèque Mazarine de Paris.* Monumenta Musica Sacrae, 5. Paris: Nouvelles Éditions Latines, 1981.

Hewitt, Helen, ed. *Harmonice musices odhecaton A.* Medieval Academy of America Publications, 42. Cambridge, MA: Medieval Academy of America, 1942; repr. New York, 1978.

Husmann, Heinrich, ed. *Die drei- und vierstimmigen Notre-Dame-Organa.* Publikationen Älterer Musik, 11. Leipzig: Breitkopf & Härtel, 1940.

Intabulatura de lauto libro primo. Venice: Ottaviano Petrucci, 1507 (facsimile ed. François Lesure [Geneva and Paris: Éditions Minkoff, 1978]; reproduced at https://bit.ly/3a8lXGM).

Intabulatura de lauto libro secondo. Venice: Ottaviano Petrucci, 1507 (facsimile ed. François Lesure [Geneva and Paris: Éditions Minkoff, 1978]; and ed. Albert Reyerman, 2 vols. [n.p.: Tree Edition, 2011]; reproduced at https://bit.ly/2XEB0my).

Ives, Charles. *Symphony no. 4.* New York: Associated Music Publishers, 1965.

Karp, Theodore. *The Polyphony of Saint Martial and Santiago de Compostela.* 2 vols. Berkeley and Los Angeles: University of California Press, 1992.

Kelly, Thomas Forrest, and Matthew Peattie, eds. *The Music of the Beneventan Rite.* Monumenta Monodica Medii Aevi, 9. Kassel: Bärenreiter, 2016.

Lesure, François, ed. See Gaultier, Denis.

Machaut, Guillaume de. *The Works of Guillaume de Machaut*, ed. Leo Schrade. 2 vols. Polyphonic Music of the Fourteenth Century, 2–3. Les Remparts, Monaco: Éditions de l'Oiseau-Lyre, 1956.

Maître, Claire, ed. *Graduel de l'abbaye royale de Saint-Denis, début XIe siècle: Paris, Bibliothèque Mazarine, ms. 384.* Manuscrits notés, 3. N.p.: Éditions Actes Sud, 2005.

McGee, Timothy J., ed. *Medieval Instrumental Dances.* Music: Scholarship and Performance. Bloomington and Indianapolis: Indiana University Press, 1989.

Memelsdorff, Pedro, ed. *The Codex Faenza 117: Instrumental Polyphony in Late Medieval Italy.* 2 vols. Ars Nova, nuova ser., 3. Lucca: Libreria Musicale Italiana, 2013.

Milán, Luis de. *Libro de musica de vihuela de mano, intitulado El maestro.* Valencia: Francisco Diaz Romano, 1536 (facsimile ed. Francisco Roa [Madrid: Sociedad de la Vihuela, 2008]; reproduced at http://bdh-rd.bne.es/viewer.vm?id=0000022795).

El maestro, ed. Charles Jacobs. University Park and London: Pennsylvania State University Press, 1971.

Monteverdi, Claudio. *Madrigali guerrieri, et amorosi.* 9 vols. Venice: Alessandro Vincenti, 1638 (facsimile, Monteverdi, *Madrigali guerrieri, et amorosi libro ottavo*, ed. Vacchelli, 1: 107–91).

Madrigali guerrieri, et amorosi libro ottavo, ed. Anna Maria Vacchelli. 2 vols. Claudio Monteverdi Opera Omnia, 14. Cremona: Fondazione Claudio Monteverdi, 2004.

L'Orfeo. Venice: Ricciardo Amadino, 1609 (facsimile, Monteverdi, *L'Orfeo*, ed. Vacchelli, 1: 329–55; ed. Piero Mioli, Archivum Musicum, Musica Drammatica, 1 [Florence: Studio per Edizioni Scelte, 1993]; and ed. Elisabeth Schmierer, Meisterwerke der Musik im Faksimile, 1 [Laaber: Laaber-Verlag, 1998]).

L'Orfeo, ed. Anna Maria Vacchelli. 2 vols. Claudio Monteverdi Opera Omnia, 8. Cremona: Fondazione Claudio Monteverdi, 2014–16.

Mozart, Wolfgang Amadeus. *Don Giovanni*, ed. Albert Richard, Guy Mollat du Jourdin, François Lesure, René Dumesnil and Jacques Duron. 9 vols. Paris: La Revue Musicale, 1967.

Klaviersonaten, ed. Wolfgang Plath and Wolfgang Rehm. Neue Ausgabe Sämtlicher Werke, ser. 9, 25/2. Kassel: Bärenreiter, 1986 (reproduced at http://dme.mozarteum.at/DME/nma/nmapub_srch.php?l=1).

Piano Concerto No. 21 in C Major, K. 467: The Autograph Score, ed. Jan LaRue. The Pierpont Morgan Library Music Manuscript Reprint Series. New York: Dover, 1985.

MPG 3 *Die Handschrift St. Gallen Stiftsbibliothek 359 Cantatorium*. Monumenta Palaeographica Gregoriana, 3. Münsterschwarzach: Studien des Gregorianischen Chorals, n.d.

MPG 4, 1 *Die Handschrift St. Gallen Stiftsbibliothek 390 Antiphonarium Hartkeri*. Monumenta Palaeographica Gregoriana, 4, 1. Münsterschwarzach: Studien des Gregorianischen Chorals, n.d.

MPG 4, 2 *Die Handschrift St. Gallen Stiftsbibliothek 391 Antiphonarium Hartkeri*. Monumenta Palaeographica Gregoriana, 4, 2. Münsterschwarzach: Studien des Gregorianischen Chorals, n.d.

Mudarra, Alonso. *Tres libros de musica en cifra para vihuela*. Seville: Juan de León, 1546 (facsimile ed. James Tyler [Monaco: Éditions Chanterelle, 1980]; reproduced at http://bdh-rd.bne.es/viewer.vm?id=0000108275&page=1).

Tres libros de musica en cifra para vihuela (Sevilla, 1546), ed. Emilio Pujol. Monumentos de la Música Española, 7. Barcelona: Consejo Superior de Investigaciones Científicas, 1949.

Newsidler, Hans. *Ein newgeordent küntslich Lautenbuch*. Nürnberg: Johannes Petreius, 1536 (facsimile ed. Peter Päffgen, 2 vols., Institutio pro arte testudinis, ser. A, 1 and 3 [Neuss: Junghänel-Päffgen-Schäffer, 1974–76]; and in Faksimile-Edition Laute, 6 [Stuttgart: Cornetto, 2004]; reproduced at https://bit.ly/3i2zJgK; and at https://bit.ly/33hjUib). English translation of preface, Marc Southard and Suzana Cooper, trans., "A Translation of Hans Newsidler's *Ein newgeordent kunstlich Lautenbuch*... (1536)," *Journal of the Lute Society of America* 11 (1978): 5–25.

PalMus 8 *Antiphonarium tonale missarum XI siècle: Codex H. 159 de la Bibliothèque de l'École de Médecine de Montpellier.* Paléographie Musicale, 8. Tournai: Desclée, Lefebvre et Cie, 1901–5; repr. Bern, 1972.

PalMus 10 *Antiphonale missarum sancti Gregorii IXe–Xe siècle: Codex 239 de la Bibliothèque de Laon.* Paléographie Musicale, 10. Tournai: Desclée, 1909–12; repr. Bern, 1971.

PalMus 11 *Antiphonale missarum sancti Gregorii (Xe siècle): Codex 47 de la Bibliothèque de Chartres.* Paléographie Musicale, 11. Tournai: Desclée, 1912–21; repr. Bern, 1972.

PalMus ser. 2, 1 *Antiphonale officii monastici écrit par le B. Hartker: No 390–391 de la Bibliothèque de Saint-Gall.* 2nd ed., ed. Jacques Froger. Paléographie Musicale, ser. 2, 1. Bern: Lang, 1970.

PalMus ser. 2, 2 *Cantatorium (IXe siècle): No 359 de la Bibliothèque de Saint-Gall.* Paléographie Musicale, ser. 2, 2. Tournai: Société de Saint-Jean l'Évangeliste and Desclée, 1924; repr. Bern, 1968.

Payne, Thomas B., ed. *Le Magnus liber organi de Notre-Dame de Paris*, 6a: *Les organa à deux voix du manuscrit de Wolfenbüttel, Hertzog August Bibliothek, cod. guelf. 1099 Helmst.* Les Remparts, Monaco: Éditions de l'Oiseau-Lyre, 1996.

Penderecki, Krzysztof. *For the Victims of Hiroshima, Threnody for 52 Stringed Instruments.* Kraków: Polskie Wydawnictwo Muzyczne, 1960.

Peri, Jacopo. *Le musiche sopra l'Euridice.* Florence: G. Marescotti, 1600; repr. in Bibliotheca Musica Bononiensis, sezione 4, 2 (Bologna, 1969); and in Monuments of Music and Music Literature in Facsimile, Second Series, Music, 28 (New York, 1973).

Plumley, Yolanda, and Anne Stone, eds. *Codex Chantilly: Chantilly, Bibliothèque du château de Chantilly, MS 564, facsimilé.* 2 vols. Épitome Musical. Turnhout: Brepols, 2008.

Poulenc, Francis. *Sonata, Flute and Piano.* London: J. and W. Chester, 1958.

Rankin, Susan, ed. *The Winchester Troper: Facsimile Edition and Introduction.* Early English Church Music, 50. London: Stainer & Bell for the British Academy, 2007.

Reaney, Gilbert, ed. *The Manuscript London, British Museum, Additional 29987.* Musicological Studies and Documents, 13. N.p.: American Institute of Musicology, 1965.

Roesner, Edward H., ed. *Antiphonarium, seu, Magnus liber organi de gradali et antiphonario: Color Microfiche Edition of the Manuscript, Firenze, Biblioteca medicea laurenziana, Pluteus 29.1.* Munich: H. Lengenfelder, 1996.

— ed. *Le Magnus liber organi de Notre-Dame de Paris*, 1: *Les quadrupla et tripla de Paris.* Les Remparts, Monaco: Éditions de l'Oiseau-Lyre, 1993.

— ed. *Le Magnus liber organi de Notre-Dame de Paris*, 7: *Les organa et les clausules à deux voix du manuscrit de Wolfenbüttel, Herzog August Bibliothek, cod. guelf. 628 Helmst.* Les Remparts, Monaco: Éditions de l'Oiseau-Lyre, 2009.

Rokseth, Yvonne, ed. *Polyphonies du XIIIe siècle: Le manuscrit H 196 de la Faculté de médecine de Montpellier.* 4 vols. Paris: Éditions de l'Oiseau-Lyre, 1935–39.

Rore, Cipriano de. *Il primo libro de madrigali a quattro voci.* 4 vols. Ferrara: Giovanni de Buglhat et Antonio Hocher, 1550. (1569 edition [Venice: Gardano]; reproduced at https://bit.ly/2PxHmzK).

Opera omnia. 8 vols., ed. Bernhard Meier. Corpus Mensurabilis Musicae, 14. N. p.: American Institute of Musicology, 1959–77.

Schönberg, Arnold. *Das Buch der hängenden Gärten,* Op. 15, in *Lieder mit Klavierbegleitung,* ed. Josef Rufer. Arnold Schönberg Sämtliche Werke, riehe A, 1. Mainz and Vienna: B. Schott's Söhne and Universal Edition, 1966, pp. 113–49.

Five Pieces for Orchestra, Opus 16. New York: C. F. Peters, 1952.

Fünf Orchesterstücke, Opus 16. Leipzig: C. F. Peters, 1912.

Schumann, Robert. *Carnaval,* Op. 9. Leipzig: Breitkopf & Härtel, 1837 (reproduced at brahms-institut.de).

Concert für das Pianoforte mit Begleitung des Orchesters. Leipzig: Breitkopf und Härtel, n.d.

Fantasiestücke, Op. 12. Leipzig: Breitkopf & Härtel, 1838 (reproduced at brahms-institut.de).

Humoreske, Op. 20. Vienna: Petro Mechetti quondam Carlo, 1839 (reproduced at brahms-institut.de).

Kinderscenen, Op. 15, in *Robert Schumann's Werke,* ed. Clara Schumann, ser. VII, vol. 3. Leipzig: Breitkopf & Härtel, 1880, pp. 64–73.

Staehelin, Martin, ed. *Die mittelalterliche Musikhandschrift, W_1: Vollständige Reproduktion des "Notre Dame"-Manuskripts der Herzog August Bibliothek Wolfenbüttel Cod. Guelf. 628 Hemst.* Wiesbaden: Harrosowitz, 1995.

Stockhausen, Karlheinz. *Nr. 14: Plus Minus.* N.p.: Universal Edition, 1963.

Nr. 27: Spiral für einen Solisten. Vienna: Universal Edition, 1973.

Strawinsky, Igor. *Pétrouchka.* Berlin: Édition Russe de Musique, n.d.

Variations, Aldous Huxley in Memoriam. London: Boosey & Hawkes, 1965.

Tischler, Hans, ed. *The Montpellier Codex.* 7 vols. in 4. Recent Researches in the Music of the Middle Ages and Early Renaissance, 2–8. Madison, WI: A-R Editions, 1978.

ed. *The Parisian Two-Part Organa: The Complete Comparative Edition.* 2 vols. Stuyvesant NY: Pendragon Press, 1988.

Usula, Nicola, ed. See Cavalli, Francesco.

Valente, Antonio. *Intavolatura de cimbalo recercate fantasie et canzoni francese desminuite con alcuni enori balli et vare sorte de contraponti, libro primo.* Naples: Giuseppe Caccio dall'Aquila, 1576 (partially reproduced at https://bit.ly/2DB6frZ).

Intavolatura de cimbalo (Naples 1576), ed. Charles Jacobs. Oxford: Oxford University Press, 1973.

van der Werf, Hendrik. *The Oldest Extant Part Music and the Origin of Western Polyphony*. 2 vols. Rochester NY: The author, 1993.

Wallner, Bertha Antonia, ed. *Das Buxheimer Orgelbuch: Handschrift mus. 3725 der Bayerischen Staatsbibliothek, München*. Documenta Musicologica, ser. 2: Handschriften-Faksimiles, 1. Kassel: Bärenreiter, 1955.

———, ed. *Das Buxheimer Orgelbuch*. 3 vols. Das Erbe Deutscher Music, 37–39. Kassel: Bärenreiter, 1958–59.

Wooldridge, H. E., and H. E. Hughes, eds. *Early English Harmony from the 10th to the 15th Century*. 2 vols. London: Bernard Quaritch and the Plainsong and Mediaeval Music Society, 1897–1913; repr. New York, 1976.

Books and Articles

Agricola, Mart. *Musica instrumentalis deudsch*. Wittemberg: Georg Rhau, 1529; repr. ed. Rob. Eitner, Publikation Älterer Praktischer und Theoretischer Musik-Werke, 20 (Leipzig: Breitkopf & Härtel, 1896). English translation: *The 'Musica instrumentalis deudsch' of Martin Agricola: A Treatise on Musical Instruments, 1529 and 1545*, trans. William E. Hettrick, Cambridge Musical Texts and Monographs (Cambridge: Cambridge University Press, 1994).

Albertus Magnus. *De causis proprietatum elementorum*, ed. Paul Hossfeld. Alberti Magni Opera Omnia, 5, 2. Aschendorf: Monasterii Westfalorum, 1980, pp. 47–104. English translation: *On the Causes of the Properties of the Elements = (Liber de causis proprietatum elementorum)*, trans. Irwen M. Resnick (Milwaukee: Marquette University Press, 2010).

Alexander de Villa-Dei. *Das Doctrinale des Alexander de Villa-Dei: Kritisch-exegetische Ausgabe*, ed. Dietrich Reichling. Monumenta Germaniae Paedagogica, 12. Berlin: A. Hofmann & Comp., 1893.

Anonymous of St. Emmeram. *De musica mensurata*, ed. and trans. Jeremy Yudkin. Music: Scholarship and Performance. Bloomington and Indianapolis: Indiana University Press, 1990.

Antico, Andrea. *Frottole intabulate da sonare organi*, ed. Peter Sterzinger. Diletto Musicale, 891. Vienna: Doblinger, 1987.

Apel, Willi. *The Notation of Polyphonic Music 900–1600*. 5th ed. Medieval Academy of America Publications, 38. Cambridge, MA: Medieval Academy of America, 1961.

———. "The Partial Signatures in the Sources up to 1450." *Acta Musicologica* 10 (1938): 1–13.

Aribo. *De musica*, ed. Jos. Smits van Waesberghe. Corpus Scriptorum de Musica, 2. Rome: American Institute of Musicology, 1951.

Arlt, Wulf. "A propos de la notation 'paléofranque': Observations spécifiques et generales extraites de mon carnet d'atelier," in *Actes du Colloque de Royaumont*, ed. Colette and Massip, pp. 51–72.

Arnold, Denis. *Giovanni Gabrieli and the Music of the Venetian High Renaissance*. London: Oxford University Press, 1979.

Arnold, F. T. *The Art of Accompaniment from a Thorough-Bass as Practised in the 17th and 18th Centuries*. London: Oxford University Press, 1931; repr. London, 1961.

Atkinson, Charles M. "The Anonymous Vaticanus *in speculo*," in *Actes du Colloque d'Auxerre*, ed. Aubert and Rankin, pp. 29–56.

 The Critical Nexus: Tone-System, Mode, and Notation in Early Medieval Music. AMS Studies in Music. New York: Oxford University Press, 2009.

 "*De Accentibus Toni Oritur Nota Quae Dicitur Neuma*: Prosodic Accents, the Accent Theory, and the Paleofrankish Script," in *Essays on Medieval Music in Honor of David G. Hughes*, ed. Graeme M. Boone. Isham Library Papers, 4. Cambridge MA: Harvard University Press, 1995, pp. 17–42.

 "Franco of Cologne on the Rhythm of Organum Purum." *Early Music History* 9 (1990): 1–26.

 "Glosses on Music and Grammar and the Advent of Music Writing in the West," in *Western Plainchant in the First Millennium*, ed. Gallagher *et al.*, pp. 199–215.

Aubert, Eduardo Henrik, and Susan Rankin, eds. *Actes du Colloque d'Auxerre: Notarum figura: L'écriture musicale et le monde des signes au 9e siècle Auxerre, Centre d'études médiévales, 17–18 juin 2011 = Études Grégoriennes* 40 (2013).

Augustine of Hippo. *De musica*, ed. and trans. Maria Bettetini. Testi a Fronte, 55. Milan: Rusconi, 1997. English translation: *On Music*, trans. Robert Catesby Taliaferro, The Fathers of the Church: Saint Augustine, 4 (Washington: Catholic University of America Press, 1947), pp. 151–379.

Aurelian of Réôme. *Musica disciplina*, ed. Lawrence Gushee. Corpus Scriptorum de Musica, 21. N.p.: American Institute of Musicology, 1975. English translation: *The Discipline of Music (Musica Disciplina)*, trans. Joseph Ponte, Colorado College Music Press Translations, 3 (Colorado Springs: Colorado College Music Press, 1968).

Babb, Warren, trans. *Hucbald, Guido, and John on Music: Three Medieval Treatises*, ed. Claude V. Palisca. Music Theory Translation Series, 3. New Haven: Yale University Press, 1978.

Bach, Johann Sebastian. *Precepts and Principles for Playing the Thorough-Bass or Accompanying in Four* Parts, *Leipzig, 1738*, ed. and trans. Pamela L. Poulin. Early Music Series, 16. Oxford: Oxford University Press, 1994.

Bailey, Derek. *Improvisation: Its Nature and Practice in Music*. London: The British Library National Sound Archive, 1992.

Bain, Jennifer. "'Messy Structure'? Multiple Tonal Centers in the Music of Machaut." *Music Theory Spectrum* 20 (2008): 195–237.

 "Tonal Structure and the Melodic Role of Chromatic Inflections in the Music of Machaut." *Plainsong & Medieval Music* 14 (2005): 59–88.

Baltzer, Rebecca A. "How Long was Notre-Dame Organum Performed?" in *Beyond the Moon*, ed. Gillingham and Merkley, pp. 118-43.

"The Decoration of Montpellier 8: Its Place in the Continuum of Parisian Manuscript Illumination," in *The Montpellier Codex*, ed. Bradley and Desmond, pp. 78-89.

Bank, J. A. *Tactus, Tempo and Notation in Mensural Music from the 13th to the 17th Century*. Amsterdam: Annie Bank, 1972.

Barker, Andrew. *Scientific Method in Ptolemy's 'Harmonics'*. Cambridge: Cambridge University Press, 2000.

Baroffio, Giacomo. "Music Writing Styles in Medieval Italy," trans. Giovanni Varelli, in *The Calligraphy of Medieval Music*, ed. Haines, pp. 101-24.

Bartholomaeus Anglicus. *De genuinis rerum coelestium, terrestrium et inferarum proprietatibus*. Frankfurt: Wolfgang Richertum, 1601; repr. Frankfurt am Main, 1964.

De proprietatibus rerum, ed. Christel Meier, Heinz Meyer, Baudouin Van den Abeele and Iolanda Ventura. Vol. 1. De Diversis Artibus, 78 (n.s. 41). Turnhout: Brepols, 2007.

Bean, Kenneth L. "An Experimental Approach to the Reading of Music." *Psychological Monographs* 50 no. 6 (1938): 1-80.

Bent, Margaret. *Magister Jacobus de Ispania, Author of the* Speculum musicae. Royal Musical Association Monographs, 28. Farnham: Ashgate, 2015.

Berger, Anna Maria Busse. *Medieval Music and the Art of Memory*. Berkeley, Los Angeles and London: University of California Press, 2005.

Mensuration and Proportion Signs: Origins and Evolution. Oxford Monographs on Music. Oxford: Oxford University Press, 1993.

Berger, Christian. *Hexachord, Mensur und Textstruktur: Studien zum französischen Lied des 14. Jahrhunderts*. Beihefte zum Archiv für Musikwissenschaft, 35. Stuttgart: Franz Steiner, 1992.

Berger, Karol. *"Musica ficta": Theories of Accidental Inflections in Vocal Polyphony from Marchetto da Padova to Gioseffo Zarlino*. Cambridge: Cambridge University Press, 1987.

Bernard, Jonathan W. "The Evolution of Elliott Carter's Rhythmic Practice." *Perspectives of New Music* 26 no. 2 (Summer, 1988): 164-203.

Bernard, Philippe. *Du chant romain au chant grégorien (IVe-XIIIe siècle)*. Patrimoines Christianisme. Paris: Éditions du Cerf, 1996.

Bernhard, Michael. "Die Überlieferung der Neumennamen im lateinischen Mittelalter," in *Quellen und Studien zur Musiktheorie des Mittelalters*, 2, ed. Michael Bernhard, Bayerische Akademie der Wissenschaften, Veröffentlichungen der Musikhistorischen Kommission, 13. Munich: Verlag der Bayerische Akademie der Wissenschaften, 1997, pp. 13-91.

Betteray, Dirk van. *Quomodo cantabimus canticum Domini in terra aliena: Liqueszenzen als Schlüssel zur Textinterpretation, eine semiologische*

Untersuchung an Sankt Galler Quellen. Studien und Materialien zur Musikwissenschaft, 45. Hildesheim: Georg Olms, 2007.

Białkowski, Mariusz. "Alcune osservazioni sulla notazione sangallese nei contesti liquescenti e melodicamente unisonici." *Beiträge zur Gregorianik* 59–60 (2015): 111–21.

Bielitz, Mathias. *Zum Bezeichneten der Neumen, insbesondere der Liqueszenz: Ein Hypothesenansatz zum Verhältnis von Musik und Sprache, zur diatonischen Rationalität, zur Bewegungs- und Raum-Analogie, zur Enstehung der Neumenschrift und zur Rezeption des Gregorianischen Chorals in Benevent.* Neckargemünd: Männeles Verlag, 1998.

Billecocq, Marie-Claire. "Lettres ajoutées à la notation neumatique du codex 239 de Laon." *Études Grégoriennes* 17 (1978): 7–144.

Bischoff, Bernhard. *Paläographie des römischen Altertums und des abendländischen Mittelalters.* Grundlagen der Germanistik, 24. Berlin: Erich Schmidt Verlag, 1979.

Blackburn, Bonnie J. "The Lascivious Career of B-Flat," in *Eroticism in Early Modern Music*, ed. Bonnie J. Blackburn and Laurie Stras. Farnham: Ashgate, 2015, pp. 19–42.

Boethius, Anicius Manlius Severinus. *De institutione musica*, ed. Gottfried Friedlein, in *De institutione arithmetica libri duo, De institutione musica libri quinque, accedit Geometria quae fertur Boetii.* Bibliotheca Scriptorum Graecorum et Romanorum Teubneriana. Leipzig: Teubner, 1867; repr. Frankfurt am Main, 1966, pp. 175–371. English translation: *Fundamentals of Music*, trans. Calvin M. Bower, ed. Claude V. Palisca, Music Theory Translation Series (New Haven: Yale University Press, 1989).

Bohlman, Philip V. "Musicology as a Political Act." *Journal of Musicology* 11 (1993): 411–36.

Bonderup, Jens. *The Saint Martial Polyphony–Texture and Tonality: A Contribution to Research in the Development of Polyphonic Style in the Middle Ages*, trans. Stephanie Olsen and Jean McVeigh. Studier og publikationer fra Musikvidenskabeligt Institut Aarhus Universitet, 4. Copenhagen: Dan Fog Musikforlag, 1982.

Boorman, Stanley. *Ottaviano Petrucci: Catalogue Raisonné.* Oxford: Oxford University Press, 2006.

Boretz, Benjamin, and Edward T. Cone, eds. *Perspectives on Notation and Performance.* Perspectives of New Music. New York: W. W. Norton, 1976.

Boulez, Pierre. "L'écriture du musicien: Le regard du sourd?" *Critique* 36 (1981): 443–64; repr. Pierre Boulez, *Jalons (pour une décennie): Dix ans d'enseignement au Collège de France (1978–1988)*, ed. Jean-Jacques Nattiez, Musique/Passé/Présent (n.p.: Christian Bourgois, 1989), pp. 293–315; and Pierre Boulez, *Points de repère, 2: Regards sur autrui*, ed. Jean-Jacques Nattiez and Sophie Galaise, Musique/Passé/Présent (n.p.: Christian Bourgois, 2005), pp. 268–92.

Bradley, Catherine A., and Karen Desmond, eds. *The Montpellier Codex, the Final Fascicle: Contents, Contexts, Chronologies*. Studies in Medieval and Renaissance Music. Woodbridge: The Boydell Press, 2018.

Bragard, Roger. "Le Speculum musicae du compilateur Jacques de Liège." *Musica Disciplina* 7 (1953): 59–105; *ibid.* 8 (1954): 1–17.

Brinkmann, Reinhold, ed., *Improvisation und neue Musik*. Veröffentlichungen des Instituts für Neue Musik und Musikerziehung, 20. Mainz: B. Schott's Söhne, 1979.

Brodsky, Warren, Avishai Henik, Bat-Sheva Rubinstein and Moshe Zorman. "Auditory Imagery from Musical Notation in Expert Musicians." *Perception & Psychophysics* 65 (2003): 602–12.

Brodsky, Warren, Yoav Kessler, Bat-Sheva Rubinstein, Jane Ginsborg and Avishai Henik. "The Mental Representation of Music Notation: Notational Audiation." *Journal of Experimental Psychology: Human Perception and Performance* 34 (2008): 427–45.

Brothers, Thomas. *Chromatic Beauty in the Late Medieval Chanson: An Interpretation of Manuscript Accidentals*. Cambridge: Cambridge University Press, 1997.

Brown, Earle. "Notation und Ausführung neuer Musik." *Darmstadter Beiträge zur neuen Musik* 9 (1965): 64–86.

Bukofzer, Manfred F. *Studies in Medieval and Renaissance Music*. New York: W. W. Norton, 1950.

Byo, James L. "Effects of Barlines, Pitch, and Meter on Musicians' Rhythmn [sic] Reading Performance." *Journal of Band Research* 27 (1991–92): 34–44.

Cahn, Peter, and Ann-Katrin Heimer, eds. *De musica et cantu: Studien zur Geschichte der Kirchenmusik und der Oper. Helmut Hucke zum 60. Geburtstag*. Musikwissenschaftliche Publikationen, Hochschule für Darstellende Kunst, 2. Hildesheim: Georg Olms Verlag, 1993.

Campagne, Augusta. *Simone Verovio: Music Printing, Intabulations and Basso Continuo in Rome around 1600*. Wiener Veröffentlichungen zur Musikgeschichte, 13. Vienna: Böhlau Verlag, 2018.

CANTUS. *An Aquitanian Antiphoner: Toledo, Biblioteca capitular, 44.2*. Wissenschaftliche Abhandlungen, 55, no. 1. Ottawa: Institute of Mediaeval Music, 1992.

Caplin, William E. "Theories of Musical Rhythm in the Eighteenth and Nineteenth Centuries," in *The Cambridge History of Western Music Theory*, ed. Christensen, pp. 657–94.

Cardine, Eugène. *Semiologia gregoriana*. Rome: Pontificio Istituto di Musica Sacra, 1968. English translation: *Gregorian Semiology*, trans. Robert M. Fowels (Solesmes: Abbaye Saint Pierre de Solesmes, 1983).

Carter, Elliott. "Music and the Time Screen," in *Current Thought in Musicology*, ed. John W. Grubbs. Symposia in the Arts and the Humanities, 4. Austin: University of Texas Press, 1976, pp. 63–88; repr. in Elliott Carter, *The*

Writings of Elliott Carter: An American Composer Looks at Modern Music, ed. Else Stone and Kurt Stone (Bloomington: Indiana University Press, 1977), pp. 343–67.

"The Time Dimension in Music." *Music Journal* 23 no. 8 (November 1965): 29–30; repr. in Elliott Carter, *The Writings of Elliott Carter: An American Composer Looks at Modern Music*, ed. Else Stone and Kurt Stone (Bloomington: Indiana University Press, 1977), pp. 243–47.

Caskel, Christoph. "Notation für Schlagzeug." *Darmstadter Beiträge zur neuen Musik* 9 (1965): 110–16.

Charteris, Richard. *Giovanni Gabrieli (ca. 1555–1612): A Thematic Catalogue of His Music with a Guide to the Source Materials and Translations of His Vocal Texts*. Thematic Catalogues, 20. Stuyvesant, NY: Pendragon Press, 1996.

Chartier, Yves. "Hucbald de Saint-Amand et la notation musicale," in *Musicologie médiévale*, ed. Huglo, pp. 145–55.

Charru, Philippe. "Temps et musique dans la pensée d'Augustin." *Revue d'Études Augustiniennes et Patristiques* 55 (2009): 171–88.

Christensen, Thomas, ed. *The Cambridge History of Western Music Theory*. Cambridge History of Music. Cambridge: Cambridge University Press, 2002.

Claussen, M. A. *The Reform of the Frankish Church: Chrodegang of Metz and the Regula canonicorum in the Eighth Century*. Cambridge Studies in Medieval Life and Thought, ser. 4, 61. Cambridge: Cambridge University Press, 2004.

Coelho, Victor. *The Manuscript Sources of Seventeenth-Century Italian Lute Music*. New York: Garland Publishing, 1995.

Coelho, Victor Anand, ed. *Performance on Lute, Guitar, and Vihuela: Historical Practice and Modern Interpretation*. Cambridge Studies in Performance Practice. Cambridge: Cambridge University Press, 1997.

Coelho, Victor, and Keith Polk. *Instrumentalists and Renaissance Culture, 1420–1600*. Cambridge: Cambridge University Press, 2016.

Cole, Hugo. *Sounds and Signs: Aspects of Musical Notation*. London: Oxford University Press, 1974.

Colette, Marie-Noël, and Catherine Massip, eds. *Actes du Colloque de Royaumont: Manuscrits notés en neumes en Occident Abbaye de Royaumont 29–31 octobre 2010 = Études Grégoriennes* 39 (2012).

Collamore, Lila Diane. "Aquitanian Collections of Office Chants: A Comparative Survey." Ph.D. diss., Catholic University of America, 2000.

Collins, Michael. "The Performance of Triplets in the 17th and 18th Centuries." *Journal of the American Musicological Society* 19 (1966): 281–328.

Commentarius anonymus in Micrologum Guidonis Aretini, in *Expositiones in Micrologum Guidonis Aretini*, ed. Jos. Smits van Waesberghe. Musicologica Medii Aevi, 1. Amsterdam: North-Holland Publishing Company, 1957, pp. 95–172.

Compendium musicae mensurabilis artis antiquae, ed. F. Alberto Gallo, Corpus Scriptorum de Musica, 15. N.p.: American Institute of Musicology, 1971, pp. 59–73.

Corbin, Solange. *Die Neumen*. Palaeographie der Musik 1, fasc. 3. Cologne: Arno Volk-Verlag, Hans Gerig KG, 1977.

Coussemaker, Edmond de, ed. *Scriptorum de musica medii aevi*. 4 vols. Paris: A. Durand, 1864–76; repr. Hildesheim, 1963.

Cowell, Henry. "Our Inadequate Notation." *Modern Music* 4 no. 3 (March–April 1927): 29–33.

Craft, Robert. "'Dear Bob[sky]' (Stravinsky's Letters to Robert Craft, 1944–1949)." *The Musical Quarterly* 65 (1979): 392–439.

Crocker, Richard. "Two Recent Editions of Aquitanian Polyphony." *Plainsong & Medieval Music* 3 (1994): 57–101.

Cullin, Olivier. "Notations in Carthusian Liturgical Books: Preliminary Remarks," in *The Calligraphy of Medieval Music*, ed. Haines, pp. 175–94.

Curran, Sean. "A Palaeographical Analysis of the Verbal Text in Montpellier 8: Problems, Implications, Opportunities," in *The Montpellier Codex*, ed. Bradley and Desmond, pp. 32–65.

Dahlhaus, Carl. "Notenschrift heute." *Darmstadter Beiträge zur neuen Musik* 9 (1965): 9–34.

"Die Tactus- und Proportionenlehre des 15. bis 17. Jahrhunderts," in *Geschichte der Musiktheorie*, 6: *Hören, Messen und Rechnen in der frühen Neuzeit*, ed. Frieder Zaminer. Darmstadt: Wissenschaftliche Buchgesellschaft, 1987, pp. 335–61.

"Zur Geschichte der Synkope." *Die Musikforschung* 12 (1959): 385–91.

Dal Maso, Vania. *Teoria e pratica della musica italiana del rinascimento*. Lucca: Libreria Musicale Italiana, 2017.

Danckwardt, Marianne. "Zur Notierung, klanglichen Anlage und Rhythmisierung der Mehrstimmigkeit in den Saint-Martial-Handschriften." *Kirchenmusikalisches Jahrbuch* 68 (1984): 31–88.

Davis, Lisa Fagin. *The Gottschalk Antiphonary: Music and Liturgy in Twelfth-Century Lambach*. Cambridge Studies in Palaeography and Codicology, 8. Cambridge: Cambridge University Press, 2000.

Debrock, Mark, and Pieter Mannaerts. "Liquescence et force articulatoire: Une approche phonétique du chant grégorien." *Études Grégoriennes* 45 (2018): 71–106.

Desmond, Karen. "Did Vitry Write an *Ars vetus et nova*?" *Journal of Musicology* 32 (2015): 441–93.

Music and the moderni, 1300-1350: The ars nova in Theory and Practice. Cambridge: Cambridge University Press, 2018.

"Texts in Play: The *Ars nova* and Its Hypertexts." *Musica Disciplina* 57 (2012): 81–153.

Dorfmüller, Kurt. *Studien zur Lautenmusik in der ersten Hälfte des 16. Jahrhunderts.* Münchner Veröffentlichungen zur Musikgeschichte, 11. Tutzing: Hans Schneider, 1967.

———. "La tablature de luth allemande et les problèmes d'édition," in *Le luth et sa musique*, ed. Jacquot, pp. 245–57.

Drai-Zerbib, Véronique, and Thierry Baccino. "L'expertise dans la lecture musicale: Intégration intermodale." *L'année psychologique* 105 (2005): 387–422.

Drai-Zerbib, Véronique, Thierry Baccino and Emmanuel Bigand. "Sight-Reading Expertise: Cross-Modality Integration Investigated Using Eye Tracking." *Psychology of Music* 40 (2012): 216–35.

Dry, François. "Instructions allemandes pour le luth et instructions espagnoles pour la vihuela: Esquisse d'une comparaison," in *". . . La musique, de tous les passetemps le plus beau . . .": Hommage à Jean-Michel Vaccaro*, ed. François Lesure and Henri Vanhulst. Domaine Musicologique, 19. N.p.: Klincksieck, 1998, pp. 109–19.

Duchez, Marie-Elisabeth. "Des neumes à la portée: Élaboration et organisation rationnelles de la discontinuité musicale et de sa représentation graphique, et la formule mélodique à l'échelle monocordale." *Canadian University Music Review* 4 (1983): 22–65.

———. "La representation spatio-verticale du caractère musical grave-aigu et l'élaboration de la notion de hauteur de son dans la conscience musicale occidentale." *Acta Musicologica* 51 (1979): 54–73.

Dufourt, Hugues. "L'artifice de l'écriture dans la musique occidentale." *Critique* 37, no. 408 (May 1981): 465–77; repr. in Hugues Dufourt, *Musique, pouvoir, écriture*, Musique/Passé/Présent (n.p.: Christian Bourgois, 1991), pp. 177–89; and *ibid.*, Collection Musique & Philosophie (n.p.: Éditions Delatour France, 2014), pp. 209–23.

Duhamel, Pascale. "L'enseignement de la musique à l'Université de Paris d'après le manuscrit BnF lat.7378A." *Acta Musicologica* 79 (2007): 263–89.

Dunford, Dawn. "Optometry and Music: A Review of the Literature." *Journal of Optometric Vision Development* 31 no. 2 (Summer 2000): 76–82.

Earp, Lawrence. *Guillaume de Machaut: A Guide to Research.* Garland Composer Resource Manuals, 36. New York: Garland, 1995.

———. "Machaut's Role in the Production of Manuscripts of His Works." *Journal of the American Musicological Society* 42 (1989): 461–503.

Emerson, John A. *Albi, Bibliothèque Municipale Rochegude, Manuscript 44: A Complete Ninth-Century Gradual and Antiphoner from Southern France*, ed. Lila Collamore. Wissenschaftliche Abhandlungen, 77. Ottawa: Institute of Mediaeval Music, 2002.

Eppelsheim, Jürgen. "Buchstaben-Notation, Tabulatur und Klaviatur." *Archiv für Musikwissenschaft* 31 (1974): 57–72.

Everist, Mark. "From Paris to St. Andrews: The Origins of W_1." *Journal of the American Musicological Society* 43 (1990): 1–42.

"Montpellier 8: Anatomy of...," in *The Montpellier Codex*, ed. Bradley and Desmond, pp. 13–31.

"The Polyphonic *Rondeau c.* 1300: Repertory and Context." *Early Music History* 15 (1996): 59–96.

Fabris, Dinko. "Lute Tablature Instructions in Italy: A Survey of the *Regole* from 1507 to 1759," trans. Paul Beier, in *Performance on Lute, Guitar, and Vihuela*, ed. Coelho, pp. 16–46.

Feisst, Sabine. *Der Begriff "Improvisation" in der neuen Musik*. Berliner Musik Studien, 14. Sinzig: Studio, 1997.

"Negotiating Freedom and Control in Composition: Improvisation and Its Offshoots 1950–1980," in *The Oxford Handbook of Critical Improvisation Studies*, ed. Benjamin Piekut and George E. Lewis. 2 vols. New York: Oxford University Press, 2016, 2:206–29.

Fellin, Eugene C. "The Notation Types of Trecento Music," in *L'ars nova italiana del trecento*, 4, ed. Agostino Ziino. Certaldo: Centro di studi sull'Ars Nova Italiana del Trecento, 1978, pp. 211–23.

Fenlon, Iain. *Music, Print and Culture in Early Sixteenth-Century Italy*. Panizzi Lectures, 1994. London: British Library, 1994.

Ferretti, Bernardino. "Molti dialetti, un'unica lingua." *Studi Gregoriani* 11 (1995): 155–88.

Una notazione neumatica della Francia del nord: Saggio critico sulla notazione paleofranca. Novalesa: Comunità Benedettina dei SS. Pietro e Andrea, 2003.

Fine, Philip, Anna Berry and Burton Rosner. "The Effect of Pattern Recognition and Tonal Predictability on Sight-Singing Ability." *Psychology of Music* 34 (2006): 431–47.

Fischer, Kurt von. *Studien zur italienischen Musik des Trecento und frühen Quattrocento*. Publikationen der Schweizerischen Musikforschenden Gesellschaft, ser. 2, 5. Bern: Verlag Paul Haupt, 1956.

"Zur Entwicklung der italienischen Trecento-Notation." *Archiv für Musikwissenschaft* 16 (1959): 87–99.

Fischer, Rupert. "Chartres, Bibliothèque Municipale, cod. 47." *Beiträge zur Gregorianik* 28 (1999): 73–89.

"Einführung in Handschriften des Gregorianischen Chorals, I: St. Gallen, Stiftsbibliothek, Codex 359: Das Cantatorium von St. Gallen." *Beiträge zur Gregorianik* 19 (1995): 61–70.

"Epiphonus oder Cephalicus?" *Beiträge zur Gregorianik* 8 (1989): 5–28.

"Laon, Bibl. de la ville, 239." *Beiträge zur Gregorianik* 21 (1996): 75–91.

Floros, Constantin. *Universale Neumenkunde*. 3 vols. Kassel: Bärenreiter-Antiquariat, 1970.

Flotzinger, Rudolf. "Johannes de Garlandia und Anonymus IV: Zu ihrem Umfeld, ihren Persönlichkeiten und Traktaten," in *Gedenkschrift für Walter Pass*, ed. Martin Czernin. Tutzing: Hans Schneider, 2002, pp. 81–98.

"Zur Frage der Modalrhythmik als Antike-Rezeption." *Archiv für Musikwissenschaft* 29 (1972): 203–8.

Formarier, Marie. *Entre rhétorique et musique: Essai sur le rythme latin antique et médiéval*. Latinitates, 9. Turnhout: Brepols, 2014.

Fox, Christopher. "Opening Offer or Contractual Obligation? On the Prescriptive Function of Notation in Music Today." *Tempo* 68 no. 269 (July 2014): 6–19.

Franco of Cologne. *Ars cantus mensurabilis*, ed. and trans. Jean-Philippe Navarre. AMICVS, Moyen Age, 1. Paris: Cerf, 1997.

Ars cantus mensurabilis, ed. Gilbert Reaney and André Gilles. Corpus Scriptorum de Musica, 18. N.p.: American Institute of Musicology, 1974. English translation: "Ars cantus mensurabilis," trans. Oliver Strunk, rev. James McKinnon, in *Source Readings in Music History*, ed. Strunk., rev. ed., ed. Treitler, pp. 226–45.

Froger, Jacques. "L'épitre de Notker sur les 'lettres significatives': Édition critique." *Études Grégoriennes* 5 (1962): 23–71.

Frutiger, Adrian. *Der Mensch und seine Zeichen*. 2 vols. Echzell: Horst Heiderhoff Verlag, 1979.

Fuller, Sarah Ann. "Aquitanian Polyphony of the Eleventh and Twelfth Centuries." 3 vols. Ph.D. diss., University of California, Berkeley, 1969.

"Defending the *Dodecachordon*: Ideological Currents in Glarean's Modal Theory." *Journal of the American Musicological Society* 49 (1996): 191–224.

"Hidden Polyphony—A Reappraisal." *Journal of the American Musicological Society* 24 (1971): 169–92.

"The Myth of 'Saint Martial' Polyphony: A Study of the Sources." *Musica Disciplina* 33 (1979): 5–26.

"A Phantom Treatise of the Fourteenth Century? The *Ars nova*." *Journal of Musicology* 4 (1985–86): 23–50.

Gaffurius, Franchinus. *Practica musice*. Milan: Guillermus le Signerre, 1496; repr. Farnborough, 1967; reproduced at gallica.bnf.fr. English translation: *Practica musicae*, trans. Clement A. Miller, Musicological Studies and Documents, 20 (n.p.: American Institute of Musicology, 1968).

Gallagher, Sean, James Haar, John Nádas and Timothy Striplin, eds. *Western Plainchant in the First Millennium: Studies in the Medieval Liturgy and Its Music*. Aldershot: Ashgate, 2003.

Gallo, F. Alberto. "Die Notationslehre im 14. und 15. Jahrhundert," in *Geschichte der Musiktheorie*, 5: *Die mittelalterliche Lehre von der Mehrstimmigkeit*, ed. Frieder Zaminer. Darmstadt: Wissenschaftliche Buchgesellschaft, 1984, pp. 257–356.

La teoria della notazione in Italia dalla fine del XII all'inizio del XV secolo. Antiquae Musicae Italicae, Subsidia Theorica. Bologna: Tamari Editori, 1966.

Garlandia, Johannes de. *De mensurabili musica*, ed. Erich Reimer. 2 vols. Beihefte zum Archiv für Musikwissenschaft, 10–11. Wiesbaden: Franz Steiner, 1972.

English translation: *Concerning Measured Music (De Mensurabili Musica)*, trans. Stanley H. Birnbaum, Colorado College Music Press Translations, 9 (Colorado Springs: Colorado College Music Press, 1978).

Gasparini, Francesco. *L'armonico pratico al cimbalo*. Venice: Antonio Bortoli, 1708; repr. in Monuments of Music and Music Literature in Facsimile, Second Series, Music Literature, 14 (New York: Broude Bros., 1967). English translation: *The Practical Harmonist at the Harpsichord*, trans. Frank S. Stillings, ed. David L. Burrows, Music Theory Translation Series, 1 (New Haven: Yale University Press, 1963; repr. New York 1980).

Gillingham, Bryan. *Modal Rhythm*. Wissenschaftliche Abhandlungen, 46. Ottawa: Institute of Mediaeval Music, 1986.

"Saint-Martial Polyphony: A Catalogue Raisonné," in *Gordon Athol Anderson (1929-1981): In Memoriam*. 2 vols. Wissenschaftliche Abhandlungen, 39. Henryville, Ottawa and Binningen: Institute of Mediaeval Music, 1984, 1:211–62.

Gillingham, Bryan, and Paul Merkley, eds. *Beyond the Moon: Festschrift Luther Dittmer*. Wissenschaftliche Abhandlungen, 53. Ottawa: Institute of Mediaeval Music, 1990.

Gillman [sic], Elizabeth, Geoffrey Underwood and John Morehen. "Recognition of Visually Presented Musical Intervals." *Psychology of Music* 30 (2002): 48–57.

Gilman, Elizabeth, and Geoffrey Underwood. "Restricting the Field of View to Investigate the Perceptual Spans of Pianists." *Visual Cognition* 10 (2003): 201–32.

Glareanus, Henricus. *Dodecachordon*. Basel: n.p., 1547; repr. in Monuments of Music and Music Literature in Facsimile, Second Series, Music Literature, 65 (New York, 1967). English translation by Clement A. Miller, 2 vols., Musicological Studies and Documents, 6 (n.p.: American Institute of Musicology, 1965).

Glover, Jane. "A List of Monteverdi's Instrumental Specifications," in *Claudio Monteverdi Orfeo*, ed. John Whenham. Cambridge Opera Handbooks. Cambridge: Cambridge University Press, 1986, pp. 182–84.

Goldman, Richard F. "Current Chronicle." *The Musical Quarterly* (1951): 83–89.

Goolsby, Thomas W. "Eye Movement in Music Reading: Effects of Reading Ability, Notational Complexity, and Encounters." *Music Perception* 12 (1994): 77–96.

"Profiles of Processing: Eye Movements during Sightreading." *Music Perception* 12 (1994), 97–123.

Gordon, Edwin E. *Learning Sequences in Music: A Contemporary Music Learning Theory*. Chicago: GIA Publications, 2007.

Grainger, Percy. "The Impress of Personality in Unwritten Music." *The Musical Quarterly* 1 (1915): 416–35.

Grant, Roger Mathew. "Epistemologies of Time and Metre in the Long Eighteenth Century." *Eighteenth-Century Music* 6 (2009): 59–75.

Grier, James. "Adémar de Chabannes (989–1034) and Musical Literacy." *Journal of the American Musicological Society* 66 (2013): 605–38.

———. "Adémar de Chabannes, Carolingian Musical Practices, and *Nota Romana*." *Journal of the American Musicological Society* 56 (2003): 43–98.

———. *Ademarus Cabanennsis monachus et musicus*. Corpus Christianorum, Autographa Medii Aevi, 7. Turnhout: Brepols, 2018.

———. "Authority of the Composer, Authority of the Editor," in *Nordic Music Editions: Symposium 1–2 September 2005*, ed. Niels Krabbe. Copenhagen: The Royal Library, 2006, pp. 17–29.

———. *The Critical Editing of Music: History, Method, and Practice*. Cambridge: Cambridge University Press, 1996.

———. "The Musical Autographs of Adémar de Chabannes (989–1034)." *Early Music History* 24 (2005): 125–68.

———. *The Musical World of a Medieval Monk: Adémar de Chabannes in Eleventh-Century Aquitaine*. Cambridge: Cambridge University Press, 2006.

———. "Scribal Practices in the Aquitanian Versaria of the Twelfth Century: Towards a Typology of Error and Variant." *Journal of the American Musicological Society* 45 (1992): 373–427.

———. "Some Codicological Observations on the Aquitanian Versaria." *Musica Disciplina* 44 (1990): 5–56.

Griffiths, John. "'¿Fantasía o realidad?' La vihuela en las *Obras* de Cabezón." *Anuario Musical* 69 (2014): 193–213.

———. "La producción de libros de cifra musical en España durante el siglo XVI." *Hispánica Lyra* 12 (2010): 10–27.

———. "The Vihuela: Performance Practice, Style, and Context," in *Performance on Lute, Guitar, and Vihuela*, ed. Coelho, pp. 158–79.

Guido d'Arezzo. *Epistola ad Michahelem*, in *Guido d'Arezzo's Regule rithmice*, ed. and trans. Pesce, pp. 437–531.

———. *Micrologus*, ed. Jos. Smits van Waesberghe. Corpus Scriptorum de Musica, 4. N. p.: American Institute of Musicology, 1955. English translation in *Hucbald, Guido, and John*, trans. Babb, pp. 57–83.

———. *Prologus in Antiphonarium*, ed. Joseph Smits van Waesberghe. Divitiae Musicae Artis, ser. A, 3. Buren: F. Knuf, 1975. Also in *Guido d'Arezzo's* Regule rithmice, ed. and trans. Pesce, pp. 405–35.

———. *Regulae rhythmicae*, ed. Joseph Smits van Waesberghe and Eduard Vetter. Divitiae Musicae Artis, ser. A, 4. Buren: Knuf, 1985. Also in *Guido d'Arezzo's* Regule rithmice, ed. and trans. Pesce, pp. 327–403.

Gunter, Thomas C., Björn-Helmer Schmidt and Mireille Besson. "Let's Face the Music: A Behavioral and Electrophysiological Exploration of Score Reading." *Psychophysiology* 40 (2003): 742–51.

Günther, Ursula. "Die Mensuralnotation der Ars nova in Theorie und Praxis." *Archiv für Musikwissenschaft* 19–20 (1962–63): 9–28.

Gushee, Lawrence. "Jehan des Murs and His Milieu," in *Musik und die Geschichte der Philosophie und Naturwissenschaften im Mittelalter: Fragen zur Wechselwirkung von "Musica" und "Philosophia" im Mittelalter*, ed. Frank Hentschel. Studien und Texte zur Geistesgeschichte des Mittelalters, 62. Leiden: Brill, 1998, pp. 339–71.

Haggh, Barbara, and Michel Huglo. "*Magnus liber—Maius munus*: Origine et destinée du manuscrit F." *Revue de Musicologie* 90 (2004): 193–230.

Haines, John. "Anonymous IV as an Informant on the Craft of Music Writing." *Journal of Musicology* 23 (2006): 375–425.

"From Point to Square: Graphic Change in Medieval Music Script." *Textual Cultures* 3 no. 2 (Autumn, 2008): 30–53.

"The Origins of the Musical Staff." *The Musical Quarterly* 91 (2008): 327–78.

"*Proprietas* and *Perfectio* in Thirteenth-Century Music Theory." *Theoria* 15 (2008): 5–29.

Haines, John, ed. *The Calligraphy of Medieval Music*. Musicalia Medii Aevi, 1. Turnhout: Brepols, 2011.

Halpern Andrea R., and Gordon H. Bower. "Musical Expertise and Melodic Structure in Memory for Musical Notation." *American Journal of Psychology* 95 (1982): 31–50.

Halporn, James W., Martin Ostwald and Thomas G. Rosenmeyer. *The Meters of Greek and Latin Poetry*, rev. ed. Norman: University of Oklahoma Press, 1980.

Ham, Martin. "A Sense of Proportion: The Performance of *Sesquialtera* ca. 1515-ca. 1565." *Musica Disciplina* 56 (2011): 79–274.

Hamilton, David. "Igor Stravinsky: A Discography of the Composer's Performances," in *Perspectives on Schoenberg and Stravinsky*, rev. ed., ed. Benjamin Boretz and Edward T. Cone. New York: W. W. Norton, 1972, pp. 268–84.

Handlo, Robertus de. *Regule*, ed. and trans. Peter M. Lefferts, in *Regule = The Rules, Robertus de Handlo, and Summa = The Summa, Johannes Hanboys*. Greek and Latin Music Theory, 7. Lincoln, NE: University of Nebraska Press, 1991, pp. 80–179.

Handschin, Jacques. "Eine alte Neumenschrift." *Acta Musicologica* 22 (1950): 69–97; and 25 (1953): 87–88.

Harding, Rosamond E. M. *The Metronome and It's* [sic] *Precursors*. Henley-on-Thames: Gresham Books, 1938.

Haubenstock-Ramati, Roman. "Notation—Material und Form." *Darmstadter Beiträge zur neuen Musik* 9 (1965): 51–54.

Haug, Andreas. "Zur Interpretation der Liqueszenzneumen." *Archiv für Musikwissenschaft* 50 (1993): 85–100.

Heartz, Daniel. *Pierre Attaingnant Royal Printer of Music: A Historical Study and Bibliographical Catalogue*. Berkeley and Los Angeles: University of California Press, 1969.

"Les premières 'Instructions' pour le luth (jusque vers 1550)," in *Le luth et sa musique*, ed. Jacquot, pp. 77–92.

Hebborn, Barbara. *Die Dasia-Notation*. Orpheus Schriftenreihe zu Grundfragen der Musik, 79. Bonn: Orpheus-Verlag, 1995.

Heinichen, Johann David. *Neu erfundene und gründliche Anweisung*. Hamburg: Benjamin Schillers, 1711; repr. ed. Wolfgang Horn, Documenta Musicologica, ser. 1: Druckschriften-Faksimiles, 40 (Kassel: Bärenreiter, 2000). English translation by Benedikt Brilmayer and Casey Mongoven, Harmonologia, 17 (Hillsdale NY: Pendragon Press, 2012).

Helsen, Kate. "The Evolution of Neumes into Square Notation in Chant Manuscripts." *Journal of the Alamire Foundation* 5 (2013): 143–74.

Hemming, Rudolf. "German Lute Tablature and Conrad Paumann," trans. Uta Henning. *Lute Society Journal* 15 (1973): 7–10.

Hen, Yitzhak. *The Royal Patronage of Liturgy in Frankish Gaul to the Death of Charles the Bald (877)*. Henry Bradshaw Society, Subsidia, 3. London: Boydell Press, 2001.

Hentschel, Frank. "The Sensuous Music Aesthetics of the Middle Ages: The Cases of Augustine, Jacques de Liège and Guido of Arezzo." *Plainsong & Medieval Music* 20 (2011): 1–29.

Herbst, Johann-Andreas. *Musica moderna prattica, ouero maniera del buon canto*. Frankfurt: Georg Mullers Verlag, 1658; repr. ed. Florian Grampp, in *Deutsche Gesangstraktate des 17. Jahrhunderts*, Documenta Musicologica, ser. 1: Druckschriften-Faksimiles, 43 (Kassel: Bärenreiter, 2006).

Hieronymus de Moravia. *Tractatus de musica*, ed. Christian Meyer and Guy Lobrichon. Corpus Christianorum Continuatio Mediaevalis, 250. Turnhout: Brepols, 2012. English translation of *Discantus positio uulgaris*: "Discantus positio vulgaris," in "Two XIII Century Treatises on Modal Rhythm and the Discant: Discantus positio vulgaris, De musica libellus (Anonymous VII)," trans. Janet Knapp, *Journal of Music Theory* 6 (1962): 200–15 at 203–7. Also trans. James McKinnon, in *Source Readings in Music History*, ed. Strunk, rev. ed., ed. Treitler, pp. 218–22.

Highben, Zebulon, and Caroline Palmer. "Effects of Auditory and Motor Mental Practice in Memorized Piano Performance." *Bulletin of the Council for Research in Music Education* 159 (Winter 2004): 58–65.

Hiley, David, and Janka Szendrei. "Notation, §III, 1: History of Western Notation: Plainchant," in *Grove Music Online*, www.oxfordmusiconline.com.

Hindemith, Paul. *Elementary Training for Musicians*, 2nd ed. New York: Schott Music, 1949.

Holschneider, Andreas. *Die Organa von Winchester: Studien zum ältesten Repertoire polyphoner Musik*. Hildesheim: Georg Olms Verlagsbuchhandlung, 1968.

Hoppin, Richard H. "Conflicting Signatures Reviewed." *Journal of the American Musicological Society* 9 (1956): 97–117.

"Partial Signatures and Musica Ficta in Some Early 15th-Century Sources." *Journal of the American Musicological Society* 6 (1953): 197–215.

Hourlier, J. "Le domaine de la notation messine." *Revue Grégorienne* 30 (1951): 96–113, 150–58.

Hucbald of Saint Amand. *Musica*, ed. Yves Chartier, in *L'oeuvre musicale d'Hucbald de Saint-Amand: Les compositions et le traité de musique*. Cahiers d'Études Médiévales, Cahier spécial, 5. Montreal: Bellarmin, 1995, pp. 136–213. English translation in *Hucbald, Guido, and John*, trans. Babb, pp. 13–44.

Huck, Oliver. "Double Motet Layouts in the Montpellier Codex and Contemporaneous *Libri motetorum*," in *The Montpellier Codex*, ed. Bradley and Desmond, pp. 90–99.

Hucke, Helmut. "Toward a New Historical View of Gregorian Chant." *Journal of the American Musicological Society* 33 (1980): 437–67.

Hughes, Andrew. *Manuscript Accidentals: Ficta in Focus 1350–1450*. Musicological Studies and Documents, 27. N.p.: American Institute of Musicology, 1972.

Hughes, David G. "Evidence for the Traditional View of the Transmission of Gregorian Chant." *Journal of the American Musicological Society* 40 (1987): 377–404.

"From the Advent Project to the Late Middle Ages: Some Issues of Transmission," in *Western Plainchant in the First Millennium*, ed. Gallagher *et al.*, pp. 181–98.

Huglo, Michel. "The Earliest Developments in Square Notation: Twelfth-Century Aquitaine," trans. Barbara Haggh, in *The Calligraphy of Medieval Music*, ed. Haines, pp. 163–71.

"Observations codicologiques sur l'antiphonaire de Compiègne (Paris, B.N. lat. 17436)," in *De musica et cantu*, ed. Cahn and Heimer, pp. 117–30.

"Toward a Scientific Palaeography of Music," trans. John Haines, in *The Calligraphy of Medieval Music*, ed. Haines, pp. 13–21.

"La tradition musicale aquitaine: Répertoire et notation," in *Liturgie et musique (IXe – XIVe s.)*. Cahiers de Fanjeaux, 17. Toulouse: E. Privat, 1982, pp. 253–68.

Huglo, Michel, ed. *Musicologie médiévale: Notations et séquences*. Paris: Librairie Honoré Champion, 1987.

Huglo, Michel, and Haggh-Huglo, Barbara. "Des lettres de la passion aux lettres significatives notkériennes," in *"Quod ore cantas corde credas": Studi in onore di Giacomo Baroffio Dahnk*, ed. Leandra Scappaticci. Monumenta Studia Instrumenta Liturgica, 70. Vatican City: Libreria Editrice Vaticana, 2013, pp. 427–36.

"Interview with Stravinsky." *The Observer* no. 6788 (3 July 1921): 9.

Jackson, Roland. "Guillaume de Machaut and Dissonance in Fourteenth Century French Music." *Musica Disciplina* 53 (2003–8): 7–49.

Jacquot, Jean, ed. *Le luth et sa musique: Neuilly-sur-Seine, 10–14 septembre 1957.* Le Choeur des Muses. Paris: Éditions du Centre National de la Recherche Scientifique, 1958.

Jacques of Liège. *Speculum musicae,* ed. Roger Bragard. 7 vols. in 8. Corpus Scriptorum de Musica, 3. Rome: Institute of Musicology, 1955–73. Partial English translation: "From *Speculum musicae,*" trans. Oliver Strunk, rev. James McKinnon, in *Source Readings in Music History,* ed. Strunk., rev. ed., ed. Treitler, pp. 269–78.

Jammers, Ewald. "Die palaeofraenkische Neumenschrift." *Scriptorium* 7 (1953): 235–59.

"Studien zu Neumenschrift, Neumenhandschriften und neumierter Musik." *Bibliothek und Wissenschaft* 2 (1965): 85–161.

Tafeln zur Neumenschrift. Tutzing: H. Schneider, 1965.

Janovka, Tomáš Baltazar. *Clavis ad thesaurum magnae artis musicae.* Prague: Georgius Labaun, 1701; repr. in Dictionarium Musicum, 2 (Amsterdam: Frits Knuf, 1973). Partial English translation in Lester, *Between Modes and Keys,* pp. 163–77.

Jean, Georges. *Langage de signes: L'écriture et son double.* Découvertes Gallimard, Archéologie. N.p.: Gallimard, 1989.

Judd, Cristle Collins. *Reading Renaissance Music Theory: Hearing with the Eyes.* Cambridge Studies in Music Theory and Analysis, 14. Cambridge: Cambridge University Press, 2000.

"Renaissance Modal Theory: Theoretical, Compositional, and Editorial Perspectives," in *The Cambridge History of Western Music Theory,* ed. Christensen, pp. 364–406.

Kagel, Mauricio. "Komposition—Notation—Interpretation." *Darmstadter Beiträge zur neuen Musik* 9 (1965): 55–63.

Karkoschka, Erhard. *Das Schriftbild der neuen Musik: Bestandsaufnahme neuer Notationssymbole, Anleitung zu deren Deutung, Realisation und Kritik.* Celle: Moeck, 1966. English translation: *Notation in New Music: A Critical Guide to Interpretation and Realisation,* trans. Ruth Koenig (New York: Praeger, 1972).

Kirnberger, Joh. Phil. *Die Kunst des reinen Satzes in der Musik.* 2 vols. in 4. Berlin: C. F. Voss (vol. 1); Berlin and Königsberg: G. J. Decker and G. L. Hartung (vol. 2), 1776–79; repr. ed. Gregor Herzfeld (Kassel, 2004). English translation: *The Art of Strict Musical Composition,* trans. David Beach and Jurgen Thym, Music Theory Translation Series, 4 (New Haven and London: Yale University Press, 1982).

Klauser, Theodor. "Die liturgischen Austauschbeziehungen zwischen der römischen und der fränkischen Kirche vom achten bis zum elften Jahrhundert." *Historisches Jahrbuch* 53 (1933): 169–89.

Klöckner, Stefan. "Cod. H 159 der Bibliothek der Medizinischen Fakultät von Montpellier (Tonar von Saint-Bénigne, Dijon)." *Beiträge zur Gregorianik* 30 (2000): 77–93.

Koehler, Laurie. *Pythagoreisch-platonische Proportionen in Werken der ars nova und ars subtilior*. 2 vols. Göttinger Musikwissenschaftliche Arbeiten, 12. Kassel: Bärenreiter, 1990.

Kolisch, Rudolf. *Tempo und Charakter in Beethovens Musik*, ed. Regina Busch and David Satz. *Musik-Konzepte*, 76/77. Munich: Edition Text + Kritik, 1992. English translation: "Tempo and Character in Beethoven's Music," trans. Thomas Y. Levin and David Satz, *The Musical Quarterly* 77 (1993): 90–131, 268–342.

Kontarsky, Aloys. "Notationen für Klavier." *Darmstadter Beiträge zur neuen Musik* 9 (1965): 92–109.

Kornicke, Eloise. "An Exploratory Study of Individual Difference Variables in Piano Sight-Reading Achievement." *Quarterly Journal of Music Teaching and Learning* 6 (1995): 56–79.

Kreitner, Kenneth, Louis Jambou, Desmond Hunter, Stewart A. Carter, Peter Walls, Kah-Ming Ng, David Schulenberg and Clive Brown. "Ornaments," in *The New Grove Dictionary of Music and Musicians*, ed. Stanley Sadie. 2nd ed. 29 vols. London: Macmillan, 2001, 18:708a–746b.

Kügle, Karl. *The Manuscript Ivrea, Biblioteca Capitolare 115: Studies in the Transmission and Composition of Ars Nova Polyphony*. Wissenschaftliche Abhandlungen, 69. Ottawa: Institute of Mediaeval Music, 1997.

Lambertus. *Musica mensurabilis*, in *The "Ars musica" Attributed to Magister Lambertus/Aristoteles*, ed. Christian Meyer, trans. Karen Desmond. Royal Musical Association Monographs, 27. Farnham: Ashgate, 2015, pp. 60–115.

Law, Vivien. "The Study of Grammar," in *Carolingian Culture: Emulation and Innovation*, ed. Rosamond McKitterick. Cambridge: Cambridge University Press, 1994, pp. 88–110.

Leach, Elizabeth Evas. "Machaut's First Single-Author Compilation," in *Manuscripts and Medieval Song: Inscription, Performance, Context*, ed. Helen Deeming and Elizabeth Eva Leech. Music in Context. Cambridge: Cambridge University Press, 2015, pp. 247–70.

Lee, Ji In. "The Role of Inner Hearing in Sight Reading Music as an Example of Inter-Modal Perception." *Musikpsychologie* 18 (2006): 35–52.

Leech-Wilkinson, Daniel. "The Emergence of *ars nova*." *Journal of Musicology* 13 (1995): 285–317.

Lersch, Irmgard. "Mensuralnotation zwischen Ars Antiqua und Ars Nova." *Musica Disciplina* 54 (2009): 5–38.

Lester, Joel. *Between Modes and Keys: German Theory 1592–1802*. Harmonologia, 3. Stuyvesant, NY: Pendragon Press, 1989.

Compositional Theory in the Eighteenth Century. Cambridge MA: Harvard University Press, 1992.

Levy, Kenneth. "Abbot Helisachar's Antiphoner." *Journal of the American Musicological Society* 48 (1995): 171–86.

"Charlemagne's Archetype of Gregorian Chant." *Journal of the American Musicological Society* 40 (1987): 1–30.

Gregorian Chant and the Carolingians. Princeton: Princeton University Press, 1998.

"On the Origins of Neumes." *Early Music History* 7 (1987): 59–90.

Ligeti, György. "Neue Notation—Kommunikationsmittel oder Selbstzweck?" *Darmstadter Beiträge zur neuen Musik* 9 (1965): 35–50.

Lipman, Samuel. "Stravinsky: Rerecording History," in *The House of Music: Art in an Era of Institutions*. Boston: David R. Godine, 1984, pp. 120–32 (originally published in *The New Criterion*, 1982).

Llewellyn, Jeremy. "Grammar, Writing and Chant: Notker the Editor and the *Epistola ad Lantbertum*," in *Actes du Colloque d'Auxerre*, ed. Aubert and Rankin, pp. 225–41.

Lloyd, Angela. "Ordering and Reordering in Cipriano de Rore's 1542 and 1550 Madrigal Books." *Muziek & Wetenschap* 6 (1997): 3–25.

Loesch, Heinz von. "Musica—Musica practica—Musica poetica," in *Geschichte der Musiktheorie*, 8/1: *Deutsche Musiktheorie des 15. bis 17. Jahrhunderts*, erster Teil, *Von Paumann bis Calvisius*, ed. Thomas Ertelt and Frieder Zaminer. Darmstadt: Wissenschaftliche Buchgesellschaft, 2003, pp. 99–264.

Lombardi, Daniele. *Scrittura e suono: La notazione nella music contemporanea*. Rome: Edipan, 1980.

Lowery, H. "On Reading Music." *The Dioptric Review and the British Journal of Physiological Optics* new series, 1 (1940): 78–88.

Lowinsky, Edward E. "Conflicting Views on Conflicting Signatures." *Journal of the American Musicological Society* 7 (1954): 181–204.

"Early Scores in Manuscript." *Journal of the American Musicological Society* 13 (1960): 126–73.

"The Function of Conflicting Signatures in Early Polyphonic Music." *The Musical Quarterly* 31 (1945): 227–60.

"On the Use of Scores by Sixteenth-Century Musicians." *Journal of the American Musicological Society* 1 (1948): 17–23.

Madell, Jaime, and Sylvie Hébert. "Eye Movements and Music Reading: Where Do We Look Next?" *Music Perception* 26 (2008): 157–70.

Marchetto of Padua. *Pomerium in arte musicae mensuratae*, ed. Joseph Vecchi. Corpus Scriptorum de Musica, 6. N.p.: American Institute of Musicology, 1961.

Marshall, Robert. L. "J. S. Bach's Compositions for Solo Flute." *Journal of the American Musicological Society* 32 (1979): 463–98.

Martin, Henri-Jean. *Histoire et pouvoirs de l'écrit*. Collection Histoire et Décadence. Paris: Librairie Académique Perrin, 1988. English translation: *The History and Power of Writing*, trans. Lydia G. Cochrane (Chicago: University of Chicago Press, 1994).

Mathiesen, Thomas J. *Apollo's Lyre: Greek Music and Music Theory in Antiquity and the Middle Ages*. Publications of the Center for the History of Music

Theory and Literature, 2. Lincoln and London: University of Nebraska Press, 1999.

Matthesson, Johann. *Das neu-eröffnete Orchestre*. Hamburg: B. Schillers, 1713; repr. ed. Dietrich Bartel, *Die drei Orchestre-Schriften*, 1 (Laaber: Laaber-Verlag, 2002).

Maw, David. "*Je le temoin en mon chant*: The Art of Diminution in the Petronian Triplum," in *The Montpellier Codex*, ed. Bradley and Desmond, pp. 161–83.

McClary, Susan. *Modal Subjectivities: Self-Fashioning in the Italian Madrigal*. Berkeley, Los Angeles and London: University of California Press, 2004.

McGee, Timothy J. "*Dança amorosa*: A Newly-Discovered Medieval Dance Pair," in *Beyond the Moon*, ed. Gillingham and Merkley, pp. 295–306.

"'Ornamental' Neumes and Early Notation." *Performance Practice Review* 9 (1996): 39–65.

The Sound of Medieval Song: Ornamentation and Vocal Style According to the Treatises. Oxford Monographs on Music. Oxford: Oxford University Press, 1998.

McKitterick, Rosamond. *The Carolingians and the Written Word*. Cambridge: Cambridge University Press, 1989.

"Royal Patronage of Culture in the Frankish Kingdoms under the Carolingians: Motives and Consequences," in *Committenti e produzione artistico-letteraria nell'alto medioevo occidentale, 4–10 aprile 1991*. 2 vols. Settimane di studio del Centro italiano di studi sull'alto medioevo, 39. Spoleto: Presso la Sede del Centro, 1992, 1:93–129.

Meier, Bernhard. *Die Tonarten der klassischen Vokalpolyphonie*. Utrecht: Oosthoek, Scheltema & Holkema, 1974. English translation: *The Modes of Classical Vocal Polyphony Described According to the Sources*, trans. Ellen S. Beebe (New York: Broude Brothers, 1988).

Meyer, Christian. "Zur 'Konstruktion' der antiken Musiktheorie bei Glarean," in *Heinrich Glarean*, ed. Schwindt, pp. 147–59.

Michels, Ulrich. *Die Musiktraktate des Johannes de Muris*. Beihefte zum Archiv für Musikwissenschaft, 8. Wiesbaden: Franz Steiner, 1970.

Miller, Clement A. "Gaffurius' *Practica Musicae*: Origin and Contents." *Musica Disciplina* 22 (1968): 105–29.

Minamino, Hiroyuki. "Conrad Paumann and the Evolution of Solo Lute Practice in the Fifteenth Century." *Journal of Musicological Research* 6 (1986): 291–310.

"Production and Reception of Petrucci's Lute Books." *Journal of the Lute Society of America* 41 (2008): 37–55.

Mocquereau, André. *Le nombre musical grégorien ou rythmique grégorienne: Théorie et pratique*. 2 vols. Rome and Tournai: Société de Saint-Jean l'Évangéliste, 1908–27.

Morley, Thomas. *A Plaine and Easie Introduction to Practicall Musicke*. London: Peter Short, 1597 (facsimile in The English Experience, 207 [Amsterdam and New York: Theatrum Orbis Terrarum and Da Capo Press, 1969]).

Muris, Johannes de. *Ars practica mensurabilis cantus secundum Iohannem de Muris: Die Recensio maior des sogenannten "Libellus practice cantus mensurabilis,"* ed. Christian Berktold. Bayerische Akademie der Wissenschaften, Veröffentlichungen der Musikhistorischen Kommission, 14. Munich: Verlag der Bayerische Akademie der Wissenschaften, 1999.

——— *Écrits sur la musique*, trans. Christian Meyer. Collection Sciences de la Musique. N.p.: CNRS Editions, 2000.

——— *Notitia artis musicae et Compendium musicae practicae*, Petrus de Sancto Dionysio, *Tractatus de musica*, ed. Ulrich Michels. Corpus Scriptorum de Musica, 17. N.p.: American Institute of Musicology, 1972. Partial English translation: "From *Notitia artis musicae*," trans. Oliver Strunk, rev. James McKinnon, in *Source Readings in Music History*, ed. Strunk., rev. ed., ed. Treitler, pp. 261–69.

Nakada, Tsutomu, Yukihiko Fujii, Kiyotaka Suzuki and Ingrid L. Kwee. "'Musical Brain' Revealed by High-Field (3 Tesla) Functional MRI." *NeuroReport* 9 (1998): 3853–56.

Nelson, Janet L. "Literacy in Carolingian Government," in *The Uses of Literacy in Early Medieval Europe*, ed. Rosamond McKitterick. Cambridge: Cambridge University Press, 1990, pp. 258–96.

Odenkirchen, Andreas. "13 Neumentafeln in tabellarischer Übersicht," in *De musica et cantu*, ed. Cahn and Heimer, pp. 257–62.

Oesch, Hans. *Guido von Arezzo: Biographisches und Theoretisches unter besonderer Berücksichtigung der sogenannten odonischen Traktate*. Publikationen der Schweizerischen Musikforschenden Gesellschaft, ser. 2, 4. Bern: Verlag Paul Haupt, 1954.

Ongaro, Guilio M. "All Work and No Play? The Organization of Work among Musicians in Late Renaissance Venice." *Journal of Medieval and Renaissance Studies* 25 (1995): 55–72.

Ostheimer, Andreas. "Die Niederschrift von Musik mit Dasiazeichen: Untersuchungen zur praktischen Anwendung eines 'theoretischen' Schriftsystems." *Beiträge zur Gregorianik* 28 (1999): 51–72.

Owens, Jessie Ann. "The Milan Partbooks: Evidence of Cipriano de Rore's Compositional Process." *Journal of the American Musicological Society* 37 (1984): 270–98.

——— "Mode in the Madrigals of Cipriano de Rore," in *Altro Polo: Essays on Italian Music in the Cinquecento*, ed. Richard Charteris. Sydney: Frederick May Foundation for Italian Studies, 1990, pp. 1–15.

Page, Christopher. *The Christian West and Its Singers: The First Thousand Years*. New Haven and London: Yale University Press, 2010.

Palisca, Claude V. "Die Jahrzehnte um 1600 in Italien," trans. Horst Leuchtmann, in *Geschichte der Musiktheorie, 7: Italienische Musiktheorie im 16. und 17. Jahrhundert*, ed. Frieder Zaminer. Darmstadt: Wissenschaftliche Buchgesellschaft, 1989, pp. 221–306.

Palm, Siegfried. "Zur Notation für Streichinstrumente." *Darmstadter Beiträge zur neuen Musik* 9 (1965): 87–91.

Peirce, Charles S. *Collected Papers of Charles Sanders Peirce*, 8 vols., ed. Charles Hartshorne and Paul Weiss. Cambridge, MA: Harvard University Press, 1931–58.

Penttinen, Marjaana, and Erkki Huovinen. "The Early Development of Sight-Reading Skills in Adulthood: A Study of Eye Movements." *Journal of Research in Music Education* 59 (2011): 196–220.

Pesce, Dolores. *The Affinities and Medieval Transposition*. Music: Scholarship and Performance. Bloomington and Indianapolis: Indiana University Press, 1987.

Pesce, Dolores, ed. and trans. *Guido d'Arezzo's* Regule rithmice, Prologus in Antiphonarium, *and* Epistola ad Michahelem: *A Critical Text and Translation*. Wissenschaftliche Abhandlungen, 73. Ottawa: Institute of Mediaeval Music, 1999.

Phillips, Nancy. "The Dasia Notation and Its Manuscript Tradition," in *Musicologie médiévale*, ed. Huglo, pp. 157–73.

"Notationen und Notationslehren von Boethius bis zum 12. Jahrhundert," trans. Gudrun Tillmann-Budde, in *Geschichte der Musiktheorie*, 4: *Die Lehre von einstimmigen liturgischen Gesang*, ed. Thomas Ertelt and Frieder Zaminer. Darmstadt: Wissenschaftliche Buchgesellschaft, 2000, pp. 293–623.

Phillips, Nancy, and Michel Huglo. "Le *De musica* de saint Augustin et l'organisation de la durée musicale du IXe au XIIe siècles." *Recherches Augustiniennes* 20 (1985): 117–31.

Pierce, Todd. *The International Pictograms Standard*. Cincinnati: ST Publications, 1996.

Pinegar, Sandra. "On Rhythmic Modes." *Theoria* 8 (1994): 73–112.

Planchart, Alejandro Enrique. *The Repertory of Tropes at Winchester*. 2 vols. Princeton: Princeton University Press, 1977.

Powers, Harold. "From Psalmody to Tonality," in *Tonal Structures in Early Music*, ed. Cristle Collins Judd. Criticism and Analysis of Early Music, 1. New York and London: Garland Publishing, 1998, pp. 275–340.

"Monteverdi's Model for a Multimodal Madrigal," in *In cantu et in sermone: For Nino Pirrotta on His 80th Birthday*, ed. Fabrizio Della Seta and Franco Piperno. Italian Medieval and Renaissance Studies, The University of Western Australia, 2. Florence: Leo S. Olschki, 1989, pp. 185–219.

Prosdocimus de Beldemandis. *Tractatus practice de musica mensurabili*, in *Scriptorum de musica medii aevi*, ed. Coussemaker, 3:200–28.

Tractatus practice de musica mensurabili ad modum ytalicorum, in Sartori, *La notazione italiana*, pp. 35–71.

Pseudo-Odo. *Dialogus*, ed. Martin Gerbert, in *Scriptores ecclesiastici de musica*. 3 vols. St. Blasien: Typis San-Blasianis, 1784; repr. Hildesheim, 1963, 1:251–64.

Ptolemy, Claudius. *The Harmonics*, trans. Andrew Barker, in *Greek Musical Writings, 2: Harmonic and Acoustic Theory*. Cambridge Readings in the Literature of Music. Cambridge: Cambridge University Press, 1989, pp. 270–391.

Quantz, Johann Joachim. *Versuch einer Anweisung die Flute traversiere zu spielen*. 3rd ed. Breslau: Johann Friedrich Korn der älter, 1789. English translation: *On Playing the Flute*, trans. Edward R. Reilly (New York: The Free Press, 1966).

Quintilian. *Institutio oratoria*, ed. M. Winterbottom. 2 vols. Scriptorum Classicorum Bibliotheca Oxoniensis. Oxford: Oxford University Press, 1970. English translation: *The Orator's Education*, ed. and trans. Donald A. Russell, 5 vols., Loeb Classical Library (Cambridge, MA, and London: Harvard University Press, 2001).

Radke, Hans. "Zur Spieltechnik der deutschen Lautenisten des 16. Jahrhunderts." *Acta Musicologica* 52 (1980): 134–47.

Rankin, Susan. "Calligraphy and the Study of Neumatic Notations," in *The Calligraphy of Medieval Music*, ed. Haines, pp. 47–62.

"Identity and Diversity: The Idea of Regional Musical Notations," in *Nationes, Gentes und die Musik im Mittelalter*, ed. Frank Hentschel and Marie Winkelmüller. Berlin: Walter de Gruyter, 2014, pp. 375–93.

"Neumatic Notations in Anglo-Saxon England," in *Musicologie médiévale*, ed. Huglo, pp. 129–44.

"On the Treatment of Pitch in Early Music Writing." *Early Music History* 30 (2011): 105–75.

"The Song School of St Gall in the Later Ninth Century," in *Sangallensia in Washington: The Arts and Letters in Medieval and Baroque St. Gall Viewed from the Late Twentieth Century*, ed. James C. King. New York: P. Lang, 1993, pp. 173–98.

"Typologies of Ninth-Century Music Notations," in *Actes du Colloque de Royaumont*, ed. Colette and Massip, pp. 33–49.

"Winchester Polyphony: The Early Theory and Practice of Organum," in *Music in the Medieval English Liturgy: Plainsong and Mediaeval Music Society Centennial Essays*, ed. Susan Rankin and David Hiley. Oxford: Oxford University Press, 1993, pp. 59–99.

Writing Sounds in Carolingian Europe: The Invention of Musical Notation. Cambridge Studies in Palaeography and Codicology. Cambridge: Cambridge University Press, 2018.

Rastall, Richard. *The Notation of Western Music: An Introduction*. New York: St. Martin's Press, 1982.

Raven, D. S. *Latin Metre*. London: Faber and Faber, 1965; repr. London, 1998.

Read, Gardner. *20th-Century Microtonal Notation*. Contributions to the Study of Music and Dance, 18. New York: Greenwood Press, 1990.

Compendium of Modern Instrumental Techniques. Westport, CT: Greenwood Press, 1993.

Contemporary Instrumental Techniques. New York: Schirmer Books, 1976.

Modern Rhythmic Notation. Bloomington: Indiana University Press, 1978.

Pictographic Score Notation: A Compendium. Westport, CT: Greenwood Press, 1998.

Source Book of Proposed Music Notation Reforms. Music Reference Collection, 11. New York: Greenwood Press, 1987.

Reaney, Gilbert. "The Manuscript Chantilly, Musée Condé 1047." *Musica Disciplina* 8 (1954): 59–113.

Manuscripts of Polyphonic Music, 11th–Early 14th Century. Répertoire International des Sources Musicales, B/4, 1. Munich-Duisburg: Henle, 1966.

"A Postscript to 'The Manuscript Chantilly, Musée Condé 1047'." *Musica Disciplina* 10 (1956): 55–59.

Reckow, Fritz. *Die Copula: Über einige Zusammenhänge zwischen Setzweise, Formbildung, Rhythmus und Vortragsstil in der Mehrstimmigkeit von Notre-Dame*. Akademie der Wissenschaften und der Literatur, Abhandlungen der Geistes- und Sozialwissenschaftlichen Klasse, Jahrgang 1972, no. 13. Mainz and Wiesbaden: Verlag der Akademie der Wissenschaften und der Literatur, and F. Steiner, 1972.

"Proprietas und perfectio: Zur Geschichte des Rhythmus, seiner Aufzeichnung und Terminologie im 13. Jahrhundert." *Acta Musicologica* 39 (1967): 115–43.

Reckow, Fritz, ed. *Der Musiktraktat des Anonymus 4*. 2 vols. Beihefte zum Archiv für Musikwissenschaft, 4–5. Wiesbaden: Franz Steiner, 1967. English translation: *The Music Treatise of Anonymous IV: A New Translation*, trans. Jeremy Yudkin, Musicological Studies and Documents, 41 (Neuhausen-Stuttgart: American Institute of Musicology, Hänssler-Verlag, 1985).

Riché, Pierre. *Les écoles et l'enseignement dans l'occident chrétien de la fin du Ve siècle au milieu du XIe siècle*. 3rd ed. Paris: Picard, 1999.

Risatti, Howard. *New Music Vocabulary: A Guide to Notational Signs for Contemporary Music*. Urbana, Chicago and London: University of Illinois Press, 1975.

Ristory, Heinz. *Denkmodelle zur französischen Mensuraltheorie des 14. Jahrhunderts*. 2 vols. Wissenschaftliche Abhandlungen, 81. Ottawa: Institute of Mediaeval Music, 2004–16.

Post-franconische Theorie und Früh-Trecento: Die Petrus de Cruce-Neuerungen und ihre Bedeutung für die italienische Mensuralnotenschrift zu Beginn des 14. Jahrhunderts. Europäische Hochschulschriften, ser. 36, Musikwissenschaft, 26. Frankfurt am Main: Peter Lang, 1988.

Robertson, Anne Walters. *The Service-Books of the Royal Abbey of Saint-Denis: Images of Ritual and Music in the Middle Ages*. Oxford Monographs on Music. Oxford: Oxford University Press, 1991.

Roesner, Edward H. "The Emergence of *musica mensurabilis*," in *Studies in Musical Sources and Styles: Essays in Honor of Jan LaRue*, ed. Eugene K. Wolf and Edward H. Rosener. Madison, WI: A-R Editions, 1990, pp. 41–74.

——— "Johannes de Garlandia on *organum in speciali*." *Early Music History* 2 (1982): 129–60.

Rumphorst, Heinrich. "Verhältnis von St. Galler und Metzer Notation." *Beiträge zur Gregorianik* 52 (2011): 61–87.

Sanders, Ernest H. "Consonance and Rhythm in the Organum of the 12th and 13th Centuries." *Journal of the American Musicological Society* 33 (1980): 264–86.

——— "The Early Motets of Philippe de Vitry." *Journal of the American Musicological Society* 28 (1975): 24–45.

Sanders, Ernest H., and Peter M. Lefferts. "Petrus de Cruce," in *Grove Music Online*, www.oxfordmusiconline.com.

Santosuosso, Alma Colk. *Letter Notations in the Middle Ages*. Wissenschaftliche Abhandlungen, 52. Ottawa: Institute of Mediaeval Music, 1989.

Sartori, Claudio. *La notazione italiana del trecento in una redazione inedita del "Tractatus practice cantus mensurabilis ad modum ytalicorum" de Prosdocimo de Beldemandis*. Florence: Leo S. Olschki, 1938.

Saussure, Ferdinand de. *Cours de linguistique générale*, ed. Charles Bally and Albert Sechehaye. Paris: Payot, 1972 (originally published Lausanne: Payot, 1916). English translation: *Course in General Linguistics*, trans. Wade Baskin (New York: McGraw-Hill, 1959).

Sbordoni, Alessandro, and Antonio Rostagno, eds. *Free Improvisation: History and Perspectives*. Lucca: Libreria Musicale Italiana, 2018.

Schoenberg, Arnold. "About Metronome Markings," trans. Leo Black, in *Style and Idea: Selected Writings of Arnold Schoenberg*, ed. Leonard Stein. Rev. ed. Berkeley and Los Angeles: University of California Press, 1984, pp. 342–43.

Schön, Daniele, and Mireille Besson. "Visually Induced Auditory Expectancy in Music Reading: A Behavioral and Electrophysiological Study." *Journal of Cognitive Neuroscience* 17 (2005): 694–705.

Schürmann, Martin, Tommi Raij, Nobuya Fujiki and Riitta Hari. "Mind's Ear in a Musician: Where and When in the Brain." *NeuroImage* 16 (2002): 434–40.

Schwindt, Nicole, ed. *Heinrich Glarean oder: Die Rettung der Musik aus dem Geist der Antike?* Trossinger Jahrbuch für Renaissancemusik, 5. Kassel: Bärenreiter, 2005.

Scully, Terence. "French Songs in Aragon: The Place of Origin of the *Chansonnier Chantilly, Musée Condé 564*," in *Courtly Literature: Culture and Context*, ed. Keith Busby and Erik Kooper. Utrecht Publications in General and Comparative Literature, 25. Amsterdam and Philadelphia: John Benjamins Publishing Company, 1990, pp. 509–21.

Seeger, Charles. "Prescriptive and Descriptive Music-Writing." *The Musical Quarterly* 44 (1958): 184–95.

Selfridge-Field, Eleanor. *Venetian Instrumental Music from Gabrieli to Vivaldi.* Blackwell's Music Series. Oxford: Basil Blackwell, 1975.

Sergent, Justine. "Music, the Brain and Ravel." *Trends in Neurosciences* 16 (1993): 168–72.

Sergent, Justine, Eric Zuck, Sean Terriah and Brennan MacDonald. "Distributed Neural Network Underlying Musical Sight-Reading and Keyboard Performance." *Science* 257 (2 July 1992): 106b–109.

Servant, Isabelle, and Thierry Baccino. "Lire Beethoven: Une étude exploratoire des mouvements des yeux." *Musicae Scientiae* 3 (1999): 67–94.

Sheldon, Deborah A. "Visual Representation of Music: Effects of Beamed and Beamless Notation on Music Performance." *Journal of Band Research* 31 (1995–96): 86–101.

Sloboda, John A. "Experimental Studies of Music Reading: A Review." *Music Perception* 2 (1984): 222–36.

"The Eye-Hand Span—An Approach to the Study of Sight Reading." *Psychology of Music* 2 (1974): 4–10.

"Phrase Units as Determinants of Visual Processing in Music Reading." *British Journal of Psychology* 68 (1977): 117–24.

"The Psychology of Music Reading." *Psychology of Music* 6 (1978): 3–20.

Smith, F. Joseph. *Iacobi Leodiensis Speculum musicae: A Commentary.* 3 vols. Wissenschaftliche Abhandlungen, 13, 22 and 43. Brooklyn: Institute of Mediaeval Music, 1966–83.

"Jacques de Liège, an Anti-Modernist?" *Revue belge de musicologie* 17 (1963): 3–10.

"Jacques de Liège's Criticism of the Notational Innovations of the Ars Nova." *Journal of Musicological Research* 4 (1982–83): 267–313.

Smits van Waesberghe, Jos. *De musico-paedagogico et theoretico Guidone Aretino eiusque vita et moribus.* Florence: L. S. Olschki, 1953.

"The Musical Notation of Guido of Arezzo." *Musica Disciplina* 5 (1951): 15–53.

Muziekgeschiedenis der Middeleeuwen, 2: Verklaring der Letterteekens (litterae significatiuae) in het gregoriaansche Neumenschrift van Sint Gallen: Een Onderzoek naar de historische Waarde van den zoogenaamden Notker-Brief en naar den Oorsprong en de Beteekenis der Letterteekens in St. Gallen. Nederlandsche Muziekhistorische en Muziekpaedagogische Studiën, A. Tilburg: W. Bergmans, 1939–42.

Solomon, Maynard. *Beethoven.* New York: Schirmer, 1977.

Southern, Eileen. *The Buxheim Organ Book.* Wissenschaftliche Abhandlungen, 6. Brooklyn: Institute of Mediaeval Music, 1963.

Stäblein, Bruno. "Modale Rhythmen im Saint-Martial-Repertoire?" in *Festschrift Friedrich Blume zum 70. Geburtstag,* ed. Anna Amalie Abert and Wilhem Pfannkuch. Kassel: Bärenreiter, 1963, pp. 340–62.

Schriftbild der einstimmigen Musik. Musikgeschichte in Bildern, 3, lief. 4. Leipzig: Veb Deutscher Verlag für Musik, 1975.

Stewart, Lauren, Vincent Walsh and Uta Frith. "Reading Music Modifies Spatial Mapping in Pianists." *Perception & Psychophysics* 66 (2004): 183–95.

Stockhausen, Karlheinz. "Musik und Graphik." *Darmstadter Beiträge zur neuen Musik* 3 (1960): 5–25.

Stone, Kurt. *Music Notation in the Twentieth Century: A Practical Guidebook*. New York and London: W. W. Norton, 1980.

Stones, Alison. "Les manuscrits du Cardinal Jean Cholet et l'enluminure beauvaisienne vers la fin du XIIIeme siècle," in *L'art gothique dans l'Oise et ses environs (XIIeme–XIVeme siècle)*. N.p.: GEMOB, 2001, pp. 239–68.

"The Style and Iconography of Montpellier folio 350r," in *The Montpellier Codex*, ed. Bradley and Desmond, pp. 66–77.

Strawinsky, Igor. *Chroniques de ma vie*. Bibliothèque Méditations. Paris: Denöel/Gonthier, 1962.

Poétique musicale sous forme de six leçons. Charles Eliot Norton Lectures for 1939–1940. Cambridge MA: Harvard University Press, 1942. English translation: *Poetics of Music in the Form of Six Lessons*, trans. Arthur Knodel and Ingolf Dahl (Cambridge MA: Harvard University Press, 1947).

Strunk, Oliver, ed. *Source Readings in Music History*, rev. ed., ed. Leo Treitler. New York: Norton, 1998.

Sullivan, Blair. "Alphabetic Notation and Hucbald's *artificiales notae*," in *Quellen und Studien zur Musiktheorie des Mittelalters*, 3, ed. Michael Bernhard. Bayerische Akademie der Wissenschaften, Veröffentlichungen der Musikhistorischen Kommission, 15. Munich: Verlag der Bayerische Akademie der Wissenschaften, 2001, pp. 63–80.

Sunyol, Gregori M. *Introducció a la paleografia musical gregoriana*. Montserrat: Abbey of Montserrat, 1925.

Tanay, Dorit. *Noting Music, Marking Culture: The Intellectual Context of Rhythmic Notation, 1250–1400*. Musicological Studies and Documents, 46. Holzgerlingen: American Institute of Musicology, Hänssler-Verlag, 1999.

"The Transition from the Ars Antiqua to the Ars Nova: Evolution or Revolution?" *Musica Disciplina* 46 (1992): 79–104.

Tinctoris, Johannes. *Opera theoretica*, ed. Albert Seay. 2 vols. in 3. Corpus Scriptorum de Musica, 22. N.p. and Neuhausen-Stuttgart: American Institute of Musicology, 1975–78. English translation of *Proportionale musices: Proportions in Music (Proportionale musices)*, trans. Albert Seay, Colorado College Music Press Translations, 10 (Colorado Springs: Colorado College Music Press, 1979).

Tonda, Mario Stefano. "Nuove osservazioni sull'*Intavolatura de cimbalo* del 1576 de Antonio Valente." *Informazione Organistica* 10–11 (2005): 3–21.

Treitler, Leo. "The Early History of Music Writing in the West." *Journal of the American Musicological Society* 35 (1982): 237–79.

"Homer and Gregory: The Transmission of Epic Poetry and Plainchant." *The Musical Quarterly* 60 (1974): 333–72.

"Observations on the Transmission of Some Aquitanian Tropes," in *Forum musicologicum: Basler Beiträge zur Musikgeschichte*, 3: *Aktuelle Fragen der musikbezogenen Mittelalterforschung: Texte zu einem Basler Kolloquium des Jahres 1975*, ed. Hans Oesch and Wulf Arlt. Winterthur: Amadeus, 1982, pp. 11–60.

"Oral, Written, and Literate Process in the Transmission of Medieval Music." *Speculum* 56 (1981): 471–91.

"Reading and Singing: On the Genesis of Occidental Music-Writing." *Early Music History* 4 (1984): 135–208.

"Regarding Meter and Rhythm in the *Ars Antiqua*." *The Musical Quarterly* 65 (1979): 524–58.

Truitt, Frances E., Charles Clifton Jr., Alexander Pollatsek and Keith Rayner. "The Perceptual Span and the Eye-Hand Span in Sight Reading Music." *Visual Cognition* 4 (1997): 143–61.

Unverricht, Hubert. "Die Dasia-Notation und ihre Interpretation," in *Ars musica musica scientia: Festschrift Heinrich Hüschen*, ed. Detlef Altenburg. Beiträge zur Rheinischen Musikgeschichte, 126. Cologne: Verlag der Arbeitsgemeinschaft für Rheinische Musikgeschichte, 1980, pp. 444–48.

Upton, Elizabeth Randell. "Aligning Words and Music: Scribal Procedures for the Placement of Text and Notes in the Chantilly Codex," in *A Late Medieval Songbook and Its Context: New Perspectives on the Chantilly Codex (Bibilothèque du Château de Chantilly, Ms. 564)*, ed. Yolanda Plumley and Anne Stone. Collection "Épitome musical." Turnhout: Brepols, 2009, pp. 115–32.

"Inventing the Chantilly Codex." *Studi Musicali* 31 (2002): 181–231.

van Dijk, S. J. P. "Papal Schola *versus* Charlemagne," in *Organicae voces: Festschrift Joseph Smits van Waesberghe*. Amsterdam: Instituut voor Middeleeuwse Muziekwetenschap, 1963, pp. 21–30.

Van Doren, Rombaut. *Étude sur l'influence de l'abbaye de Saint-Gall (VIIIe au XIe siècle)*. Académie Royale de Belgique, Classe des Beaux-Arts, Mémoires, 2, fasc. 3. Brussels: Maurice Lamertin, 1925 (also published as Université de Louvain, Recueil de Travaux Publiés par les Membres des Conférences d'Histoire et de Philologie, ser. 2, 6 [Louvain: Librairie Universitaire, Uystpruyst, 1925]).

Vendrix, Philippe. "La notation à la Renaissance," in *Histoire de la notation du Moyen Âge à la Renaissance*. Musique Ouverte. N.p.: Minerve, 2003, pp. 135–94.

Vicentino, Nicola. *L'antica musica ridotta alla moderna prattica*. Rome: Antonio Barre, 1555; repr. ed. Edward Lowinsky, Documenta Musicologica, ser. 1: Druckschriften-Faksimiles, 17 (Kassel: Bärenreiter, 1959). English translation: *Ancient Music Adapted to Modern Practice*, trans. Maria Rika Maniates, ed. Claude V. Palisca, Music Theory Translation Series. New Haven and London: Yale University Press, 1996.

Virdung, Sebastian. *Musica getutscht*. Basel, 1511; repr. ed. Klaus Wolfgang Niemöller, Documenta Musicologica, ser. 1: Druckschriften-Faksimiles, 31 (Kassel: Bärenreiter, 1970). English translation: *Musica getutscht: A Treatise on Musical Instruments (1511) by Sebastian Virdung*, trans. and ed. Beth Bullard, Cambridge Musical Texts and Monographs. Cambridge: Cambridge University Press, 1993.

Vitry, Philippe de. *Ars nova*, ed. Gilbert Reaney, André Gilles and Jean Maillard. Corpus Scriptorum de Musica, 8. N.p.: Institute of Musicology, 1964. English translation: "Philippe de Vitry's Ars Nova: A Translation," trans. Leon Plantinga, *Journal of Music Theory* 5 (1961): 204–23.

Vogel, Cyrille. "Les motifs de la romanisation du culte sous Pepin [sic] le Bréf [sic] (751–768) et Charlemagne," in *Culto cristiano, politica imperiale carolingia: 9–12 ottobre 1977*. Convegni del Centro di studi sulla spiritualità medievale, Università degli Studi di Perugia, 18. Todi: Presso l'Accademia Tudertina, 1979, pp. 9–41.

La reforme cultuelle sous Pepin le Bref et sous Charlemagne (deuxième motitié du VIIIe siècle et premier quart du IXe siècle). Graz: Akademische Druck- und Verlagsanstalt, 1965.

Vollaerts, J. W. A. *Rhythmic Proportions in Early Medieval Ecclesiastical Chant*. 2nd ed. Leiden: E. J. Brill, 1960.

Wagner, Peter. *Einführung in die gregorianischen Melodien: Ein Handbuch der Choralwissenschaft*, 2: *Neumenkunde: Paläographie des liturgischen Gesanges*. 2nd ed. Leipzig: Breitkopf & Härtel, 1912.

Wagner, Pierre-Édouard. "Chant romain et chant messin: L'école de Metz (VIIIe–IXe siècles)," in *L'art du chantre carolingien: Découvrir l'esthéthique première du chant grégorien*, ed. Christian-Jacques Demollière. Metz: Éditions Serpenoise, 2004, pp. 13–26.

Wagner, Richard. *Richard Wagner's Prose Works*, trans. William Ashton Ellis. 2nd ed. 8 vols. London: Kegan Paul and Co., 1892–99.

Sämtliche Schriften und Dichtungen, 6th ed. 16 vols. in 8. Leipzig: Breitkopf und Härtel, n.d.

Über das Dirigieren. Leipzig: C. F. Kahnt, 1870. Originally published in instalments in the *Neue Zeitschrift für Musik*, November 1869 through January 1870. Reprinted in Wagner, *Sämtliche Schriften*, 8: 261–337. English translation: *About Conducting*, trans. Ellis, in *Richard Wagner's Prose Works*, 4:289–364.

Über die Aufführung des "Tannhäuser": Eine Mitteilung an die Dirigenten und Darsteller dieser Oper. Published privately, 1852. Reprinted in Wagner, *Sämtliche Schriften*, 5: 123–59. English translation: *On the Performing of "Tannhäuser,"* trans. Ellis, in *Richard Wagner's Prose Works*, 3:167–205.

Waite, William G. *The Rhythm of Twelfth-Century Polyphony, Its Theory and Practice*. Yale Studies in the History of Music, 2. New Haven: Yale University Press, 1954.

Warfield, Gerald. *Writings on Contemporary Music Notation: An Annotated Bibliography*. Ann Arbor: Music Library Association, 1976.

Waters, Andrew J., Ellen Townsend and Geoffrey Underwood. "Expertise in Musical Sight Reading: A Study of Pianists." *British Journal of Psychology* 89 (1998): 123–49.

Waters, Andrew J., and Geoffrey Underwood. "Eye Movements in a Simple Music Reading Task: A Study of Expert and Novice Musicians." *Psychology of Music* 26 (1998): 46–60.

Wathey, Andrew. "Philippe de Vitry's Books," in *Books and Collectors 1200–1700: Essays Presented to Andrew Watson*, ed. James P. Carley and Colini G. C. Tite. British Library Studies in the History of the Book. London: The British Library, 1997, pp. 145–52.

Wegman, Rob C. "The World According to Anonymous IV," in *Qui musicam in se habet: Studies in Honor of Alejandro Enrique Planchart*, ed. Anna Zayaruznaya, Bonnie J. Blackburn and Stanley Boorman. Miscellanea, 8. Middleton, WI: American Institute of Musicology, 2015, pp. 693–729.

Werbeck, Walter. "Glareans Vorstellung von modaler Stimmigkeit – Die für das *Dodekachordon* bestellten Kompositionen," in *Heinrich Glarean*, ed. Schwindt, pp. 177–97.

Wiora, Walter. "Zum Problem des Ursprungs der mittelalterlichen Solmisation." *Die Musikforschung* 9 (1956): 263–74.

Wolf, Thomas. "A Cognitive Model of Musical Sight-Reading." *Journal of Psycholinguistic Research* 5 (1976): 143–71.

Wolinski, Mary E. "The Compilation of the Montpellier Codex." *Early Music History* 11 (1992): 263–301.

Wright, Craig. "Leoninus, Poet and Musician." *Journal of the American Musicological Society* 39 (1986): 1–35.

  Music and Ceremony at Notre Dame of Paris, 500–1550. Cambridge Studies in Music. Cambridge: Cambridge University Press, 1989.

Wright, Roger. *Late Latin and Early Romance in Spain and Carolingian France*. ARCA Classical and Medieval Texts, Papers and Monographs, 8. Liverpool: Francis Cairns, 1982.

Yudkin, Jeremy. "The Anonymous Music Treatise of 1279: Why St. Emmeram?" *Music & Letters* 72 (1991): 177–96.

  "The Anonymous of St. Emmeram and Anonymous IV on the *Copula*." *The Musical Quarterly* 70 (1984): 1–22.

  "The *Copula* According to Johannes de Garlandia." *Musica Disciplina* 34 (1980): 67–84.

  "Notre Dame Theory: A Study of the Terminology, Including a New Translation of the Music Treatise of Anonymous IV." Ph.D. dissertation, Stanford University, 1982.

  "The Rhythm of Organum Purum." *Journal of Musicology* 2 (1983): 355–76.

Yumoto, Masato, Maki Matsuda, Kenji Itoh, Akira Uno, Shotaro Karino, Osamu Saitoh, Yuu Kaneko, Yukata Yatomi and Kimitaka Kaga. "Auditory Imagery Mismatch Negativity Elicited in Musicians." *NeuroReport* 16 (2005): 1175–78.

Zapke, Susana. "Notation Systems in the Iberian Peninsula: From Spanish Notations to Aquitanian Notation (9th–12th Centuries)," in *Hispania vetus: Musical-Liturgical Manuscripts from Visigothic Origins to the Franco-Roman Transition (9th to 12th Centuries)*, ed. Susana Zapke. Bilbao: Fundación BBVA, 2007, pp. 189–243.

Zarlino, Gioseffo. *Le istitutioni harmoniche*. Venice: n. p., 1558; repr. in Monuments of Music and Music Literature in Facsimile, Second Series, Music Literature, 1 (New York, 1965). English translation of part 4: *On the Modes: Part Four of* Le Istitutioni Harmoniche, *1558*, trans. Vered Cohen, ed. Claude V. Palisca, Music Theory Translation Series (New Haven: Yale University Press, 1983).

Zenck, Claudia Maurer. *Vom Takt: Untersuchungen zur Theorie und kompositorischen Praxis im ausgehenden 18. und beginnenden 19. Jahrhundert*. Vienna: Böhlau Verlag, 2001.

Zhukov, Katie. "Evaluating New Approaches to Teaching of Sight-Reading Skills to Advanced Pianists." *Music Education Research* 16 (2014): 70–87.

Zöbeley, Hans Rudolf. *Die Musik des Buxheimer Orgelbuchs: Spielvorgang, Niederschrift, Herkunft, Faktur*. Münchner Veröffentlichungen zur Musikgeschichte, 10. Tutzing: Hans Schneider, 1964.

Index

accidentals, 45, 46, 50, 51, 145, 146, 149, 150, 162
Adam de la Halle, 203
Adémar de Chabannes, 12, 13, 14, 38, 39, 57, 59, 201, 208
Admonitio generalis, 11, 15
Agricola, Martin, 156
Albert the Great, 72, 76
Alcuin of York, 8–9
Alexander de Villa-Dei, 68
alteration, 67–68
Amadino, Ricciardo, 186
Ammerbach, Elias Nikolaus, 158
   Orgel oder Instrument Tabulaturbuch, 145
Anonymous IV, 64–65, 66, 67, 68, 73, 74, 76, 78, 79, 80, 81, 84, 85, 86, 98
Anonymous of Saint Emmeram, 64–65, 66, 67, 68, 70, 74, 75–76, 78, 79, 80, 82, 84, 85, 86, 88, 94, 98
Antico, Andrea
   Frottole intabulate da sonare organi libro primo, 128–130, 132, 136, 139, 160
ars subtilior, 112
articulation, 179, 211
Attaingnant, Pierre, 156, 157
   Tres breue et familiere introduction, 154–156
audiation, 207, 209, 210–211
Augustine of Hippo
   De musica, 69–70
Aurelian of Réôme, 9–10, 12–13, 14

Bach, Johann Sebastian, 140, 163, 187, 188
   Klavierbüchlein für Wilhelm Friedemann Bach, 179
   Mass in B minor, BWV 232, 187
   Sonata for Flute and Harpsichord, BWV 1030, 177
   Sonatas for Flute and Harpsichord, BWV 1030–32, 163
   Sonatas and Partitas for Violin Solo, BWV 1001–6, 132
   Toccata and Fugue in D minor, BWV 538, 175
   Well-Tempered Clavier, BWV 846–69, 175
Banchieri, Adriano
   L'organo suonarino, 177
bar line, 128–130, 136–137, 143, 149, 153, 155, 183, 209
Bartholomaeus Anglicus, 72, 76
Bartók, Béla, 164
   Mikrokosmos, 141
beam, 144, 145, 158, 193, 195, 196, 209
Beethoven, Ludwig van, 178
   Piano Concerto, Op. 37, 188
   Piano Concerto, Op. 73, 188
   Sonatas for Pianoforte, Op. 2, 191
   Sonata for Pianoforte, Op. 13, 177
   Sonata for Pianoforte, Op. 106, 190–191
   Symphony no. 3, Op. 55, 140
   Symphony no. 9, Op. 125, 187, 188
Berio, Luciano
   Sequenza III per voce femminile, 193, 194
   Sequenza VII per oboe solo, 193, 194–195
Boethius, 13, 53, 69
Boosey & Hawkes, 217
Boulez, Pierre, 6–7
Brahms, Johannes
   Piano Concerto, Op. 15, 188
   Piano Concerto, Op. 83, 188
Breitkopf und Härtel, 189
Brown, Earle
   Available Forms 1, 197
Brumel, Antoine, 154

Cabezón, Antonio de, 151, 154, 159
   Obras de música para tecla arpa y vihuela, 146–151
Caccini, Giulio
   L'Euridice, 162
Carter, Elliott, 206
   Eight Pieces for Four Timpani, 195–196
Cavalieri, Emilio
   Rappresentatione di Anima e di Corpo, 162
Cavalli, Francesco
   Il novello Giasone, 131, 186
   Scipione Africano, 131

cephalicus, 29, 31, 44, 47–48, 220
Charlemagne, 8–9, 11, 12, 14, 16, 37, 201
clef, 45, 46, 50, 51, 54–55, 59, 174, 211
climacus, 19, 20, 24, 35, 41, 44, 48
cliuis, 19, 20, 22, 23, 25, 26, 30, 43, 44, 46–47, 48, 49, 51, 217, 220, 221
Codex Calixtinus, 182
coloration, 97, 105–108, 110, 203
Compere, Loyset
   Garisses moy, 122
Corelli, Arcangelo
   Sonatas for Violin, Op. 5, 132
   Trio Sonata, Op. 1, no. 3, 177
Cowell, Henry, 192
currentes, 80

Debussy, Claude
   La demoiselle élue, 133
   La mer, 133
des Prez, Josquin
   Missa De beata virgine, 139
Discantus positio uulgaris, 63–64, 66, 67, 74
dot of addition, 5, 100, 103, 122–000, 128–130, 131, 134
dot of perfection, 100–102, 103, 118
Du Fay, Guillaume
   Flos florum, 171–173
Dufourt, Hugues, 6–7
dynamics, 190, 211, 214

eptaphonus, 28, 42, 44, 47–48, 220
expression, 190

Feldman, Morton
   Intersection 2 for Piano Solo, 197
fixation, 210, 214
Fox, Christopher, 198, 204–205
Franco of Cologne, 64–65, 67–68, 76–78, 81, 82, 84, 97, 101–102, 103, 105, 106, 110, 132, 183, 202, 203
Frescobaldi, Girolamo, 136
Fulda, Adam of, 173

Gabrieli, Giovanni, 143
   Sacrae symphoniae, 160–161, 176, 180, 184, 186, 190
Gaffurius, Franchinus
   Practica musice, 119–121, 126–128
Garlandia, Johannes de, 63, 64, 66, 67, 72–74, 75, 76, 78–80, 82, 84, 85, 89, 95, 132, 135, 137
Gasparini, Francesco, 174
Gaultier, Denis
   La rhétorique des dieux, 156
Gershwin, George
   Rhapsody in Blue, 207
Glarean, Heinrich, 173
Gonzaga, Francesco, 186
Grainger, Percy, 200–201
Guido d'Arezzo, 22, 45, 51, 54–55, 57–59, 110, 166
   Micrologus, 167
   Prologus in Antiphonarium, 39–40

Handel, Georg Friedrich
   Sonata for Flute and Continuo in G minor, HWV 360, 177
   Water Music, 140
Handlo, Robertus de, 95
Hauptstimme, 214, 215
Heinichen, Johann, 175
Helisachar, 10, 11, 15
hemiola, 140
Herbst, Johann-Andreas
   Musica moderna prattica, 178
hexachords, 45, 58, 166, 167–173
Hindemith, Paul, 2
Hucbald of Saint Amand, 13–14, 22, 53, 201

imperfection, 87–88, 91, 94–95, 97–103, 105–106, 108–110, 111–112, 117–119, 122, 130–131
Ives, Charles
   Symphony no.4, 175, 196

Jacobus de Ispania, 95, 96, 97, 98–99, 101, 102, 103, 109
Jacques of Liège. *See* Jacobus de Ispania
Janovka, Tomáš, 174
Jerome of Moravia, 63–64
John the Deacon, 11–12, 14
Kirnberger, Johann Philipp
   Die Kunst des reinen Satzes in der Musik, 133, 138–139, 140
Lambertus, 64–65, 97, 99
language, symbolic, 4–5
leger line, 156, 211
Leoninus, 202
ligatures, 17, 19–20, 35, 36, 41–43, 44, 46, 49, 69, 71, 72, 73–74, 75–80, 81–84, 86, 89–91, 94, 95, 108, 118, 119, 209, 217, 218, 219
line of division, 87
liquescents, 16, 25, 28–29, 35, 36, 42–43, 46, 50, 220
litterae significatiuae, 27, 32–35, 42, 53, 176, 220–221

Machaut, Guillaume de, 203
  Biaute qui toutes autres pere, 106–110, 118, 122, 168
Mälzel, Johann Nepomuk, 178
manuscripts
  Albi, Bibliothèque municipale Rochegude, MS 44, 15–16, 17–18, 28, 29, 35
  Bamberg, Staatsbibliothek, MS Lit.115, 169–171, 172
  Berlin, Staatliche Museen Preußischer Kulturbesitz, Kupferstichkabinett, MS 78 C 12, 156
  Berlin, Staatsbibliothek Preußischer Kulturbesitz, Mus. ms. Autogr., L. v. Beethoven, 2, and Artaria 204, 187
  Berlin, Staatsbibliothek Preußischer Kulturbesitz, Mus. ms. Autogr., L. v. Beethoven 14, 188
  Berlin, Staatsbibliothek Preußischer Kulturbesitz, Mus. ms. Autogr., L. v. Beethoven 15, 188
  Berlin, Staatsbibliothek Preußischer Kulturbesitz, Mus. ms. Bach P 180, 187
  Berlin, Staatsbibliothek Preußischer Kulturbesitz, Mus. ms. Bach P 967, 132
  Bologna, Museo Internazionale et Biblioteca della Musica di Bologna, MS Q.15, 171, 172, 173
  Cambridge, Corpus Christi College, MS 473, 26, 61
  Chantilly, Bibliothèque du château de Chantilly, MS 564, 112–119, 120, 122, 125–127, 136
  Chartres, Bibliothèque municipale, MS 47, 15, 17–18, 21, 23, 24, 25, 26, 27, 28, 29, 30–31, 33, 34, 35, 220
  Faenza, Biblioteca comunale, MS 117, 128, 136, 137, 142, 144, 160
  Florence, Archivio di Stato, Notarile Antecosimiano, No.17879, 137
  Florence, Biblioteca Medicea Laurenziana, MS Pluteo 29,1, 61, 63, 81, 82–84, 91, 182
  Laon, Bibliothèque municipale, MS 239, 15, 17–18, 21, 23, 24, 25, 26, 28, 29, 30–31, 33–34, 35
  London, British Library, Additional MS 28550, 142
  London, British Library, Additional MS 29987, 142
  London, British Library, Additional MS 36881, 48, 61
  Montpellier, Bibliothèque Interuniversitaire Médecine, MS H. 159, 53, 167
  Montpellier, Bibliothèque Interuniversitaire Médecine, MS H. 196, 65, 85, 91–94, 95, 182–183
  Munich, Bayerische Staatsbibliothek, Mus. ms. 3725, 143
  New York, Pierpont Morgan Library, MS Heineman 266, 188
  Paris, Bibliothèque Mazarine, MS 384, 41–43, 44, 45, 46–48, 49
  Paris, Bibliothèque nationale de France, département Musique, MS 967, 133
  Paris, Bibliothèque nationale de France, département Musique, MS 1548 (1–8), 187
  Paris, Bibliothèque nationale de France, MS français 844, 137, 139, 142
  Paris, Bibliothèque nationale de France, MS français 1584, 106–110, 168, 203
  Paris, Bibliothèque nationale de France, MS français 9221, 106–110, 203
  Paris, Bibliothèque nationale de France, MS latin 909, 38, 59
  Paris, Bibliothèque nationale de France, MS latin 1107, 41, 46–48, 49, 50, 51, 52, 54, 82
  Paris, Bibliothèque nationale de France, MS latin 1121, 38, 59
  Paris, Bibliothèque nationale de France, MS latin 1138, 39
  Paris, Bibliothèque nationale de France, MS latin 1139, 61, 181
  Paris, Bibliothèque nationale de France, MS latin 1338, 39
  Paris, Bibliothèque nationale de France, MS latin 3549, 39, 61
  Paris, Bibliothèque nationale de France, MS latin 3719, 39, 61, 182
  Paris, Bibliothèque nationale de France, MS latin 5240, 39, 59
  Paris, Bibliothèque nationale de France, MS latin 7378A, 96, 99–105, 109, 117, 118, 122, 126, 135–136, 137
  Paris, Bibliothèque nationale de France, MS latin 17296, 41, 44–48, 49, 52, 54, 57
  Paris, Bibliothèque nationale de France, MS latin 17436, 21
  Saint Gall, Stiftsbibliothek, MS 359, 15, 17–18, 21, 23, 25, 26–27, 28, 29, 30–31, 33, 34, 35, 217–223
  Toledo, Biblioteca Capitular, MS, 20, 167

manuscripts (cont.)
    Wolfenbüttel, Herzog August Bibliothek,
      MS Helmstedt 628, 61, 63, 91, 182
    Wolfenbüttel, Herzog August Bibliothek,
      MS Helmstedt 1099, 61, 65, 91, 182
Marchetto of Padua
    Pomerium in arte musicae mensuratae, 111
Mattheson, Johann, 175
mensuration signs, 102–103, 110–111, 112,
    122, 135, 140, 149, 153, 155
Mensurstrich, 136
metre, classical quantitative, 68–71
metronome, 178, 179, 195, 211
Metz, 14, 16, 35, 36, 37, 43
microtones, 175, 196, 207
Milán, Luis de, 151, 155, 159
    Libro de musica de vihuela de mano, intitulado El maestro, 154
mode (in mensuration), 99–101, 104
modulation, metrical, 195–196, 206
Monteverdi, Claudio, 136
    Lamento della Ninfa, 130, 139
    L'Orfeo, 161–162, 184–186, 187
Morley, Thomas
    A Plaine and Easie Introduction to Practicall Musicke, 133
Mozart, Wolfgang Amadeus, 187, 188
    Don Giovanni, KV 527, 187
    Piano Concerto, KV 467, 188
    Sonata for Pianoforte, KV 570, 191
    Sonata for Pianoforte, KV 576, 191
Mudarra, Alonso
    Tres libros de música en cifra para vihuela, 154
Muris, Johannes de, 96–98, 203
    Ars practica mensurabilis cantus, 98, 100, 102, 104–105, 106, 109, 122
    Compendium musicae practicae, 102
    Notitia artis musicae, 97–98, 100–102, 103, 104, 109, 117, 122, 135–136, 137
    Quadripartitum numerorum, 96
Musica enchiriadis, 40

Nebenstimme, 214, 215, 217
Newsidler, Hans
    Ein newgeordent küntslich Lautenbuch, 158–159
notation, alphabetic, 53
notation, Anglo-Saxon, 36
notation, Aquitanian, 16, 17, 21, 22–23, 24, 38, 39, 40, 41, 46, 48–49, 51, 59–60
notation, Beneventan, 36
notation, Breton, 22, 23, 41, 44

notation, dasian, 16–17, 40, 53, 221
notation, descriptive, 1–2, 56–57
notation, figured bass, 163, 204
notation, Italian, chant, 36
notation, Italian, mensural, 111
notation, literal, 142, 145
notation, Messine, 21, 22, 23, 41, 44
notation, palaeofrankish, 10, 16–17, 20, 53, 221
notation, prescriptive, 1–2, 56–57, 203
notation, proportional, 193, 194–195, 196, 197, 206
notation, Saint Gall, 17, 20, 22, 23, 24, 33, 41, 42, 43
notation, square, 41, 43, 45, 46, 48–51, 52
notation, successive, 181
notation, Visigothic, 36
notation, void, 121, 122
Notker Balbulus, 11–12, 14

Obrecht, Jacob, 173
Omni desideranti notitiam, 97, 99, 100, 102, 103, 104, 106, 122
oriscus, 29–31, 42–43, 47, 50, 51
ornaments, 145, 179, 211, 220, 222

Paumann, Konrad, 156–157
pedalling, 190, 191
Peirce, Charles Sanders, 3–4, 142
Penderecki, Krzysztof
    For the Victims of Hiroshima, Threnody for 52 Stringed Instruments, 193, 196
perfection, 85–88, 94–95, 98, 99–103, 104–106, 108–110, 111–112, 117–119, 122, 130–131
Peri, Jacopo
    Le musiche sopra l'Euridice, 162
Perotinus, 202
Petrucci, Ottaviano, 152, 153, 154, 155, 156, 157
    Harmonice musices odhecaton, 121–122
Petrus de Cruce, 95–96, 102, 183, 202
Petrus de Domarto, 120
Pippin the Short, 8–9, 11, 14, 15, 201
plica, 88, 91, 94
podatus, 19, 20, 21, 23, 25–26, 44, 47, 217
porrectus, 19, 20, 22, 23, 31, 32, 43, 44, 46–47, 49, 50, 217, 219
Poulenc, Francis
    Sonata for Flute and Piano, 211–214, 222
prolation (in mensuration), 100, 104, 109, 110, 112, 116, 117, 118–119, 122
proportions, 97, 203
Prosdocimus de Beldemandis

Tractatus practice de musica mensurabili, 110, 111, 126
Tractatus practice de musica mensurabili ad modum ytalicorum, 111
Pseudo-Odo
   Dialogus, 167
Ptolemy, Claudius, 173
punctum, 18–22, 23, 24, 25, 26, 41, 46, 48, 217–218, 221

Quantz, Johann Joachim
   Versuch einer Anweisung die Flute traversiere zu spielen, 133
quilisma, 12, 13, 16, 29–32, 35, 42–43, 44, 47, 50, 176, 220

rests, 89, 95, 149
Rore, Cipriano de
   Il primo libro de madrigali a quattro voci, 173–174

saccade, 210
Saint Denis, abbey of, Paris, 41, 54
Saint Martial, abbey of, Limoges, 38, 39, 59–60
San Marco, basilica of, Venice, 161
Saussure, Ferdinand de, 2, 5, 19
scandicus, 24, 44
Schoenberg, Arnold, 178, 217
   Das Buch der hängenden Gärten, Op. 15, 175
   Five Pieces for Orchestra, Op. 16, 214–217
Schotts Sohnen, B., 187, 188
Schumann, Robert
   Carnaval, Op. 9, 133
   Fantasiestücke, Op. 12, 133
   Humoreske, Op. 20, 133
   Kinderscenen, Op. 15, no. 10, 140
   Piano Concerto, Op. 54, 188
Seeger, Charles, 1–2, 56, 203
semiotics, 2–4
signature, key, 5, 55, 173–175
signature, time, 5, 140, 141, 211
signatures, conflicting, 169
signs, iconic, 3–4, 5, 17, 20, 24, 31, 35–36, 41, 43, 44, 50, 51, 81, 84, 94, 95, 103, 134, 142, 163, 167, 176
signs, indexical, 3–4, 142, 143, 151, 154, 159, 167
signs, symbolic, 3–4, 19, 20, 24, 31, 35–36, 41, 46, 50, 51, 63, 81, 84, 103, 121, 142, 167, 193
slur, 163, 211

solmization, 55, 57–58, 168, 169
Spinacino, Francesco, 152–154, 155, 156
staff, 39–40, 45, 46, 50, 51, 59, 110, 152
Stockhausen, Karlheinz, 192, 207
   Plus Minus, 197–199
   Spiral, 199
Stravinsky, Igor, 178–179, 190, 191, 204, 206, 207
   Firebird, 192
   Petrushka, 141
   Poétique musicale sous forme de six leçons, 1, 200
   Variations, Aldous Huxley in Memoriam, 217
syncopation, 104–105, 106, 109, 110, 111, 117–118, 122, 126, 135–136, 137, 140, 203

tablature, 142–143
tempo, 138, 190
tempus (in mensuration), 100, 104, 108, 110, 112, 116, 118–119, 122
tie, 128–130, 136
Tinctoris, Johannes
   Proportionale musices, 119–121
   Super punctis musicalibus, 126, 127
torculus, 19, 23, 41, 44, 46, 221
tractulus, 23, 220
transposition, 189
Treitler, Leo, 2, 3, 9, 12, 15, 16, 17, 19, 20, 31–32, 36, 45, 62
tristrophe, 12, 13

uirga, 18–22, 23, 24–25, 26, 29, 31, 41, 44, 46–47, 48, 49, 217–218, 221,
uncinus, 23
Universal Editions, 194

Valente, Antonio, 151, 153, 154, 158, 159
   Intavolatura de cimbalo, 146–151
Vicentino, Nicola, 139
   L'antica musica ridotta alla moderna prattica, 176, 177
Vincenti, Alessandro, 130
Virdung, Sebastian, 156
Vitry, Philippe de, 96–97, 99, 105, 203
   Ars nova, 99, 102, 103, 105–106

Wagner, Richard, 1, 178, 179, 191, 207

Zarlino, Gioseffo, 139

CAMBRIDGE INTRODUCTIONS TO MUSIC

'Cambridge University Press is to be congratulated for formulating the idea of an "Introductions to Music" series.' *Nicholas Jones, The Musical Times*

Each book in this series focuses on a topic fundamental to the study of music at undergraduate and graduate level. The introductions will also appeal to readers who want to broaden their understanding of the music they enjoy.

Books in the series

Musical Notation in the West James Grier
Renaissance Polyphony Fabrice Fitch
Music Sketches Friedemann Sallis
Program Music Jonathan Kregor
Electronic Music Nicholas Collins, Margaret Schedel and Scott Wilson
Gregorian Chant David Hiley
Music Technology Julio D'Escrivan
Opera Robert Cannon
Postmodernism in Music Kenneth Gloag
Serialism Arnold Whittall
The Sonata Thomas Schmidt-Beste
The Song Cycle Laura Tunbridge

Made in the USA
Monee, IL
28 April 2026

49136491R00160